Catholic Social Thought

This series focuses on Catholic social thought and its application to current social, political, economic, and cultural issues. The titles in this series are written and edited by members of the Society of Catholic Social Scientists. They survey and analyze Catholic approaches to politics, sociology, law, economics, history, and other disciplines. Within these broad themes, authors explore the Church's role and influence in contemporary society.

The Society of Catholic Social Scientists was formed in 1992 to rejuvenate a distinctively Catholic scholarship in the social sciences.

1. *The Public Order and the Sacred Order*, by Stephen M. Krason, 2009.
2. *Bioethics, Law, and Human Life Issues*, by D. Brian Scarnecchia, 2010.
3. *Pope Pius XII on the Economic Order*, by Rupert J. Ederer, 2011.
4. *Economics As If God Matters*, by Rupert J. Ederer, 2011.
5. *Toward the Common Good*, edited by Robert F. Gorman, 2011.
6. *Sociology and Catholic Social Teaching*, edited by Stephen R. Sharkey, 2012.

Sociology and Catholic Social Teaching

Contemporary Theory and Research

Edited by
Stephen R. Sharkey

Catholic Social Thought, No. 6

THE SCARECROW PRESS, INC.
Lanham • Toronto • Plymouth, UK
2012

Published by Scarecrow Press, Inc.
A wholly owned subsidiary of The Rowman & Littlefield Publishing Group, Inc.
4501 Forbes Boulevard, Suite 200, Lanham, Maryland 20706
http://www.scarecrowpress.com

Estover Road, Plymouth PL6 7PY, United Kingdom

British Library Cataloguing in Publication Information Available

Library of Congress Cataloging-in-Publication Data

Sociology and Catholic social teaching : contemporary theory and research / edited by Stephen R. Sharkey.
    p. cm. — (Catholic social thought ; no. 6)
  Includes bibliographical references and index.
  ISBN 978-0-8108-8297-3 (cloth : alk. paper) — ISBN 978-0-8108-8327-7 (ebook)
  1. Christian sociology—Catholic Church. 2. Church and social problems—Catholic Church. I. Sharkey, Stephen Richard.
  BX1753.S636 2012
  261.8088'282—dc23
2012017731

Contents

Acknowledgments

First of all I would like to thank the Society of Catholic Social Scientists (SCSS) and President Stephen Krason for offering me the opportunity to develop this book, and for encouraging sociologists within the Society to contribute their thoughts and expertise. The Pontifical Academy of Social Sciences at the Vatican in Rome was very gracious and accommodating in allowing me access to the materials in Part Two, and granting permission to reprint them.

I would also like to thank Kenneth Grasso and Robert Gorman, SCSS editors of the Catholic Social Thought series to which this volume belongs, and Bennett Graff, editor at Scarecrow Press, for their invaluable support and advice. Alverno College made it possible for me to complete a substantial portion of the early work on this volume by supporting my sabbatical during Spring 2011.

Finally, I would like to acknowledge and thank my beloved wife of forty years, Mirella, for her patience, sacrifices, and thoughtful discussions during the entire period I was occupied with this project. Two decades ago we came back to the Catholic Church together after many years away, which has been a true blessing, and we share all of our life and work in the light of the Faith.

Introduction

The Society of Catholic Social Scientists (SCSS) is very pleased to present *Sociology and Catholic Social Teaching: Contemporary Theory and Research* as part of its ongoing series on Catholic social thought, developed in collaboration with Scarecrow Press.[1] This book is meant to illustrate some of the topics and approaches explored by sociologists who propose Catholic social teaching to both academics and the broader public as a valuable framework for social analysis and problem-solving; and at the same time seek to help the Catholic Church better understand contemporary society and refine its social teaching. It is not a comprehensive survey of the growing body of work in sociology done by Catholic scholars with such interests, but rather a sampling of conceptual and empirical studies to give you, the reader, an idea of what is being explored, and to encourage your further interest.

While often differing in their particular political outlooks, all the authors included here come to the study of society aware of how the Catholic faith shapes both their intellectual interests and their value judgments concerning best ways to address pressing social problems in light of our collective need to pursue holiness. Furthermore, while professionally active in various (often secular) contexts and also committed to their academic discipline in and of itself, they share a willingness to think about sociology in light of their faith, and use the best ideas from secular sociology to help advance a more authentically Christian culture in our era. They see Catholicism and sociology as mutually benefitting from a deep conversation. The idea of such a conversation may seem unusual today, even rather provocative—after all, aren't "science" and "religion" not supposed to mix? But in fact it has a long tradition and is experiencing a comeback or renewal, as social scientists and Church leaders seek out more complex, spiritually and empirically informed understandings of the human issues of our times.

Entering the conversation inevitably introduces questions about how sociology has been defined and practiced in the past as well as how the Church perceived it. Sociology is indeed an expression of modernism, and more recently postmodernism, and all too often its mainstream has ignored or looked askance at religion itself, perhaps at best admitting that people may believe they have religious motives for behavior. The Catholic Church, too, has had her doubts about the intellectual merits and moral worth of sociology and has had to reconsider those doubts. As will be explored in several papers here, professionalizing sociology quite intentionally differentiated itself over the 20th century from theology, the Social Gospel, emerging Catholic and Christian social thought, and religiously-inspired social work, claiming a specialized naturalistic and materialistic form of intellectual practice. This had major consequences for how mainstream sociological activity was framed and rewarded: what was included and excluded from research agendas, college curricula, conferences and publications. On the other hand, the Church tended to lead with theology and moral philosophy in its effort to develop an interpretation of social systems. A wide and serious rift occurred.

Yet while there are good scientific reasons to maintain some distinctions between sociological and religious frames of reference and ways of thinking, we believe the rift has ultimately been stifling and dysfunctional. It needed to be overcome, replaced with a more nuanced complementarity. Thus we see ourselves as part of a larger, happy renewal of social science in general, including other fields like history, economics, psychology, and political science, all of which have movements like ours aimed at *reintegrating reason and faith* into a more holistic and complex approach to the study of human experience. As the Mission of the SCSS states,[2]

> The contemporary social sciences are primarily dependent on secular assumptions, concepts and theories. Consequently, the role of faith and Catholic social teaching is hardly considered in today's body of social science. The Society of Catholic Social Scientists (SCSS), founded in 1992, boldly challenges this secularized approach to the social sciences by combining objective scholarly analysis with fidelity to the Magisterium.
>
> Through a collegiality of Catholic scholars, professors, researchers, practitioners, and writers, the SCSS brings rigorous, credible scholarship to political, social and economic questions. SCSS members approach their work in both a scholarly and evangelical spirit. They are expected to strictly observe the highest scholarly and professional requirements of their disciplines as they examine their data in light of Church teaching and the Natural Law. In this way, the Society seeks to obtain objective knowledge about the social order, provide solutions to vexing social problems, and further the cause of Christ.

The above point about "fidelity to the Magisterium" is also crucial to note up-front. Catholic or not, you are probably aware that in contemporary Christianity there is a wide spectrum of views and positions on core moral and social teachings, and at times disputes among them are severe. We acknowledge the existence of such differences within Catholicism, but in our efforts here we start from and rely on the official teachings of the Catholic Church as expressed by its formal teaching arm, the Magisterium. Teachings and principles about the faith and their application to social life are summarized in two main documents, the *Catechism of the Catholic Church* (2003) and especially the *Compendium of the Social Doctrine of the Church* (Pontifical Council of Justice and Peace

2004). The former contains firm teachings set forth with the highest level of dogmatic teaching authority contained in Church Council proceedings and *ex cathedra* encyclicals. The latter contains such teachings also, but further includes material whose sources have important but somewhat lower levels of authority, such as documents from episcopal conferences and pontifical councils or academies. Out of that mix the *Compendium* provides both core truths that will not change, for example on human sexuality and the right to life from conception to natural death, and also guidelines that are meant to frame discussions of specific social policies, what may be called "matters of prudential judgment" about which well-intentioned Catholics may disagree. For example, Catholic social teaching says we must always design social policies that respect the inherent dignity of individuals; but whether a particular poverty reduction program does or does not manifest this respect is a matter for social scientific analysis and debate. We can say that on core topics Catholic social teaching creates bottom-line criteria for judging what happens in society, and at other times, where there is some room for disagreement, offers a framework for setting up ways to make such judgments better. In this volume our goal is not to tear down or redirect core Catholic doctrines or teachings, but to help the Church think about society in a way consistent with its principles using the best available information, and evolve a better social science the Church may use to analyze the contemporary world.

Overview of the Articles

The articles here reflect a range of perspectives on what the conversation between Catholicism and sociology should entail or emphasize, and thus they contribute to it in different ways. In their overall scholarly history some of our authors have stressed more the value of keeping sociological and religious ways of thinking distinct, while others put more emphasis on developing some type of integrated Catholic sociology. I think debating such differences is important in the long run for a couple of reasons. First, it could potentially contribute to healthy changes in the academic boundaries of disciplines and foster useful interdisciplinarity: here I am anticipating more and more collaboration between social science and religion on research and theory building. And second, it could create a healthy space where future sociologists interested in helping the Catholic Church can believe their work will be truly valued: here I am personally hoping that sociologists whose faith is important and visible do not have to bracket that part of their mental lives so much in their scholarly work. But for the present purpose of *introducing* the current conversation between sociology and Catholicism to a diverse audience, we don't need to emphasize the details of such debates in this anthology. Suffice it to invite you to reflect on how you would characterize the relationship between sociology and Catholic social thought as you work your way through each of the articles offered here.

My own papers try to offer a frame to put around this range of approaches by, first, reviewing some of the history of the relationship between mainstream sociology and Catholic social thought and synthesizing what we might learn about putting sociology and Catholic social thought together; and then second, identifying some trends in contemporary mainstream sociology that offer promise for that convergence. The way I put it is that each article in this volume is designed to blend theory and conceptual discussion with a concrete analysis of specific problems or issues, so the reader can see *how a Catholic sociological imagination works in practice.* This type of sociology involves, first of all, the re-examination of basic disciplinary concepts and frameworks used to understand culture and social structure to see how they fit with Catholic teaching, and revising them if necessary; and secondly, the application of qualitative and quantitative methods to study social patterns in light of that teaching. Thus each article is both conceptual and empirical in some way.

Part One: Contributions from the Society of Catholic Social Scientists

Part One contains original works prepared especially for this volume by members of SCSS on a range of important topics, chosen because they address key sociological questions or concerns of Catholics and fellow travelers today. The first article, entitled "Toward a Catholic Sociological Imagination: Sociologies in the Service of Catholic Social Teaching" by myself, provides *some of the history of sociology's relationship to Catholicism, and offers a sketch of the notion of a Catholic sociological imagination as an adaptation of the classical formulation of C.W. Mills.* This form of imagination, I argue, responds in a multidimensional way to the societal need for data and interpretation that can help us bring into focus a moral compass grounded in Christ. It is an imagination in which faith and reason seek each other out.

The next article by Fr. D. Paul Sullins, entitled "Imagined Communions: The Virtual Nation for Virtuous Nations," examines *the Catholic Church's concrete socio-political and spiritual role in world affairs, its organizational presence and work on the global stage.* It can carry out such a role because of its unique nature as both a historical/human and transcendent/divine structure. To be sure its worldly actions can be better or worse in motive and consequence, affected as they are by all too human limits of its members; but its guiding light retains its glow because it is the mystical body of Christ on earth guided by a profound grace running beneath its organizational and teaching work.

Next are discussions of two particular, yet related, subfields of the wider discipline of sociology which contribute much to discerning and diagnosing particularly troubling aspects of our culture. First is a critique and reframing of the *sociology of knowledge,* by Joseph Varacalli, entitled "Beyond the 'Dictatorship of Relativism': Toward a Sociology of Knowledge, Catholic-Style." The sociology of knowledge specializes in analyzing the "social location" of ideas, how the context in which their authors set them forth shapes the content of the ideas themselves and our perceptions of their truth or worth or even plausibility. Many standard concepts and theories sociology employs in its discourse about social stability and social change, about the nature of the person, and about how cultures work were shaped by the strong anti-religious, even anti-Catholic views of their originators. Examples include the notion that objective truth and religious values are and should be two entirely separate realms of human thinking, or that it is impossible to judge or rank norms and values of different subgroups in a diverse, pluralistic society since all are "equally true for their believers." Varacalli goes to the heart of the debate on the relativism and uncertainties of our culture and offers a clearly Catholic alternative to the usual sociological models of how knowledge is created and legitimated.

Then we have a critique and reframing of the subfield of *deviance*, in "Catholic Social Teachings and the Sociology of Deviance" by Anne Hendershott. Deviance studies how societies establish and enforce notions of what is normal and acceptable thought and behavior, and how these notions can change over time under certain circumstances and why. Some societies' systems of norms and values endure for a very long time. But in societies like ours, rapid change in how we think and act is the order of the day. Many of the changes we observe around us, for example in family life, personal relationships, sexuality, and how we can earn a living are happening so fast we can hardly keep up. Hendershott explores how some major changes are particularly destructive for us objectively yet have lost their status as deviant; further, many changes are advocated by specific groups whose goal is to attack the core of the Christian and Catholic worldview. She illustrates her analysis with the example of the "normalization" of homosexuality. Thus we need a different sociological view of deviance that acknowledges these destructive effects of "the new normal" and calls us back to our root traditions, even if in a new way.

Next are two articles concerning the light *quantitative studies shed on main trends and patterns in social customs, laws and beliefs with regard to human bonding and happiness.* What happens when foundational orienting norms and values, described for example by the term Natural Law, are lost or not adhered to in how people pursue these goods? The first of these is by Patrick Fagan, called "How a Catholic Grounding Can Contribute to the Empirical Social Sciences." Fagan is a Senior Fellow at the Washington-based Family Research Council, and routinely publishes empirical syntheses of trend data on marriage and family structure, sexuality, and related topics for use in public policy debates. The Council's mission is to champion "marriage and family as the foundation of civilization, the seedbed of virtue, and the wellspring of society."[3] It is a major player in our current "culture war" over family and relationship issues, and a frequent ally of the Catholic Church in those political, ideological battles. Fagan reflects on some exemplar empirical findings that reveal what happens when the natural law is weakened and the social institution of the family is transmogrified, compared to when it is solidly based in perennial wisdom. He also explains how he thinks Catholic social teaching can benefit from well done sociology.

Then is offered *a recent study of how recent dramatic social change has impacted "emerging adults" for better or worse* by G. Alexander Ross and his associate Michael Wagner, titled "A Cohort Analysis of Happiness among Young Adults." Using a widely available national longitudinal data set commonly employed by sociologists for many purposes, Ross and Wagner compare happiness and other attitudes among 18–26 year-old males and females in the cohorts of the 1950s to the 1980s—a period of dramatic social change for the emerging adult age group. They analyze the impact of these changes and explore the effects among young adults when they accept responsibility for others and reject the self-focused life. The authors discuss how the findings reflect the Catholic understanding that people flourish when they strive to make a free gift of their full selves to others.

Part One then concludes with a second paper of mine entitled "Responding to the Challenge of Postmodernism: Potential Grounds for Future Collaboration between Sociology and Catholic Social Thought." As I briefly mentioned above, here I attempt to identify some key currents entirely within mainstream sociology whose conceptual implications and empirical findings offer, I think, a door to greater collaboration between the discipline and scholars of Catholic social thought. They represent shifts in how sociology defines itself, theorizes, and frames research questions. These currents create openings to the conversation between sociology and Catholicism which the present volume advocates. I explore two trends, personalist critical realism and public sociology.

Part Two: Contributions from the Pontifical Academy of Social Sciences

Part Two contains articles written not by members of SCSS, but rather members of the Catholic Church's international Pontifical Academy of Social Sciences (PASS). Since it is likely that most North American readers are not very familiar with PASS, it was founded in 1994 by Pope John Paul II, who sought to create a forum for creating and debating social scientific information that could help the Magisterium fulfill its responsibilities and refine its social teaching. As the Pope's founding statement declares, "The Pontifical Academy of Social Sciences has the aim of promoting the study and progress of the social, economic, political and juridical sciences, offering the Church the elements which she can use in the study and development of her social doctrine. The Academy also reflects on the application of that doctrine in contemporary society" (John Paul II 1994, 1). It has met each year since its founding, and conference themes have focused on such topics as Work and Employment (1996, 1997, and 1999); Globalization (2001, 2003, and 2005); Intergenerational Solidarity (2002, 2004, and 2006); Human Rights (2009); and Religious Freedom (2011).[4]

In 2004 the renowned American legal scholar and eventual U.S. ambassador to the Vatican, Mary Ann Glendon, was appointed President of the Academy, a position she retains as of this writing. At that year's tenth anniversary conference, Glendon (2004) remarked that when John Paul II established the Academy, he exhorted the original members to "Be not afraid" in their quest for knowledge. "He urged us to search for 'all the grains of truth present in the various intellectual and empirical approaches' of the disciplines gathered under this roof" (49), and to work unceasingly to bring the results of scholarship to bear on human realities "with a 'view to finding solutions to people's concrete problems, solutions based on social justice.'" I am struck by how the mission and activities of PASS express an eagerness about and opening to conversation with sociology and other fields that perhaps many are not aware of, and may even believe is not typical of Catholicism. They also parallel the goals and work of the Society of Catholic Social Scientists very closely, though on a much larger scale to be sure.

That said, we are especially pleased to offer writings here by two highly respected international colleagues in sociology, Margaret Archer from the UK and Pierpaolo Donati from Italy. Both share SCSS's interest in helping the Church develop her social thinking and actively shape the future of society for the better. These articles are taken from the proceedings of the 2008 Vatican conference of the Academy on "Pursuing the Common Good: How Solidarity and Subsidiarity Can Work Together," which our colleagues organized. *Solidarity and subsidiarity are two pillars of Catholic social teaching whose meanings have tended to become unclear or confused over time, and need major refocusing.* The articles in this section reveal how sociology can help with the process of their clarification and precision.

In his article "Discovering the Relational Character of the Common Good," Donati elaborates on the definitional problems that have arisen in the two concepts, and explains how a particular type of relational sociology, one solidly grounded in sociological reality yet incorporating the transcendent as a natural aspect of social life, can inform and help re-establish the authentic meaning of solidarity and subsidiarity as useful principles. Then, in her paper "Education, Subsidiarity, and Solidarity: Past, Present, and Future," Archer explores what these principled terms mean concretely and applies them to a study and evaluation of centralized higher educational systems in Europe. The intent of those systems would seem to be to make life better for more people through training and self-actualization. It does not usually work that way, Archer finds, precisely because Catholic social teaching principles are not in play in how the systems are designed and delivered.

Because the articles by Archer and Donati were part of a larger conference, we thought it would be interesting and informative to set them in that context by accompanying them with additional material. Thus we include with their articles the Greetings to the Academy by Pope Benedict XVI, Greetings to the Pope by Archer, and the conference Opening Address by Archer and Donati to all attendees.

Lastly, a brief word about formatting. All the papers in Part Two were originally written in or translated into English following continental style for usage and citations, and formatted to meet Vatican publication guidelines. For publication in the present volume, they have been slightly adapted and edited, without introducing any change in meaning, to meet our publishing conventions as far as possible. Some differences from American conventions do remain, however, that reflect the authors' European voices and scholarly style.

Part Three: About the Authors

One final point. We also believe that the sociology presented here is not some abstract enterprise, but emerges out of each author's own life journey as a scholar and person of faith. So to help the reader better understand where these particular sociologists are coming from and why they go where they go, we've included a section at the end of the book with both the usual *biographical* information about each author's professional accomplishments, and also some *autobiographical* comments on his or her personal path as a sociologist thinking with the Church. We hope this will invite you, the reader, to think about your own walk toward integrating faith and reason in your professional and personal life, and in your sociology.

Notes

1. So far these include the *Encyclopedia of Catholic Social Thought, Social Science, and Social Policy, Vols. 1, 2* and 3 (Coulter, Krason, Myers, and Varacalli 2007/2011); *The Public Order and the Sacred Order: Contemporary Issues, Catholic Social Thought and the Western and American Traditions, Vols. 1 and 2* (Krason 2009); *Bioethics, Law, and Human Life Issues* (Scarnecchia 2010); a volume on political science entitled *Toward the Common Good: A Catholic Critique of Political Science* (Gorman 2011), and several monographs related to economics by Rupert Ederer, including most recently *Pope Pius XII on the Economic Order* (Ederer 2011).

2. See www.catholicsocialscientists.org.

3. See www.frc.org.

4. Many conference documents are now becoming available as downloadable computer files from the PASS website at the Vatican. See http://www.vatican.va/roman _curia/pontifical_academies/acdscien/index_social_en.htm.

Bibliography

Catechism of the Catholic Church. 2nd edition. 2003. New York: Doubleday.

Coulter, Michael, Stephen Krason, Richard Myers, and Joseph Varacalli, eds. 2007 (Vol. 3 update 2011). *Encyclopedia of Catholic Social Thought, Social Science, and Social Policy, Vols. 1, 2, and 3.* Lanham, MD: Scarecrow Press.

Ederer, Rupert. 2011. *Pope Pius XII on the Economic Order.* Lanham, MD: Scarecrow Press.

Glendon, Mary Ann. 2004. "The First Ten Years of the Pontifical Academy of Social Sciences." In *Traditions in Turmoil,* by Mary Ann Glendon (49–51). Ann Arbor, MI: Sapientia Press.

Gorman, Robert, ed. 2011. *Toward the Common Good: A Catholic Critique of the Discipline of Political Science.* Lanham, MD: Scarecrow Press.

John Paul II. 1994. "*Motu Proprio* Establishing the Pontifical Academy of the Social Sciences." Accessed at http://vatican.va/roman_curia/pontifical_academies.

Krason, Stephen. 2009. *The Public Order and the Sacred Order: Contemporary Issues, Catholic Social Thought, and the Western and American Traditions, Vols. 1 and 2.* Lanham, MD: Scarecrow Press.

Pontifical Council of Justice and Peace. 2004. *Compendium of the Social Doctrine of the Church.* Washington, DC: United States Conference of Catholic Bishops.

Scarnecchia, Brian. 2010. *Bioethics, Law, and Human Life Issues: A Catholic Perspective on Marriage, Family, Contraception, Abortion, Reproductive Technology, and Death and Dying.* Lanham, MD: Scarecrow Press.

PART ONE

**Contributions from the
Society of Catholic Social Scientists**

1

Toward a Catholic Sociological Imagination: Sociologies in the Service of Catholic Social Teaching

Stephen R. Sharkey

The regenerate science I have in mind would not do even to minerals and vegetables what modern science threatens to do to man himself. When it explained it would not explain away. When it spoke of the parts it would remember the whole. While studying the It it would not lose what Martin Buber calls the Thou-situation.
C.S. Lewis, *The Abolition of Man,* 1947[1]

In this opening article of the collection, my goal is to provide some general background and context to the work being done by these sociologists to create a bridge between their secular discipline and the corpus of Catholic Social Teaching (CST). In the first major section, I try to define what it means conceptually to advance a "Catholic sociological imagination" in service to the Church's social Magisterium; and in the second, I offer what I believe are some signature historic moments in the development of the role Catholic sociologists have played in contributing to Catholic social thought and social teaching.

Throughout this introductory piece and other contributions to the anthology, there will be references to various similar-sounding but distinct terms: Catholic Social Teaching (CST), Catholic social thought, and Catholic sociology. And all of these particular domains are part of a larger territory called Catholic intellectual culture. What are these, and how do they stand in relation to each other? Not every author in this anthology speaks exactly the same language on these matters, but in general they acknowledge three different interconnected domains in the Catholic intellectual culture territory this book deals with. Such a tripartite distinction is also common elsewhere in the relevant literature, employed quite recently for example by Williams (2011) in his excellent book *The World as It Could Be: Catholic Social Thought for a New Generation*. Thus, firstly, by *Catholic Social Teaching* (CST) we generally mean the formal Magisterial social teachings of the Church as set forth in the various papal social encyclicals, and also most comprehensively in the *Compendium of the Social Doctrine of the Church* (Pontifical Council of Justice and Peace 2005). The *Compendium* includes dogmatic teachings derived from sources of highest doctrinal authority, such as Church council documents and papal encyclicals; as well as teachings derived from elsewhere, such as Vatican congregations and academies, that have a very high but not absolute authority and strongly complement dogmatic truths (*Compendium*, #8). This CST consists of core principles for reflection and focus, criteria for judgment, and directives for action (*Compendium*, #7) regarding social problems; the four permanent, core principles are the dignity of the human person, the common good, subsidiarity, and solidarity (#160).[2] CST is intended and designed to balance stability and universality with evolution and contextuality—what the authors call "continuity and renewal," where the former depends on universal values drawn from Revelation and the latter on the study of particular historical conditions (#85).

CST is a body of formal doctrine defined by the Church through a complex process of reflection and dialogue over decades, grounded in a cumulative review of prior teaching; it has the most stable, firm content and boundaries of any of the three domains here. Blasi and Sullins (2009) call CST as set forth in the *Compendium* a *centripetal* force: a stabilizing center which, while certainly evolving (indeed in paragraph 860 its authors refer to the *Compendium* as a "work site where the work is always in progress"), also changes, albeit cautiously, and forms a kind of general template one can always reliably turn and return to. Williams (2011) uses the same adjective, "centripetal," to describe the Catholic effort to achieve social cohesion and coherence in a world of societal multiplicity and defined by tensions between universalism and localism, the one and the many, unity and diversity, the common good and individual freedoms.

Next, *by Catholic social thought* is meant a considerably broader and more fluid territory of multidisciplinary scholarship surrounding and including official CST, with a dialectical flow of interaction among its contributors. On the one hand it comprises the social scientific and social philosophical discourse and scholarship that draws on extant CST to influence society, to bring the teachings into the world through application. On the other hand, it seeks to explore issues and concepts, use research findings to influence the evolution of CST doctrine itself, clarify CST's implications and impacts in particular settings, and identify new social issues on the horizon that CST will eventually have to address. Catholic social thought is thus a more expansive, and at times contentious, *centrifu-*

gal force that seeks to probe and stretch CST's meanings and applications through interaction with relevant scholarship about faith and society. In other words, it is where a fairly broad range of perspectives about social realities and their application to Catholic theory and practice are aired, and the boundaries of orthodoxy are often tested.

Finally by *Catholic sociology* is meant academic sociologies built from or including frameworks in the secular discipline that are broadly compatible with Catholic principles, developed by sociologists who are often but not always Catholic. They are offered *for the purpose of contributing to Catholic social thought*, thus having the capacity to directly or indirectly influence CST's profile and development. What makes such sociologies Catholic is their compatibility with Catholic social analytic principles and their being aimed at developing those principles through theory and research. Catholic sociology—like Catholic economics or Catholic political science or Catholic psychology or Catholic history, understood in the terms defined here and all of which flow into Catholic social thought—sits on the cultural and spiritual bridge between the secular and sacred in academia and in the broader idea-sphere of society. It is *not* a confessional sociology that starts and ends all empirical and/or theoretical questions with biblical analysis and exegesis.[3] Rather it is sociology broadly derived, done and shaped in light of Catholic thought. Its moral and value foundations for analyzing the meaning of well-researched empirical findings are grounded in Catholic social thought, while its theories are rooted in or are compatible with the Catholic intellectual tradition. And it draws on secular ideas and research whenever useful and appropriate.

These domains often interrelate and interconnect, as ideas and people move across this multilayered territory. Altogether, these domains (plus other related scholarly disciplines and institutions involved with advancing the Catholic social idea) contribute to what may overarchingly be called a Catholic intellectual culture.

Sociology Contributing Its Imagination to Catholic Intellectual Culture

The focus of this paper and the anthology as a whole is on the vector that runs from the discipline of secular sociology through its contributions to Catholic social thought, and on toward the evolution of CST. I am interested in what can help us, as academically-trained sociologists, do a better job fostering the principles of CST in the broader society by using some developments in contemporary sociology to build a substantial Catholic reply to the problems of postmodern society. This is a matter of both improving social theory and offering evidence of ways to live better—that is, in a manner more in accordance with

Catholic Social Teaching. In this way we can make a conceptual contribution to rebuilding some of the collapsed plausibility structure of orthodox Catholicism in our era and revitalize the role of CST principles in public life or civil society.

This will require some discernment about what in academic sociology can and should be drawn upon or adapted for this purpose. Papers in this anthology often try to do just that: they draw on sociology in all its theoretical and empirical breadth to contribute to an understanding of society through a Catholic lens. This is not often easy to do. While the overall academic discipline of sociology did share some common social reform interests with Catholic social thought early in its history, especially during the era of rapid expansion of industrial capitalism with all its social dislocations, that affinity truly fragmented as "science" and "religion" came to be seen as different and essentially incompatible realms of human endeavor. As I shall discuss later, in recent decades academic sociology has been indifferent and even hostile to explicit collaboration with religion in general and Catholicism in particular (Varacalli 1992; Sullins 2007). As scientifically-framed sociology parted ways with religion, the discipline also parried with the formation quite early of the subspecialty called the "sociology of religion" so that religious topics could still be considered under the disciplinary canopy of legitimacy. After all, religion was in fact a major preoccupation of the discipline's founding fathers like Weber and Durkheim. But in its pursuit of general theories of religion the subfield was strongly influenced by positivist and materialist intellectual currents in theory and research, which valued the sort of universalist stance of "objectivity" and "neutrality" meant to situate the sociology of religion firmly in the camp of science and not religion. While believing sociologists often migrated to the sociology of religion, it could be a rather ambiguous home at best, since sociology as a discipline is, I would say, often scandalized by the particularity of religious adherence and found a way to explore religion as a datum without having to strongly and personally engage its reflexive meanings.

In this volume we are trying to light a path beyond that type of sociology of religion. Perhaps the closest cousin to the sociology we present is the kind of research that gets used to help the Church read the signs of the times or to help critics make a point—for example by documenting patterns in Catholic organizational structures and beliefs and in social trends that impact upon the nature of religious experiences and worldviews, often comparatively. Even so, we seek something more and different than a sociology which happens to be about Catholicism as a significant institution, though it would include that: we emphasize here a sociology whose authors intend to directly engage Catholic social thought and CST in order to explore or advance them, thereby placing Catholic social thought into the sociological quiver along with many other analytic resources, and at the same time placing a range of sociological thinking and research into the Catholic quiver to help the Church and us find our way.

I think this is more possible today than it has been for decades. There are valuable developments in current sociology we may draw upon, which build upon models of man and society more directly compatible with Catholic principles and shaped by values consistent with Catholic concerns about the direction of our culture. In fact I will review some specific examples of these recent developments in the valedictory paper at the end of Part One. At the moment, let me focus on my belief that these recent developments in sociology invite us to articulate a particular Catholic adaptation of the classic Millsian sociological imagination—an imagination which can become part of the fabric of a *stronger Catholic intellectual culture*. Recently Sullins (2010) defined a Catholic intellectual culture as including the *unity of faith and reason, the acceptance of Magisterial teachings of the Church, and an active critique of culture*. Each factor is crucial and been the subject of much rich discussion leading to the affirmation of the elements Sullins has set forth. Just to indicate a few examples, consider John Paul II's encyclicals *Fides et Ratio* and *Veritatis Splendor*; Romano Guardini's ([1923] 2004) early twentieth century foundational work on the "Catholic worldview" as inherently rooted in orthodox Church teachings—work upon which Pope Benedict XVI often in fact admiringly builds his social and theological views; George Weigel's (2004) recent portrait of a Catholic sensibility as both rooted in enduring truths and open to new understandings; and Michael Gallagher's (2003) work on the centrality of cultural analysis for the advancement of the Faith. Sullins argues that, taken together, these three features will "foster Catholic intellectuals and dispose students to the truth, and ha[ve] the potential to preserve and restore elements of reason and humanity that are being lost in Western civilization."

What specifically is needed to adapt contemporary secular sociology to the purpose of serving CST by incorporating Sullins' list of three features? If any concept has informed the contemporary discipline of sociology in a comprehensive way, it has been C. Wright Mills' notion of the sociological imagination. It is therefore useful to start our consideration of reframing sociology so it may serve CST right there.

Problems with Mills' Idea in Principle and Practice

Sociologists will readily recognize the widely employed phrase "sociological imagination" set forth in 1959 by Mills, and used in almost every basic sociology textbook to introduce a main goal of the discipline: i.e., to develop students' intellectual and moral capacities to connect biography and social context, to see the larger structural forces operating behind social problems often perceived in individualistic or psychologistic ways. In articulating this idea Mills made the pedagogically helpful distinction between "private troubles" and "public issues." Private troubles are problems that are the result of an individual's circumstances or capacities, local situations and conditions, the ups and downs of life. We all know particular women and men who may struggle in marriage, Mills wrote: they have private troubles in their married life. But what is going on when a huge percentage of marriages in a society are ending in divorce? Something else must be occurring besides the private struggles of some couples. Public issues are widespread problems affecting large numbers of individuals whose causes lie in some aspect of the broader society, in what will be called the "social structure."

While highly engaging especially for new students, insofar as it opens the door to seeing sociology and its concern for social structures as personally relevant, from a Catholic point of view there are at least two significant problems with the way the term *sociological imagination* was used by Mills and is commonly deployed today in the sociological mainstream. First, the concept tends to be implicitly or explicitly loaded with the driving politics of its author. Mills' sociology was essentially a secular-left political framework grounded in Marxian conflict theory, which inspires its adherents by coupling outrage and a preponderant hermeneutic of suspicion to a reductionist class analysis, and then framing sociological research as a form of leftist political consciousness raising. Mills' goal was to quite literally wake a complacent people up to various forms of oppression they might not be aware of—in itself certainly not a bad thing. But the means to get there involve supplanting inherited moral traditions with materialist factors to interpret the malaise. One is to get politically angry at capitalism and elites and all hierarchies, and pursue explicitly socialist goals. Those inherited traditions are in fact part of the problem from Mills' point of view.

I argue that learning or inquiry based essentially on outrage and a utopian socialist vision that rejects all religion has its empirical and moral limits. The Millsian project's useful pedagogical purposes and critical stance may begin well, but in the end too easily take us in a direction *away* from Catholic social thought ontologically and epistemologically. Despite its salutary effort to connect sociology as a science with values and a prophetic stance, Mills' sociological imagination is in effect yet another enlightenment-style version of sociology *replacing* religion. In this sense, though sensitive to the personal and biographical aspects of social life, it essentially updates the Comtean substitution of sociology for religion from which a core of the discipline draws its energies. Mills' own life and work reveal a fundamental antagonism to religion as a source of authentic meaning and understanding of society: though raised Catholic himself as a boy and having served at the altar, he never took on the Faith and in fact once wrote, during the time he was working on his book supporting Castro and Cuban revolution, that Catholics "haven't got me" (Shannon 2006, especially chapter 6; Sharkey 2005; Mills and Mills 2000). In the Marxist tradition his sociology declares religion as but an expression of false consciousness; his take on biography is historico-critical, to use a theological term, and fails to develop the deep personalism so essential to a Catholic understanding of the human condition. The Millsian sociologist is a heroic outcast from bourgeois culture and its religious trappings who dares to serve as a humanistic social critic engaging the plight of the oppressed. To authentically stand outside, a Millsian sociologist must cast aside all his cherished ideas and affiliations, even looking very askance at his own intellectual home; thus he will also turn on those cadres within the discipline that serve corporate and other hierarchical interests. Such heroic and eradicating scrutiny makes Millsian reflexivity seem complex and morally worthy. But despite the value of the goals the process is actually an endlessly looping critique of critique, which in my own personal experience as a student learning the field, reminded me of the "crit-self-crit" sessions central to the culture of Marxist fringe parties ascertaining who was worthy of the label "true radical."

Second, and related, these politics of the concept are merged with an excessively strong social constructionism that fits well with the contemporary subculture of sociology. Christian Smith's (2010) remarks about this are helpful to quote at length, since his perspective on the matter involves both theoretical and personal considerations about how sociologists engage the strong constructionism rampant in the field, and which several authors in the present anthology in fact also critique:

> The phrase "The Social Construction of_____," has become a ubiquitous framing device for sociological and other social scientific analyses of nearly every subject conceivable. Most sociologists today seem as comfortable using the phrase "social construction" as say, "social structure," "social stratification," or any other elementary disciplinary concept.
>
> Something about the idea of social constructionism resonates strongly with the sociological imagination, namely, that much of human social life that appears to many people as "natural," taken-for-granted facts of an objective, fixed order is not determined by the essential properties of nature but are variable artifacts of human cultural creation through social definition, interaction, and institutionalization. The social thus displaces nature in this perspective as the source of much if not all of human experience. A closely related reason why social constructionism attracts many sociologists is the ironic form of analysis that it readily engenders. Most interesting and influential sociological works are those that show that something we previously understood in one way is best really understood quite differently. Usually the difference comes with an ironic twist. For instance, we previously thought that mental asylums were institutions provided by humane societies to care for their psychologically impaired members, until Erving Goffman showed us that asylums are essentially totalitarian concentration camps. Social constructionism thus provides sociologists a powerful analytic tool to perform the assumption-upending ironic twists that make for interesting storytelling. Social constructionism also appeals to many sociologists because its unmasking of the seemingly natural as contingently constructed open up possibilities for intentional personal and social change toward greater justice, freedom, equality, and human fulfillment....This theoretical leaning fits nicely with the personal progressive politics of most social scientists. (120–21)

Smith goes on to say that, like many of us, he too was strongly shaped in his sociological formation by the likes of Peter Berger, and appreciates the social critical approach sociological constructionism can foster. Nevertheless, he says—and with this I strongly concur—today's sociological/social construction-ist imagination has "run amok" with wild claims, intellectual naivetè, half truths, rhetorical hyperbole, and trendiness, where the person as an acting responsible agent tends to dissolve in a cascade of social determinism, along with the possi-bility of higher human purpose beyond the will to power of ideologies. It is strongly bound up with liberationist and individualist ideology.

Toward a Catholic Sociological Imagination

All this cries out for some counterposing temperance and balance, as well as greater theoretical sophistication, and I think putting a Catholic dimension into the mix can accomplish these. So in using the term "*Catholic* sociological imag-ination" I mean to *adapt* the standard Millsian usage, and offer one such coun-terposition. I want to preserve and value Mills' basic question about how peo-ples' lives connect to structures—or put another way, how biography connects to history—and acknowledge the value of constructionist insights, but allow in a role for religious and spiritual realities as both motives for research and, very importantly, as part of the *ontological* reality of society we study. It is important to break down the academic and theoretical barriers between sociology and reli-gion, so as to expand the intellectual freedom available to anyone developing a sociological imagination useful for our purposes.

As Swatos (1987) put it, I and my colleagues advocate a "sociology as if re-ligion is real." Or, as Keenan (2003) expressed it, we seek a "transfigurational sociology" (his use of a religious term is quite intentionally provocative), by which he means a sociology that opens space for sociologists grounded in a ra-ther closed materialist and naturalistic universe of analysis and understanding to be able to confront a bit more comfortably the anxiety that can be provoked by the clearly spiritual import of their science, and the non-material dimension of human individual and social experience—what Peter Berger once called "signals of transcendence." It is also a sociology that moves from the sort of non-individualistic, profoundly *social relational* model of the person, an image of God and thus carrying the dynamic nature of the Trinity within, described by Pope Benedict in many of his works[4] and often enough affirmed even in secular language by much perceptive social science (Douglas and Ney 1998). Of keen interest is also the fact that this relational model of the person correlates with a part of the sociological tradition that always emphasized non-atomistic, relation-al dynamics as the *sine qua non* of social systems; this relational view is now enjoying renewed interest, and explicitly recalls attention to the role of real reli-gious experiences at the heart of any society (Donati 2010).

To return to Sullins' terminology, a scholarly and passionate Catholic sociological imagination pursues the understanding of the relationship between biography and history, of why social life is as it is in various times and places, by drawing on the learnings of both faith and reason, seen as two intrinsically related ways of knowing, and by accepting the reality of religion and transcendence in the people being studied. It starts ethically or morally from the position that the Church's basic teachings about the transcendent meaning of life, the relational nature of man, and the ultimate purposes of society are true. And it develops its objective analysis of culture and social structure by posing and answering empirical questions suggested by CST principles and their application to real social issues.

It is interesting to me that recently some sociologists, conscious of the intensely reflexive character of sociological thought and practice in this postpositivist era, are pushing the boundaries even of an apparently secular sociological imagination to include domains that can readily encompass the sacred or transcendent in the sociological gaze. What is it that we see, when we see sociologically with the necessary depth and openness? What does such a sociological imagination open us to that the normal version doesn't? Kieran Flanagan (2007) explores this question in depth, starting from the premise that what sociologists are often most concerned with, social structures, are not in fact clearly visible at first to those inside them or to the sociological observer, but they are made real by thought and behavior and can come into focus for sociologists with the right gaze. Pushing out the limits of the Millsian perspective, Flanagan cites Zygmunt Bauman's take on the Millsian sociological imagination: in a 2002 interview, Bauman argued that sociology involves a "sixth sense" we can develop to make those structures more visible. For Bauman (2002)—hardly in a religious camp himself—Mills' sociological imagination involves the realization that "there is more to what you see and hear than meets the eye, that the most important part is hidden from view, and that there is a huge and dense tissue of inter-human connections below the visible tip of the iceberg. An insight that triggers imagination, that if worked on properly, sediments sociology." While it is not clear that Mills would put it this way, even the materialist Bauman has to acknowledge sociology's capacity to make mystery more visible. Flanagan then extends the implications of this point, arguing that this kind of sociological search can indeed lead to the theological, to the Spirit working in people's lives as well as in the life of the sociologist doing the searching. Catholic sociologies of various sorts press toward this type of expansive imagination which can make visible the invisible, including the spiritual.

Sociology Engaging CST, but in a Different Key

There are indeed many possible micro, meso, and macro-level sociologies that could thus serve the project of advancing Catholic Social Teaching and its four constituent principles or pillars of the spiritually sane society: namely, the dignity of the human person, the common good, subsidiarity, and solidarity. However, it is important to state that the focus in our anthology is on those sociologies which implicitly or explicitly rest on, are compatible with, or point toward, Magisterial doctrines. In this anthology we seek to advance CST's principles within those orthodox parameters, even as the criteria for applying those principles in concrete societal policy situations are prudential and somewhat elastic. Discussing this territory requires caution because CST discourse has become caught up in the politicization of the Church and often reflects political agendas regarding key doctrines.

As is well known, the Church does not build CST around particular politics or forms of government—though it does favor democracies at this time. Yet while there are some who've tried to develop social scientific analyses employing CST in a way "beyond left and right" (e.g., Cochran and Cochran 2003), the fact is that the American CST terrain has often been dominated by liberal-leaning and even heterodox scholars and activists, who bend CST's frequently legitimate press for significant change in the broader society back toward the specific ideological purpose of protestantizing Catholicism, of moving Catholicism to embrace the organizational structure and doctrines of episcopalianism. This usually occurs in the name of a misunderstood interpretation of Vatican II, said to demand the acculturation of the Church's norms and structures to contemporary society's norms and values in order to achieve social acceptability and relevance among a population more at ease with a generic individualistic humanism than the challenge of traditional Catholicism. This is hardly a new problem for the Church: as G.K. Chesterton observed in 1910, "The huge modern heresy is to alter the human soul to fit modern social conditions, instead of altering modern social conditions to fit the human soul" (Chesterton 1910, 104). Today's CST discourse too often serves to accomplish the former by making it easier for Catholics to be modern in Chesterton's sense. Many popular presentations of CST have functioned to challenge not just prudential positions but core Church doctrines on all manner of topics both social and theological, especially by advocating an emphasis on historico-critical methodologies and a supposedly more flexible cultural relativism that melt away the Church's reliance on "absolutes" in its doctrine and pastoral work (e.g., Mich 2001; Curran 2002; Maguire 2001; Thompson 2010). In the United States this often ends up, for example, as support for a variety of feminist positions on women's ordination and contraception, normalization of homosexuality and support for LGBT legal goals, embracing of liberation theology abroad, and frank advocacy of the policy preferences of the left wing of the Democratic Party on everything from military deployments to abortion.[5] In fact on many campuses CST can be an appealing lever for organizing new generations of weakly catechized and loosely attached Catholic students against the hierarchical Church: looking for some sort of spirituality and ways to dedicate themselves to service, and ripe for a target for their genuine moral indignation and search for justice, they are intentionally led away from the heart of the Church by its liberal and radical critics who are in a position to shape ministry and curricula, as the Cardinal Newman Society so often sadly documents.

This process occurred because of what has been termed a "secularization from within" (Sharkey 2004–5; Varacalli 2000, especially chapter 9; Hendershott 2009; Burtchaell 1998; Shaw 2011). For a generation now, "social justice" was too often discussed in a way that, while employing Catholic terminology and moral urgency, was actually *detached* from the orthodox doctrines underlying CST principles such as the authority of the Magisterium to make decisions and foundations of sexual morality. By usually overemphasizing one side of an authentically Catholic teaching whose actual complexity a lay audience might not appreciate, dissidents or apostates could seem publicly Catholic in their rhetoric, goals, and activity but actually hollow out Catholic identity in parishes, retreat centers, and on campuses.[6] For example, starting with a valid criticism of the very real problem of clericalism, and using a technically accurate statement that the Body of Christ is all inclusive and encompasses the laity, the baby is promptly thrown out with the bathwater. The Church is said to be "not merely" the Pope and the hierarchy, but rather "is really" a more democratic and diverse, more congregational "people of God" who are probably even more capable of discussing social justice and establishing doctrines than the curia ever could be because of their "more real" involvement with the realities of life in society where ambiguity rather than absolute moral standards prevail. Thus if the People of God and their preferred theologians disagree with the hierarchy, so what? They are their own best magisterium and their own best agents for challenging injustices.[7]

The liberal tendencies of the dominant CST discourse also dovetailed strongly with the well-known ideological bias of sociology itself. As Peter Berger (2002) himself ruefully observed, the field has been dominated by not only a certain methodological fetishism that has its origins in the radical positivism of its post-founding period, but perhaps worse an "ideologization" that has "deformed science into an instrument of agitation and propaganda (the Communists used to call this 'agitprop'), invariably for causes on the left of the ideological spectrum." Sociology has been swept by derivatives of the Marxism of the 1960s, mixed with certain strands of feminism and multiculturalism. And as Smith noted earlier, another major problem is the prevalence of strong social constructionism and its cousin, radical moral relativism.

To be sure, core elites within sociology praise this development as part of sociology's heroic struggle against bourgeois hegemony in society and within the discipline itself. The struggle was always there but became most prominent starting with Mills and his cohort in the 1960s; since then the radicalism of the period diffused itself throughout the profession, though in an often diluted form, as undergraduates became graduate students who became teachers and researchers who became department chairs and leaders in the associations. Today, sociology finds itself often at odds with "fat cat sociology" in the service of corporate elites, as well as with conservatism in general—understood as Republican political power, popular support for militarism, state-level refusal to legalize same sex marriage, and so forth. As Michael Burawoy (2005) approvingly assessed the disciplinary scene with specific examples in his 2004 American Sociological Association presidential address,

> The increased presence and participation of women and racial minorities, the ascent of the 1960s generation to leadership positions in departments and our association, marked a critical drift that is echoed in the content of sociology.
>
> Thus, political sociology turned from the virtues of American electoral democracy to studying the state and its relation to classes, social movements as political processes, and the deepening of democratic participation. Sociology of work turned from processes of adaptation to the study of domination and labor movements. Stratification shifted from the study of social mobility within a hierarchy of occupational prestige to the examination of changing structures of social and economic inequality—class, race and gender. The sociology of development abandoned modernization theory for underdevelopment theory, world systems analysis, and state-orchestrated growth. Race theory moved from theories of assimilation to political economy to the study of race formations. Social theory introduced more radical interpretations of Weber and Durkheim and incorporated Marx into the canon.

I believe it is accurate to say that in every domain of social justice thinking within the Catholic orbit that sociology could touch, sociology touched it with the approaches Burawoy mentions here. Thus to the extent that there has been a considerable presence of sociological ideas in social justice thinking—ideas about social stratification, discrimination, colonialism, and power in particular—they tended to be the ideas derived from Marxian conflict theory: in particular race theory, feminism, and social constructionism aimed at liberations from authority structures. The authority of the Church's teachings, qua authority system, also became a target for sociological disdain insofar as the Church was understood with a small c, as essentially a reactionary monarchical social organization needing *aggiornamento* in a really big way.

Since sociology and Catholicism did not often find common ground historically in recent decades, this particular case of convergence or synergy between a certain type of liberation-oriented sociology and liberation Catholicism needs some accounting. Though that detailed accounting must be left for another time, I suspect the convergence can be explained in terms of the strong tendency toward *antinomianism* underlying both perspectives: that is, the view of law or principles of order as externalities that can hamper the authentic freedom of individuals. In religion this is a conviction, as Reno (2011) recently put it, that the letter of the law kills: "To affirm any limiting norms—moral principles, confessional or creedal standards, and even the authority of the Bible—is to fall victim to 'legalism.'" In social analysis, postmodern sociological cultural theory's antinomianism amounts to asserting an antagonism between form and freedom, between order and authenticity. Thus contemporary sociology's preoccupation in empirical research with documenting the experiences of various groups have with confining or restraining social customs and laws, the celebration of diversity for its own sake, and the discipline's abandonment of any notion of overriding social metanarrative except that of seeking liberation through radical acceptance of difference. Speaking from personal knowledge it became harder and harder to attend sociology meetings and talk about being a loyal Catholic, or attempt to rebut a sociological argument of this antinomian sort with an idea from CST—and not just intellectually difficult, but also interpersonally difficult. Being a non-antinomian Catholic was equivalent to being religiously judgmental, culturally narrow-minded and intellectually retrograde.

This synergy of liberalisms has been a potent cocktail—and it has made efforts to carry out sociology that acknowledges the reality of ultimate values and sees the person in more than social constructionist terms particularly difficult from both directions. Thus a key part of our task is to take sociologies compatible with solid CST doctrine and enter the zone of Catholic social thought with them, and not leave that territory only to the Church's liberal and heterodox critics. Varacalli (1987, 1989, 1996, 2000) has repeatedly stated that sociologies reflecting orthodox teachings are very important to put on the table at this time because they can contribute enormously to rebuilding the collapsed plausibility structures—ideas and the social institutions built upon those ideas—that Catholicism needs to be a viable alternative voice in contemporary society. For these plausibility structures have truly withered. As the broader culture privatized and secularized Christianity, and what remained of the latter was dominated by the Evangelical and non-denominational mega-churches, Catholicism's mechanisms for producing a next generation of faithful Catholics were eaten away through errant revisions of traditions and an incapacity to effectively catechize. Catholicism could not sustain itself even as one of several plausible alternatives in a diverse society.

I am not rhapsodizing about a loss of the golden days of the 1950s when everyone watched Archbishop Sheen on television and nuns were everywhere: if that period were so golden how could the Church's appeal and authority have collapsed so quickly? No, it is something deeper about failing to come to terms with asserting Catholicism as a realistic and important worldview in ways beyond simple assimilation into the American mainstream. In any case, the factual results of this eviscerating process have been clearly documented, for example, in the excellent longitudinal National Study of Youth and Religion,[8] which demonstrates the almost unbelievably weak connection today's Catholic teens and then young adults have to the Church as a habitus and source of identity, and their almost non-existent understanding of basic Catholic doctrine, social or otherwise. They are part of a larger social trend toward cafeteria religion, to be sure; but tragically, Catholics "score low" even in a range of low scoring among all groups, except Mormons and some Evangelicals, on many empirical indicators of strength of participation in, and knowledge of, their faith.

A shorthand way to summarize these related trends is to say a "culture war" has been running through the middle of the heart of every social institution, including the Church. The concept of "culture war" is itself contentious, having been challenged by liberal sociologists such as Alan Wolfe (2006) as overdramatizing the normal conflicts among different perspectives in a democratic society. But I argue—with Hunter (1991, 2006), George (2001), Varacalli (2000), Little (1995), and many others—that the war is real. It has constricted both the width of contemporary sociology and the development of Catholic social teaching, and challenges the ability of sociologists who serve the Church with loyalty to the Church's Magisterium to have a significant voice. Sociology ought to be diverse, and Catholic social teaching ought to be a big tent. The sway of leftist ideology artificially narrowed both territories.

Is this the whole story? No, because the trend is starting to shift. Within sociology, there exists a strong renewal of interest in the reflexive aspects of social life, including religious experiences; efforts to reframe models of the person upon which sociological theory is built; and the role religion has played as a core conceptual arena and empirical concern of sociology from the very first (Flanagan 1996, 2007).[9] This interest is bolstered by the collapse of certain modernist sociological claims concerning secularization's inevitable destruction of Religion, which by any empirical measure has *not* increased with modernization as predicted. On the contrary, Religion is alive and growing in certain ways, though often viewed with alarm by secular liberals in particular as a "resurgence of fundamentalism." Thus sociology is opening to some degree to thinking in a religious key. Also, as I will argue in the last paper in this Part, even within the strong leftist call to arms for sociology to more effectively engage public policy and social change, a door is paradoxically opened for the renewed examination of a range of value foundations for such public sociological work—and this can include values espoused by orthodox Catholics.

At the same time, within the Church the dominance of liberal critics in the culture war that had lasted for a generation (Kelly 1981)—often on the basis of faulty ideas made possible by certain vaguenesses or weaknesses in Vatican II texts themselves (Rourke 2011)—has also definitely waned. Especially under the influence of the current and previous popes, there is fortunately today a new opening to orthodoxy in the arena of CST teachings and to a growing understanding of Vatican II documents as grounded deeply in foundational Church teachings. The *Compendium* is itself a major expression of this. And of special interest for us here is the definite healing of the old breach between Catholicism and social sciences on the part of the Church. In fact, citing especially John Paul II's 1991 encyclical *Centesimus Annus* and his *motu proprio* establishing the Pontifical Academy of the Social Sciences in 1994, the *Compendium* explicitly states its appreciation and need for what the various branches of social science can contribute to social doctrine:

> *A significant contribution to the Church's social doctrine comes also from human sciences and the social sciences. In view of that particular part of the truth that it may reveal, no branch of knowledge is excluded.* The church recognizes and receives everything that contributes to the understanding of man in the ever broader, more fluid and more complex network of his social relationships. She is aware of the fact that a profound understanding of man does not come from theology alone, without the contributions of many branches of knowledge to which theology itself refers.
>
> This attentive and constant openness to other branches of knowledge makes the Church's social doctrine reliable, concrete and relevant. Thanks to the sciences, the Church can gain a more precise understanding of man in society, speak to the men and women of her own day in a more convincing manner and more effectively fulfill her task of incarnating in the conscience and social responsibility of our time, the word of God and the faith from which social doctrine flows. (Pontifical Council for Justice and Peace 2005, #78)

The *Compendium* also calls upon the laity to step up to the plate to work to transform social life in the secular realm (#83) following orthodox Church teachings, and this too may be observed: the hegemony of liberalism is attenuating with the generational rise of what Allen (2009) and Weigel (2011b) call "evangelical" or "John Paul II" Catholics, who for two decades now have been seeking to reverse the sad dilution of Catholicism in the waters of individualism, relativism, and materialism.

This generation and its allies in the Curia need social scientific scholarship about culture and society to shine light on ways to build a renewed and world-tested orthodox Catholicism, and turn to social scientists both lay and clerical to provide it. It is not that the influence of Call to Action and liberation theology have entirely disappeared from the Church and parish staffs; nor have the parallel radical social constructionism and Marxism faded from sociology. Rather a new generation of ideas, based often on *resourcement* of the traditions, is rising up in both settings and gaining traction.

In such a shifting context Varacalli (1992) pointed to a "calling" for a particular kind of contemporary sociology that serves the Church, which following some very broad principles could play out in many different specific ways. It is not necessarily conservative or liberal on matters of prudential judgment, but it operates past the historically prevailing confines of liberal orthodoxies and political correctness. That calling is

1) To provide objective social research;

2) To assist the Catholic Church in the tasks of a) understanding how surrounding forces affect the Faith and b) reconstructing the social order along Christian principles;
3) To apply, where applicable, Catholic principles to the existing body of sound social scientific theory, concepts and methods; and
4) To do so through a thorough public intellectual exchange.

For my money this is a good description of what a Catholic sociological imagination for our time entails—and what the materials in this anthology try in various ways to do.

Getting Here Historically: Building Foundations for Sociology to Contribute to CST Today

Varacalli's statement of how sociology can work with Catholic social thought may seem relatively uncontroversial and simple, but it stands on a rich and complex—though sometimes dismaying—intellectual and spiritual history. On the one hand there has been a considerable struggle between academic sociology as a discipline and Catholicism. Here I tend to emphasize the American setting but this antagonism between sociology and religion played out also in Europe, in somewhat diverse ways. John Brewer (2007, 23–24) summarizes some of the central national patterns as follows:

> Irrespective of the Christian input into early US sociology, the subject developed quickly there as a secular one, as in France, so that those sociologists who maintained their religiosity were placed mostly in a side-flow, although a few like Peter Berger managed to successfully negotiate the mainstream. The vast number of educational establishments in the United States with a religious ethos ensured religious sociologists had an institutional space to keep Christian sociology alive but this kind of sociology was marginalized. Because they felt professional incongruity as sociologists (rather than as Christians), religious sociologists in the United States directed their attention to working out an engagement with mainstream secular sociology rather than theology, and with the exception of Protestant evangelical sociologists, they tried to denude their sociology of institutional markers of faith, as the French Catholic sociologists eventually did. They did not look to theology to buttress their Christianity within sociology, and when theologians began serious engagement with sociology in the 1970s, US sociologists were slow to respond. By contrast, Christian sociology in Britain lasted until the early 1950s but only got in the way of effective engagement between sociology and theology. [British] Christian sociology was isolationist and separatist and unlike in the USA, it declined to be a bridge to mainstream sociology.

On the other hand, however, there is also a parallel history of strong *positive* contributions by Catholic sociologists to Catholic social thought, to the application of CST to concrete politics and policies in many countries, and to core CST doctrine itself. We presently stand on the shoulders of past Catholic social scientists who helped us construct a platform for our work today.[10] In this section I discuss examples of three ways in which this platform-building proceeded. First, Catholic sociologists tried to heal the epistemological and philosophical tensions between sociology and Catholicism, and find a way for the discipline and the Church to accept religiously inspired social science as legitimate. Second, sociologists helped Catholicism play a more significant and direct role in sociopolitical life in democracies. And third, sociologists made important scholarly contributions to the formal CST corpus.

Saving Sociology for the Church: Catholic Rebuttals of Positivism

A key problem Catholic sociologists in this country and elsewhere have confronted for decades was—and still can be—the chilly climate afforded religious beliefs within the academic discipline. As sociology emerged as a professionalizing body it tended strongly to position itself as a version of objectivist natural science, which sat at the top of the academic prestige hierarchy in both Europe and this country. Sociology's prevailing intellectual and cultural origins involved a blend of Comtean positivism, Spencerian evolutionism related to Darwinian thought, and Marxian materialism. These were deployed to better understand the rise and consequences of the industrial revolution and provide laws for designing social improvement of various sorts. But this frequently involved an explicit and often hostile effort to *supplant* the cultural and institutional power of religion in general, and Catholicism in particular, with a new scientific or scientific/political elite with a secular belief system. Varacalli (1990) called this "an enlightened substitute for religious commitment." Hunter (1987, cited in Gay 1998) went so far as to say that secular humanism became the intelligentsia's "fourth faith," a meaning system or cosmology every bit as powerful for irreligious sociologists as the three pillars of Catholicism, Protestantism, and Judaism had been for society in earlier days.[11] It is well known that Comte, Spencer, and Marx, as well as other founding fathers of the discipline were atheists and often explicitly hostile to Catholicism or Christianity in their goals and scholarship.[12] In the words of Benton Johnson (1987), at the core of all three of these diverse theoretical perspectives

> were two indictments of religion—or more specifically Christianity—in the name of human reason and well-being. The first indictment was the charge that religious teachings are not true; the second indictment was that religion had encouraged many practices that are inimical to human welfare. The basic message

of this theoretical tradition, then, is that religion is neither good nor true by the standards of an enlightened age. The practical implication of these indictments was obvious: The sooner our historic religions are done away with, the better.

Johnson goes on to say that contemporary sociological theory picks up these general indictments and adapts them in disciplinary ways: religious matters are inadmissible as scientific propositions, the methods of science do not allow for moral judgments, and religious ideas refer to a realm that is essentially non-empirical and thus not amenable to scientific investigation. He argues that the overall result in academia, and in the broader culture, was a kind of détente between religion and social science: an uneasy truce and academic partition (some might say apartheid) with clear boundary patrolling on sociology's side of the line of demarcation. Recent scholarship on the paradigms of theology (Flanagan 2007) suggests, consistent with Brewer's observations cited above, that while sociology has had a very strong impact on contemporary theology for several decades—for example, in feminist and liberation theologies—there has not been much flow back across the boundary until quite recently.

The Catholic Church, too, was suspicious of sociology for its thoroughly secular modernism, and for a long period tended to favor deductive analyses and criticism of societal issues in terms of moral and theological principles. It was skeptical about the use of information about current social conditions to shape doctrine as temperocentric, preferring the longer view embedded in the scholastic tradition. The somewhat infamous (and I think usually unread!) 1907 encyclical by Pius X, *On the Doctrines of the Moderns,* and Fr. Peter Palombelli's *Syllabus Condemning the Errors of the Modernists* of the same year (Palombelli is identified as the Notary to the Holy Roman and Universal Inquisition) do not mention sociology or social science by name, but strongly condemn historicism, naturalism, and any science that declares Catholic beliefs as myths, better replaced by a vague Protestant and generic Christianity unencumbered by superstitions (Pius X [1907] n.d.). The Pope was right: these points were certainly prevalent within the emerging positivist social science of the time. Yet, in the very same era, the social encyclicals starting with *Rerum Novarum* were opening the door to a more empirically-based perspective: sociological concepts like class, industrialization, culture, and power were more and more frequently employed in Church documents.

American Catholic sociologists in the early-to-mid 1900s (a growing number of Catholics were acquiring advanced degrees in that field) were thus caught between a rock and a hard place. On the one hand they wanted Catholic ideas to be seen as valuable and legitimate by colleagues in what was a very chilly disciplinary climate: as Brewer indicated, they really wanted to stay connected to the growing discipline and have a voice in it. On the other, they wanted the skeptical Church to accept sociology as a partner for its social mission, by recognizing that radical positivism was not the only sociological paradigm available, and that the field could successfully carry out values-based research and theorizing compatible with the Church's ontology and epistemology. Catholic sociologists worked to challenge the secularist and rationalist biases of the mainstream, and sustain a closer relationship between their discipline and their faith, in both conceptual and organizational ways.

Especially during the 1930s and '40s, a number of Catholic scholars wrote books for collegiate sociology courses which attempted to *widen sociology's boundaries conceptually* by including an explicitly spiritual dimension or content in the discipline's field of vision. In effect they were trying to write the reality of the presence of God in creation, in the person, and in society into the legitimate scholarly territory of the field, by collapsing the secular modernist distinctions between sociology, social philosophy, and theology. Thus emerged a kind of integralist Catholic sociology intentionally meant to challenge the materialist premises and boundaries of the discipline. Organizationally, in the U.S. this translated into an effort to create a distinctive professional community more friendly to nurturing sociologists with Catholic culture and ideas, that could also serve as a kind of haven for Catholics in a heartless disciplinary world: namely, the American Catholic Sociological Society (ACSS), which existed from 1938 to 1970.

Many examples of Catholic sociological work emerging out of ACSS with this more integralist approach could be cited here: to name three, there was Fr. Paul Hanley Furfey's *Three Theories of Society* (1937); Fr. Raymond Murray's *Introductory Sociology* ([1935] 1946); and Don Luigi Sturzo's *The True Life: Sociology of the Supernatural* (1947), which in its English translation from the Italian influenced American Catholic social thought although Sturzo was never an ACSS member. In one way or another all such works frame the substance of sociological inquiry to be about the working of grace and nature in society. Just to give a flavor of the approach I cannot resist looking to Eva Ross' 1939 *Fundamental Sociology*, a college-level introductory textbook with wide circulation at the time. Ross was trained as a labor economist in England, converted to Catholicism, emigrated to the United States, and got her PhD in sociology from Yale in 1937. She founded the Sociology Department at Trinity University in Washington, DC, where she taught for many years, and was a long-standing member and officer within ACSS. Like many similar texts Ross' version first notes the impact of the ex-Catholic Comte's anti-religious evolutionism on the process of separating sociology from religious thought; then she argues how this process, together with Darwinism and political liberalism, fostered a very lame, one-sided system for analyzing society.

A "Catholic sociology" is for Ross a necessary corrective and deserves status as a distinct paradigm within the discipline, as we might say today. In her *Fundamental Sociology* she argues that the cure for Comte's absurd perspective is a sociology that is more than just a reporting science: it is an *interpretive* science that, in the "wider" view mentioned above, definitely includes social philosophy: "The Catholic sociologist, therefore, differs from the majority of the sociologists whose work we outlined in the last chapter, chiefly in that his theory is not based on working hypotheses alone; but he integrates his inductive work with a social philosophy based on certain postulates, and thus he can interpret social facts in the light of reason, and produce a well-rounded theory of use in guiding societal organization" (Ross 1939, 135). Ross then draws out her list of postulates, which are specifically titled "The Postulates of Sociology" and *not* postulates of social philosophy:

> The Catholic sociologist, therefore, does not regard sociology in the narrow positivistic sense, and in his work presupposes the following, which he considers to be satisfactorily proved by philosophy, by historical events, by revelation, and in other ways:
>   That God exists, who is the Creator of all things, man included.
>   That Christ, the Son of God, established the Church to which He gave divine authority to guide men in matters related to their supernatural destiny.
>   That man has a spiritual soul which is immortal; hence he has an eternal destiny.
>   That man is endowed with a free will.
>   That man is not only subject to physical (necessary) laws, but also to the moral law.
>   That man is a social being, and has certain rights and duties which are common to all mankind. (Ross 1939, 135–36)

This is a list that certainly startled or dismayed her more secular disciplinary contemporaries, yet that her textbook not only survived but thrived through several editions attests to the plausibility of this sort of position in her milieu. Nevertheless such socio-religious integralism, while evocative, did not prevail even within the ACSS. Within a couple of decades Ross herself, Paul Hanley Furfey, and others changed their views about the effectiveness of this approach, which did not translate well into clear sociological differences between the works of Catholics and the works of those who were not, except perhaps in topics chosen for study. Within the ACSS some members were more pluralist, expecting a distinctively Catholic sociology to emerge and assume a rightful place among the other respected theoretical traditions in the field, marked by its religious foundations and goals and perhaps even research methods, but still sociology. Others were more assimilationist, and expected to eventually merge into the mainstream over time; they saw themselves adopting the concern for social justice and the moral focus of Catholicism as a personal motive for engaging in research and writing, but not really doing anything different *qua* sociologists than anyone else (Kivisto 1989). They believed there were valuable Catholic motives for doing good sociology that could be foregrounded and argued as legitimate; but there was no such thing, really, as a "Catholic sociology" per se. The history shows a victory for the assimilationists, who at most wanted to keep sociology and religion more conceptually distinct while still in some sort of conversation: a perhaps warmer version of the "détente" referred to by Johnson earlier. They might even agree personally with the sort of Rossian postulates laid out above, but argued they should not enter explicitly into sociological work and discourse in order for sociology to retain its scientific persona and credibility.

The ACSS continued to meet and gather adherents throughout the post-war period and into the early 1960s; but by the late 1960s the ACSS had lost its *raison d'etre* for various reasons, including:

- A failure to have clearly defined or developed consensus around the notion of Catholic sociology;
- The weakening of past prejudice and discrimination toward Catholic sociologists in the ASA and other professional bodies, coupled with a desire on the part of many sociologists and social science teachers with Catholic roots to be more a part of the mainstream of the discipline—i.e., a dynamic of assimilation;
- A shift in the vocational background, professional credentialing, and academic socialization of sociologists with Catholic roots, as less were members of religious orders, and more received training in secular institutions and felt their religious identification decline relative to their academic identification; and
- The conceptual ascendancy of the "sociology *of* Catholicism" and, more broadly the "sociology *of* religion," in place of a religiously-grounded and inspired sociology, as more discipline-oriented and non-Catholic researchers came into the organization who sought to pursue the sociology of religion as a specialization, thus fostering a diffusion of mission and constituency.

In short, the desire of a majority of ACSS members became less to preserve a haven for Catholics than to participate in the mainstream of the profession. Catholics entering the discipline by the 1960s had more likely acquired degrees from secular institutions or Catholic institutions trying to shed or "broaden" their Catholic heritage; they interacted more widely with secular and ecumenical colleagues in professional networks and conferences; and worked more often on secular campuses and on Catholic campuses whose missions were drifting toward the secular. This process overcame their predecessors' and opponents' need to build up and maintain a zone of difference; a split emerged between what were perceived by the newer cohorts as religious "traditionalists" versus what the first generation members saw as "young turks and progressive democrats" more gung ho about sociology as a modern science that should be less encumbered by religious ideology. The "young turks" perceived that the ACSS was too clubby, organizationally, and worse, functioned to stigmatize their professional identities in a "Catholic ghetto." They were probably right about both of these, various scholars of the ACSS agree; but it is also unfortunately true that the "traditionalists" did not show an ability to solve the problems that plagued the ACSS from its inception, and could not now develop a viable approach to healing this emerging split or making a strong case for retaining the concept of a Catholic sociology.

In 1964 the Society's journal, long known as the *American Catholic Sociological Review*, was renamed *Sociological Analysis: A Journal in the Sociology of Religion*. And in 1970 the ACSS went out of formal existence, renaming itself the Association for the Sociology of Religion (ASR). The language of these two changes clearly indicates the shift to a more secular, mainstream focus on religion and religious behavior as objects of study, away from a religiously inspired endeavor meant to examine social life from a particular religious stance. Scholars of this historical chapter diverge in their interpretation of this qualitative shift, from seeing it as a failure of Catholics to seize the moment and stay true to their origins, to applauding it as a victory for Catholics finally able to traverse out of their parochial religious ghetto and join a more cosmopolitan academic culture (Sharkey 2004–5; Varacalli 1990; Kivisto 1989). Whatever one's interpretation, it is clear that the effort to produce a distinctive Catholic sociological paradigm of this genre withered.

And yet, this type of twentieth century effort to integrate sociology and Catholic Faith should not simply be dismissed as quaint. Regardless of how one views the history, I believe that ACSS' decades-long effort to keep open a bridge between sociology and faith contributed to three things important to us now.

First is *a gadfly-like role in the emergence of a moral and reflexive paradigm of sociology that enabled the eventual collapse of the radical positivist hegemony in sociology* under the weight of its demonstrably false claims of naturalistic value-neutrality in theory and research. ACSS members, even those who favored more of a separation between faith and science, made the self-consciously reflexive critique of sociologistic positivism, naturalism, and behaviorism very strongly and very early. Their critique prefigured the type of criticism of sociology that eventually became an avowed "prophetic" and value-laden critical approach to the discipline fostered later by the likes of Alvin Gouldner and Robert Friedrichs. ACSS sociologists had offered their own early version of a prophetic sociology, and their heirs within the emergent subfield of the sociology of religion kept that substantive social topic ensconced within the boundaries of the discipline. ACSS stars like Fr. Paul Hanley Furfey (despite his sometime dubious sociological individualism and predilection for liberation theology later in his career)[13] were part of the inspirational generation searching for a morally persuasive sociology that helped foster the strong ethics-based encounter with social justice and social equality that has characterized sociology since the 1960s.[14] In effect religion never really went away in the field even as its more confessional manifestations, like a camp of organized "Christian sociologies," did not fare well (Flanagan 1996). We even see an echo of this rather recently in the surprising common cause found among religiously minded sociologists, new left-oriented neo-marxist critical theorists, and the political theologians of the Anglican-inspired Radical Orthodoxy movement, in their so-called liturgical critique of society and traditional materialist sociology.[15]

Second is the *organizational persistence of a core tradition of specifically Catholic critique and pursuit of sociology,* and other related fields, which found its way some decades later into the foundation of the Society of Catholic Social Scientists (SCSS) in 1992—an interdisciplinary organization that exists today for many of the same reasons that ACSS existed half a century ago. Scholars within this Society often discuss the ideological or paradigmatic constraints on, and coolness to, religious discourse that are quite prevalent within disciplines like history, economics, psychology, and of course sociology. They are still discussing how best to link their faith with their scientific practices—though now strongly buttressed by much Church encouragement of such analytic exploration that was not much available to the ACSS a generation ago. The bottom line here is that the very existence of ACSS and its efforts to test out an integral sociology remind us today to seek some way to bring faith and science back into conversation in sociological practice if we hope to advance CST as a moral policy framework. Further, an important feature of this organizational heritage is the effort to create a structural, formal organizational forum *for active collaboration between lay experts, vowed religious experts, and clerical experts on social issues.* ACSS membership included significant numbers of each whose routine collaborations and interactions played an important role in trying to heal the breach between sociology and Catholicism that had formed during the first half of the twentieth century over the problems over modernism. SCSS has the same kind of membership profile today. That secular outsiders often saw and today see this collaboration as too cozy, and that professionalizing Catholic sociologists perhaps began to feel they should expand their collegial circle further out into the secular discipline for career and intellectual reasons, do not detract from the core fact that a tradition of collaboration between clergy, religious, and laity was built up during the twentieth century and endures now.

Third, the history of ACSS' struggles *reminds us of how deeply rooted and persistent is sociology's wariness of scholars whose faith figures explicitly in their work; and how deeply embedded is the need to separate science and religion into entirely distinct categories in the discipline's culture and socialization processes for forming professional identity.* While there is empirical research documenting some increase of openness to discussion of values or religious matters in the context of scientific work, according to Ecklund (2011) about 80% of natural and social scientists still prefer a strong separation of religion and science into what Stephen Jay Gould once called "non-overlapping magisteria." And we either are ourselves or have all met Catholic and Evangelical believers who feel they must "stay in the closet" in sociological gatherings to avoid ostracism, subtle or strong. Thus whether one wishes to engage the debate over integralist sociology that occurred within ACSS or not, that group and its heirs laid a foundation for sociology stepping outside of its secular and liberal mainstream to provide a Catholic-based critique of contemporary societal trends which academically trained social scientists could attend to. As noted earlier, this critique is now welcomed by a discerning Church in need of good data and theories to explore and implement its CST principles, as exemplified in the 1994 establishment of the Pontifical Academy of Social Sciences by John Paul II to serve as the think tank for the Pontifical Council of Justice and Peace, wherein sociologists play a prominent role.

Catholic Sociologists Helping to Forge the State's Social Policy and the Church's Social Teaching

Next to consider is how Catholic sociologists played significant historical roles in the formation and refinement of CST and its application to policy in specific societies. It is interesting to think that "prototypical" sociological ideas related to human rights and cultural relativism were being developed in the Church well before an academic discipline called sociology appeared in the 19th century. As early as the late 1500s, for example, theologians Francisco Suarez and Francisco de Vitoria, in the face of the Church's need to develop its perspective on the often brutal treatment of indigenous peoples by ostensibly Catholic explorers and colonists, worked out the implications of reason and freedom embedded in scholastic philosophy for our view of man wherever he is encountered, thus making an early case for universal human rights, the need for international law, and religious freedom as part of the Catholic Enlightenment. Later, throughout the period of the early rise of capitalism, there existed a strong "social Catholicism" that condemned the miseries being wrought by growing socio-economic upheavals and offered particular social reform models based on social solidarity, such as "corporatism," labor legislation, and advocacy of democratic freedom—all of which influenced Pope Leo XIII's vision of realizing social justice and combating the potential human degradations offered by socialism in the first social encyclical, *Rerum Novarum* (Pope 1994; McGuire 2007; Charles 1998).

As the challenges of industrialization unfolded and the social encyclicals called for more humane conditions of living and employment and better moral formation of individuals and families, there emerged a framework of Catholic response to societal misery based not only on the traditional forms of personal or group charity and almsgiving, perhaps writ larger, but rather on *social justice structured and protected by larger social institutions,* such as government. With the Church (quite appropriately) no longer operating in the realm of government and international relations as a major landholder or nation-state herself, there needed to be ways to influence the behavior of governments and the process of social policy formation from the inside, as it were: for example, through the workings of civil society, labor unions, political parties, and governmental policy formation groups.

Catholic sociologists were prominent in the formation of both new structures for social welfare and political action, and the consolidation of Catholic social teaching that could be used as an overarching framework for Catholic activities regarding the "social question." Sullins observes that there were many Catholic sociologists during the early twentieth century who worked to advance "themes of the Church's nascent social teaching by means of a scientific analysis that commended them to a wider critical audience." A few examples of such sociologists, discussed in rough chronological order, may provide a sense of the *range* of types of activity and positions taken in this regard. I selected three who were *clergy*, to make the point that sociological thinking was clearly ensconced and being developed within the Church despite the climate of skepticism toward social science that may have prevailed in some sectors. None of these three individuals have an academic degree in sociology for such degrees were either not yet available or rare. But their work is replete with the empirical and theoretical study of social life and social change, of groups, institutions, and structures, typically in a highly interdisciplinary manner, which we would recognize today as sociological. In effect they have sociological minds and in fact were often responsible for introducing or strengthening sociological thinking in the discourse of the Church.

Monsignor John Ryan and the Politics of Socio-economic Justice

The first is Monsignor John Ryan (1869–1945), whose work in political economics, especially on the living wage, involved extensive collaboration with other social reform groups to influence governmental wage policies, as well as personal activism and scholarship on economic justice.[16] Born in Minnesota and exposed early on to agrarian populism, Ryan became very interested in the moral foundations of economic activity and policy. Degreed in theology he nevertheless read widely in the social sciences, and when he eventually became a Minnesota seminary faculty member he introduced courses on sociology and economics into the curriculum—the first ever such seminary courses in this country. His 1906 book *The Living Wage* and his 1916 work *Distributive Justice* were foundational for American Catholic social thought regarding social justice and its possible realization in capitalist society. Throughout the first decades of the 1900s Ryan was a vocal and thoughtful advocate for minimum wage and workers' unionization rights laws. In 1913 he even wrote a minimum wage law for women and children in Minnesota that passed, but was overturned a decade later at the federal level through the action of the Supreme Court, during the period when the Court was interpreting the fourteenth amendment to the Constitution as freedom of contract rather than worker protection. In 1915 he joined the political science faculty at Catholic University of America in Washington, and right after World War I he helped the Church delineate and propose specific economic plans for post-war reconstruction and stabilization. From 1920 until he passed away in 1945 he directed the Social Action committee of the National Catholic Welfare Conference, the precursor to today's U.S. Bishops Conference. From the early 1930s on Ryan became a prominent advisor in various capacities to the Roosevelt administration's New Deal, where his ideas on economic justice had significant influence.

Always the progressive, but in agreement with the anti-socialism of *Rerum Novarum*, he was the first Catholic priest to serve on the national board of the American Civil Liberties Union, and he was personally embroiled in controversies regarding the relationship between Church and state that were being fueled by the anti-Catholicism of the period. Despite such controversies and activism, Msgr. Ryan reminds us of the possibility of taking Catholic social teaching directly into the political arena through the process of influencing legislation and helping to build Catholic social organizational infrastructure to operate in the democratic public square. In this Ryan modeled what today we would call the role of *the public intellectual,* who spoke from the Church broadly understood (i.e., as a clergy and faculty member from a Catholic university) to society through its governing and opinion-shaping structures. In this he helped combat the powerful anti-Catholicism then prevalent in American society and showed that Catholics could contribute constructively not only to grassroots social action and charity, but also policy formation at the highest level.

Fr. Luigi Sturzo and the Formation of the Christian Democratic Movement

A second, slightly more contemporary example is Sicilian born Don Luigi Sturzo (1871–1959).[17] He shares with Ryan certain commonalities. Like Ryan, Sturzo was also degreed in theology (and philosophy, and he was ordained in 1894) but taught the relatively new discipline of sociology in his first seminary faculty assignment, where in fact at quite a young age he was appointed Professor of Political Economy, Philosophy, and Sociology. Like Ryan, Sturzo was from a rural area which experienced much poverty and injustice at the hands of its local ruling elites. Like Ryan, Sturzo helped form workers and students associations and advocated socio-economic reforms at the local and regional levels.

But Don Sturzo went farther than Msgr. Ryan in a key sense. That is, he advocated a much more direct participation of Catholics in electoral political activities—and did so in a context where such participation was considered problematic, indeed forbidden, by the Pope at the time as an outcome of the political and spiritual struggle between the Papacy and the emerging Italian nation-state during the anti-clerical *Risorgimento*. Thus the priest Sturzo was not only an officer in the civil association Catholic Action, he *also served as elected mayor* of his home town of Caltagirone for many years as well as a provincial

Councilor for Catania. In 1915 he convinced Pope Benedict XV to drop the ban on Catholic involvement in Italian politics which opened a door to wider Catholic political activities, and during World War I served on various Italian government commissions. Then in 1919, during the turbulent years immediately after World War I which would eventually spawn the rise of Italian Fascism, he founded the first Christian Democratic political party, the Partito Popolare Italiano (PPI), with a platform based on the Catholic social principles articulated in *Rerum Novarum*. With Mussolini's rise to governmental power Sturzo and his allies fought against fascism for several years until the PPI was ordered dissolved by government decree in 1926; at that point Sturzo went into exile. He first lived elsewhere in Europe; he wrote a major work called *Church and State* while in France in 1938, that appeared in English a year later and brought Sturzo considerable attention. As the Germans swamped Europe early in World War II he came to the United States, in 1940. Throughout his career in the U.S. and back in Italy after the war, Sturzo was interested in merging sociological analysis with Catholic social teachings as a foundation for direct Catholic political action.

As I mentioned earlier, Sturzo was one of the sociologists who wrote his own integral sociology text, which in translation was a significant influence on the work of Paul Hanley Furfey, among others.[18] The ideas in this text reflect how, throughout his career, Sturzo could integrate spiritual truths with secular action, or put religious principles directly into political work. In *The True Life: Sociology of the Supernatural* (1947) a key question for Sturzo is how sociology, "sired by positivism" and "held within the boundaries of nature," can be carried into the realm of the supernatural so as to be more encompassing of the concrete life in society of human beings. He observes that in Genesis we see the founding of society in the relationship between Adam and Eve, the first fellowship. Larger and more complex societies are essentially larger and larger projections of such fellowship and association working in an inexhaustible process, unified underneath its diversity by the working of grace. As Graham (2000) put it,

> Sturzo understood that grace is present in history. The supernatural is not something accidental added to man's natural life; it is a real transformation of human existence and activity. Grace is an inner principle which unifies the lives of individuals and societies, giving them a supernatural imprint. Because of this presence of grace, the study of society without considering that presence is a methodological abstraction, a running away from reality.

The very notion of a Christian democratic party or political movement can only make sense if one has already established a conceptual framework such as this upon which to base action, action aimed at helping grace work in people and social systems. But the specifics of structuring such action depend a lot on the context, as we can see in comparing the socio-political approaches taken by

Sturzo and Ryan to bring Catholic social teaching into the political policy arena of their respective cultures. In the American two-party system of secular representative democracy, adapted to a pluralist but predominantly Protestant culture with no established religion, and one not infrequently anti-Catholic, it made more sense for Catholics advocating social betterment—for Ryan—to try to influence society through shaping public opinion and the policies of the existing parties and elected officials. Third parties almost never worked, for starters, and trying to build a Catholic front would have seemed monolithically alien and threatening to the mainstream of society—an organized invasion of papists. Catholicism was coming out of its ghetto, to be sure, but had to work its influence within the parameters of the given political structures. However in multiparty parliamentary democracies like Italy, especially those with the added factor of Catholicism being the established legal religion, the path to a public voice for CST could more readily and more likely be attained through direct political action: party formation, running candidates for elections, and parliamentary coalition building. This was the general route Sturzo followed. Though silenced under Mussolini, the circle of intellectuals and activists who had been part of the formation of Sturzo's Partito Populare eventually became or inspired leaders in the post-World War II Christian Democratic Movement, which generated postwar political parties not only in Italy but also elsewhere in Europe and Latin America.

Despite early successes especially in the fight against the powerful Communist and Socialist parties during the cold war, The Partito Democristiano in Italy unfortunately became highly oligarchical and suffered great corruption: while powerful and enduring it was often criticized for its hypocrisy and deals with the devil. Today, Christian democratic parties endure in Europe and Latin America but often in unfortunate alliances with the ruling elites of their societies. The Christian Democratic party in Italy has in fact cracked under the weight of its spiritual and secular failures into many factions at this point. But Christian democratic ideals persist in Italian and European political culture, and certainly Benedict XVI is doing what he can to revivify them and detach them from their historically corrupted past. Sturzo's influence as a sociologist is still felt through the work of a vibrant Sturzo Institute, and considerable interest in reexamining his social thought exists in academia especially among Europeans who struggle to recover their cultural and political roots in the wake of postmodern social fragmentations.

Joseph Cardinal Hoffner and the Lead-up to the Compendium

A third example reveals yet another pathway for linking sociology with Catholic social teaching. Joseph Cardinal Hoffner (1906–1987)[19] was first and foremost a scholar strongly influenced by the emerging social teaching of his era, in particular Pope Pius XI's *Quadragesimo Anno* published in 1931.

Hoffner, like Ryan and Sturzo, came from a rural family; he entered the local seminary, but was soon identified as having intellectual abilities meriting advanced study. Thus he was sent to the Gregorian in Rome, received ordination in 1932, and completed a theology doctorate there in 1934 on the theme "Social Justice and Social Love." He also received a second theology doctorate from Freiburg in Germany in 1938 with a thesis on the relationships between peasants and the Church in medieval Germany, while also studying economics. In 1944 he also wrote a postdoctoral thesis on "Christianity and Human Dignity," concerning ethical issues in Spanish colonialism.

During the Nazi terror Hoffner and his sister did what they could to oppose anti-Semitism by secretly harboring Jews in their own homes, such that they both eventually were named "Righteous" by the state of Israel and listed at *Yad Yashem* in Jerusalem. In 1945 after the end of the war, Hoffner was appointed professor of Pastoral Theology and Christian Social Teaching at the seminary in Trier; then in 1951 he went to the University of Munster as professor of Christian Social Science (the oldest known university chair of this type), where a few years later he founded an eventually highly influential Institute of Christian Social Sciences and the *Yearbook of Christian Social Sciences.* He was made Bishop of Munster in 1962, attended Vatican II as part of the commission for education and culture, and strongly supported the development of *Gaudium et Spes.* He became Archbishop of Cologne in 1968, was appointed Cardinal in 1969, then became chair of the influential and controversy-laden German Bishops Conference in 1976, where he was part of the struggle to address the heretical positions of Hans Küng, and to confront growing political and theological challenges to the Church's teachings on abortion and family life. He was a strong backer of the election of John Paul II, and Cardinal Ratzinger from the Congregation for the Doctrine of the Faith sent him to South America to inspect and report on Brazilian seminary formation programs there with special attention to the problems of Marxist liberation theology.

In civil and political society Hoffner also had a major influence on German social justice policies in several ways: through his work in the German Bishops conference, as a force in various German Catholic lay associations dealing with economic and social problems, and as a consultant to the post-World War II German government on such matters as pensions, housing, and labor-management relations. Hoffner thus resembles both Ryan and Sturzo in this active involvement with social policy questions and engagement with governing political parties. He consistently advocated that the Church's role in contemporary society had to be founded on social doctrine as laid out originally in modern times by Bishop Kettler and Pope Leo XIII and destined to evolve through a combination of historical-theoretical analysis, empirical study of social conditions, and the application of a strong core of universal truths through which to interpret such data.

All these accomplishments in themselves qualify Hoffner for appointment to our CST pantheon of historical heroes. But the key reason I cite him here as an example of sociology shaping CST is because of the remarkable textbook-style summary of Catholic social doctrine he first published in 1962, which became extremely popular and in fact was republished in eight editions over a twenty year period in multiple languages (even Korean and Japanese). It really was the fullest and most comprehensive statement on social teaching there was at the time. In this aspect Hoffner's book serves as a prime example of a coherent summary of extant CST that enjoyed a more global reach. The fruits of this approach eventually became manifest in today's universal *Compendium*.

I personally first learned of Hoffner's existence because his textbook was mentioned in a 1993 paper by SCSS founder Stephen Krason called "What the Catholic Finds Wrong with Secular Social Science," which outlined a number of epistemological, philosophical, and theoretical divergences between especially positivist-inspired social science and a Catholic counterpart. Krason's last objection to secular social science focused on what college students might be exposed to in their course materials; he argued for a resurgence of Catholic materials for that audience that might look like updated versions of works "from only a generation ago." And what might some examples of such texts from only a generation ago be? Krason's first example was Joseph Cardinal Hoffner's 1962 *Fundamentals of Christian Sociology*, and by listing some of its striking—by contrast to today's typical introductory sociology book—chapter headings gave some clue as to what a Catholic sociology text would have involved. Hoffner developed sections on "The Social Nature of Man," "The Principle of Subsidiarity," "The Characteristics of Natural Law," "The Family as a 'Cell' in Human Society," "Work and the Professions," "The Origin and Meaning of the State," and the global "Unity of the Human Race," just to name a few.

The translated title of this book is interesting; the edition Krason referred to and which I personally acquired later was an Irish imprint also released in the U.S., that rendered the German title *Christliche Gesellschaftslehre* as *Fundamentals of Christian Sociology* (Hoffner 1962)—a title I jumped at for its use of the word *sociology* in a way similar to others, like Furfey and Sturzo. Later it was often translated more generically as *Christian Social Teaching*, and that is the title used for the currently available version in English, put out online by a German group interested in preserving Hoffner's legacy called Ordo Socialis, the Academic Association for the Promotion of Christian Social Teaching. The editor, Lothar Roos (1997), uses the last published edition of the book from 1983 as a base text, then incorporates supplements to Hoffner's original material in a different font that "add the substance of recent papal pronouncements" on a given topic from encyclicals that appeared after 1983. I was dubious about this approach initially, but eventually concluded that it does work to make Hoffner's opus come alive, because Hoffner's core text is so consistent with the heart of

CST and anticipates many of the specific developments that occurred in CST after his own death, for example in *Centesimus Annus*.

Hoffner's text certainly has its limits and emphases: in a review of the Roos text Krason (1999) observed that while he is very strong on such topics as disarmament, the uniqueness of cultures in the context of a deeper universality of human experience, and many economic issues such as just wages and the need for social security, Hoffner does not deal sufficiently with moral snarls like deterrence and the ever-growing power of the state that fills the void left by the diminishment of religious authority. Nevertheless, Hoffner's text serves as a vibrant prototype of a synthesis of CST, meant to reach a broad audience and display the breathtaking range of social topics and issues about which the Church has thought and spoken. In fact, Blasi and Sullins (2009) make a compelling case that the *Compendium* is strongly influenced in content and structure by Hoffner's text, even though Hoffner is never actually cited in the *Compendium* as a specific source:

> The systematization of Catholic social teaching presented in the *Compendium* is clearly patterned on that of Hoffner's text. The table of contents is virtually identical to the arrangement of topics provided in the *Compendium*. Part 1 of Hoffner's book, for example, after setting forth the social nature of man, propounds three principles of a Christian understanding of the social order—solidarity, the common good, and subsidiarity—exactly as does the *Compendium*. These principles are then applied, in Part 2, to the range of social institutions, with sections on marriage and the family; work and profession; the economy; the state; and the community of nations. With additional chapters on the environment and peace, this is the same list, and in the same order, of the topical outline found in Part 2 of the *Compendium*. (ix)

Blasi and Sullins go on to detail other parallels at the level of style and conceptual approach, for example in their extremely similar treatment of the concept of social justice, how it emerged in use and how it is identical with "legal justice" if the latter is correctly understood. Another example relates to how Hoffner and the *Compendium* both discuss "scarcity" and the human response to limitations of goods and resources.

I leave it to the reader, as do Blasi and Sullins, to delve into such connections more fully. But it is clear that Hoffner's legacy as a social scientist is twofold: his efforts to directly influence social policies through civic action and political engagement, and through a direct and, in fact, global contribution to the formation of contemporary CST.

Final Remarks

Our Catholic sociological forebearers have contributed to developing a wider view of sociology than the positivist project would allow; to organizing collaboration between clergy, religious, and lay social scientists on the analysis of social issues; to projecting Catholic social principles into the public square—indeed the very institutions of politics—in diverse ways; and to the very generation of formal social doctrine in the Magisterium of the Church. Thanks in part to their work, and to the scholarly and spiritual fortitude of Catholic sociologists who followed such as those often cited in this paper, today we have potentially available a Catholic sociological imagination to bring to bear on pressing matters of concern in all institutional arenas of society. The articles in this reader all build on this legacy of action and conceptual foundation. They explore how the Church herself is gradually adapting its shape to meet the societal challenges of international interaction; reflexively analyze the limits of current sociological thinking and explore potential avenues for a more spiritually open perspective; document empirical trends that attest to the importance of natural law as an underlying force in social life; and use core concepts in CST to empirically and theoretically study the dynamics of particular social institutions. It is my hope that these materials may both introduce newcomers to the richness of sociology's work vis-à-vis Catholic social teaching, and also inspire further work in this arena for the Church.

Notes

1. C.S. Lewis, *The Abolition of Man* (1947, 89–90). With thanks to Stratford Caldecott (2009), who also used this quote as an epigram in his recent book *Beauty for Truth's Sake: On the Re-enchantment of Education*.

2. It is well known that other groups and Bishops conferences adapt these basic four principles and amplify them, even adding additional principles. For example, the United States Conference of Catholic Bishops employ seven, adding themes on family life and environmental concern (USCCB 2005).

3. Sociologies of the confessional sort are not sufficiently inclusive of the gamut of sociological frameworks, I think; nevertheless they can inspire and inform. A very recent scripturally-centered example from Protestant Christian sociology would be Vern Poythress' *Redeeming Sociology: A God-Centered Approach* (2011). Something quite a bit closer to the sociology reflected in the present volume would be Craig Gay's (1998) didactically titled but wide-ranging and intellectually rich volume *The Way of the (Modern) World Or, Why It's Tempting to Live as If God Doesn't Exist*, which I would highly recommend for Gay's ability to draw on all manner of sociologies to examine religion in postmodernism. A Christian Sociological Society still meets today, often piggybacking their gathering with the annual meetings of the American Sociological Association.

4. See Thomas Rourke's (2011) splendid overview of Pope Benedict XVI's social teachings, including on this particular theme.

5. For a broad analysis of the often dramatic divergences between contemporary Democratic Party positions and Catholic teachings, see Carlin (2006); and for some anecdotal evidence on the situation of the Catholic "social justice left" after the November 2010 elections in which Democrats were often defeated, see Neumeyr (2010). While most specific policy consideration within CST are considered prudential—with the exception of life issues—and thus open to a range of political positions, the alliance of current Catholic liberals with the Democratic Party is tragically hegemonic and in that context CST positions and Democratic Party platform positions, including those on abortion, are blurred together. Consider, for example, the recent open letter sent to House Speaker John Boehner (a Catholic) on the occasion of his selection as May 2011 commencement speaker at the Catholic University of America, by 75 academics from various Catholic universities. The group admonishes his political positions on economic policy for violating Catholic social teachings on the preferential option for the poor and as such are anti-life, arguing they are in effect out of step with settled CST consensus in this country, which they claim to represent. For the text of the letter and a brief supportive commentary, see Winter (2011). For critique of the letter, see Weigel (2011a) and Fitzpatrick (2011).

6. For links to current articles, presentations, and Church statements about this problem of Catholic identity on campuses, see the Catholic Education Project of the Cardinal Newman Society, available at http://www.cardinalnewmansociety.org/.

7. For an excellent example of this outlook, see well-known CST textbook author David O'Brien's (2011) recent opinion piece attacking the 2011 appointment of Archbishop Chaput to head the Archdiocese of Philadelpia.

8. See Smith and Denton (2005) and Smith and Snell (2009) for an abundance of qualitative and quantitative data from this sociologically compelling study.

9. At one point Flanagan goes so far as to remark that sociology as a discipline has its own Hound of Heaven: no matter how far and long sociology tried to run and hide from religion, it kept catching up and beckoning the field.

10. For a much richer and detailed account than can be provided here of the Catholic critique of modernism and the emergence of a positive Catholic intellectual and social scientific tradition engaging the contemporary world, starting in the Progressive era, see Woods (2004).

11. Craig Gay (1998, 203) cites Hunter's resume of this fourth faith as follows:
Humanism is...a meaning system or a cosmology. It is built upon certain unstated assumptions, as well as formal propositions about the nature of the universe (a closed, naturalistic system), the origin of the human race (evolutionary), the nature and origin of knowledge (scientistic if not positivistic), the nature of human values (relativistic, subjectivistic, and in part, scientifically derived), and the goal of human life (the full "realization" and "actualization" of human potentiality at both the individual and societal level)....Humanity as a symbol and as a reality is, for all practical purposes, sacralized, as is the chief mechanism or humanity's progress and development—science/technology.

12. See, for example, De Lubac's *The Drama of Atheist Humanism* (1995) and DeMarco and Wiker's *Architects of the Culture of Death* (2004).

13. See Sullins (2005).

14. See, for example, Furfey's 1944 classic *The Mystery of Iniquity*, his 1966 *The Respectable Murderers*, and his 1978 *Love and the Urban Ghetto*. All three and others

illustrate well a fervently moral sociology addressing structures of sin using Catholic language.

   15. See Hollon (2009), especially chapter 5; and a special issue of *Telos* called "The Liturgical Critique of Modernity," edited by Berman (1998).

   16. For further summary information about Ryan and his remarkable career, see Kelly (2007) and the website of the John A. Ryan Center for Catholic Studies at the University of St. Thomas, http://www.stthomas.edu/cathstudies/cst/aboutus/ryaninfo/html.

   17. For fuller accounts of Sturzo's life and work, see Graham (2000, 2007).

   18. See Villa (2005).

   19. For further brief overviews of Hoffner's life and work, see Rauscher (2007) and Roos (1997).

Bibliography

Allen, John. 2009. *The Future Church: How Ten Trends Are Revolutionizing the Catholic Church.* New York: Doubleday.

Bauman, Zygmunt. 2002. Interview by Tony Blackshaw. *Network: Newsletter of the British Sociological Association,* October (83): 1–3.

Berger, Peter. 2002. "Whatever Happened to Sociology?" *First Things,* October: 27–29.

Berman, Russell, ed. 1998. "Toward a Liturgical Critique of Modernity." Special issue, *Telos,* Fall (113).

Blasi, Anthony J., and D. Paul Sullins. 2009. "Introduction." In *Catholic Social Thought: American Reflections on the "Compendium,"* edited by D. Paul Sullins and Anthony J. Blasi, vii–xiv. New York: Lexington Books.

Brewer, John. 2007. "Sociology and Theology Reconsidered: Religious Sociology and the Sociology of Religion in Britain." *History of the Human Sciences,* 20 (2): 7–28.

Burawoy, Michael. 2005. "2004 ASA Presidential Address: For Public Sociology." *American Sociological Review,* 70 (1): 4–28.

Burtchaell, James, C.S.C. 1998. *The Dying of the Light: The Disengagement of Colleges and Universities from Their Christian Churches.* Grand Rapids, MI: Eerdmans.

Caldecott, Stratford. 2009. *Beauty for Truth's Sake: On the Re-enchantment of Education.* Grand Rapids, MI: Brazos Press.

Carlin, David. 2006. *Can a Catholic Be a Democrat?* Manchester, NH: Sophia Institute Press.

Charles, Rodger, S.J. 1998. "Leo XIII." In *Christian Social Witness and Teaching. Volume II,* by Rodger Charles, 3–30. Herefordshire, UK: Gracewing Books.

Chesterton, G.K. 1910. *What's Wrong with the World?* New York: Sheed and Ward.

Cochran, Clarke E., and David Carroll Cochran. 2003. *Catholics, Politics, and Public Policy: Beyond Left and Right.* Maryknoll, NY: Orbis Books.

Curran, Charles. 2002. *Catholic Social Teaching 1891–Present: A Historical, Theological, and Ethical Analysis.* Washington, DC: Georgetown University Press.

De Lubac, Henri. 1995. *The Drama of Atheist Humanism.* San Francisco: Ignatius Press. Originally published 1944 in French.

DeMarco, Donald, and Benjamin Wiker. 2004. *Architects of the Culture of Death.* San Francisco: Ignatius Press.

Donati, Pierpaolo. 2010. *La matrice teologica della societa.* Soveria Mannelli, Italy: Rubbettino Editore.

Douglas, Mary, and Steven Ney. 1998. *Missing Persons: A Critique of Personhood in the Social Sciences.* Berkeley: University of California Press.

Ecklund, Elaine. 2011. "Science on Faith." *The Chronicle of Higher Education,* February 11: B9–B10.

Fitzpatrick, James. 2011. "John Boehner and the Professors." *The Wanderer,* June 2: 4.

Flanagan, Kieran. 1996. *The Enchantment of Sociology: A Study of Theology and Culture.* New York: St. Martin's Press.

———. 2007. *Sociology in Theology: Reflexivity and Belief.* New York: Palgrave Macmillan.

Furfey, Paul Hanly, S.J. 1937. *Three Theories of Society.* New York: Macmillan.

———. 1944. *The Mystery of Iniquity.* Milwaukee: The Bruce Publishing Co.

———. 1966. *The Respectable Murderers.* New York: Herder and Herder.

———. 1978. *Love and the Urban Ghetto.* Maryknoll, NY: Orbis Books.

Gallagher, Michael, S.J. 2003. *Clashing Symbols: An Introduction to Faith and Culture.* New York: Paulist Press.

Gay, Craig M. 1998. *The Way of the (Modern) World Or, Why It's Tempting to Live as If God Doesn't Exist.* Grand Rapids, MI: Eerdmans.

George, Robert. 2001. *The Clash of Orthodoxies: Law, Religion and Morality in Crisis.* Wilmington, DE: ISI Books.

Graham, Msgr. George. 2000. "Luigi Sturzo: A Prophet for Today." *Homiletic and Pastoral Review,* May: 16–24.

———. 2007. "Sturzo, Don Luigi." In *Encyclopedia of Catholic Social Thought, Social Science, and Social Policy,* edited by Michael Coulter, Stephen Krason, Richard Myers, and Joseph Varacalli, 1036–37. Lanham, MD: Scarecrow Press.

Guardini, Romano. (1923) 2004. *La visione cattolica del mondo.* Brescia, Italy: Editrice Morcelliana.

Hendershott, Anne. 2009. *Status Envy: The Politics of Catholic Higher Education.* New Brunswick, NJ: Transaction Publishers.

Hoffner, Right Rev. Joseph. 1962. *Fundamentals of Christian Sociology.* Cork, Ireland: The Mercier Press.

Hollon, Bryan. 2009. *Everything Is Sacred: Spiritual Exegesis in the Political Theology of Henri de Lubac.* Eugene, OR: Cascade Books.

Hunter, James Davison. 1987. "America's Fourth Faith? A Sociological Perspective on Secular Humanism." *This World,* Fall: 103–4

———. 1991. *Culture Wars: The Struggle to Define America.* New York: Basic Books.

———. 2006. "The Enduring Culture War." In *Is There a Culture War? A Dialogue on Values and American Public Life,* by James Davison Hunter and Alan Wolfe, 10–40. Washington, DC: Pew Research Center, Brookings Institution Press.

Johnson, Benton. 1987. "Faith, Facts, and Values in the Sociology of Religion." In *Religious Sociology: Interfaces and Boundaries,* edited by William Swatos, 3–14. New York: Greenwood Press.

Keenan, William. 2003. "Rediscovering the Theological in Sociology: Foundations and Possibilities." *Theory, Culture, and Society,* 20 (1): 19–42.

Kelly, Eileen. 2007. "Ryan, John Augustine." In *Encyclopedia of Catholic Social Thought, Social Science, and Social Policy,* edited by Michael Coulter, Stephen

Krason, Richard Myers, and Joseph Varacalli, 927–28. Lanham, MD: Scarecrow Press.

Kelly, Msgr. George. 1981. *The Battle for the American Church*. Garden City, NY: Image Books.

Kivisto, Peter. 1989. "The Brief Career of Catholic Sociology." *Sociological Analysis*, 50: 403–8.

Krason, Stephen. 1993. "What the Catholic Finds Wrong with Secular Social Science." *Social Justice Review*, January/February: 5–11.

———. 1999. "Review of Lothar Roos' edited version of Hoffner's *Christian Social Teaching*." *Catholic Social Science Review*, IV: 275–78.

Lewis. C.S. 1947. *The Abolition of Man: How Education Develops Man's Sense of Morality*. New York: Macmillan.

Little, Joyce. 1995. *The Church and the Culture War: Secular Anarchy or Sacred Order*. San Francisco: Ignatius Press.

Maguire, Daniel. 2001. *Sacred Choices*. Minneapolis: Fortress Press.

McGuire, Daniel. 2007. "Rerum Novarum." In *Encyclopedia of Catholic Social Thought, Social Science, and Social Policy*, edited by Michael Coulter, Stephen Krason, Richard Myers, and Joseph Varacalli, 913–14. Lanham, MD: Scarecrow Press.

Mich, Marvin L. 2001. *Catholic Social Teaching and Movements*. Mystic, CT: Twenty-Third Publications.

Mills, C. Wright. 1959. *The Sociological Imagination*. New York: Oxford University Press.

Mills, Kathryn, with Pamela Mills, eds. 2000. *C. Wright Mills: Letters and Autobiographical Writings*. Berkeley: University of California Press.

Murray, Rev. Raymond. (1935) 1946. *Introductory Sociology*. 2nd Edition. New York: Appleton-Century Crofts.

Neumeyr, George. 2010. "'Social Justice' and the New Politics: The Ground Shifts beneath the Catholic Left." *The Catholic World Report*, December: 1.

O'Brien, David. 2011. "For Archbishop's Camp, the Church Is the Hierarchy." *Philadelphia Inquirer*, July 26. Accessed August 1, 2011, http://articles.philly.com/2011-07-26/news/29816769_1_female-priests-catholic-church-bishops.

Pontifical Council for Justice and Peace. 2005. *Compendium of the Social Doctrine of the Church*. Washington, DC: United States Conference of Catholic Bishops and the *Libreria Editrice Vaticana*.

Pius X. (1907) n.d. *On the Doctrine of the Modernists* and *Syllabus Condemning the Errors of the Modernists*. Boston: St. Paul Editions.

Pope, Stephen. 1994. "Rerum Novarum." In *The New Dictionary of Catholic Social Thought*, edited by Judith Dwyer, 828–44. Collegeville, MN: The Liturgical Press.

Poythress, Vern. 2011. *Redeeming Sociology: A God-Centered Approach*. Wheaton, IL: Crossway Books.

Rauscher, Anton. 2007. "Hoffner, Cardinal Joseph." In *Encyclopedia of Catholic Social Thought, Social Science, and Social Policy*, edited by Michael Coulter, Stephen Krason, Richard Myers, and Joseph Varacalli, 507–9. Lanham, MD: Scarecrow Press.

Reno, R.R. 2011. "Loving the Law." *First Things*, January: 33–38.

Roos, Lothar. 1997. "Introduction to the English Edition" of *Christian Social Teaching* by Joseph Cardinal Hoffner. Available online at http://www.catholicsocial scientists.org/CSSR/Archival/1999/1999_275.pdf.

Ross, Eva. 1939. *Fundamental Sociology.* Milwaukee: The Bruce Publishing Company.

Rourke, Thomas. 2011. *The Social and Political Thought of Benedict XVI.* Lanham, MD: Lexington Books.

Shannon, Christopher. 2006. *Conspicuous Criticism: Tradition, the Individual, and Culture in Modern American Social Thought.* Scranton: University of Scranton Press.

Sharkey, Stephen. 2004–5. "Framing a Catholic Sociology for Today's College Students: Lessons from Furfey, Ross, and Murray, Parts I and II." *Catholic Social Science Review,* IX: 265–98 and X: 235–70.

———. 2005. "Beyond Mills' Sociological Imagination: Using a Pedagogy Based on Sorokin's Integralism to Reach Today's Introductory Sociology Students." *Catholic Social Science Review,* X: 53–81.

Shaw, Russell. 2011. "Only Part of the Story: The Conventional Wisdom Operative in American Social Justice Circles Neglects the Role of Virtue." *The Catholic World Report,* August/September: 43–44.

Smith, Christian. 2010. *What Is a Person? Rethinking Humanity, Social Life, and the Moral Good from the Person Up.* Chicago: University of Chicago Press.

Smith, Christian, with Melinda L. Denton. 2005. *Soul Searching: The Religious and Spiritual Lives of American Teenagers.* New York: Oxford University Press.

Smith, Christian, with Patricia Snell. 2009. *Souls in Transition: The Religious and Spiritual Lives of Emerging Adults.* New York: Oxford University Press.

Sturzo, Don Luigi. 1947. *The True Life: Sociology of the Supernatural.* London: Geoffrey Bles: The Centenary Press. Originally published 1943 in Italian.

Sullins, Rev. D. Paul. 2005. "Paul Hanly Furfey and the Catholic Intellectual Tradition." In *Paul Hanley Furfey's Quest for the Good Society,* edited by Bronislaw Misztal, Francesco Villa, and Eric Williams, 125–47. Washington, DC: Council for Research in Values and Philosophy, Catholic University of America.

———. 2007. "Sociology: A Catholic Critique." In *Encyclopedia of Catholic Social Thought, Social Science, and Social Policy,* edited by Michael Coulter, Stephen Krason, Richard Myers, and Joseph Varacalli, 1004–7. Lanham, MD: Scarecrow Press.

———. 2010. "Enhancing a Catholic Intellectual Culture." In *Studies in Catholic Higher Education,* by Center of the Advancement of Higher Education, March. Accessed May 10, 2011, http://www.CatholicHigherEd.org.

Swatos, William Jr. 1987. "Preface." In *Religious Sociology: Interfaces and Boundaries,* edited by William Swatos, Jr., vii–xiv. New York: Greenwood Press.

Thompson, J. Milburn. 2010. *Introducing Catholic Social Thought.* Maryknoll, NY: Orbis Books.

United States Conference of Catholic Bishops. 2005. "Seven Themes of Catholic Social Teaching." Washington, DC: USCCB Communications.

Varacalli, Joseph. 1987. "The Resurrection of 'Catholic Sociologies': Toward a Catholic Center." *Social Justice Review,* May/June: 100–106.

———. 1989. "Sociology, Feminism, and the Magisterium." *Homiletic and Pastoral Review,* LXXXIX (10): 60–66.

———. 1990. "Catholic Sociology in America: A Comment on the Fiftieth Anniversary Issue of *Sociological Analysis.*" *International Journal of Politics, Culture, and Society,* 4 (2): 249–62.

———. 1992. "Secular Sociology's War Against *Familiaris Consortio* and the Traditional Family: Whither Catholic Higher Education and Catholic Sociology?" In *The*

Church and the Universal Catechism, edited by Anthony Mastroeni, 161–86. Steubenville, OH: Franciscan University Press.

————. 1996. "Catholic Social Science and the Reconstruction of the Social Order." Faith and Reason, XXII (1–2): 3–14.

————. 2000. *Bright Promise, Failed Community: Catholics and the American Public Order.* Lanham, MD: Lexington Books.

Villa, Francesco. 2005. "Sociology and Metasociology: A Journey of Over Half a Century." In *Paul Hanley Furfey's Quest for the Good Society,* edited by Bronislaw Misztal, Francesco Villa, and Eric Williams, 45–71. Washington, DC: Council for Research in Values and Philosophy, Catholic University of America.

Weigel, George. 2004. *Letters to a Young Catholic.* New York: Basic Books.

————. 2011a. "Reactionary Liberalism and Catholic Social Doctrine." Accessed June 8, 2011, http://www.eppc.org/publications/publID.4460/pub_detail.sap.

————. 2011b. "Benedict XVI and the Future of the West." Ethics and Public Policy Center website, accessed July 11, 2011, http://www.eppc.org/publications/publID.4511/pub_detail.sap

Williams, Thomas. 2011. *The World as It Could Be: Catholic Social Thought for a New Generation.* Chestnut Ridge, NY: The Crossroad Publishing Company.

Winter, Michael. 2011. "Catholic Academics Challenge Boehner." *National Catholic Reporter,* May 11. Accessed August 1, 2011, http://ncronline.org/blogs/distinctly-catholic/breaking-news-catholic-academics-challenge-boehner.

Wolfe, Alan. 2006. "The Culture War that Never Came." In *Is There a Culture War? A Dialogue on Values and American Public Life,* by James Davison Hunter and Alan Wolfe, 41–73. Washington, DC: The Pew Research Center and Brookings Institution Press.

Woods, Thomas, Jr. 2004. *The Church Confronts Modernity: Catholic Intellectuals and the Progressive Era.* New York: Columbia University Press.

2

Imagined Communions:
The Virtual Nation for Virtuous Nations

D. Paul Sullins

If it is the work of Catholics to discern God's purpose in the modern world not only through piety and theology but also through (in the oft-repeated phrase of the Second Vatican Council) "discerning the signs of the times," then a theoretically Catholic sociology—by which I mean a sociology which examines social life from a theoretical standpoint which incorporates the truth-claims of the Catholic faith, in contrast to one which studies particular features of Catholic institutions, which I would call an "applied Catholic sociology"—has a uniquely important contribution to make to comprehending God's work in the world and the role of the Church in it. This may have always been true, but in the situation today of advanced modernity, in which the Catholic Church has explicitly adopted the disposition and self-understanding of being one actor among many other legitimate religious and quasi-religious actors, it is strongly and emphatically the case. A Catholic understanding of the role and structures of the Church among the social arrangements of modernity cannot be arrived at by appending a discrete concept of the Church, no matter how internally coherent or theologically insightful, to an otherwise secular theory of the modern world. Today more than ever, we must try to understand the meaning of the social world in light of Catholic truth as a preliminary and means to understanding the meaning of and God's purposes for the Church itself, and for all of us must live both in the Church and in the world.

This essay is an exercise in such a theoretically Catholic sociological analysis, in this case of the development of the role and disposition of the Holy See in relation to the changing role of the nation-state and the rise of a transnational order through the latter half of the 20th century. The impetus for this development, I will suggest, lies not only in the Enlightenment ideal of the nation-state and the emergence of a secular ideal of human dignity, but in the interaction of both of these cultural forces with the social arrangements and emerging social teachings of the Catholic Church. This collision of sociocultural factors has shaped not only the emergence of a universal political order but also the rise of the modern papacy, creating the possibility not only of national interests and peoples but also of national virtues.

The issues addressed in this case implicate one of the central problematics of sociology (and one which is crucial for the possibility of Catholic sociology): do human social arrangements cohere around a moral consensus, what Durkheim termed a "collective conscience," or are they patterned according to interests and power as in the familiar Marxian view? At the same time this analysis also challenges the (secular and secularizing) division of social forces into "secular" and "sacred," another contrivance of Durkheim's, in favor of a Catholic/catholic perspective that sees the social forces of the Enlightenment as precipitating both secular and sacred forms. The same set of forces that led to the rise of the nation-state also led to the universality and recognized infallibility of the papacy; they also led, simultaneously and not incidentally, to the emergence of human society as a recognized subject of action and object of study, and to the precipitation of the social sciences, and later sociology, from less differentiated conceptions of the scholastic project. Recently these forces have also led, I argue, to the restructuring of Catholic diversity and dissent, and to the reconstitution of the nation-state, in ways that mirror each other. The questions addressed in this study, finally, have growing practical relevance, in a global order in which the moral deficiencies of national economic arrangements result in transferred pain throughout the world economic system; and which increasingly looks to universal structures to provide moral direction and restraint, not only for violent aggression and international disputes, but also for such (bi- or multi-) lateral national concerns as trade, population, immigration, and environmental degradation.

Accommodating the Nation-state

The relation of the Roman Catholic Church to the modern nation-state has always been an uneasy one. Perhaps alone among current international actors, the Church is not a modern institution, and it has not recently globalized. Now entering its third millennium of existence, the Church's institutional structures and identity were formed a thousand years before the emergence of modern nations. It became a global institution, extending to the perimeter of the known world as the dominant, universally established religion, fifteen hundred years before the current trends of world globalization. Unlike any other religious or secular institution, the center of the Catholic Church today is not in any nation. Although its ruling structures are in Italy, it is not in any constitutive sense the Italian Catholic Church. The offices of the Pope, in fact, technically reside in a separate virtual nation, Vatican City, the only universally recognized national entity that is not a member of the United Nations.

Although the Vatican City State, with its own juridical existence and territory, enters into international agreements in its own right, it has, unlike all other nations, no diplomatic representation, nor can it advance any national or territorial interests. No nation has diplomatic relations with the Vatican. Rather, the Vatican State serves, in the words of the Holy See's U.N. Mission, merely as a "pedestal upon which is posed a much larger and unique independent and sovereign authority/rule: that of the Holy See" (Holy See 2006). As an actor in international diplomacy the Holy See has diplomatic relations with most nations, but represents, not (except in certain specific circumstances) the national interests of the Vatican, but "the central government of the Roman Catholic Church," specifically the juridical person of "the Pope as Bishop of Rome and head of the college of Bishops." This unique arrangement is designed to preserve and clarify the unique independence and neutrality of the Holy See among world actors. A pertinent analogy is the capital city of the United States, which, in order to preserve the unique independence of the national government, is located in a district which does not itself, technically, have separate representation in national affairs. For the same reason, the Holy See has elected not to adopt the status of a full or voting member of the United Nations, but rather that of a "permanent observer," in order, in the words of the Holy See's U.N. Mission, "to maintain absolute neutrality in specific political problems" (Holy See 2006).

If social arrangements have religious affinities, the nation-state has had an affinity for Protestant, as opposed to Catholic, Christianity. It is widely recognized today that modern nations are in large part socially constructed regimes—subjective realms of communicative action in Habermas' thought, or, in Anderson's (1991) apt definition, *imagined communities*. Anderson theorizes that nations are imagined, in that the image of communion with all members of the nation, a kind of "national consciousness" analogous to the Marxian notion of class consciousness, resides in millions of individuals who will never actually interact; communities, that is, characterized by a deep horizontal fraternity among otherwise unrelated persons; sovereign, that is, comprising a sphere of freedom for autonomous individuals; and limited, that is, conceived not as universal, but as having borders beyond which lay other nations (Anderson 1991, 7–8).

In this view, the Durkheimian affinity between social arrangements and religious activities is expressed in the acknowledgment that nations embody subjective views of ultimate meaning that can be properly termed religious. If, as Anderson suggests, nations are in some senses mythic realms, the particular mythos of the modern nation-state is not that of universal Catholicism, but that of

Protestant pluralism. As Anderson (1991, 7) puts it: "Coming to maturity at a stage of human history when even the most devout adherents of any universal religion were inescapably confronted with the living *pluralism* of such religions, and the allomorphism between each faith's ontological claims and territorial stretch, nations dream of being free, and, if under God, directly so. The gage and emblem of this freedom is the sovereign state."

Since the days of Roman persecution, of course, a universal religious regime such as Christianity has always existed in some tension with political authority. Medieval Christendom sought to resolve this tension by subsuming multiple political arrangements under a single religious ideal; in the nation-state modernity has adopted the opposite strategy, attempting to subsume multiple religious ideals under a single political authority. As an accommodation to religious pluralism, national sovereignty has been problematic for Catholicism since the Enlightenment. It has also, as secularization demonstrates, grown to be problematic for Protestantism. And for at least the last hundred years, it has become increasingly problematic for nation-states themselves.

The problem for sovereignty so construed is that the pluralism that called it into being does not cooperate with the noted imagined allomorphism of ontology and territory. Pascal, who noted in the 17th century that what is truth on one side of the Pyrenees is error on the other, would have to greatly shorten the geographical scope of such a comparison today. The problem of pluralism between nations eventually gave rise to the problem of pluralism within nations, and thus began to corrode rather than reinforce the national mythos. For a time, national religions (or effectively dominant religions) created a bulwark against such pluralism, but with the rise of world consciousness and scientific rationality, national religions gave way to the myth of the secular state.

Surely Casanova (1994) is correct in arguing that, in such a situation, the pre-eminent imperative for religious regimes is to become legitimately public religions. The Yale historian and Muslim expert Lamin Sanneh makes a similar point when he observes that the church—by which he means Christianity generically—has, in contrast to Islam, no native political language, but that the "language" of the Church must be translation. In this view, which is also characteristic of Stanley Hauerwas and similar theological ethicists, the state of Christianity relative to nation-states today is something like that of a benign parasite, or a permanent invader (Hauerwas and Willimon 1989).

These assessments, however, assign too much objectivity to the state and too little to the Church. As Durkheim noted, religion does not merely receive from the state, but also offers important desiderata to the state. The nature and extent of these benefits are debated, but even the most restrictive Marxist view on the matter acknowledges that they have at minimum historically comprised what are generally termed legitimacy, with regard to rulers, and internalization, with regard to the ruled. Until the modern era, and even today with regard to pre-modern regimes, such were universally considered essential qualities of a functioning state.

The modern myth is that these ancient imperatives of church-state relations somehow no longer apply. This is, of course, a self-reinforcing notion, necessary by definition to imagine a secular state. But is it true? Much evidence suggests otherwise. At the prime of nationhood, the 20th century witnessed the proliferation, not of mature secular states in which religion and governance both thrived, but of militantly ideological totalitarian regimes of the right and the left, on the one hand, and of comprehensive yet assertively secular welfare states, on the other hand. In both outcomes, as religion conceded the power to govern to the state, the state began to assume some of the functions formerly filled by religion, such as personal security or identity or compassion (even by means of a vestigial state religion), in order to govern legitimately. The decline of strong functioning state religions, it appears, has led inevitably to the rise of religious or quasi-religious states.

How then to explain the progress and attraction of the secular ideal? If the church-state imperatives still do apply, then the official ignorance by the state of religious matters is part of their current application. As noted above, the separation from religion of the Western secular state is as much a result of religious outcomes as political ones. Thus I suggest that, ironically, the state today is secular because secularity serves religion. The state does not serve religion, but that the state does not serve religion serves religion. And it serves most particularly the world-reforming religions that spring from the Jewish/Christian/Islamic tradition.

Virtual Nationality

In this light it is not too surprising that, in an era of *quasi-religious nations*, the Catholic Church has adopted the form of a *quasi-national religion*. The nature of its diplomatic presence, that of a virtual state with effectively no territory, reflects the persistence of the church-state imperative, in the same way as does elaborate national social service or health care or educational bureaucracies in a state with effectively no religious commitments. Both developments are concomitant responses to the transition from "late nationality" to the emerging international world system. The Catholic Church, as a transnational actor, imagines itself to be a holder of sovereignty absent an actual state as an accommodation to a world system in which nations, as transreligious actors, imagine themselves to be holders of meaning absent an actual religion. In both cases the meaning and the sovereignty are virtual, subjective realities, which in their contingency open up national and religious arrangements to emerging possibilities. The fictive character of Catholic nationality, therefore, mirrors the fictive character of secular meaningfulness, and by extension of state sovereignty itself.

The onset of modernity involved closely related philosophical, political, and religious transformations, which we know today as the contiguous rise of the Enlightenment, the nation-state, and the Protestant Reformation. Similarly, today's processes of globalization involve a confluence of philosophical, political, and religious changes which will likely recast the modern tension among these three movements. The Catholic Church's current unique status in world affairs reflects a meeting of globalizing processes with internal developments in Catholicism that began to emerge only recently, in response to the modern settlement, and have accelerated since the Second Vatican Council.

Four crucial components of these developments, which respectively address the philosophical, economic, political, and religious challenges of modernity, are the recognition of the development of doctrine, the centralization of Church authority structures furthered by the definition of papal infallibility, the emergence and dominance of Catholic social ideals and teaching, and the universalization of the Catholic mission. I will leave discussion of the doctrinal, philosophical developments for another time, and here focus on the issues of centralization, the contribution of Catholic social thought to human rights ideals, and universalization in turn, followed by a discussion of two possible effects, or differences these make: the restructuring of Catholic diversity and dissent, and the reconstitution of the nation-state.

Centralization

It is often recognized that the Catholic Church's centralized hierarchical organization, unique among world religions, is a major factor in its diplomatic effectiveness, expediting its international role and activities and permitting the articulation of a clear global agenda. It is common today to think of the Catholic Church as having always been a steeply hierarchical institution, but the level of centralization and worldwide integration of authority that exists in the Church today is, in historical terms, a fairly recent development, which is connected to the putative decline of the nation-state.

The congruence between national and religious identity that emerged at the Reformation inhibited both the inherently disintegrative tendencies of the new Protestantism and the inherently cohesive inclinations in Catholicism. Today, as the nation-state secularizes and faces challenges of legitimacy, global Protestant organizations and alliances are fracturing in the face of a corrosive post-denominationalism, while Catholicism is in the process of becoming more highly centralized.

Through most of the Church's history the type of pre-eminent authority the Pope exercises today has been challenged by the centrifugal forces of conciliarism (rule by church councils) and gallicanism (rule by national assemblies of bishops). Eight hundred years ago conciliarism was at its height; during most of the twelfth century there were two rival popes supported by competing councils. Gallicanism was in ascendancy just two centuries ago, when the prerogatives of the Pope were severely circumscribed following the French revolution.[1]

The essential components of the current transnational identity of the Catholic Church, formed as a specific response to the Reformation nation-state, can be traced directly to the First Vatican Council in 1870. The major product of this council, of course, was the definition of the doctrine popularly known as papal infallibility, which specifically establishes that the Pope's interpretation of doctrine cannot be over-ridden by a council or national assembly. There had, in fact, been an attempt to define papal infallibility at the Council of Trent (1545–1563), but the success of the proposal had to wait until 1870, by which time the bishops were far less powerful, and a military threat to the Papal States was imminent. Significantly, at the same that Vatican I declared the Pope a supreme moral authority internally, the Council also renounced all use of physical force by the Church against external actors. The immediate effect was to clarify and finally settle the nature of the Church relative to the nation-state. Mart Bax (1991, 14), in a history of these developments, concludes, "Vatican I transformed the Roman Catholic Church into a centralized, hierarchical and supra-national religious regime in which moral interdependencies were carefully formulated....The Roman Catholic regime adopted a stand that was detached from the state and transcended the interests of national states. For these reasons, it developed into an opponent to be reckoned with."

A century later the centralization of the Church was ratified and extended by the Second Vatican Council of the 1960s. Ironically, while progressive Catholics received Vatican II as a manifesto for local autonomy, the net effect of the Council was as much to direct and regulate as to promote and legitimate local variation in the Church. The Council documents strongly reaffirmed papal infallibility (Vatican Council II 1964, #18) and, in language that presaged current global developments, called for increased unity and the elimination of dissent under papal leadership: "Since the human race today is tending more and more towards civil, economic and social unity, it is all the more necessary that priests should unite their efforts and combine their resources under the leadership of the bishops and the Supreme Pontiff and thus eliminate division and dissension in every shape and form, so that all mankind may be led into the unity of the family of God" (Vatican Council II 1964, #28; this passage is quoted in Wojtyla [Pope John Paul II] 1979, 154). It is often forgotten that it was the losing forces of *ressourcement* at the Council who advocated the return to a less Rome-centered Church. With regard to the sociological centralization of the Church, the most obvious fact of Vatican II is almost never noticed: that it was held at the Vatican. After two millennia of councils held everywhere else, with Vatican II the Catholic Church belatedly held two successive councils in under a century at the center of church power.

As a matter of simple fact, in the period following the Council, assertions of centralized regulation have occurred at a pace seldom if ever before matched in the history of the Church. In the last forty years the Catholic Church has issued (a) new or updated universal: lectionary, code of canon law, catechism (the first in 400 years), general instruction for the liturgy, general directory for catechesis, and norms for Catholic universities and schools, to mention only the most significant. During the same period the Pope has issued more universal teaching documents, not just slightly more but several times as many, than at any previous time in the history of the Church. By some measures, more doctrine and discipline has been promulgated from Rome during the last 40 years than in all the previous ages of the Church combined. In historical terms, we may well be at only the beginning of a period of growing centralization in the Catholic Church.

Such centralization is made possible (as we have seen) by the revocation by the Church of statist ambitions. It is made necessary by the de facto articulation of the faith in a growing and sometimes incompatible variety of cultural forms. Here it must be remembered that the Catholic Church understands itself to have a pre-eminent institutional mission, i.e., to faithfully preserve and transmit the historically conditioned revelation of God in Jesus Christ. This imperative affects the Church's institutional elaboration directly, in that the Church extends the incarnation of its founder in the fiction that the Pope incarnates the Church in international affairs.

Thus, along with the global centralization of the Church in the Vatican and its curia has been a trend toward the formalization and centralization of national Catholic churches (Casanova 1997, 136–37). In contrast to national Protestant churches, Catholic national churches have more often prophetically challenged prevailing social and moral norms that counter the Catholic understanding of the Christian faith. The U.S. Conference of Catholic Bishops (USCCB) has often taken diplomatic positions on international issues that are in sync with those of the Vatican even when these positions are not popular in the U.S. For example, the USCCB has repeatedly advocated U.S. ratification of international treaties, already signed by the Vatican and every European nation, to impose environmental standards and eliminate the use of landmines—none of which have ever attained the support of a majority of Americans or been ratified by the U.S. In September 2002 the U.S. bishops, in a just war critique closely modeled on one articulated earlier by the Vatican, publicly denounced plans by the Bush administration to invade Iraq, despite overwhelming support for such an action in the U.S. Congress and among the American public, including a large majority of American Catholics. The U.S. Catholic Church has persistently opposed such generally accepted practices as contraception, elective abortion, normalization of homosexual relations, and even (technically) divorce, as well as maintaining uncharacteristically non-democratic and gender-stratified forms of institutional leadership. The Church maintains these positions and structures in conformity with global church norms, in the face of a strong social consensus to the contrary among the U.S. population and even among national Catholic elites. By contrast, the Anglican Communion, the largest and arguably most cohesive international Protestant affiliation, has been unable to prevent the American Episcopal Church from taking steps to normalize homosexual relations, with the result that both the American and international Anglican churches are undergoing various levels of conflict, disaggregation, and realignment.

Catholic Social Thought and Universal Human Rights

The Holy See's effectiveness in the international order is also due, in part, to the current dominance of Christian ideals and forms in the international order. It is common today to think of American power, or perhaps the allied power of the West, as the lynchpin of world order. However, the dominance of the West in world affairs is not primarily a hegemony of political power but a dominance of cultural values and forms; and primary among these values and forms is the Christian faith. The Christian faith, in varying forms and to varying degrees, has been proposed by scholars as the common root of capitalism, democracy, rationalization, the ideal of progress, the project of modern science, even Marxism and secular humanism. To the extent that such forms have promoted global development and comity to date, and considering the actual transitions of power that have occurred and the growing belligerence of the United States with the decline of the cold war, it may be more accurate today to speak of the possibilities of a *pax Christiana* than of a *pax Americana*.

At the center of the norms and ideals that guide the international order is a Christian understanding of human persons. The ideals of human dignity, human rights, freedom, and self-determination are direct elaborations of Christian themes and doctrines. It may be instructive to recall that those who labored to institute the Universal Declaration of Human Rights, which forms the juridical constitution of today's international order and legitimacy, as well as the United Nations, did so out of an explicit application of Christian principles. Franklin Roosevelt declared that the United Nations "shall seek...the establishment of an international order in which the spirit of Christ shall rule the hearts of men and nations" (*New York Herald Tribune*, January 7, 1939; quoted in Maritain 1944, 58).

It does not detract from the universal appeal and applicability of the ideals of human dignity to note that their articulation in such form and force reflected the central theme and language of the relatively new body of Catholic social thought. In the establishment and promotion of ideals of universal rights, Catholics were more than marginally implicated. Catholic intellectuals, from Jacques Maritain to John Courtney Murray, argued that world peace, democracy, and the Christian faith were inextricably linked, a line of reasoning which pervades Catholic social thought to this day.

The body of doctrines known as Catholic Social Thought (CST) is remarkable in that it emerged relatively late and developed relatively quickly in the long history of Christian tradition. The first recognized social encyclical—aptly named *Rerum Novarum*, the "New Things"—did not appear until the year 1891, that is, until almost 19 of the 20 centuries we have experienced since the time of Christ's incarnation had already passed. Since their late emergence, furthermore, the social teachings have developed into an identifiable and important part of the Church's teaching with a speed that is, in terms of doctrinal history, nothing short of unprecedented. From the first articulation in *Rerum Novarum* to the mature systematization of the *Compendium* (Pontifical Council for Justice and Peace 2005) spans little more than a century.

Some will object that the social teachings did not emerge entirely de novo, but grew from seeds that are evident far earlier in the tradition. This is undoubtedly true; indeed, many of the themes of CST are expressed in Scripture; but this does not weigh against, but rather strengthens, the point I am making. The more the social teachings are implicated in the Christian idea theologically, the less understandable it is on theological grounds why they came so late chronologically. Imagine the degree of social injustice the West might have been spared if the principle of subsidiarity or the equal and inalienable dignity of human persons had been articulated during the feudal era. No, the theological continuity of the social teachings with the central themes of the Christian faith only sharpens the question: if they are so theologically central and essential, why were they not articulated much earlier?

The answer is that CST came to light when and how it did not as a result of an internal theological problematic but in response to emergent changes in the sociocultural order. It is commonly recognized that the social teachings appeared in response to industrialization, particularly the development of commodity wages and growing property inequality that inhibited human freedom among the wage-earning classes. But CST is also far more than a critique of industrialization; it articulates a vision of human being and human society that addresses the root problems of modernity itself. Solidarity, for example, counteracts the atomic individualism of Enlightenment thinking about man in a recognition and promotion of human sociality that goes far beyond mere labor coalitions. The principle of subsidiarity not only creates space for human freedom in intimate associations, but also redresses the tendency toward vertical sovereignty and total control of subordinates which is expressed no less in the rational bureaucratic state than in the divine right of kings. The ideal of the common good provides a justification for collective political arrangements that both challenges and affirms modern voluntaristic or utilitarian ideals of popular sovereignty.

But the primary and most successful exemplar of CST's response to Enlightenment modernity has been the ideal of the dignity of the human person. This formulation has been universally accepted by religious and secular regimes, and, with the related concept of human rights, lays at the root of the modern world order. The Preamble of the Universal Declaration of Human Rights begins with "the recognition of the inherent dignity...of all members of the human family." The formal idea of human dignity, of course, expresses a central impulse of Enlightenment, specifically Kantian, moral philosophy. It was in Catholic social reflection, however, that the idea of human dignity took concrete shape in the expression of moral social arrangements.

In the international realm, the principles of Catholic Social Thought form the context for, and are in turn advocated principally by, the international activity of the Holy See. Just as the Holy See does not pursue national interests in the ordinary sense, so in this arena CST functions not as an ideology but truly as principle, as unapologetically Catholic ideas of human life and freedom are brought to bear, for the most part, for the benefit of all humanity rather than the material interests of the Catholic Church.

Increasingly, the Catholic Church has adopted the role of advocacy for the spirit of Christ, expressed in support of universal human freedoms and values, thus becoming a kind of civil religion of the emerging international order. For at least two decades, and explicitly since *Ut Unam Sint* (John Paul II 1995), the Pope has envisioned the possibility of speaking for all Christians, not just Catholics. In many regards this recognizes what is already a de facto representation, that extends, not without some irony, even as far as other religions (as discussed further in a moment). As a matter of practice, the Holy See's international diplomacy in recent times has been directed far less to the relation of the Church to nations than to the relations of nations with each other. The Holy See's U.N. Mission explicitly acknowledges this role: "[W]hy do so many countries seek official contacts with the Holy See?...What they do seek is what the Holy See, by its very nature and tradition, can offer: orientation and spiritual inspiration that should animate the life of nations and their mutual relationships" (Holy See 2006). Its primary messages in United Nations discourse include: the equality of all nations; the solidarity among nations, particularly across differentials of wealth and power; the priority, in international disputes, of negotiation and jurisprudence over war; and, more recently, the defense of unborn life and natural forms of the family (Tauran 2002).

Universalism

The recent process of centralization of Catholic authority has been accompanied in the 20th century by an increasing universalism in its evangelistic and public policy activities. The social encyclicals, beginning with *Rerum Novarum* in 1891 (Leo XIII 1891), increasingly addressed matters of social and economic life that had traditionally been considered external to Christian doctrine proper. In 1931's *Quadragesimo Anno*, subtitled "On the Reconstruction of the Social Order," Pope Pius XI dedicated the first portion of the document to defending the still novel thesis that "there resides in Us the right and duty to pronounce with supreme authority upon social and economic matters" (Pius XI 1931, #41). Beginning with *Pacem in Terris* in 1963, papal encyclicals (with a few exceptions) began to be addressed, not only to bishops and Catholic faithful, but also to "all persons of good will." At the same time as the Church, due to centralization, increasingly spoke with one voice, it aspired to speak for and address its message to one common humanity.

The process was also accelerated by the Second Vatican Council, particularly as a result of its groundbreaking declaration on religious liberty, which affirmed that even error had rights of conscientious assent. As the implications of this idea have worked themselves into the Church's diplomatic activities since the Council, the policy of *libertas ecclesiae* has been transmuted into an advocacy of *libertas humanae*. Whereas prior to the 1960s the Church sought to defend the particular freedom, and dominance if possible, of the Catholic faith, since the Second Vatican Council the Holy See has supported not just religious freedom for Catholics as an institutional strategy, but religious freedom for all religions as a matter of principle. Consequently global Catholicism has been engaged, not always consistently, in a project of renouncing national institutional privilege in favor of participation as one voluntary religious institution among many in a civil society comprised, within nations, of ideally unconstrained religious discourse. The good of the Church is now bound up with the good of the human person.

Increasingly, the Church seeks to ensure the freedom of the faith, not primarily through negotiating institutional conditions or arrangements but by focusing on structures that promote religious freedom for all persons and religious actors. Where at one time the Church sought to dominate, today it seeks only not to be dominated. Just as, and for many of the same reasons as, a multinational business corporation, the Church ideally seeks a free and open market of ideas, but also, for its own good, no monopoly on the expression of truth. In its current self-understanding, the Church sits more comfortably in the marketplace of religion than in the seat of power.

There are good reasons to worry that in the protection of its institutional interests the Church must engage in a realpolitik that may compromise its social justice ideals. But the Church has no ability to counter the coercive violence of realpolitik in kind; it has no borders to protect; and its institutional force is scant at best. In fact, the ability to compromise and nuance the Church's position is built into its principles regarding the articulation of moral truth. On the whole, the maintenance of centralized authority promotes flexibility, not rigidity, in the articulation and application of Catholic convictions in particular situations. Whether by irony or design, the effect of this policy has been to place the Church in a powerful position in the formation of international civil structures.

Enabling and Reclaiming Dissent

The nation-state enabled not only the Protestant schism but also a variety of less severe centripetal forces in Catholicism. To be sure, cultural pluralism has characterized the Christian faith since its beginning, when, on the Day of Pentecost, persons of many nationalities and cultures received the Gospel proclamation, so it is recorded, in their own tongue. Since the emergence of the modern world order a wide variety of perspectives, interpretations, disciplines, and liturgical expressions of the faith have been, to a large extent, a resultant of diverse national languages, cultures, sensibilities, ethnicities, and political arrangements. In our day this diversity is being re-ordered.

It has been widely recognized that the ongoing process of globalization simultaneously encourages both global conformity and local diversity. As rationalized norms become universal, disparate oppositional extremes are empowered. In the Catholic Church a similar dual dynamic has led to the strengthening of oppositional forces at the same time as papal authority has become largely universalized. Centralized papal authority, like global trade agreements, is effective for boundary maintenance, limiting diversity when it crosses the line into dissent or is particularly prominent, but cannot efficiently impose the internalization of norms and ideals or desired behavior in local, that is, national settings. Some (e.g., Hervieu-Leger 1997, looking at the Catholic charismatic movement and world youth days) have argued, moreover, that opposition or diversity is decreasingly associated with nations and increasingly resident in cultural elaborations and a network of international organizations that have emerged since the mid-20th century. Like religious orders of an earlier day, modern lay apostolates pursue particular visions of the faith largely unhindered by hierarchical oversight, and increasingly these develop transnational presences and sensibilities.

There is little doubt that this is occurring; however, it is unlikely that, with the possible exception of certain religious elites, such international linkages will effectively homogenize Catholic religious culture. National differences in religious life will persist, and strengthen. Figure 2.1 presents evidence of such persistence and enhancement of national diversity among Catholics worldwide. The figure reports findings from the World Values Surveys (total n = 63,729 Catholic respondents in up to 49 nations) in 1981, 1990, and 1997 on the diversity of opinion among Catholics worldwide on abortion. In Catholic moral teaching, elective abortion is never justifiable; over this period the Holy See engaged in consistent and extensive advocacy to prohibit the practice of abortion. To the question, "Is abortion ever justified?" respondents were invited to indicate their view on a 10-point scale ranging from "Never" to "Always." The figure reports the mean square variance of opinion between nations and within nations, and the corresponding F statistic for each year. It is clear that in every period the variance of opinion within nations is much smaller than that between nations; the between-nation variance is several hundred times larger than the within-nation

variance, the bars for which are barely visible in the figure. Since 1981, moreover, the variance between nations has almost doubled (from 415 to 802) while
within-nation variance has increased only slightly (from 6.5 to 7.2). These results show directly that the consistent and public opposition of the Holy See to
abortion in the international sphere has not prevented the existence and growth
of local diversity, largely correlated with national—political and cultural—
differences, on this key Catholic issue.

Figure 2.1. Diversity of Catholic opinion on abortion within and between nations: World Values Surveys 1981–1997.

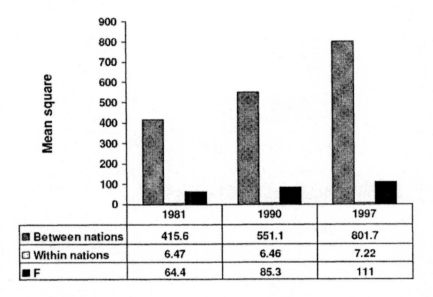

	1981	1990	1997
▨ Between nations	415.6	551.1	801.7
▢ Within nations	6.47	6.46	7.22
▪ F	64.4	85.3	111

In his 2000 McGinley lecture, the late Cardinal Avery Dulles suggested that
there are certain structural arrangements in the Catholic Church today that promote the simultaneous development of centralization and local diversity in institutional Catholicism. He presents an image of centralization and decentralization
as two tendencies that co-exist in a dynamic tension in the Church, such that a
greater force in one direction leads to a greater countering force in the other.
"Precisely because of the increased activity of particular churches and conferences," Dulles observes, "Rome is required to exercise greater vigilance than
ever, lest the unity of the church be jeopardized" (Dulles 2000). To some extent,
as well, the agency of the Holy See operates to preserve local diversity in the
face of international oppositional tendencies. By appealing to the Holy See, local churches have recourse to balance the intrusion of centrifugal forces. Dulles

presents several cases where this has functioned with regard to translations of church texts, concluding "...as in many [cases], the authority of Rome functions to protect local churches from questionable exercises of power by national or international agencies" (Dulles 2000).

However, the larger reality that opposes the centralizing forces in world Catholicism is ongoing secularization—individual secularization in Bryan Wilson's (1982) sense—manifested in the growing tendency for culture to carry religion rather than the other way around. Increasingly, for most Catholics worldwide, the rise of personal choice in religion is leading to the selective appropriation of religious goods and the assimilation of religious values to humanistic ones elaborated along the lines of cultural, that is, effectively national, differences. As authority is becoming more centralized, explicit, and resident in formal institutional arrangements, elements of diversity or dissent are becoming more globally diffuse, implicit, and resident in informal cultural appropriations of the faith. Although the particular issues in question may be different, Catholics in Africa and South America, no less than in North America, experience little cognitive dissonance in simultaneously affirming strong allegiance to the Pope and selectively ignoring his directives in their private personal behavior.

Ironically, this secularization is in some ways enabled by the advocacy of the Holy See itself. If persons are free in conscience to choose their religion, then dissenting Catholics can claim to be free in conscience to select among Catholic doctrines. If the truths of faith express the truths of humanity, then secularists can claim that humanistic values circumscribe Catholic religious truths. The very values advocated by the highest Catholic authority are capable of misappropriation by a Catholic religious culture that, up to an extent, protests them.

In this irony lies a unique and fundamentally catholic or ecumenical opportunity for the Holy See, for protest is a central problematic of both religious and secular culture today; and if global Catholicism may struggle with too much centralization, global Protestantism struggles much harder with too little. While Catholic diversity today risks being muted, Protestant diversity risks becoming incoherent and self-defeating. As the Holy See increasingly represents universal religious realities and rights in the international sphere, it benefits most strongly, next to Catholic interests, the interests of those separated Christian communities that are most similar to Catholicism, namely, Protestant Christians. Many of the realities and rights involved, moreover, are more characteristic of Protestantism than they are of Catholicism.

When the Pope advocates the primacy of conscience, free religious discourse, the rights of religious minorities, freedom to convert, even unhindered access to religious scriptures and worship in the common language, he is advocating positions that Protestants maintained in the face of Catholic opposition from the Reformation until as recently as the 1960s. In its international role, therefore, the Holy See serves as a unifying agent, not only for the Catholic Church, but also for the myriad Christian expressions of an increasingly disintegrated Protestantism. For all Protestant groups, the Holy See's framing of moral discourse in the international sphere provides a reference for their own proclamation of the Gospel. In the United States, fundamentalists make common cause with Catholics in opposition to abortion and gay marriage at the same time as liberals appropriate Catholic social teachings in economic policy. In this sense, the Holy See's international agency moves more than a little toward recapturing an *unam catholicam ecclesiam.*

Toward Virtuous Nations

As the forces of globalization, post-modernity, and multinational capitalism, among others, pose ongoing challenges to the legitimacy and autonomy of nation-states, the Catholic Church appears now to be entering an era in which it functions once again in the liminal space between nations and in the emerging international civil society. One of the strong contributions of the virtual nation which is the Catholic Church to the international order in years to come will be a clear articulation of the necessity and proper mission of nations. This situation bears some resemblance to the medieval *res publica Christiana,* in which a common religious faith formed the basis for a civilized world order among relatively weak political actors. Jose Casanova has referred to the emerging era as "neomedieval," and Philip Jenkins has famously called it the "next Christendom." While it is not all certain that the current challenges will ultimately result in an erosion of national power, it is clear that nations, as imagined communities, are being broadly re-imagined on a global scale today. In this process it is crucial that the spiritual potential of nation-states be encouraged and elaborated, that they may mature, as it were, from imagined communities to imagined communions.

This development is crucial to the continued progression of the modern ideal of human rights which lies at the heart of the international order. In a global national order, human rights are not merely individual rights, but also entail the rights of nations. Indeed, it was the weakness of national religions to posit human rights in individuals. Just as it is important to affirm that human rights are not ontologically conferred by the state, but inhere in each person by the action of God, so it is also important to affirm that human rights is an empty concept apart from membership in a nation that makes their attainment sociologically possible. So the 2005 *Compendium of the Social Doctrine of the Church* (Pontifical Council for Justice and Peace, #435) explicitly calls for "national rights" to extend and secure "human rights."

Yet the relation between human and national rights is not just functional; it is not merely that the rights of nations in international discourse must be established in order that the rights of persons in national discourse can be secured. Rather, national rights are an essential species of human rights, because nationhood is an essential human activity. As Aristotle recognized that man is by nature a political animal, so Catholic social doctrine has recognized that, in the modern world system, the formation of nations is a rational, that is, human, activity. The discovery of new and limiting responsibilities in the elaboration of a transnational world order betokens the transformation, adjustment, and maturing of the nation-state, but not its disappearance or even its weakening. Nations, no less than religions and economies, are called to serve the human person, and it will be the ongoing role of the Church, speaking as a nation to the nations, to call all nations to discover and enact their own virtues.

Notes

1. This paragraph and the two following are adapted from D. Paul Sullins, "Beyond Christendom: Protestant/Catholic Distinctions in the Coming Global Christianity," *Religion* 36 (November 2006): 197–213.

Bibliography

Anderson, Benedict. 1991. *Imagined Communities: Reflections on the Origin and Spread of Nationalism.* New York: Verso.

Bax, Mart. 1991. "Religious Regimes and State-formation: Toward a Research Perspective." In *Religious Regimes and State-Formation: Perspectives from European Ethnology,* edited by Eric Wolf, 7–53. Albany, NY: SUNY Press.

Casanova, Jose. 1994. *Public Religions in the Modern World.* Chicago: University of Chicago Press.

———. 1997. "Globalizing Catholicism and the Return to a 'Universal' Church." In *Transnational Religion and Fading States,* edited by Susanne Rudolph and James Piscatori, 121–43. Boulder, CO: Westview Press.

Dulles, Avery. 2000. "The Papacy for a Global Church." McGinley Lecture, Fordham University, New York, March 22. Reprinted in *America,* July 15, 2000.

Hauerwas, Stanley, and William Willimon. 1989. *Resident Aliens: Life in the Christian Colony.* Nashville, TN: Abingdon Press.

Hervieu-Leger, Daniele. 1997. "Faces of Catholic Transnationalism: In and Beyond France." In *Transnational Religion and Fading States,* edited by Susanne Rudolph and James Piscatori, 104–20. Boulder, CO: Westview Press.

Holy See. 2006. "A Short History of the Holy See's Diplomacy." Accessed April 15, 2006, http://www.holyseemission.org/short_history.html.

John Paul II. 1995, March 25. *Ut Unum Sint* [On Commitment to Ecumenism]. Encyclical letter. Vatican website, http://www.vatican.va/holy_father/john_paul_ii/encyclicals/documents/hf_jp-ii_enc_25051995_ut-unum-sint_en.html.

Leo XIII. 1891, May 15. *Rerum Novarum* [On Capital and Labor]. Encyclical letter. Vatican website, http://www.vatican.va/holy_father/leo_xiii/encyclicals/documents/hf_l-xiii_enc_15051891_rerum-novarum_en.html.

Maritain, Jacques. 1944. *Christianity and Democracy*. New York: Scribner's Press.

Pius XI. 1931. *Quadragesimo Anno*. Encyclical letter. Vatican website, http://www
.vatican.va/holy_father/pius_xi/encyclicals/documents/hf_pxi_enc_19310515_quadr
agesimo-anno_it.html.

Pontifical Council for Justice and Peace. 2005. *Compendium of the Social Doctrine of the
Church*. Washington, DC: USCCB Publishing.

Sullins, D. Paul. 2006. "Beyond Christendom: Protestant/Catholic Distinctions in the
Coming Global Christianity." *Religion* 36 (4): 197–213.

Tauran, Jean-Louis. 2002. "The Presence of the Holy See in the International Organizations." Presentation, Catholic University of the Sacred Heart, Milan, Italy, April 22.
Accessed April 15, 2006, http://www.vatican.va/roman_curia/secretariat_state
/documents/rc_seg-st_doc_20020422_tauran_en.html.

Vatican Council II. 1964, November 21. *Lumen Gentium*. [Dogmatic Constitution on the
Church]. Vatican website, http://www.vatican.va/archive/hist_councils/ii_vatican
_council/documents/vat-ii_const_19641121_lumen-gentium_en.html.

Wilson, Bryan. 1982. *Religion in Sociological Perspective*. New York: Oxford University
Press.

Wojtyla, Karol. (1972) 1979. *Sources of Renewal: The Implementation of the Second
Vatican Council*. San Francisco: Harper and Row.

3

Beyond the "Dictatorship of Relativism": Toward a Sociology of Knowledge, Catholic-Style

Joseph A. Varacalli

Introduction

This essay has multiple and related goals, all of which deal with the implications of relativity for the intellectual and moral life as understood from an authentically Catholic frame of reference. It should be stated at the outset that the Catholic vision is not opposed to relativity, per se. Catholicism posits an incarnational, sacramental, and integrationist understanding of reality in which both the truth of Jesus Christ and of the natural law written into the heart can impregnate, center, and define much of the diversity and pluralism of social and historical existence. However, empirically it is the case that, especially in the modern and postmodern context, many social constructions of reality, whether of a cultural or academic nature, lack or violate a universal standard of evaluation. In general, this essay deals with the relationship of the absolute to the relative in both civilization at large and within the academic discipline of sociology.

One specific goal of this essay is to explain what Pope Benedict XVI/Cardinal Ratzinger means by the "dictatorship of relativism" and to discuss what he sees as its deleterious consequences for civilization. A second is to sociologically analyze the dispersion and institutionalization of cultural/religious/moral relativism in a Christian West undergoing significant secularization and the social and individual dysfunctions it encourages. A third is to historically account for the emergence and development of the "sociology of knowledge," explicating how this sociological sub-discipline arose as a response to secularization and pluralism and, in large part, is itself reflective of the relativism it attempts to explain. Fourth, the attempt is made to move in the direction of developing a "sociology of knowledge, Catholic style" that attempts to at least partially transcend relativism. Such a construction takes clues from the work of such sociologists of knowledge as Max Scheler and Werner Stark. Fifth, the central sociological issue of social stratification will be used as an example of how a Catholicized "sociology of knowledge" investigation would differ from the two mainstream approaches on the topic, i.e., from Karl Marx and Max Weber, and some of the contemporary research indebted to them. Sixth, included will be a discussion of other Catholic and non-Catholic intellectuals who attempt to integrate into their respective analyses some conception of a natural law or universal norm analysis, as well as from selected "Catholic-friendly" non-Catholic social science research that, while not explicitly introducing any metaphysical dimension, nonetheless provide empirical research findings consistent with those of a Catholic social science. Finally, provided will be a few examples from a brief, preliminary, and possible "research agenda" for a Catholicized and contemporary sociology of knowledge perspective.

Two quick caveats are in order. The first is that some of what I call "Catholic friendly" non-Catholic social science research is actually conducted by scholars who may (or may not) be devotionally Catholic; the point is that they do not introduce consciously or explicitly either any metaphysical dimension, natural law analysis, or ideas and concepts from the corpus of Catholic social thought in their scholarship. The second is that the subject matter addressed in this essay could easily constitute at least a full-length monograph. What will be provided, as such and practically, is only a selection of authors, ideas, theories, concepts, and research findings that are illustrative, representative, and suggestive of a prospective, expanded version of the essay.

Relativism: From Subjectivization to Totalitarianism

A couple of years before he ascended to the throne of Peter, Joseph Cardinal Ratzinger had addressed the reality of relativism—in its related religious, moral, cultural, and intellectual manifestations—as a central problem of modern civilization, at least in Europe, Canada, and for significant sectors of the United States (Ratzinger 2004). However, the phrase—the "dictatorship of relativism"—that would focus great attention to, and generate significant controversy over, the topic was issued by the Cardinal in his last address, qua Cardinal, the day before becoming Pope Benedict XVI. In his Address to the College of Cardinals in the Vatican Basilica on April 18, 2005, "Homily *Pro Eligendo Romano Pontifice*" ("For the election of the Roman Pontiff"), Cardinal Ratzinger asked rhetorically:

How many winds of doctrine have we known in recent decades, how many ideological currents, how many ways of thinking. The small boat of the thought of many Christians has often been tossed about by these waves—flung from one extreme to another: from Marxism to liberalism, even to libertinism; from collectivism to radical individualism; from atheism to a vague religious mysticism; from agnosticism to syncretism; and so forth....Today, having a clear faith based on the Creed of the Church is often labeled as fundamentalism. Whereas relativism...seems to be the only attitude that can cope with modern times. We are building a dictatorship of relativism that does not recognize anything as definitive and whose ultimate goal...(or standard of judgment)...is solely one's own ego and desires. (Perl 2007, 452–53)

It is important to point out that, in his Address to the College of Cardinals, the then Cardinal Ratzinger's discussion of relativism focused primarily on its individual consequences promoting the subjectivization of human consciousness and the pluralization—and in some cases, the paralysis—of individual cognitive and normative judgments. (In my own scholarship, I have referred to this phenomenon as "multicultural relativism" [Varacalli 1994].) In other writings, however, Pope Benedict XVI/Cardinal Ratzinger makes clear that relativism takes on a social and institutional dimension breeding an unjustifiable intolerance and indefensible discrimination. (Again, I have previously referred to this phenomenon as "radical multiculturalism" [Varacalli 1994].) As he states in *Christianity and the Crisis of Cultures*), "[R]elativism...becomes a dogmatism that believes itself in possession of the definitive knowledge of human reason, with the right to consider everything else merely as a stage of human history that is basically obsolete and deserves to be relativized" (Benedict XVI 2006, 45). In *Without Roots: The West, Relativism, Christianity, Islam* (Benedict XVI and Pera 2006, 128), he elaborates further on this inevitable extension of relativism into society:

In recent years I find myself noting how the more relativism becomes the generally accepted way of thinking, the more it tends toward intolerance, thereby becoming a new dogmatism....Its relativism creates the illusion that it has reached greater heights than the loftiest philosophical achievements of the past. It prescribes itself as the only way to think and speak—if, that is, one wishes to stay in fashion. Being faithful to traditional values and to the knowledge that upholds them is labeled as intolerance, and relativism becomes the required norm. I think it is vital that we oppose this imposition of a new pseudo-enlightenment, which threatens freedom of thought as well as freedom of religion.

And on his trip to the United Kingdom (September 16–19, 2010), Pope Benedict XVI "warned against 'aggressive forms of secularism' which no longer value, or even tolerate, religious voices in public life" (Allen 2010, 1). He also stated bluntly that "there are some who seek to exclude religious belief from public discourse, to privatize it, or even to paint it as a threat to equality and liberty" (2). It is both interesting and important to point out that Pope Benedict XVI's long-time collaborator and friend, Pope John Paul II, had arrived at a similar conclusion in his 1993 encyclical, *Veritatis Splendor* (*The Splendor of Truth*), arguing that relativism inexorably leads to totalitarianism, whether of a "hard" or "soft" variety. For John Paul II:

> Totalitarianism arises out of a denial of truth in the objective sense. If there is no transcendent truth, in obedience to which man achieves his full identity, then there is no sure principle for guaranteeing just relations between people. Their self-interest as a class, group, or nation would inevitably set them in opposition to one another. If one does not acknowledge transcendent truth, then the force of power takes over, and each person tends to make full use of the means at his disposal in order to impose his own interests or his own opinion, with no regard for the rights of others....Thus, the root of modern totalitarianism is to be found in the denial of the transcendent dignity of the human person who, as the visible image of the invisible God, is therefore by his very nature the subject of rights which no one may violate—no individual, group, class, nation, or state. Not even the majority of a social body may violate these rights, by going against the minority, by isolating, oppressing, or exploiting it, or by attempting to annihilate it. (John Paul II 1993, 120–21)

Given Pope Benedict XVI's "Christocentric" *theological* focus, his primary solution to the dictatorship of the proletariat is adherence to "the Son of God, the true man...the measure of true humanism..." which "opens us up to all that is good and gives us a criterion by which to distinguish the true from the false, and deceit from truth" (Perl 2007, 453). It should be noted that others opposed to an extreme relativism—whether Catholic or not or religious believer or not—could make main recourse to a *philosophical* solution, i.e., the natural law or universal moral law tradition, that would offer a yardstick producing essentially the same cognitive and normative analysis of contemporary civilization. Pope John Paul II seemed to be equally at ease with employing both complementary approaches in his analysis of modern life. It is the case, however, that it has been Pope Benedict XVI's discussion that has generated recently a great deal of reflection on the consequences of relativism, this essay included.

Creation/Dispersion/Institutionalization/ Consequences of Relativism

There is no one single cause for the development of deep-seated relativism within certain civilizations and classes of individuals at certain junctures in time. In the contemporary era, the relativistic worldview, which questions the very existence of any conception of absolute truth and universal standards, has been dialectically shaped in relation to various historical developments. Among the most prominent would be the secularization of Judaism and Christianity in the Western world, especially among those successfully socialized into a formal educational system that has no significant place for a transcendent otherworldly religious perspective; the empirical reality of pluralism brought about by increased travel, economic and intellectual exchange, and communication; the growth and dispersion of science and, derivatively, of an outlook shaped fundamentally by positivism and scientism; destructive wars which have weakened Western civilization and have shaken its confidence in its own cultural and religious roots; and the growth of an unrestrained freedom and "autonomous" individualism which increasingly forms the ultimate locus of everyday decision making and authority in those private sphere sectors that have, thus far, escaped the increasingly monopolistic control of the State.

Relativism in its varied forms can be found in both its high and low cultural forms. In the former case, one witnesses its embrace by a cultural and educational elite who dominate the public sphere of life and serve as its gatekeepers. These modern day gnostics significantly control which perspectives are to be considered "acceptable" and mainstream, i.e., those significantly, and variously, materialistic, utilitarian, subjective, existentialist, "absurdist," deconstructionist, and nihilistic in composition. In the latter case, one witnesses a less articulated version that is pervasive among some elements of the broader society, but especially among non-evangelical Protestant and non-Mormon college youth and upper-middle class "bourgeois" adults. Relevant here are the more theoretical works of the philosopher, Allan Bloom (1987, *The Closing of the American Mind*) and the sociologist John Cuddihy (1978, *No Offense: Civil Religion and American Faith*) and the more empirically based sociological studies associated with Christian Smith and his *National Study of Youth and Religion* research team (Smith and Lundquist Denton 2005; Smith and Snell 2009).

Relativism is, in part, an extreme reaction against and attempt to counter a fundamental "ethnocentrism" grounded into all human beings as the result of their socialization into a particular worldview (Varacalli 2007). The concept of ethnocentrism was coined by the early American sociologist, William Graham Sumner (1906), defined as when "one group is the center of everything and all others are scaled and rated with reference to it" (Henslin 2011, 37). For the prominent cultural anthropologist and defender of relativism, Clifford Geertz (1984, 265), "what the relativists...want us to worry about is provincialism—the danger that our perceptions will be dulled, our intellects constricted, and our sympathies narrowed by the overlearned and overvalued acceptance of our own society."

The contemporary widespread institutionalization of relativity, according to Christian sociologist Charles Garrison (1988, *Two Different Worlds: Christian Absolutes and the Relativism of the Social Sciences*), finds one of its beginnings in the attempt to develop the concept of cultural relativity *as a methodology* to oppose the ethnocentrism of some Western scholars in the human and social sciences who interpreted the less industrialized civilizations outside of the northwestern European orbit to be primitive and inferior and who had everything to learn by imitating the worldview and lifestyle of the latter. Sociologist James Henslin (2011, 37) defines "cultural relativism" as a methodology as trying "to understand a culture on its own terms (and)…looking at how elements of a culture fit together without judging those elements as superior or inferior." Many times the ethnocentric worldview utilized by some of the early European and American social scientists operated out of a "social Darwinist" perspective influenced by the work of the British philosopher and sociologist Herbert Spencer (1820–1903), who proposed the idea that civilizations were inevitably involved in a "survival of the fittest." It is of little surprise that, at the time, Spencer saw the West as the victor, temporarily at least, in this conflict. The use of cultural relativism as a method to challenge hidden cultural and intellectual assumptions is crucial to the overall sociological enterprise and represents one of the discipline's many positive contributions.

Over time, however, cultural relativism as a methodology for social research has been expanded to a more widely-accepted relativism, in all of its manifestations, as a mode of understanding social reality, either consciously by secular/progressive intellectuals or more unconsciously and to a less internalized degree and manner, by the man-in-the-street. Cultural relativity is undergirded by some underlying social realities. For one thing, it makes it easier for individuals in a pluralistic context to offer, in John Cuddihy's phrase, "no offense" and to appear, as Allan Bloom analyzes it, as "open" and "tolerant," thus, in the short run, at least, making social intercourse easier and less full of conflict. For another, it promotes a more unconstrained sense of freedom increasing the chances that, when human beings violate the natural law or commit sinful acts, they can "rationalize" (in the Freudian, not Weberian sense) their deviant behavior instead of admitting one's transgression, owning up to the dysfunctional consequences of participating in pathological behavior, and vowing to attempt, in essence, "to sin no more." This rationalizing activity is an example of what Daniel Patrick Moynihan (1993) meant with the phrase, "defining deviance down." Individual psychological uses of cultural relativism, in turn, have been institutionalized by progressive secular elites, who dominate the society-defining public sphere "megastructural" social institutions of modern life, as a mechanism of socially controlling which definitions of social reality are to be considered "acceptable." As both the analyses of Popes John Paul II and Benedict XVI have argued, relativism ultimately tends toward the monopolistic control of ideas and, derivatively, of societal power and economic resources.

A Catholic social scientist would reject both the ethnocentric and relativist options. In its place, the Catholic social scientist would attempt to develop a third option, an alternative that would provide a universal yardstick that would necessarily incorporate some supernatural/metaphysical dimension. This yardstick would be either theological in the form of the Word made Flesh in the figure of Jesus Christ, the preferred approach of Pope Benedict XVI, or through the application of the universal moral law or natural ,law (Hittinger 2007; Budziszewski 1997; Rice 1999) as presented in the work of, among many others, the Catholic philosopher-sociologist, Jacques Leclercq (1947). It is, of course the case, that such an incorporation would be vehemently rejected by most whose consciousness is circumscribed by a purely and exclusively empirical plane of analysis dismissive of the existence or relevance of any metaphysical realm.

Relativism is intimately related to the emergence, recently, of the social worldview and academic policy of "multiculturalism." Given this intimate relationship, it isn't surprising that serious Catholics, believers in the Judeo-Christian orbit, and advocates of the universal moral law, reject the concept as it has been actualized in the West. However, as I've argued previously (Varacalli 1994), there are three variations of multiculturalism, with only two, "multicultural relativism" and "radical multiculturalism," inimical to sound thinking and social practice. Multicultural relativism makes the unfounded leap from the empirical reality of pluralism to falsely equating the validity of all differing worldviews and lifestyles in terms of the dimensions of truth, beauty, holiness, and utility. Multicultural radicalism, for its part, is one in which the alleged concern for pluralism and diversity, in actuality, is nothing more than a thin veneer, a smoke screen, for the attempted and calculated substitution of traditional Judeo-Christian and natural law thinking and acting for some utopian (e.g., Marxist, radical feminist, homosexualist) alternative in philosophy and lifestyle. However, a third variation, i.e., "multicultural realism," is consistent with the Mind of the Church. It is ultimately based on the recognition of the Catholic Church that God's hand can be found outside of the divine structure of the Church, i.e., in creation itself. To the degree that the Catholic Church, following St. Paul, affirms the principle that the natural law is written into the heart of all, and, following *Nostra Aetate* (Vatican II's "Declaration on the Relationship of the Church to Non-Christian Religions") that many non-Christian religions "often reflect a ray of that Truth which enlightens all men," then the concept of multicultural realism logically represents a legitimate Catholic approach to relating the absolute to the relative. While judgments about the compatibility of non-Catholic religions and cultures ultimately belong to the Vicar of Christ and to the Magisterium, there is no logical reason to conclude that the concept of multicultural realism remains outside of the orbit of orthodox Catholic thinking. No less a figure than Pope John Paul II seemingly has given legitimacy to the idea through his advocacy of the thesis that "evangelization" and "inculturation" are not necessarily antithetical, that, in some cases at least, one can best spread and apply the Catholic faith by building on whatever elements are true, moral, beautiful, and useful in the various cultural formations found throughout time and space.

The Sociology of Knowledge as Effect and Cause of Relativism

Given their avant-garde position in the creation and control of the vast plethora of ideas that are part and parcel of the modern societal stock of knowledge, it should not be a surprise that the increasing reality and acceptance of relativism has affected profoundly the activities of intellectuals and scholars. These gnostics are more interested in the "god-like" activities of exercising "creativity" and power in social relations than they are subordinating themselves to truth and morality.

With perhaps the single exception of the discipline of anthropology, which is so intimately involved with dealing with cultural diversity, the impact of relativism in the social sciences is greatest in the field of sociology. One brief but paradigmatic example of the latter is Howard S. Becker's (1966) work in the sociology of deviance and crime in which he denies that sociology can ever conclude that any human act is either inherently normal or, conversely, deviant or criminal. His statement that "it is not the act itself but the reactions to the act, that makes something deviant" (Henslin 2011, 134) quintessentially represents the kind of relativistic thinking dominant in the secularized field of the contemporary social sciences that Catholic and natural law thinkers believe it imperative to transcend.

The "sociology of knowledge," a term coined by Max Scheler (1874–1928), is a sub-discipline of sociology that specifically arose, at least *originally*, to address the intellectual, moral, and political consequences of relativism. The sociology of knowledge focuses on the relationship of "knowledge" (both cognitive and normative) in civilization to its "social location" or "social structural base" from which the former is either generated or granted plausibility. Like the broader discipline itself, the sociology of knowledge as an academic field of study and as a general intellectual perspective arose as a response to the forces of exaggerated social change and widespread pluralism that tended to undermine what the philosopher, Alfred Schutz (1962), termed the "taken-for-granted" assumptions of social life in European civilization, especially from the 18th century forward, and, more specifically, in academic circles in Germany in the 1920s.

The contemporary sociologist of knowledge, E. Doyle McCarthy (2006, 2483), states that "from its inception,...[the sociology of knowledge] described a field of inquiry closely linked to problems of European philosophy and historicism, particularly the nineteenth century German philosophical interest in problems surrounding relativism that were linked to the legacies of Karl Marx, Fredrick Nietzsche, and the historicists, whose cultural philosophy or worldview...was influential in German social science from the 1890s to the 1930s." McCarthy (2006, 2482) describes the original purpose of this new academic perspective:

outlined in early statements by Max Scheler and Karl Mannheim, the new discipline reflected the intellectual needs of an era, to bring both rationality and objectivity to bear on the problems of intellectual and ideological confusion. It was in this sense that the sociology of knowledge has been described as a discipline that reflected a new way of understanding "knowledge" within a modern and ideologically pluralistic setting. The approach defines a new "situation" (Mannheim 1936), summarily described as "modernity," a world where "knowledge" and "truth" have many faces. What we believe we *know* varies with the cognitive operations of human minds and these vary by community, class, culture, nation, generation, and so forth.

McCarthy (2006) notes, predictively enough, the present shift, within the contemporary sociology of knowledge, away from "the truth status of ideas and ideologies" (2483) to the "sociology of meaning," as meaning is communicated through various organizational settings and in light of "power" and "gender" considerations. As important as the latter issues are, this movement clearly is representative of the mainstream discipline's 1) complete rejection of metaphysical concerns; 2) increased emphasis on narrow specialized topics of investigation; and 3) almost obsessive quest for legitimation as a "scientific" endeavor. The major exceptions to points 2 and 3 above were the secular humanistically-oriented Marxist and other conflict theories that co-existed alongside of the positivists within the discipline from the mid-1960s onwards to the present day. Despite sharing some common methodological issues about the role of "values in research" and interest in "big," i.e., "macro," issues of ethical import with the small band of Catholic and evangelical Christian sociologists existing at the time, the secular humanists shared with the dominant positivists a rejection of any discussion about the incorporation of a supernatural/metaphysical dimension that was put forth, in many cases, in a simply irrational and unprofessional manner. Put another way, while a sociology of religion that includes metaphysical concerns *as objects of analysis* might, for some, be acceptable, a religious or Catholic sociology employing the metaphysical as *sources* of human thought and behavior was to be ridiculed, even if employed in the construction of hypotheses in social science research.

Toward a Sociology of Knowledge, Catholic-Style: Cues from Max Scheler and Werner Stark

In another essay, I listed what I considered to be the central issues involved in the sociology of knowledge. They are: 1) the nature and scope of the various "social locations" or "social structural bases" of knowledge; 2) the relationship between, respectively, culture and social structure, ideas and material states of being, and norms and interests; 3) the role of the individual as actor; 4) how knowledge is generated and manipulated; 5) how different theories of social change portray the present and future state of what passes for knowledge in civilization; and 6) the question of whether or not there is any universal yardstick available that can be used to judge the various manifestations of "knowledge," morality, beauty, and utility empirically found throughout world history and civilization (Varacalli 2012). While all these issues are important in the construction of a "sociology of knowledge, Catholic style," numbers 2, 3, and 6 are especially relevant.

Regarding the issue of the relationship between culture and social structure, i.e., number 2, the sub-discipline of the sociology of knowledge offers three ideal typical options: cultural determinism, structural determinism, and a dialectical understanding of the relationship between culture and structure. In the first option, exemplified by the sociological work of both Pitirim Sorokin (1970) and Talcott Parsons (1977), symbolic culture is viewed as ultimately determinative of how society is structured and how individuals think and act. The second or structural position is exemplified, par excellence, by Karl Marx (1964). In the Marxist formulation it is the "substructure" of economic class interests that overwhelmingly shapes cultural directives and normative guidelines that represent an epiphenomenal reality of social institutions termed the "superstructure." The dialectical vision, epitomized by the work of Peter L. Berger and Thomas Luckmann (1966), sees cultural and material states of being in an ongoing mutually shaping relationship with priority given to neither culture nor social structure.

The Catholic sociological position, *in nuce* as exemplified by the perspective of John Henry Cardinal Newman's theory of the organic development of doctrine, is not conterminous with any of the three options. It shares with the cultural determinists a fundamental understanding of the human being as primarily a cultural being which is modified by the awareness that cultural attachments are mediated and affected by—but not reduced to—material states of being, historical and personal realities and exigencies, and the reality of a human nature that—while variegated in its manifold expressions—is essentially common and unchanging. Furthermore, a sacramental, integrative, and incarnational Catholic worldview posits that portion of culture that is consistent with, following St. Thomas Aquinas, the natural law and the divine law as representing a semi-autonomous reality. This is a reflection of the Catholic belief that some social constructions can lay claim, in addition to being "human," to a status of representing both objective and truthful reality (Varacalli 1989).

Another issue involves the role of the individual as an actor in social context, i.e., number 3. On the one hand, all practitioners of the sociology of knowledge as a sub-discipline of sociology would reject the radically economic-like position that the human mind can be totally independent of either the cultural/socialization influences that are attendant to any social location/social structural base or the role of inherited tradition and culture. On the other hand, some sociologists of knowledge view, or come close to viewing, the human mind as passive and inert in the face of social forces, thus promoting a sociological version of determinism. (One thinks here especially of those of Marxist and structuralist bent but also perhaps of those functionalists who posit an "over-socialized conception of man" [Wrong 1961].) Any Catholic practitioner of the sociology of knowledge must grant that human beings simultaneously are influenced both by their social location and by the power of the human mind to reflect on the nature and causes of socialization (Berger 1963), thus creating the grounds for the assignment of responsibility for human thinking and actions, mitigated by such factors as the nature of one's inherited and present social environment, stage of human development, and state of mental health. Put another way and translated into common sociological terminology, Catholic sociologists must incorporate some version of an "actionist" perspective to counterbalance the typical sociological emphasis on "structure" and the environment as well as other forms of deterministic thought. Of note here is the promising sociological work of "critical realists" like Christian Smith (2010) and Douglas V. Porpora (2005) who analyze the failings of such reductionist notions as "homo sociologicus" operant throughout most sociological research and "homo economicus" as assumed in "rational-choice" theory. Conversely, the critical realists emphasize the meaning of the "person," consistent with its portrayal in the authentic Catholic worldview.

One other form of determinism that is found in the nooks and crannies of the sociological discipline are those that posit a strong role for biology, a certain understanding of an ironclad human nature. Probably the most prominent examples of this in the sub-discipline of the sociology of knowledge are the cyclical theories of social change found in the work of Vilfredo Pareto (1963) and, more subtly, in Pitirim Sorokin (1970). While appreciating the incorporation of the perennial reality of human nature into their respective frameworks, Catholic social thought would reject the deterministic bent of both and insist on modifications better incorporating an individual sense of free will and the ability of individuals to attempt to rationally construct a humane civilization enlightened by the truth of the Gospel, the natural law, and ideas consistent with Catholic social doctrine.

Regarding the issue of any universal yardstick, i.e., number 6, the discipline of sociology has offered numerous candidates of a purely secular nature for consideration (e.g., August Comte's scientism, Émile Durkheim's civil religion of humanity, Marx's communist world order, Edward Shils' consensual society, among others). From a Catholic perspective, these candidates are not universal at all, representing merely a functional equivalent and replacement for the traditional meaning systems lost as part of the secularization process in the once Christian West. They manifest a fundamental ethnocentrism of their own, although perhaps more masked because their content or inherent vision is more acceptable to the secularized, progressive mindset. In contrast, once again, the yardstick offered from a Catholic frame would be found in either the figure of Jesus Christ or through the natural law or through both used simultaneously.

Probably the most important, if not the most radical, opposition to any version of the sociology of knowledge that is compatible with a Catholic understanding of reality comes from the mainstream of a sociological profession dominated by a positivism that restricts—absolutely and religiously if you will—all academic inquiry to the empirical realm and that considers any discussion of "absolutes," in the words of perhaps America's historically most distinguished mainstream sociologist, Robert Merton, "as wholly foreign to empirical inquiry" (Merton 1957, 472). For the positivist sociologist true to his/her own logic, sociological theory must be completely generated by, and composed of, the findings of an inductive empirical analysis. Many sociologists, Catholic or not, believe that no such purely inductive intellectual animal exists. For instance, for the important Marxist sociologist, Alvin Gouldner (1965), all sociologies are undergirded by what he calls "domain assumptions," a claim that Catholic sociologists would agree with (although they would disagree with the *nature* of those domain assumptions utilized by those operating from an exclusively secularist perspective).

One interesting non-Catholic attempt to transcend relativity can be found in Karl Mannheim's (1936) advocacy, in his *Ideology and Utopia*, of the development of a "socially unattached intelligentsia" approximating objectivity in analysis. The Mannheimian method involves these thinkers juxtaposing competing existentially based social and historical perspectives in the attempt to avoid ideological distortion and any structurally based bias. All Catholic and many non-Catholic thinkers have concluded that Mannheim's methodology has not provided an escape route from what Karl Marx—in a play on Ludwig Fuerbach's name—termed the "fiery brook" of relativity. For the Catholic critic, the path to truth would have to have either some scriptural basis—the preferred method of Pope Benedict XVI—or (as I prefer) some metaphysically based natural law-like analysis or phenomenological analysis connecting an absolute realm of eternal values with the relativities involved in empirical analysis.

The acknowledgment of any metaphysical reality linked to social scientific analysis is denied by the overwhelming percentage of social scientists, past or present. For instance, the distinguished Robert Merton, in critiquing the work of philosopher and sociologist Max Scheler, states that Scheler "seeks to escape a radical relativism by resorting to a metaphysical dualism. He posits the realm of 'timeless essences' which in varying degrees enter into the content of judgment; a realm utterly distinct from that of historical and social reality" (Merton 1957, 472). A Catholic intellectual response to Merton would be that the metaphysical and empirical realms are simultaneously distinctive *and* related. As Jacques Maritain (Maritain 1968, 166–67) put it so well in his *The Peasant of the Garonne*, "between faith and reason, as between grace and nature, there is an essential distinction and one sometimes tends to lose sight of it....But between faith and reason, as between grace and nature, there is no separation. One tends to overlook that too....Things are that way, and so is life; there is distinction without separation." Put another way, the metaphysical and empirical necessarily overlap both in reality and hence in social analysis.

Note that there are most definitely metaphysical assumptions in a wide variety of sociological perspectives. Consider, for example, Comte's discussion of the role of science in the positive age; Durkheim's theory of a religion of humanity in the post-Enlightenment era; Marx's return to a this-worldly Garden of Eden after the Revolution; Shils' vision of the nature of a consensual society based on the application of reason and civility; and feminists' and homosexualists' ideals of a future society of supposed liberation in which the reality and concept of nature is defeated/denied once and for all (e.g., Shulamith Firestone 1970, *The Dialectic of Sex*). The question, at least from the frame of reference of the discipline of sociology, is not whether these metaphysical assumptions are true; rather, in the true spirit of open-minded scholarship, the question is "where do these assumptions lead when incorporated in actual analysis?" Put another way, the question should be "which metaphysical assumptions produce findings consistent with empirical reality?" As Stark himself puts it, "It may...be fruitful to consider the concrete insights resulting from empirical inquiry...*as if* they were reflections and incarnations of transcendental absolutes, and see when and how far such tactics will lead us" (Stark 1991, 342). A Catholic social science, for instance, would expect some significant degree of correspondence and correlation between metaphysical truth and empirical truth regarding the accuracy of information obtained through concrete research. As but one example, the positing of the "naturalness" of the intact nuclear family should correspond to empirical evidence regarding the salutary effects of affirming and living within an intact nuclear family setting.

The Catholic worldview affirms that there is an understanding of absolute truth that is provided both through reason, i.e., the natural law as a reflection of the divine law, and through revelation, i.e., Scripture and Tradition. This position acknowledges that eternal truth is inevitably mediated both through socio-historical context and the individual, and that there can be found varying degrees of truth within different cultures, historical contexts, groups, religions, philosophies, and in the stated beliefs of individuals throughout time and space that can be supported empirically or factually.

Indeed, this is precisely the goal of the sociologist of knowledge, Werner Stark. Stark (1991) claimed, through the use of a long and laborious phenomenological analysis of socio-historical reality, that "the absolute is recognizable...in, through, and under the relative...'to the absolute through the relative is our device'" and proposed "'a synoptic doctrine of man' as the solution to the 'problem of relativity'" (196). For Stark, by abstracting the "common human element" by way of the phenomenological method, the scholar can develop a body of knowledge that could "claim quasi-scientific status" (197), would be truly ecumenical, and would enable one to glimpse "verities that are more than the products of a narrow valley or a passing day" (346). Stark speaks, for instance, of why the new values of modern societies have not destroyed the Catholic Church. As he states: "But new values, however much they may overshadow the old ones, never kill them, because the old values…are in a sense eternal. That is why the prophecies of the Encyclopaedists with regard to 'l'infame' did not come true, and why (sociologically speaking) the Church of Rome has proven indestructible" (202).

In a compatible and related analysis, Max Scheler argued that all perception and thought presupposed the existence of an absolute realm of eternal values written into the heart that are ranked along a spiritual-material continuum. For Scheler, each civilization and individual personality has a specific "ethos." For him, the plurality of worldviews apparent in the empirical, historical world reflects, as such, the reality that various civilizations, groups, and individuals apprehend and prioritize the sphere of eternal values from different angles and with different priorities. The fact, for instance, that modern American civilization prioritizes economic and scientific/scientistic concerns over those spiritual does not deny that the latter—which are irreducible—exist. Furthermore, for Scheler, social and individual discord and pathology ("a disorder of the heart") results when values of lower rank, i.e., those that are more biological and material, are prioritized and institutionalized over those of higher rank, i.e., those closer to the spiritual and moral end point.

Both Stark and Scheler were interested in employing the sociology of knowledge as a method to produce a synthesis of the partial truths found incarnate within various cultures and individual modes of thinking found throughout time and space. Speaking about Stark, E. Doyle McCarthy (1991, xvi) states that his analysis "logically leads to a 'global synthesis' of the partial glimpses of eternal truths." Speaking about Scheler, Michael D. Barber (1993, 9) argues that he was "intensely interested in upholding the possibility and necessity of dialogue—that is, the pursuit of truth by nations, cultures, and individuals in solidarity." According to Kenneth W. Stikkers (1980, 29), "Scheler prophesied…(that)…mankind in the twentieth century…is entering a new era, an era which he termed the 'World Age of Adjustment'…characterized by a coming together of vital and spiritual principles…tending toward a harmonious integration…and the reversal of East-West polarities." Barber elaborates on Scheler's conclusion that Western and Eastern civilizations need and complement each other: "Scheler can argue that especially economic real factors have skewed the cultural developments of the West in favor of science and technology at the expense of its religious and metaphysical development. Asian culture, which has unfolded differentially, provides a dialogic counterpoint to the 'sublime and great conversations' between cultures for which Scheler hopes" (Barber 1993, 9–10).

It is important to point out here that, for both Stark and Scheler, what makes possible fruitful exchanges between civilizations and individuals is the existence of commonalities based on, variously put, underlying eternal essences, absolutes, and truths—or what Catholics and others would refer to as the "natural law." As Barber (1993, 10) observes, it is "Scheler's objective order of values...(that)...makes possible a critical intercultural dialogue" In Stark's (1991, 203) own words,

> The possibility of a comprehensive science of man...will show that all the diversities of human nature *in esse* are merely divergent manifestations of a common human nature *in posse*, and will thereby lay the ghost of relativism forever without denying the width and depth of the differences between different societies and cultures. It is a substantive and synoptic study of it we need if we are to escape from the *cul-de-sac* into which relativism has maneuvered us.

As an aside, I would personally add to the discussion of Stark and Scheler that one could also make the case that Catholicism—speaking as both institution (with a small "c") and worldview (with a capital "C")—represents the single most successful synthesis or, perhaps, collection, of all the essential, life-affirming, healthy, complementary and supplementary dimensions of a supernaturally oriented social existence. Catholicism incorporates reason and faith, nature and grace, authority and conscience, action on behalf of justice and contemplative prayer, Church doctrine and personal devotion/private religious experience, intellect and mysticism, and universalism and particularism (Varacalli 2001, 52; Weigel 2005). Here I follow the general contours of the argument put forth by Karl Adam in his magisterial *The Spirit of Catholicism*. As Adam (1954) points out, "Catholicism *is* a union of contraries. But contraries are not contradictories" (20). In his happy phrase, Catholicism represents "an infinitely various but unitary thing" which, when communicated successfully, provides a "detachment from the world, yet no denial of natural virtues" (9, 14). As Adam summarizes, "Catholicism is according to its whole being the full and strong affirmation of the whole man, in the complete sum of his life relations. Catholicism is the positive religion *par excellence*..." (28).

In sum, then: both Stark and Scheler give vent in their works to the Catholic-friendly idea that the absolute exists, although reflected differentially in both the civilizations of the world and within human consciousness. Catholic scholars looking to develop further a sociology of knowledge perspective that shares a compatibility with the Catholic worldview that transcends the dictatorship of relativism could (and should) profitably start their enterprise by reviewing the work of both Werner Stark (*The Sociology of Knowledge*) and Max Scheler (*Problems of a Sociology of Knowledge*).

A Comparative Example: A Catholic Versus Marxist and Weberian Approaches to Social Stratification

It is perhaps a useful exercise to suggest ways by which a Catholicized sociology of knowledge would make an analytical difference vis-à-vis secularized sociological approaches by choosing a concrete area of investigation. Chosen is the central issue of *social stratification*, dominated in the mainstream profession by the contemporary followers, respectively, of Karl Marx and Max Weber.

On the one hand, just about all sociologists assume that stratification in society involves three dimensions or factors or variables. They are 1) *wealth/property* (or economic status), 2) *power* (or political status), and 3) *prestige* (or honorific status). From the Marxist position, the relationship between these three variables is *unidimensional*, with power and prestige ultimately being reduced to the issue of wealth or, more precisely, to the issue of who owns and controls the means of production used to create wealth.

Any sociologist, including a Catholic sociologist, would be open to the empirical possibility that, in any specific historical instance, the Marxist assertion might be factually correct. On the other hand, however, the Catholic sociologist of knowledge, for several reasons, would argue against such an ironclad economic determinism. For one thing, and as mentioned previously, for some cultures, sub-cultures, and individuals, it is clear religious and social ideals are prioritized over those economic. Human beings are not completely understood through their material needs. For another, the inherent dignity of the human being and his/her own essential freedom allows individuals, within certain cultural and structural constraints, to consciously choose their own visions and imperatives. Human beings are not passive puppets to some alleged inexorable theory of dialectical materialism.

Thirdly, the Marxist emphasis on the social consequences of the undeniably high degree of the *concentration of wealth* in the hands of a small sliver of the general population would differ, by degree at least, from a Catholic interpretative frame that would emphasize, instead, the issue of whether or not individuals have a basically decent *standard of living*. It is indeed the case, for the Catholic, that "man does not live by bread alone." The central question, for the Catholic analyst, is whether or not satisfactory economic conditions exist that allows the average, well-formed individual to pursue his/her individual spiritual ends as well as working, in solidarity, for the integral development of the surrounding civilization that includes healthy cultural (e.g., freedom of religion and of conscience) as well as economic ends (e.g., a "living wage" for all). A Catholic social analyst would, of course, be very concerned with monopolization in *any* form, whether it be *economic* (e.g., capitalist elites), *political* (e.g., socialistic elites), or through *prestige* (e.g., theocratic or scientistic elites). In this, the Catholic thinker would be generally accepting of Lord Acton's famous adage to the effect that "power tends to corrupt and absolute power corrupts absolutely."

Part of the solution for any concentration of power for the Catholic thinker would lie in the institutionalization of effective "mediating structures" that stand between the solitary individual and the megastructures of the public sphere, the forging of a virtuous and engaged citizenry, and the development of a public philosophy based on the natural law.

Fourthly, *if* it is true that a Catholic sociology of knowledge perspective in the general tradition of Max Scheler and Werner Stark is based in reality, then there no doubt would be manifest various social and individual dysfunctions ("disorders of the heart") empirically observable in any society or historical period in which economic issues overwhelmingly trump in importance those emphasizing the good and holy life. A Catholicized sociology, thus, would bring to the fore an issue hitherto ignored or, at least, underplayed, i.e., the negative consequences of pursuing an essentially materialistically oriented life. In this, a Catholic sociology would have some overlap with sociological analyses that focus on the perpetual frustration of becoming trapped in the game of "keeping up with the Joneses" and not being able to put a lid on a never ending dissatisfaction ushered in by the "relative deprivation" structured into the capitalist West. In this, there is the basis of at least a conversation between the countercultural stance of a Catholic sociology and the "hippy-ish" sociology of someone like Philip Slater (1970) in his interesting timepiece, *The Pursuit of Loneliness*.

The Weberian-Catholic comparison would be a little less stark than the Marxist-Catholic juxtaposition. For one thing, Weber's multidimensional analysis avoids a simplistic unilinear determinism and, more importantly, allows for the empirical possibility that some societies, groups, and individuals emphasize "prestige" over "wealth/property" and "power." It is the prestige variable that acknowledges the possibility that, for some, religion, culture, and the spirit can supersede in importance some of the baser inclinations of the human species. However, it is important to note that those moved by "prestige" also include a sizable percentage of individuals not motivated by the more angelic aspects of humanity but are driven by the more superficial aspects of a commitment to prestige. In this regard, sociologists have long noted the ethical and moral shallowness and, indeed, outright silliness of some displays of prestige, as for instance through the concept of "conspicuous consumption," a concept coined by the iconoclastic and antinominian early American sociologist, Thorstein Veblen (1899), in his *The Theory of the Leisure Class*.

The Weberian point of view is most opposed to the Catholic vision in the sociology of knowledge in several fundamental ways. Betraying both its second order, Lutheran inspired Two Kingdoms-like and Kantian roots, a Weberian sociology rejects the Catholic argument for the qualified integration of the metaphysical and natural realms of analysis. Betraying its secularized understanding of reality, an agnostic Weberian sociology also rejects the Catholic claim, made by thinkers like Scheler and Stark, of the objective existence of a hierarchy of values reflecting an eternal transcendent sphere.

In part, the Weberian vision is one of a radical pluralism in which individuals, or at least the more modernized ones, live in a de-spiritualized world of "disenchantment," basically just "doing stuff" in a continual search for meaning and purpose in one's "private sphere" activities. Of relevance here is Gerhard Lenski's (1954) discussion of the "status inconsistency" between the economic, political, and prestige priorities that characterize modern, "gesellschaft" settings with its rejection of any set hierarchy of values oriented to the spiritual. In part, and related to this social-psychological claim, the Weberian vision is one in which modern day individuals are trapped by powerful modern public sphere (or "megastructural") institutions. As Weber himself put it, modern man is stuck in an "iron cage of mechanized petrification." In short, the Weberian vision for modern man simultaneously is one of existing in a state of political oppression and existential nausea. In contemporary sociology, this Weberian sociology was developed sympathetically with great insight by the work of Peter L. Berger, especially in his earlier writings (e.g., *The Sacred Canopy*, 1969).

The Catholic sociological understanding of reality does not so much deny some real utility to what a Weberian lens brings to light but argues that its empirical portrayal is incomplete and ultimately inadequate. Modern life is also characterized—following for instance the work of Edward A. Shils (2006)—by manifestations of tradition and "gemeinschaft"-like characteristics and also by the multiple and never ending intersections of the supernatural and natural planes of existence, what the scholar of religion Mircea Eliade (1957) meant by the term "hierophanies" in his classic work, *The Sacred and the Profane*. These intersections from the transcendent realm exist for the modern man, if "only one would see."

Other Catholic and Non-Catholic Thinkers

There are many other works by Catholic and non-Catholic writers that are useful in the attempt to construct a "sociology of knowledge, Catholic style" or, more simply put, to produce various sociological/social scientific schools of thought that are compatible with and influenced by Catholic social analysis and that defy relativistic conclusions. One is a work by Jacques Leclercq (1947), *Marriage and the Family: A Study in Social Philosophy*, that straddles the distinction between a Thomistic natural law-based social philosophical analysis and a historical and cultural sociological investigation. On the one hand, his analysis acknowledges a certain surface amount of diversity and relativity that existed and exists in traditional social contexts regarding marriage and the family. They are surfaced in at least two senses. The first is the claim that there exists a certain underlying universal core to marriage and family life to which, historically, have been added certain cultural variations The second is the claim that there was a taken-for-granted, pre-theoretical understanding of this core in which significant variations were viewed as deviant even by the actors involved; in other words, the empirical reality associated with what sociologists term "real culture" does not invalidate the consensus about its "ideal culture" formulations (Henslin 2011). On the other hand, he argues that fundamentally unhealthy marriage and family forms, rejecting both implicitly and explicitly natural law norms, have arisen and are increasingly becoming institutionalized since the 18th century in European civilization. Leclercq's analysis shares a certain affinity with one of the conservative founders of the secular discipline of sociology, Ferdinand Tonnies (1957), given the latter's argument about the "artificial" (as compared to "natural") characterization of social relations in a modern, or what he termed a "gesellschaft," society.

Philosophically and historically, respectively, Leclercq's (1947) presentation concludes that "the principles which underlie the family order ...[which]...flow...directly from the nature of man...are observed to be practically identical in all cultures" (v), sans the increasing pathological formulations of modern life. Marriage, for Leclercq, is a natural institution based on the necessary complementary nature between men and women equal in dignity but who perform somewhat distinctive, although overlapping, social roles (6–8). Note can be made here of how Leclercq anticipated the analysis of one of American sociology's most dominant figures of the mid-twentieth century, Talcott Parsons. Parsons, with his colleague, Robert F. Bales, made essentially the same case as that of Leclercq through their discussion of the nature-based "instrumental" activity of husbands and "expressive" activity for mothers (Parsons and Bales 1955). The family, for Leclercq (1947, 20), resting "on natural feelings...is composed of father, mother, and children." Leclercq's discussion here is essentially a defense of what contemporary sociologists refer to as the "intact, nuclear family." His analysis is consistent with that of the tripartite "trustee," "domestic," and "atomistic" family distinctions made by Catholic sociologist Carle Zimmerman (1947). For both Leclercq and Zimmerman, the nuclear or domestic family is the most superior family form, with the "stem" family tending to smother individuality and the overly individualistic "atomistic" family producing a large number of contemporary pathologies. The nuclear or domestic family represents, structurally, the most likely family form that can balance the essential dignity of the human beings within it with the idea of duty and obligation outside of the self, a formulation not essentially different from Parsons' own conclusions on the issue and certainly consistent with a Catholic sensibility.

One of the first secular feminist challenges within the sociological discipline to the analysis of Parsons was provided by Mirra Komarovsky (1953) in which she denies the claim that there is anything "natural" to traditional sex/gender roles and argues that an essentially male-dominated institution of marriage and family requires major changes along a "Swedish model" promoting androgyny through the intervention of the social welfare state. Komarovky's work provides a good example of the beginning of the dominance of social constructionism within sociology. The contemporary era in modern sociology, especially from the mid-1960s through to the present, has increasingly seen the repudiation of any sociological formulations that confer nature-based distinctions along the lines of sex/gender or assign normative status to the intact nuclear family with any inherent division of labor posited. In its stead, contemporary progressive sociologists view the relevant unit of analysis as the individual, viewed as a complete and self-sufficient entity, and promote—minimally—the idea of equally functional and numerous "alternatives in family living" and—maximally—the idea that the intact nuclear family is itself pathological and inherently abusive of women and children. As I have argued elsewhere (Varacalli 1992), the contemporary discipline of sociology is at war with the traditional family.

Non-Catholic Social Science

As is generally well-recognized, the emergence of the discipline of sociology in Europe was overwhelmingly of secular inspiration and was viewed in large part as a functional substitute for religion in social and intellectual life. In the formulation of Arthur Vidich and Stanford Lyman (1985), the discipline of sociology was itself a "sociodicy" or social explanation of human existence including explications of human suffering and the existence of evil, replacing in part the social functions of what Max Weber (1958; 1947) had previously termed "theodicies" or religious explanations of life and death. Indeed, many of the European foundational figures offered frameworks either hostile or, at best, indifferent to a religious understanding of social existence. Major examples abound: Karl Marx with his essential materialism and advocacy of violent class conflict and revolution; Auguste Comte with his scientism and promotion of modern-day gnostic elites; Émile Durkheim with his secular humanism and civil religion; Herbert Spencer positing his ruthless competition and "survival of the fittest;" Vilfredo Pareto with his biological determinism and ironclad "circulation of elites;" George Herbert Mead with his rejection of human nature and view of the seemingly limitless possibilities regarding the plasticity of the individual and with the continual reconstruction of civilization; and Max Weber's existentialist view of the modern day "disenchantment of the world" with its positing of the inability of the sacred to incarnate everyday life.

In comparison with the situation in Europe, i.e., in the pre-World War I early period of sociology in the United States, there was not so much a consistent antagonism manifested against Christianity per se, but against any version of it that was considered as conservative or orthodox. "Social gospel" or liberal Protestant versions of a proto-sociology emerged in which elements of the sociological worldview—especially as inspired by Comte—were synthesized with a progressive, this-worldly read of the Christian mission in the attempt to create

"God's Kingdom on earth." A social gospel sociology—a case of what can be termed a "secularization from within" (Berger 1969; Varacalli 2001)—crashed when the carnage of World War I encouraged a resurgence in the belief in "original sin" and demonstrated that science and technology can be just as easily used to destroy, as compared to building, civilization. The retreat of a liberal Protestant influence in sociology set the stage for a more complete rejection of any role for religion in the academic discipline, exemplified through the work of such devotees of positivism like William Ogburn (1922) and George Lundberg (1947).

On the other hand, it is incorrect to state that all aspects of the secular sociological enterprise have been antagonistic or of no use to those Catholics who have attempted to empirically understand society. Whatever the philosophical shortcomings of an American positivistic, allegedly "value-free," sociology from the post-World War I era up until the mid-1960s, it did provide research findings that—with significant qualifications and to some not insignificant degree—approximated objectivity and were useful. This, of course, should not surprise those who operate from a Catholic perspective acknowledging the reality of the natural law operating in the individual, even when the latter is unaware of its working, including scholars in their academic work.

The early to middle period of the twentieth century in America witnessed the development of the sociological discipline into a serious, if philosophically flawed and incomplete, academic enterprise promoted by secularists, Protestants, Jews, and even some Catholics, the latter overwhelmingly in favor, for a variety of reasons that include philosophical worldview, pragmatism, and self-interest, of sharply demarcating their faith commitments from their narrowly defined sociological activities. Most had no inclination to embrace what George Marsden (1997) has termed "the outrageous idea of Christian scholarship," the major exception to this represented by some of the founders and practitioners of the different versions of Catholic sociology implemented through the activities of the American Catholic Sociological Society, which was founded in 1938 and transformed and secularized by 1970 (Varacalli 1990).

Most Catholics who were sociologists, like other Catholic academics, used the well-publicized lament of the progressive Catholic historian, Monsignor John Tracy Ellis (1956) about the (alleged) inferior state of Catholic scholarly activity in the mid-twentieth century vis-à-vis that produced by the American academic mainstream to justify their assimilation into a purely secular intellectual frame of reference. Deficiencies of a truncated (and significantly non-reflexive and introspective) secular sociology notwithstanding, the prevalent non-religious, non-denominational, non-metaphysically-linked sociology was dedicated to producing studies of social life that were objective and, to a certain degree, were successful in that goal. More than a few of these American sociologists, in a phrase, "wrote and researched better than they knew."

In the mid-1960s, however, there were discernible changes in the goals of American sociology, some salutary and others absolutely destructive to the academic ethos, correctly understood (Shils 1980). One salutary change, noticeable within the discipline and in allied cultural analysis is consistent with what I've previously referred to as "multicultural realism" (Varacalli 1994). It entailed the attempt to provide marginalized groups the opportunity to redress what historian Arthur Schlesinger (1991, 22) termed the "exculpatory" history of the dominant sectors of society. Educator Diane Ravitch (1990, 338) similarly applauded the attempt of that era to "routinely incorporate the experience of women, blacks, American Indians, and various immigrant groups" into textbooks and, more generally, scholarship at large. Given the increased pluralization and multiplication of what Berger and Luckmann (1966) refer to as "sub-universes of meaning" in America over the past decades, the incorporation of the societal "periphery" into the intellectual accounts generated by the societal "center" (Shils 1975) represents, in the minds of some scholars, a movement toward a more "consensual society" (Shils 2006). The continual incorporation of marginal groups into sociological research now includes accounts about the sub-cultures, among others, of punk rockers, goth bars, and homosexuals.

Revealing the various ways of life of these groups is part of the calling of sociology and is central with the Catholic mission to pursue truth and accuracy in intellectual and scholarly activity. However, what was destructive to both the academic ethos and the natural law was the move from pursuing objectivity in analysis to politically correct advocacy. More and more, sociology was viewed as a mere means, minimally, to provide therapeutic relief for and normalize, the deviant and dysfunctional behavior of many living a bohemian lifestyle to, maximally, justifying various utopian and destructive visions. Indeed, the very goal of producing objective social research—never mind, a sociology based on truth!—was interpreted merely as a convenient rationalization to maintain a status quo of social inequality, based on the various manifestations of the (alleged) victims of injustice. Taken for granted was the relativistic assumption that all social lifestyles were equal in the truth content, morality, beauty, and utility. Honest and important pieces of research with "politically incorrect" conclusions or depictions of social life consistent with the natural law were not merely rejected but derided, variously, as racist, ideological, ignorant, or evil.

Two prominent examples of important studies during this era that were unjustifiably rejected will be offered. Both, unsurprisingly, viewed culture as more than a mere reflection of structural conditioning and would not settle for the typical interpretative conclusions of a normatively relativistic analysis. One is the famous "Moynihan Report," authored by Daniel Patrick Moynihan (1965, *The Negro Family: A Case for National Action*), which makes the case that the matriarchal, single-parent structure of the black family was at the heart of what he saw as a complex "tangle of pathology." This pathology involved dialectally-influencing aspects of culture, economics, and politics—i.e., government welfare programs. Another was the work of Edward Banfield (1970, *The Unheavenly City*), in which the author argues that the existence of poverty centrally involves the acceptance of a "culture of poverty" orientation to work, family, the law, education, and other spheres of existence characterized by a "present-orientation" to life. (Banfield's argument does not preclude the incorporation of other factors that are structural in nature—economic, demographic, technological—or that involve discrimination or misguided government policies, or are simply reflective of individual bad fortune.) Radical left wing social scientists like William Ryan (1971) all too simply saw analyses like that of Moynihan and Banfield to be merely ones "blaming the victim." Also worthy of note was the culturally conditioned and politically correct response of the American Psychological Association (2008) to reverse its long held view that homosexual behavior is, in any sense, abnormal and associated with dysfunctional consequences for both the individual and society. The APA statement, "Sexual Orientation and Homosexuality" bluntly declares that "...lesbian, gay, and bisexual orientation are not disorders" (APA 2008, 2) and explains that "since 1975, the American Psychological Association has called on psychologists to take the lead in removing the stigma of mental illness that has long been associated with lesbians, gay, and bisexual orientations" (APA 2008, 1). Since 1975, this position has been further cemented among the professional elites in psychology, psychiatry, and social work. A systematic and empirically based response to all this from Catholic social scientists is just beginning to emerge.

Many sociologists and social scientists who disagreed with the move away from objectivity silenced themselves in the attempt to survive in an increasingly hostile working environment dominated by hardened secular left-wing thought. Many who did attempt to challenge the then politically correct suffered in various ways. More and more, they were denied opportunities in employment, promotion, and publication and were generally castigated and marginalized when they did make public research findings that opposed the utopian excretions of the then dominant Marxists, feminists, racialists, and now—indicative of a movement moving even further away from the natural law and more and more in a politicized, "subjectivized," and even nihilistic direction—of strong deconstructionists and homosexuals. Speaking of the latter's ultimate denial of nature and the natural law, Stephen Sharkey (2012) has observed that "Queer theorists...attempt to 'queer' our thought and our social arrangements, to scramble the very basic categories we use to understand social life—what is biological classification, what is family, what is love, what is power—in order to achieve personal, experiential truths uncorrupted by cultural conditioning."

As with American civilization in general, there is today a movement in the American academy in reaction against these highly politicized and dysfunctional cultural and intellectual trends. This revitalization movement is stronger in the broader American body than it is in the academy given the stranglehold that the radical worldview holds—with the complicity of most liberals—in the university and teaching professions. Nonetheless, the truth is now starting to come out, albeit mostly and predictably, in a tepid manner. One major reason for this outing is that the chaos started in the 1960s has now had 50 years to demonstrate the rotten fruits it has brought into being. Another and related reason is that there are some liberal oriented academics in which ideology hasn't completely smothered the natural law written into the heart and who feel compelled, as a matter of intellectual honesty, to "follow where the data leads." In the earlier part of the revolution against the remnants of American and Western civilization, it was certainly easier ethically for such liberal scholars to let pass without comment revolutionary claims of a cognitive and normative nature when there was a dearth of concrete evidence against which to test the utopian promises.

Over the past 20 years or so, the academy has witnessed an increasing stream of secular analyses that, without making conscious or theoretical recourse to the natural law or, even far less likely, Catholic social doctrine, are providing conclusions that are increasingly consistent with a Catholic social science. Given their ingrained foundational liberal domain assumptions and their immersion into academic enclaves resistant to giving contrary perspectives and evidence a fair hearing (because of varied vested self-interests, both status and economic in nature), it is unsurprising that such secular corrections are usually tepid and incomplete. It is possible that the amount, quality, and positive impact of honest secular social science will increase in the immediate future because of two dialectically related reasons: 1) the continuing precipitous decline of the general civilization based as it has been on progressive presuppositions over the past few decades; and 2) the further development and institutionalization of Catholic/natural law-based social science in social institutions that are less likely to be held captive to politically correct thinking.

What are a few examples of some non-Catholic research that has been contributing in a salutary way to the resurrection of both the academy and broader civilization? Judith Wallerstein, Sandra Blakeslee, and Julia W. Lewis (2001), for instance, have produced research on the negative consequences of divorce over a 25-year period. Linda Waite and Maggie Gallagher (2001) have produced evidence that married couples do better than do singles along a host of different measurements. Sara McLanahan and Gary Sandefur (1994) demonstrate the significantly greater chances of children suffering various dysfunctions when raised in single-parent families. Mary Eberstadt (2004) shows the hidden price exacted on children when exposed to excessive use of day care and other "parental substitutes." Even in an anthropological discipline drowning in the swamps of relativism, there are some voices of reason. For instance, in his *Sick Societies: Challenging the Myth of Primitive Harmony*, Robert Edgerton (1992) has proposed the creation of a "quality of life" scale that would attempt to judge the degree to which various cultures enhance or, conversely, diminish the lives of their inhabitants.

In response to such studies, a Catholic social scientist can suggest to the skeptical secular sociologist to tentatively accept the *philosophical*, i.e., natural law, premises of a Catholic social science "as if they were true" and see where they lead. In this, again, I am slightly altering the *theological* proposal offered "to those outside the Church" by Joseph Cardinal Ratzinger in his *Christianity and the Crisis of Cultures*. As the then Cardinal suggested, "even the one who does not succeed in finding the path to accepting the existence of God ought nevertheless to try to live and to direct his life *veluti si Deus daretur*, as if God did indeed exist" (Benedict XVI 2006, 18). This is a pragmatic concession, given my conclusion, following the Catholic philosopher Ralph McInerny (1990), that the natural law provides greater possibilities for universal agreement among both religious and non-religious believers than does Pope Benedict XVI's Christocentric focus. Given the Catholic belief in the essential compatibility of faith and reason, a Catholic social scientific analysis led by either Catholic theological or natural law reasoning would produce the same analytical results with the latter, in essence, representing a slightly easier "sell" to the non-Christian world.) As the number of Catholic inspired social research studies prove their worth and actually serve to deepen the results of objective secular research, the plausibility of the former should increase, at least theoretically, among the more honest and open of secular/non-Catholic scholars.

Examples from a Possible Research Agenda: Some Suggested Topics for a Sociology of Knowledge, Catholic-Style

As previously noted, the specific Catholic positions on, first, the human being as a cultural creature mediated by the perennial realities of human nature and free will, and second, the existence of a hierarchically ordered realm of absolute values or essences as mediated by the contingencies of history, produces a distinctive approach to intellectual activity and social analysis. The purpose of this very brief section is to suggest how a Catholicized sociology or sociology of knowledge analysis might approach conventional topics in a manner different than the contemporary mainstream discipline of sociology or, for that matter, could suggest topics hitherto underrepresented in the field. The topics offered represent only a small tip of the iceberg of a full blown research agenda. Let me speak to the topics of government, cultural diversity, social change and social movements, evil, and finally, human sexuality.

One central and conventional topic of sociological analysis, for instance, involves the role of government. A Catholic approach, following the principle of "subsidiarity," would reject, on the one hand, a radically libertarian or minimalist understanding that would be indifferent to the obligations of government to

84 Joseph A. Varacalli

those either born into poverty, burdened by physical or mental handicaps, or subject to human tragedy. On the other hand, a Catholic approach would reject an overly therapeutic social welfare state breeding dependency and discouraging an active civic participation in society as does Pope John Paul II (1991) in *Centesimus Annus*. Even more so, a Catholic approach would reject the idolatrous worship of an all powerful State in its various historical forms (e.g., Communism, Nazism, Fascism) and the loss of the fundamental dignity of the human being that such political tyranny inevitably entails.

Another central topic of interest to sociology would be the social implications of, and reactions to, the reality of cultural diversity. A Catholicized sociology would reject, on the one hand, an acceptance of either a philosophy of "cultural relativism" or its most extreme logical extension, "nihilism." On the other hand, the Catholic scholar would reject the claim that any one civilization, group, and worldview deserves to hold a monopoly on truth, morality, beauty, and utility. Rather, a Catholic scholar would argue that a natural law or Christocentric analysis can make a compelling case that civilizations, groups, and worldviews can be placed on a scale that gauges the degree of its "healthfulness" or, conversely, "dysfunctionality" based on the degree to which it is formed and shaped by natural law and Christian precepts.

Another important topic in which a Catholicized sociology can make a distinctive contribution is in the area of studying the purpose and consequences of social change and social movements. Is it solely, as conflict theorists see it, the promotion of the material and economic interests of exploited social (e.g., economic, religious, ethnic, racial, and gender) classes? Is it, as neo-conservatives see it, the unmasking of ideological interests portrayed as altruism? Is it, as progressives of one stripe or another advocate, the promotion of some utopian vision seen as furthering socialism, communism, anarchism, or autonomous individualism? Is it, as religious fundamentalists desire, the institutionalization of religious theocracies? Or, as Catholic social scientists desire, is it the social construction of the "common good," defined as one promoting the "integral" development of the individual, both "body and soul"?

A topic underplayed in sociological analysis is that of evil. Many secular sociologists would deny that the concept even exists. When it is recognized, most sociologists would assert that it is solely or mainly a "structural" issue of gross social inequality in the social order. Or, as most secular psychologists would claim, it is merely another way of talking about a serious personality disorder. Without denying naturalistic/sociological causes, a Catholic sociologist would not merely dismiss as absurd the possibility that the concept of evil involves the intervention of some malevolent supernatural force or as being rooted in a certain understanding of human nature involving an acceptance of the concept of "original sin." Again, the Catholic sociologist does not expect the nonbeliever to accept the existence of any supernatural reality but requests that, for purposes of research, the hypothesis that "if some form of irreducible evil exists, then one can expect, as a consequence, some dysfunctional, immoral, and un-wholesome result." The methodological request is to accept the concept of evil "as if it exists" and see where the research leads in exactly the same manner that the Catholic sociologist would request the hypothetical acceptance of the ideas that either God or natural law exists.

A Catholic sociologist would also note that individuals are free to either re-sist or cooperate with the operation of evil, and would argue that evil cannot be ignored or reduced out of existence. Because of the sacrifice of Jesus Christ on the Cross, neither can evil permanently triumph. In part because of human agen-cy, however, evil can be abated and limited in its scope in terms of its conse-quences for society and the individual. This is the goal of the serious Catholic Christian, Catholic sociologists included. A Catholicized sociology requires the vision of the responsible person operating under the benevolent consideration of Jesus Christ.

Another topic in which a Catholicized sociology can make a distinctive con-tribution is in the area of human sexuality. In terms of the human hierarchy of needs, a Catholic sociologist would argue that sexual expression is healthy and natural when channeled properly but is not intended to be the dominant force in the life of the individual. Sexuality is viewed by the Catholic as structured into the very anthropology of the human being as a natural "good," but one of inter-mediate importance and non-defining self-definition in the human hierarchy of needs which requires to be institutionalized into socially responsible behavior within the existence of family life. When sexuality assumes a disproportionate role in human affairs—as certain Freudians and Freudian sociologists see as natural and inevitable—sexuality represents what Max Scheler termed a "disor-der of the heart" and will bring in its wake both social and individual dysfunc-tions. On the other hand, a Catholicized sociology would reject a Meadian soci-ology viewing sexuality as completely plastic and malleable and totally dependent on cultural conditioning and socialization into what Pitirim Sorokin would term a "sensate" culture. Like many other theoretical frameworks, a Ca-tholicized sociology would see sexuality and gender as the result of the interplay of both nature and nurture but along the lines of the inherent complementary of men and women as outlined in the *Compendium of the Social Doctrine of the Church* (Pontifical Council for Justice and Peace 2005).

Conclusion

As the author of this article readily admits, the ideas contained within this essay are not fully or sufficiently developed. Also readily admitted is that the author has not the talent, time, or a congenial social context to complete the job of de-veloping a "sociology of knowledge, Catholic style" or a "Catholic sociology" in a satisfactory fashion. What is hoped for, however, is that this essay has put forth some interesting and important observations, ideas, and suggestions on the intellectual table that might be further developed by other scholars in the Catholic intellectual and sociological tradition who are in a better situation to accomplish the task.

Bibliography

Adam, Karl. 1954. *The Spirit of Catholicism*. Garden City, NY: Image Books.

Allen, John L. 2010. "Benedict Battles the 'Dictatorship of Relativism.'" *National Catholic Reporter Today*, September 16. Accessed from http://ncronline.org/print/20274; http://ncronline.org/blogs/ncr-today/benedict-battles-dictatorship-relativism.

American Psychological Association. 2008. *Answers to Your Questions: For a Better Understanding of Sexual Orientation and Homosexuality*. Washington, DC: Author. Accessed May 27, 2011, http://www.apa.org/topics/sexuality/orientation.aspx: 1–4.

Banfield, Edward. 1970. *The Unheavenly City: The Nature and Future of Urban Crisis*. Boston: Little, Brown.

Barber, Michael D. 1993. *Guardian of Dialogue: Max Scheler's Phenomenology, Sociology of Knowledge, and Philosophy of Love*. Lewisburg, PA: Bucknell University Press.

Becker, Howard. 1966. *Outsiders: Studies in the Sociology of Deviance*. London: Free Press.

Benedict XVI, Pope. 2006. *Christianity and the Crisis of Cultures*. Translated by Brian McNeil. San Francisco: Ignatius Press.

Benedict XVI, and Marcello Pera. 2006. *Without Roots: The West, Relativism, Christianity, Islam*. Translated by Michael F. Moore. New York: Basic Books.

Berger, Peter L. 1963. *Invitation to Sociology: A Humanistic Perspective*. Garden City, NY: Doubleday.

———. 1969. *The Sacred Canopy: Elements of a Sociological Theory of Religion*. New York: Doubleday.

Berger, Peter L., and Thomas Luckmann. 1966. *The Sociology of Knowledge: A Treatise in the Sociology of Knowledge*. Garden City, NY: Doubleday.

Bloom, Alan. 1987. *The Closing of the American Mind*. New York: Simon & Schuster.

Budziszewski, J. 1997. *Written Into the Heart: The Case for Natural Law*. Downers Grove, IL: IVP Academic.

Cuddihy, John. 1978. *No Offense: Civil Religion and the American Faith*. New York: Seabury Press.

Eberstadt, Mary. 2004. *Home Alone America: The Hidden Toll of Day Care, Behavioral Drugs, and other Parental Substitutes*. New York: Sentinel Books.

Edgerton, Robert. 1992. *Sick Societies: Challenging the Myth of Primitive Harmony*. New York: Free Press.

Eliade, Mircea. 1957. *The Sacred and the Profane*. Translated by W.R. Trask. New York: Harvest Books.

Ellis, Monsignor John Tracy. 1956. *American Catholics and the Intellectual Life*. Milwaukee, WI: Bruce.

Firestone, Shulamith. 1970. *The Dialectic of Sex: The Case for Feminist Revolution*. New York: Morrow.

Garrison, Charles E. 1988. *Two Different Worlds: Christian Absolutes and the Relativism of Social Science*. Newark, NJ: University of Delaware Press.

Geertz, Clifford. 1984. "Anti-Anti-Relativism." *American Anthropologist* 86, 2: 263–78.

Gouldner, Alvin. 1965. *Enter Plato: Classical Greece and the Origins of Social Theory*. London: Routledge.

Haynor, Anthony L., and Joseph A. Varacalli. 1993. "Sociology's Fall from Grace: The Six Deadly Sins of a Discipline at the Crossroads." *Quarterly Journal of Ideology: A Critique of Conventional Wisdom* 16, 1–2: 3–29

Henslin, James M. 2011. *Essentials of Sociology: A Down-to-Earth Approach*, 9th edition. Boston: Allyn and Bacon.

Hittinger, Russell. 2007. *The First Grace: Rediscovering the Natural Law in a Post-Christian World*, 2nd edition. Wilmington, DE: Intercollegiate Studies Institute.

John Paul II, Pope. 1991. *Centesimus Annus*. Boston: Daughters of St. Paul.

———. 1993. *Veritatis Splendor*. Boston: Daughters of St. Paul.

Komarovsky, Mirra. 1953. *Women in the Modern World*. Boston: Little, Brown.

Leclercq, Jacques. 1947. *Marriage and the Family: A Study in Social Philosophy*, 3rd edition. Translated with a Preface by Thomas R. Hanley, O.S.B. New York and Cincinnati: Pustet.

Lenski, Gerhard. 1954. "Status Crystallization: A Nonvertical Dimension of Social Status." *American Sociological Review* 19: 405–13.

Lundberg, George A. 1947. *Can Science Save Us?* New York: Longmans, Green.

Mannheim, Karl. 1936. *Ideology and Utopia: An Introduction to the Sociology of Knowledge*. Translated by Louis Wirth and Edward Shils. London: Harcourt, Brace, and World.

Maritain, Jacques. 1968. *The Peasant of the Garonne: An Old Layman Questions Himself about the Present Time*. Translated by Michael Cuddihy and Elizabeth Hughes. New York: Holt, Rinehart, and Winston.

Marsden, George. 1997. *The Outrageous Idea of Christian Scholarship*. New York: Oxford University Press.

Marx, Karl. 1964. *Selected Writings in Sociology and Social Philosophy*. New York: McGraw-Hill.

McCarthy, E. Doyle 1991. "Introduction." In *The Sociology of Knowledge: Toward a Deeper Understanding of the History of Ideas*, by Werner Stark (ix–xix). New Brunswick, NJ: Transaction Books.

———. 2006. "Knowledge, Sociology of." *The Blackwell Encyclopedia of Sociology*, at www.sociologyencyclopedia.com: 2482–85.

McInerny, Ralph. 1990. *A First Glance at St. Thomas Aquinas*. Notre Dame, IN: University of Notre Dame Press.

McLanahan, Sara, and Gary Sandefur. 1994. *Growing Up with a Single Parent: What Hurts, What Helps*. Cambridge, MA: Harvard University Press.

Merton, Robert A. 1957. "The Sociology of Knowledge." In *Social Theory and Social Structure*, by Robert A. Merton (456–88). Glencoe, IL: Free Press.

Moynihan, Daniel Patrick. 1965. *The Negro Family: The Case for National Action*. Washington DC: United States Department of Labor.

———. 1993. "Defining Deviance Down: How We've Become Accustomed to Alarming Levels of Crime and Destructive Behavior." *The American Scholar* 62, 1: 17–30.

Ogburn, William. 1922. *Social Change with Respect to Culture and Human Nature*. New York: Huebsch.

Pareto, Vilfredo. 1963. *The Mind and the Society*. Mineola, NY: Dover.

Parsons, Talcott. 1977. *The Evolution of Societies*. Edgewood Cliffs, NJ: Prentice Hall.

Parsons, Talcott, and Robert F. Bales. 1955. *Family, Socialization, and Interaction Process*. Glencoe, IL: Free Press.

Perl, Jeffrey M. ed. 2007. "A Dictatorship of Relativism? Symposium in Response to Cardinal Ratzinger's Last Homily." Translated by Robert Valgenti. *Common Knowledge* 13 (2–3): 214–455.

Pontifical Council for Justice and Peace. 2005. *Compendium of the Social Doctrine of the Church*. Washington, DC: United States Conference of Catholic Bishops.

Porpora, Douglas V. 2005. "The Spiritual Turn in Critical Realism." *New Formations* 56: 147–61.

Ratzinger, Cardinal Joseph. 2004. *Truth and Tolerance: Christian Belief and World Religions*. Translated by Henry Taylor. San Francisco: Ignatius Press.

Ravitch, Diane. 1990. "Multiculturalism." *The American Scholar* 59: 3.

Rice, Charles. 1999. *50 Questions on the Natural Law: What It Is and Why We Need It*, revised edition. San Francisco: Ignatius Press.

Ryan, William. 1971. *Blaming the Victim*. New York: Pantheon Books.

Scheler, Max. 1980. *Problems of a Sociology of Knowledge*. Translated and with an Introduction by Manfred S. Frings. London: Routledge and Kegan Paul.

Schlesinger, Arthur M., Jr. 1991. *The Disuniting of America: Reflections on a Multicultural Society*. Knoxville, TN: Whittle.

Schutz, Alfred. 1962. *Collected Papers*, Volume I. The Hague: Nijhoff.

Sharkey, Stephen. 2012. "Gay/Lesbian Theory." In *Encyclopedia of Catholic Social Thought, Social Science, and Social Policy*, Volume III, edited by Michael L. Coulter, Stephen M. Krason, Richard S. Myers, and Joseph A. Varacalli, (125–29). Lanham, MD: Scarecrow Press.

Shils, Edward A. 1975. *Center and Periphery: Essays in Macro Sociology*. Chicago: University of Chicago Press.

———. 1980. *The Calling of Sociology: Essays in the Pursuit of Learning*. Chicago: University of Chicago Press.

———. 2006. *A Fragment of a Sociological Autobiography: The History of My Pursuit of a Few Ideas*. New Brunswick, NJ: Transaction Books.

Slater, Philip. 1970. *The Pursuit of Loneliness*. Boston: Beacon Press.

Smith, Christian. 2010. *What Is a Person? Rethinking Humanity, Social Life, and the Moral Life from the Person Up*. Chicago: University of Chicago Press.

Smith, Christian, and Melinda Lundquist Denton. 2005. *Soul Searching: The Religious and Spiritual Lives of American Teenagers*. New York: Oxford University Press.

Smith, Christian, and Patricia Snell. 2009. *Souls in Transition: The Religious and Spiritual Lives of Emerging Adults*. New York: Oxford University Press.

Sorokin, Pitirim. 1970. *Social and Cultural Dynamics*. New York: Sargent.

Stark, Werner. 1991. *The Sociology of Knowledge: Toward a Deeper Understanding of the History of Ideas*. New Brunswick, NJ: Transaction Books.

Stikkers, Kenneth W. 1980. "Introduction." In *Problems of a Sociology of Knowledge*, by Max Scheler, edited by Kenneth W. Stikkers and translated by Manfred S. Frings. London: Routledge and Kegan Paul.

Sumner, William Graham. 1906. *Folkways: A Study in the Sociological Importance of Usages, Manners, Customs, Mores, and Morals*. Boston: Ginn.

Tonnies, Ferdinand. 1957. *Community and Society*. East Lansing: Michigan State University Press.

Varacalli, Joseph A. 1989. "Sociology, Feminism, and the Magisterium." *Homiletic and Pastoral Review* 89, 10: 60–66.

———. 1990. "Catholic Sociology in America: A Comment on the Fiftieth Anniversary Issue of *Sociological Analysis*." *Sociological Analysis* 4, 2: 249–62.

———. 1992. "Secular Sociology's War Against *Familiaris Consortio* and the Traditional Family: Whither Catholic Higher Education and Catholic Sociology?" In *The Church and the Universal Catechism: Proceedings from the fifteenth convention of the Fellowship of Catholic Scholars*, edited by Rev. Anthony J. Mastroeni, S.T.D., J.D, (161–86). Steubenville, OH: Franciscan University.

———. 1994. "Multiculturalism, Catholicism, and American Civilization." *Homiletic and Pastoral Review* 96, 4: 47–55.

———. 2001. *Bright Promise, Failed Community: Catholics and the American Public Order*. Introduction by Stephen M. Krason. Lanham, MD: Lexington Books.

———. 2007. "Cultural Relativism." In *Encyclopedia of Catholic Social Thought, Social Science, and Social Policy*, Volume I, edited by Michael L. Coulter, Stephen M. Krason, Richard S. Myers, and Joseph A. Varacalli, (264–65). Lanham, MD: Scarecrow Press.

———. 2012. "Sociology of Knowledge: A Catholic Critique." In *Encyclopedia of Catholic Social Thought, Social Science, and Social Policy*, Volume III, edited by Michael L. Coulter, Richard S. Myers, and Joseph A. Varacalli, (339–44). Lanham, MD: Scarecrow Press.

Veblen, Thorstein. 1899. *The Theory of the Leisure Class*. New York: Macmillan.

Vidich, Arthur, and Stanford Lyman. 1985. *American Sociology: Worldly Rejections of Religion and Their Directions*. New Haven, CT: Yale University Press.

Waite, Linda, and Maggie Gallagher. 2001. *The Case for Marriage: Why Married People Are Happier, Healthier, and Better Off Financially*. New York: Broadway Books.

Wallerstein, Judith, Sandra Blakeslee, and Julia M. Lewis. 2001. *The Unexpected Legacy of Divorce: A Twenty-Five Year Landmark Study*. New York: Hyperion Press.

Weber, Max. 1947. *The Theory of Social and Economic Organization*. New York: Oxford University Press.

———. 1958. *From Max Weber*. Translated and edited by Hans Gerth and C. Wright Mills. New York: Oxford University Press.

Weigel, George. 2005. *Letters to a Young Catholic*. New York: Basic Books.

Wrong, Dennis. 1961. "The Oversocialized Conception of Man in Modern Sociology." *American Sociological Review* 26 (2):183–93.

Zimmerman, Carle C. 1947. *Family and Civilization*. New York: Harper and Row.

4

Catholic Social Teachings and the Sociology of Deviance

Anne Hendershott

In the Introduction to *Veritatis Splendor*, Pope John Paul II's 1993 encyclical on the very foundations of moral theology, he cautioned that: "No one can escape from the fundamental questions: What must I do? How do I distinguish good from evil?" (John Paul II 1993). While Pope John Paul II is speaking of revealed truth, natural law, and moral theology, the founding sociologists shared many of these same concerns about the moral choices we make and the moral order we create. In some important ways, the earliest sociologists were asking some of the same questions.

In fact, from the earliest days of the fledgling discipline of sociology, the founders were concerned about social order and the common good. They warned of the threat to the social order of the community that comes with the breakdown of traditional moral boundaries. Emerging in the midst of major social, economic, and political transformation sweeping across nineteenth century Europe as a result of the Industrial Revolution, the discipline of sociology sought to explain how societies maintain stability in the face of dramatic social change. As families moved to the cities from rural areas and family farms to work in the new factories being constructed, the potential for social disruption was great. And, from this time onward—until the social liberationist movements of the 1960s—sociologists continued to assert that social stability is founded on moral order—a common worldview that binds people to their families, to their communities, and to the larger economic and political institutions. Integral to this moral order is a shared concept of what constitutes deviant behavior—behavior that is defined as outside the norm—and a willingness to identify the boundaries of appropriate behavior.

Today, many sociologists have become reluctant to acknowledge that there are moral judgments to be made when discussing a subject like deviance. Yet, the world from which sociology emerged more than a century ago was, in many ways, similar to our own contemporary world of rapid, often overwhelming, social change. Just as the Industrial Revolution brought deplorable living conditions to the industrialized cities, including poverty, sickness, and dramatic changes within the family, so today's technological society presents profound challenges to social order and the common good. Globalization has created societies based less on shared culture than on narrow calculations of individual self-interest (Bryjak and Soroka 2001, 17). A commitment to a common moral order is much more difficult within a culture of such strong individualism.

Durkheim and the Collective Consciousness

The discipline of sociology emerged in the late 1800s from a sense that individualistic philosophies placed too little emphasis on the moral ties that link people in society. In one of the first sociology texts, *Rules of Sociological Method,* Émile Durkheim (1964), the "founding father" of the sociology of deviance, wrote that deviance is an integral part of all societies because it affirms cultural norms and values. Durkheim acknowledged that all societies require moral definition; some behaviors and attitudes must be identified as more salutary than others. As a sociologist, he saw that moral unity could be assured only if all members of a society were anchored to common assumptions about the world around them; without these assumptions, a society was bound to degenerate and decay. From this functionalist perspective, we are creatures with unlimited desires, which need to be held in check. The function of society is to constitute a "regulative force," setting limits on individual actions. At the same time, Durkheim believed that it is impossible for any society to be free of deviance—even a society of saints will have its sinners. Durkheim knew that deviance will always be present in every society at about the same rate. The challenge for the sociologist is to determine which behaviors are considered deviant and subject to sanctions by a given society during a given time. As some behaviors once considered deviant become "defined down," other behaviors which had never before been considered outside the norm are redefined as deviant. And, from Durkheim onward, most sociologists regarded the societal role in identifying and stigmatizing deviant behavior as an indispensable process, allowing us to live by shared standards.

Cognizant about what Durkheim called the collective consciousness (the ways in which any given individual comes to view herself or himself as part of any given group), sociologists were especially concerned with the controls that become internalized in individual consciousness as a result of what society defines as deviant. Published in 1895, Durkheim's *Rules of Sociological Method* introduces the idea of a "social conscience" as an integral part of his social theory. In an attempt to explain what causes individuals to act in similar and predictable ways, Durkheim asserted that "If I do not submit to the conventions of society: if in my dress I do not conform to the customs observed in my country and in my class, the ridicule I provoke, the social isolation in which I am kept, produce, although in an attenuated form, the same effects as punishment" (Durkheim [1895] 1963, 3).

Durkheim was one of the first to recognize the power of external coercion over individuals. For Durkheim, "the presence of this power may be recognized in its turn either by the existence of some specific sanction or by the resistance offered against every individual effort that tends to violate it." Convinced that society must be "present" within the individual, Durkheim was led to the study of religion as one of the forces that create within individuals a sense of obligation to adhere to society's demands. But, Durkheim's interest in religion lay primarily not with individual devotion, but with communal religious activities, the rituals that bind communities together and give meaning to the lives of the devout. An atheist, Durkheim was the son of a rabbi who grew to believe that god was really Society and Society was created by humans. For Durkheim it really did not matter if "god" exists or not. He maintained that all religions are the same because they play the same role in society, which is keeping individuals together. From this perspective, religious communities give people a sense of belonging, a source of meaning, and guidelines or norms on how to live.

For most of the twentieth century, defining deviance was considered a fundamental activity of any society. Following Durkheim's lead, sociologists like Talcott Parsons and Robert Merton, both from the Functionalist School of Sociology, believed that identifying deviant behavior was "functional" or central to the process of generating and sustaining cultural values, clarifying moral boundaries, and promoting social solidarity. But, even they had to acknowledge that defining deviance has never been an easy thing to do because definitions of deviance vary widely by social class, religion, culture, and association.

Today, most sociologists now define deviance as behavior which a specific group considers so dangerous or embarrassing or irritating that they bring special sanctions to bear against the persons who exhibit it. From this perspective, as Kai Erikson (1966, 6) points out in his book, *Wayward Puritans*, deviance is not a *property inherent in* any particular kind of behavior, it is a *property conferred upon* that behavior by the people who come into direct or indirect contact with it. For most sociologists, the only way one can tell whether or not a given behavior or set of behaviors is deviant then is to learn about the audience for deviance—or those who are responding to that behavior. As a result, each social group in question provides its own definitions of deviant behavior. For example, in San Francisco's gay community, public displays of affection by same-sex couples are common, yet there are parts of the United States—and beyond—where that same public behavior would elicit a negative response because it is defined as deviant by those witnessing it. Although the earliest sociologists pointed to the role that defining deviance plays in boundary maintenance for community members, these sociologists were still willing to identify categories of deviant behavior that are constant across all groups and at all times. Over time, that willingness declined as sociologists became committed to a form of egalitarianism that disallowed such judgments to be made.

In 1956 one of the influential voices in sociology, C. Wright Mills, published *The Power Elite*—a book which maintains that privileged groups participate in a "higher immorality" in their ability to marginalize as deviant those in society who become troublesome (Mills 1956). Targeted primarily to a working/middle class audience Mills' book helped to shape the discipline of sociology for the next four decades because his message was so appealing to the emerging liberationist movements for blacks, women, and gays. For Mills and his followers, society's elites use their wealth, prestige, and power to sustain their privilege and ensure that their interests become national policy. At the same time, sociologists like Howard Becker began to infuse sociological theory with the romantic view of the deviant as the hero. An entire generation of sociology students was formed in large measure by Becker's (1963) *The Outsiders*, which promoted the belief that "social groups create deviance by making the rules whose infraction constitutes deviance—and by applying those rules to particular people and labeling them as outsiders" (9). Students were soon being taught that the degree to which an act will be treated as deviant is dependent upon who commits the act, and who feels harmed by it.

Postmodern theory began to permeate sociological theory in the 1980s and '90s. Postmodernists like the French social historian Michel Foucault view reality as ultimately inaccessible by human investigation. They believe that all knowledge is a social construction and that truth claims are more about imposing political power than any search for truth. In fact, for postmodernists, there is no such thing as truth. Rather, there are multiple claims of truth by those who want to impose their beliefs and desire to dominate others. This theory confirmed the growing belief that the sociology of deviance was not so much a legitimate field of study as a means by which the powerful exerted control over the powerless.

In *Madness and Civilization*, Foucault wrote that the old model of deviance was merely oppressive middle-class morality dressed up in sociological language (Foucault 1967). According to Foucault, the social problems of the past, including homosexuality, madness, murder, incest, prostitution, illegal drug use, and robbery were not really deviance. Instead, Foucault believed that they were "categories of censure" which were gradually created, developed, and re-formed in the course of establishing and mapping out new systems and territories of domination.

Given the vogue of such ideas, sociologists who continued to write and teach about deviant behavior in terms of clear moral norms found themselves blamed for supporting the ongoing quest of the powerful to marginalize those they found troublesome. Courses on deviance began to be deleted from the curriculum and by the 1970s, the overt deconstruction of the concept of deviance was complete. The only recent in-depth analysis of a subject once considered basic to sociology is a book entitled *The Sociology of Deviance: An Obituary*. The author, Colin Sumner (1994), describes it as "a post-mortem of a field of sociology which has ceased to exist." In fact, Sumner cleverly advises readers that his book "deals with a corpse rather than a corpus of knowledge" (297). Sumner writes that the "death blow" was dealt to deviance when sociologist Alexander Liazos concluded that the subject not only was biased against the poor, but tended to ignore the way that the "corporate economy" was much more violent than so-called criminals. Concern about "crime in the suites" began to take precedence over "crime in the streets." Liazos pointed out that undergraduates at Yale (and elsewhere) jokingly referred to the popular introductory course on deviance as the study of "Nuts, Sluts and Perverts," because the typical subject matter included mental illness, prostitution, and all forms of sexual deviance, rather than what Liazos regarded as "real" deviance—covert, institutional deviance (Sumner 1994, ix).

In addition to the scholarly books and articles, best sellers like William Ryan's *Blaming the Victim* were lauded as providing "an impassioned and often brilliant exposé of middle class ideology which caused us to blame the powerless for their powerlessness" (Gans 1971). No longer would the culture of the underclass be seen as contributing to the entrenched poverty of those who were part of it. No longer would out-of-wedlock births, drug abuse, and the absence of a commitment to education or a work ethic be considered deviant. Instead, all this would be viewed as rational adaptations to an increasingly oppressive society. Drug abuse was transformed from a moral and legal issue into a medical one. Drug abusers were then redefined as victims either of their own genes or of an oppressive society that forced them to take drugs in order to dull the pain of their rejection. And nobody was stamped as deviant—except, of course, those unfortunate traditionalists whom the new power elite in academia and the media increasingly saw as maintaining an outworn and always suspect middle-class ideology about deviance.

Today, compelling pleas for a rational response to deviant behavior are often drowned out by the more emotional appeals—and political cunning—generated by advocacy groups. In 1965, Daniel Patrick Moynihan, a sociologist and four-term United States senator from New York, tried to warn us of the impending problems in the inner cities when he predicted that chaos would result from the alarming increase in single parent households—especially in the inner cities. Using the language of Durkheim, the late-Senator Moynihan (1965) warned that society's mechanisms for social control were breaking down. He warned of what he called a "tangle of pathologies" that accompanied single parenthood for inner city families. But, in the 1960s, many social scientists were reluctant to make that argument. The norms surrounding divorce and unmarried parenthood were loosening and many social scientists maintained that this would be a good thing for society. The Moynihan Report was attacked because it seemed to some to be saying that the problems of black America were attributable, at least in part, to choices that black Americans made about what kind of families they were going to choose. Even though Moynihan suggested that if job opportunities were improved, family structure would improve, most social scientists at the time believed he was blaming the victims of poverty. So for the past 40 years, instead of attacking the problem of fatherless children in the inner cities, social scientists have been more likely to attack the senator and any other sociologist who dared to look at the choices people make about their family structure.

In 1992, Senator Moynihan addressed the 87th Annual Meeting of the American Sociological Association. In a presentation entitled "Defining Deviancy Down," the senator spoke of a worrisome increase in deviant behavior and warned that for the previous decades, "society has chosen not to notice behavior that would be otherwise controlled, disapproved, or even punished." According to Moynihan, the sociologists in the audience had been complicit in this neglect: "Over the past generation, the amount of deviant behavior in American society has increased beyond the levels the community can afford to recognize. Accordingly, we have been redefining deviancy so as to exempt much conduct previously stigmatized and also quietly raising the normal level in categories where behavior is now abnormal by any earlier standard" (Moynihan 1996, 144).

The speech was received with subdued applause as few of those present were willing to be disrespectful toward someone who was one of their own in his academic origins, and who as a legislator had always been supportive of social science research. But, there were many sociologists at the meeting who thought Daniel Patrick Moynihan was wrong about deviance—just as he had once been wrong, they believed, about single parent families.

Still, in his clever alliteration of "defining deviancy down," Moynihan had captured the essence of a disturbing trend in the United States: the decline of our quality of life through our unqualified acceptance of too many activities formerly considered unacceptable. Out of wedlock births, teenage pregnancy, promiscuity, abortion, drug abuse, welfare dependency, and homelessness all seemed to be increasing, even in a climate of prosperity. Worse, these behaviors appeared to be nominally condoned.

At the same time, there was a parallel but opposite development that the senator did not touch on in his speech—a movement of "defining deviancy up." Powerful advocacy groups have been successfully stigmatizing behaviors that had formerly been regarded as "normal" and even benign. Some of these redefinitions have had positive consequences for society. For example, the efforts of advocacy groups like Mothers Against Drunk Drivers to stigmatize drunk driving has achieved success and saved lives. And, the civil rights movement to stigmatize racism in any form has been so tremendously successful that if anyone dares utter a racist joke or attempts to make a negative racial comment, that person will be immediately stigmatized as a racist deserving of punitive sanctions. This redefinition of the deviance of racism has had positive societal consequences. But, in some ways, "defining deviancy up" has negatively affected faithful Catholics who speak out to support traditional marriage or a pro-life perspective. These Catholics now find themselves labeled as deviant by women's rights groups or gay rights supporters because of their adherence to Church teaching on abortion or gay marriage in a secular culture that has defined the deviancy of these behaviors down.

These new definitions of deviance prove that Émile Durkheim was correct when he suggested that the rate of deviance recognized by any society is constant, and that deviance will occur and be identified in every society—even in a society of saints. But in ways that he and the earliest sociologists would have found startling, the forms of deviance and the targets of the new labeling system of deviance have changed: from those at the margins of society to those at the center as advocacy groups now have tremendous power to stigmatize and silence speech by those with whom they disagree.

For most of today's postmodern sociologists—those who continue to maintain that all reality is socially constructed—definitions of deviance that remain consistent across all groups and communities cannot exist in a society that has been so dramatically changed by shifts in values, politics, and social relations. The commitment to egalitarianism, along with a growing reluctance to judge the behavior of others, has made discussions of deviance difficult. Entire academic careers have been built on a clever criticism of Talcott Parsons' functionalist theory of deviance, or a hostile attack on the conservative thought of Émile Durkheim. Sumner (1994, 297) maintains that the concept of social deviance disappeared because it had run its course: "Fatally damaged by waves of successive criticism and undercut by its own logical contradictions, it ceased to be a living force. Its time had passed and it did not recover."

Because of this lack of consensus within the discipline on definitions of deviance, few sociologists teach about deviance and even fewer write about it. Edited collections of classic articles on deviance are republished every so often, but only, it seems, so that we can wonder over how backward we were to take such thinking seriously. No wonder that most sociologists, in the face of this juggernaut, have been disinclined even to speak of the concept of deviance anymore. To do so would require a willingness to discuss behavior such as homosexuality, teenage promiscuity, adultery, abortion, and addiction in relation to standards of "acceptable conduct." Defining by consensus what is acceptable is exactly what has disappeared over the last 40 years. In the aftermath of the radical egalitarianism of the 1960s, merely to label a behavior as deviant came to be viewed as rejecting the equality—perhaps the very humanity—of those engaging in it. Most sociologists became convinced that the sociology of deviance was more about the imposition of selective censure by the dominant elements of society—the "construction of deviance"—than it was about deviant behavior itself. The shift within the sociology deviance from Functionalism to Phenomenological and Conflict theories was complete as the role of power trumped the functional view of deviance.

In defending the marginal or powerless, sociologists shifted the focus of deviance to those persons and groups in society with the power to propose definitions. Attention moved from the criminal, the prostitute, and the homosexual to those who were seen to have caused their labeling as deviant. Each of these formerly defined as deviant sub-groups was allowed to define for itself its boundaries and language of identity, rejecting external definitions and labels as oppressive. Criminals were redefined as victims of an unfair economy that locked them out of legitimate opportunities. The economist Gary Becker provided this view in the 1960s when he argued that crime is a rational act, committed when the perpetrator's "expected gains exceeded his costs." He predicted that when less legal work is available, more illegal "work" takes place. Still, the most recent crime statistics provided by the FBI reveals that violent crime in the U.S. had reached a 40-year low in 2010. This was counter to the predictions made by most sociologists for the past four decades who maintain that poverty and unemployment cause crime. The late social scientist James Q. Wilson (2011) suggests that it is possible that crime in the United States is falling because of an improvement in the culture. People may actually be taking self-control more seriously—unlike the quest for self-expression, at society's cost that took place in the 1960s when crime skyrocketed (Wilson 2011, C-1). This is what the sociology of deviance is all about.

Like other criminals, prostitutes were re-defined in the 1960s and '70s as "sex-workers" who most likely had been victims of a male patriarchy which had closed the door to financial success through gender discrimination. Many countries have sex-worker advocacy groups which lobby against criminalization and discrimination of prostitutes. Sociologist Valerie Jenness (1993) provides an excellent overview of the ways in which sex workers have achieved loose, localized organizations or occasionally larger politically oriented organizations for the promotion of some goal common to them all including legalization. Claiming that prostitution is labor like any other profession, these advocacy groups are opposed to any government regulation and oversight of their profession. In the United States, one such group is COYOTE (an abbreviation for Call Off Your Old Tired Ethics) and the other is the North American Task Force on Prostitution.

Likewise, homosexuals began to make tremendous strides toward neutralizing the deviance label in the 1960s and '70s. The following section of this chapter will describe in detail the process of redefinition that was used to help convince a once skeptical public that gay men and lesbian women were not deviant—in fact, they were as the title of gay activist, Andrew Sullivan's (1996) book proclaims, *Virtually Normal*. Rather than engaging in deviant behavior, gay men and lesbian women began to be redefined as following their natural inclination in their choice of sexual partners. Homosexuality moved from something that was increasingly tolerated by society to something that is now celebrated by many groups.

Of course, it is not just the activists who have contributed to redefining homosexual behavior, abortion, and other forms of behavior once considered deviant. The legal system has played an important role in helping to define down deviance. In 1973, the Supreme Court ended all legal impediments to abortion in *Roe v Wade*. And, in 2003, *Lawrence v. Texas* struck down the sodomy law in Texas maintaining that intimate consensual sexual contact was part of the liberty protected by substantive due process under the Fourteenth Amendment. *Lawrence* invalidated all laws against sodomy between consenting same-sex adults—making homosexual genital acts legal in all states. In both *Roe* and *Lawrence*, the Supreme Court rulings followed a long period of redefinition in public opinion—defining down the deviance of abortion and homosexuality (U. S. Supreme Court ruling in *Lawrence v. Texas* 2003). The history of legalizing abortion is well known as both the pro-life and the pro-abortion sides commemorate the 1973 Supreme Court ruling with marches and inspiring speeches. Yet, as the next section will demonstrate, the process of defining down the deviance of homosexuality is less well known because it was a much slower process, and the progress toward full acceptance has not been linear. Progress toward acceptance of the gay lifestyle has been followed by periods when this progress was stymied by new charges of deviance in the 1980s as the AIDS virus was identified as being spread sexually within the gay community.

Defining Down the Deviance of Homosexuality

The most important moment in the quest toward defining down the deviance of homosexual behavior occurred on a summer evening in New York City's Greenwich Village. On June 27, 1969, in what is now recognized as a gay Boston Tea Party of sorts, the gay rights movement began to receive public attention and support. It started with a police raid at a gay bar in Greenwich Village when eight New York City police officers raided the Stonewall Inn and attempted to arrest the dancing cross-dressed patrons. As the gay couples who had been dancing in the bar were handcuffed and escorted to the waiting police vans, jeers were directed at the police. Someone threw a handful of coins, and in response, the police expanded their arrests to include those milling around outside the bar. The gay men and lesbian women escalated their resistance and the crowd began to grow as gay patrons from nearby bars arrived on the scene. Coins were thrown and then beer bottles, and later, bricks from a construction site were thrown at the arresting officers. Someone dislodged a parking meter and used it as a battering ram on the door of the now-locked Stonewall Inn. Someone else hurled a burning garbage can at a plate-glass window. The riot that fueled the gay rights movement had begun (Hendershott 2002, 94). And, even today, the Stonewall riots are celebrated as part of the gay pride revelry that occurs each June in major cities throughout the country to commemorate the beginning of the gay liberation movement.

Progress continued throughout the 1970s, emboldened in 1974, when the American Psychiatric Association (APA) helped to define down the deviance of homosexuality by removing homosexuality from the list of "disorders" in their *Diagnostic and Statistical Manual*—the "bible" used by psychiatric practitioners for diagnosing psychological disorders. Under fire from the emerging gay rights movement, the members of the APA voted at their annual meeting to delete homosexuality from the list of mental disorders in the *DSM*—thus removing any stigma from homosexual behavior. The vote had nothing to do with new research or groundbreaking genetic findings, but was instead a political response to what was becoming a powerful social movement. For years before the APA's reassessment of homosexuality, gay rights advocates had lobbied the association at the annual meetings. There were boycotts of the cities in which the APA held its conventions, and there was a well-planned media attack on the association. Given the intensity of this lobbying effort, it was no surprise when the APA finally bowed to the pressure (Hendershott 2002, 92).

Still, the progress that gays and lesbians made after Stonewall stalled as the 1980s brought unfavorable attention to the gay community in the form of fear over the primary role that gay men played in the spread of the AIDS virus. When epidemiologists and sociologists first demonstrated that AIDS was being spread sexually through the gay community, most gay men reacted with denial—rejecting the risk-reduction guidelines that were based on the growing realization that the disease was spreading through promiscuous sexuality with multiple partners. The bathhouses remained open in the Castro, San Francisco's gay district, and many gay men continued to engage in high risk sexual behavior throughout much of the decade. Even at the height of the AIDS crisis, when there were no longer any doubts about the origins or the risks of AIDS, gay activists in New York, San Francisco, Los Angeles, and Boston opposed any attempts to close the bathhouses which they characterized as "centers of gay culture" (Bawer 1993, 31).

Images of promiscuity, and reckless endangerment of others, and the pursuit of pleasure at all costs supported the stigma attached to what became again to be regarded as a deviant population. This shows how tenuous a redefinition of deviance can be as one-third of all respondents to a 1985 Gallup poll said that AIDS has worsened their opinion of homosexuality (Kirk and Madsen 1989, 172). But at the close of the disastrous AIDS-afflicted decade of the 1980s an influential book provided an understanding of how the gay community could escape the label of deviance. *After the Ball: How America Will Conquer Its Fear and Hatred of Gays in the '90s*, by Marshall Kirk and Hunter Madsen (1989), demanded that gays realize that how they were presenting themselves was the most important structural impediment to acceptance. Even more remarkably, Kirk and Madsen suggested that the gay men needed to view the AIDS epidemic as presenting them with a unique opportunity for full acceptance and inclusion. Acknowledging that Americans are basically fair-minded, they wrote, "As cynical as it may seem, AIDS gives us a chance, however brief, to establish ourselves as a victimized minority—legitimately deserving of America's special protection and care" (xxvii).

Applying a marketplace metaphor to redefining the deviance of homosexuality, savvy salesmen (both having been trained in psychological methods of operant conditioning and both with professional experience in designing marketing campaigns) Kirk and Madsen (1989) showed how the "deviants" of the past could be repackaged as the "victims" of the present. They provided gay activists with a blueprint for what they called "a conversion of the average American's emotions, mind, and will through a planned psychological attack" (154). To change public opinion, Kirk and Madsen suggested three important tactics of persuasion: *desensitization, jamming,* and *conversion*. All are designed to define down the deviance of homosexuality through a system of propaganda which includes, most importantly, a stigmatizing of those who do not agree with the goodness of homosexual acts.

Kirk and Madsen knew that in order to define down the deviance of homosexuality, they had to redefine homosexuals themselves as non-threatening. To do that, they created desensitization strategies. *Desensitization* is an effort to present gays as unthreatening and inoffensive: "They are your neighbors, your friends, your teachers, and your co-workers—they are all around you." To achieve the goal of desensitization, Kirk and Madsen (1989) advised that the gay community needed to inundate the heterosexual world with a continuous flood of gay-related advertising, presented in the least offensive fashion possible, meant to convince the consumer of the ads that homosexuals are perfectly—not just virtually—normal (149). The advertisements were coupled with a campaign to educate the heterosexual community about all of the great contributions gay men and lesbian women have made through history. Learning from the success of Black History Month, Kirk and Madsen realized that desensitization would be more likely to occur if people appreciated the contributions of gays and lesbians "from Socrates to Eleanor Roosevelt, Tchaikovsky to Bessie Smith, Alexander the Great to Alexander Hamilton, and Leonardo da Vinci to Walt Whitman" (188).

Desensitization techniques are even more powerful when combined with *jamming*, defined by Kirk and Madsen as moving people to a different opinion about homosexuality through a form of operant conditioning. The "trick" of jamming, according to Kirk and Madsen (1989) is to make the person who does not agree with the goodness of same sexual relations to "feel a sense of shame whenever his homo-hatred surfaces." The authors write that "propagandistic advertisement can depict homo-hating bigots as crude loudmouths—people who say not only faggot, but nigger, kike, and other shameful epithets" (151). In the redefinition of deviance then, anyone who dares to question the morality of gay sexual behavior is labeled a "homophobe." The efforts of the newly labeled homophobe to stigmatize homosexuality as deviant will rebound on him and cause him to unlearn such intolerant behavior. Ads to help in the jamming process include those that link prejudice against homosexuals to hate crimes such as lynchings and cross burnings. A few years ago a television advertisement shown during a Grammy Music Awards show presented teenage boys who were casually using the word "gay" in a pejorative manner. The ad then coupled these ordinary looking teenage boys with a shocking image of the brutal slaying of Matthew Shepard, the young gay man who was murdered in Wyoming over a decade ago. The message was that "hate speech" will kill gays.

The third and most important approach that Kirk and Madsen (1989) suggest to reverse the prejudice against gay men and lesbian women is *conversion,* or what they call "subverting the mechanism of prejudice through the use of associative conditioning." They write: "It isn't enough that antigay bigots should become confused about us, or even indifferent about us—we are safest, in the long run, if we can actually make them like us" (153). Conversion aims to achieve this by presenting attractive and unthreatening homosexuals in magazines, on billboards, and on television to show how normal and nice gay people are. One appealing ad promoted by the Los Angeles-based Lesbian and Gay Public Awareness Project shows an attractive middle-aged woman flanked by her two attractive daughters. The caption reads: "I'm proud of my lesbian daughter" (241).

The success of the marketplace model of defining down of the deviance of homosexuality was predicted—and decried—throughout many of the social teachings of the Catholic Church—especially in *Veritatis Splendor.*

Veritatis Splendor and Deviant Behavior

Veritatis Splendor (John Paul II 1993) opens with a reminder that as a result of original sin, we are constantly tempted to turn our gaze away from the living and true God in order to direct it toward idols, exchanging "the truth about God for a lie" (Romans 1:25). Reflecting concerns about the use of social power in redefining deviance, Pope John Paul II warns that the very foundations of moral theology are "being undermined by certain present day tendencies." Although he was speaking as a theologian, Pope John Paul II, a sociologist by training, is consciously addressing and requesting collaboration with social scientists.

In *Veritatis Splendor*, the Pope demonstrates that the root of the problem in identifying what is morally right and wrong is the detachment of human freedom from its essential and constitutive relationship to truth. Thus, the traditional doctrine regarding the natural law, and the universality and permanent validity of its precepts, is rejected. Certain of the Church's moral teachings are found simply unacceptable; and the Magisterium itself is considered capable of intervening in matters of morality only in order to "propose values in the light of which individual will independently make his or her decisions and life choices" (John Paul II 1993, #4).

Still, Pope John Paul II also reminded us that no darkness of error or sin can totally take away from man the light of God the Creator: "In the depths of his heart there always remains a yearning for absolute truth and a thirst to attain full knowledge of it." Sacred Scripture remains the source of the Church's moral doctrine—"the source of all saving truth and moral teaching." In the opening pages of his encyclical, Pope John Paul II wrote that his intention is to set forth certain aspects of doctrine which are of "crucial importance" in facing what is certainly a genuine crisis.

For Pope John Paul II, the root of these problems has been the "detachment of human freedom from its essential and constitutive relationship to truth" (#84). He added that one of the reasons that *Veritatis Splendor* was being published at this time was because it seemed fitting for it to be preceded by the release of the *Catechism of the Catholic Church* which contains a complete and systematic exposition of Christian moral teaching. For Catholics, the *Catechism* presents a guide for living a moral life.

In his encyclical, Pope John Paul II deals with a common objection to moral norms, namely, that defending objective precepts is often seen as intolerant or not taking into account the complexity of an individual's particular situation. He noted that the bond between truth, the good, and freedom is often overlooked, and warns that too often truth is not accepted, and "freedom alone, uprooted from any objectivity, is left to decide by itself what is good and what is evil" (#84). For Pope John Paul II, in the depths of our hearts there always remains a yearning for absolute truth and a thirst to attain full knowledge of it. Yet, in a secular society, most believe—including most sociologists—that there are no objective properties which all deviant acts can be said to share in common—even within the confines of a given group.

Unfortunately, there has been little help in discerning good from evil from many Catholic theologians. Swept up in the same wave of postmodernism that engulfed the sociologists, many theologians refuse to look to the Gospel as the source for saving truth. Pope John Paul II clearly identified this problem in his encyclical when he says that "while respecting the methods and requirements of theological sciences, theologians must look for a more appropriate way of communicating doctrine to the people of their time; since there is a difference between the deposit or the truths of faith and the manner in which they are expressed" (#29). The Pope warned that there have been developed "certain inter-pretations of Christian morality which are not consistent with sound teaching" (#29). And, he called upon his "Brother Bishops" to draw attention to those el-ements of the Church's moral teaching which today appear particularly exposed to error, ambiguity, or neglect (#30).

While Pope John Paul II called upon the bishops, the theologians, and the faithful to uphold the truth on moral issues, he also reminded them that this does not mean the Church is lacking in compassion. However, in today's non-judgmental culture filled with relativism on issues surrounding marriage, sexual behavior, reproductive rights, and gender relations, it is difficult for Catholics to make moral judgments—especially on homosexuality—without being viewed as lacking in empathy. The Pope pointed out that the Church is both a mother and teacher, and concealing or weakening moral truth is not consistent with genuine understanding and compassion. Yet, when Catholics attempt to draw upon Church teachings to pronounce activities like abortion or homosexual relations as morally wrong these same Catholics are often stigmatized by gay activists or pro-choice feminists as behaving in a deviant manner themselves.

Catholic Social Teachings on Homosexual Acts

Looking closely at the ways in which the deviance of homosexual behavior was defined down helps us understand both the process of societal redefinition, as well as the response to this redefinition by the Magisterium of the Catholic Church. While the *Catechism of the Catholic Church* is clear on the sanctity of marriage between one man and one woman, and the immorality of homosexual acts, much of secular society—including many self-identified Catholics—have defined down the deviance of engaging in same sex behavior. In fact, some groups of Catholics (those who attend Mass irregularly) have been even more supportive than those of other religious denominations of legislation allowing same sex couples to marry than others. Using techniques of desensitization, jamming, and conversion, these dissidents have achieved some measure of suc-cess—especially within the younger cohort of Catholics.

Research by Catholic University sociology professor Rev. Paul Sullins (2000) has revealed that the younger the Catholic, the more likely he or she is to support gay rights—including access to civil unions and same sex marriage. In a study that compared support for same sex marriage in America, Fr. Sullins found that Catholics support same sex marriage more strongly than Protestants. States with Catholic majorities are much more likely to regularize homosexual relations. Fr. Sullins also found that younger persons support same sex marriage more strongly than older Catholics, suggesting that support will continue to grow and concludes that this growing support may reflect "catechetical ambigui-ty and equivocation among the U.S. bishops" (97–123).

A *Washington Post/ABC News Poll* recently found that 63 percent of self-identified Catholics support legalizing marriage between gay men and lesbian women. This is compared with only 53 percent of the general population demonstrating such support for same sex marriage (Jones 2011). These findings mirror the results of a 2010 *American Values Survey* which revealed that 53 percent of self-identified Catholics supported allowing gay and lesbian couples to marry compared with 48 percent of the public (Jones and Cox 2010). And, a recent study by the Public Religion Institute two years after the passage of Proposition 8, the Marriage Amendment which protects traditional marriage by maintaining that marriage is restricted to a union between one man and one woman, reveals that the majority of Catholics in California (54%) now say that they would support allowing gay and lesbian couples to marry, compared with 51% of Californians overall (Jones and Cox 2010).

Although there have been questions about the failure of some of the authors of these surveys to differentiate between those Catholics who attend Mass regularly and those who do not, the data point to some concerns about the teaching role of the Magisterium on homosexual acts. The *Catechism of the Catholic Church* (USCCB, #2357) states clearly that "Basing itself on Sacred Scripture, which presents homosexual acts as acts of grave depravity, tradition has always declared that homosexual acts are intrinsically disordered. They are contrary to the natural law. They close the sexual act to the gift of life. They do not proceed from a genuine affective and sexual complementarity. Under no circumstances can they be approved."

Recognizing the changing societal norms, the *Catechism* also points out that homosexuality has taken a "great variety of forms through the centuries and in different cultures," and also acknowledges that "its psychological genesis remains largely unexplained" (USCCB, #2357). Yet, the *Catechism* maintains that even though the secular culture and a supportive media have redefined or "defined down" the deviance of homosexual acts, the Church has never approved—and can never approve—of this behavior.

The Catholic Church opposes homosexual activity because it is "intrinsically disordered." The Church is saying that the form of sex acts that homosexuals engage in are an abuse of our human nature. Many scholars—beyond the Catholic Church—have made that same argument. Jeffrey Satinover (1996), a Fellow in Psychiatry and Child Psychiatry at Yale University and former William James Lecturer in Psychology and Religion at Harvard, makes a similar argument in his book, *Homosexuality and the Politics of Truth*.

Satinover (1996) warns that "the hallmark of a society in which all sexual constraints have been set aside is that finally it sanctions homosexuality as well...without constraints civilization would lose its discipline and vitality." For Satinover, "it is a simple and sobering fact that no society that has sanctioned unconstrained sexuality has long survived" (18). Princeton professor Robert George (2002) has long argued that homosexual behavior violates not only tradition but also human reason. Maintaining that marriage is anchored in the unitive act of bodily sharing of one man and one woman whose bodies complement each other, George argues that reason alone shows that homosexual sex and heterosexual sodomy are morally wrong, just as the Catholic Church, classical philosophers, and other religious traditions have historically taught.

When the Catholic Church declares that homosexuality is disordered, this does not mean that the Church is not compassionate to those who suffer from the disorder. The *Catechism* also states that "men and women who have deep-seated homosexual tendencies must be accepted with respect, compassion, and sensitivity. Every sign of unjust discrimination in their regard should be avoided" (USCCB 2003, #2358).

Still, many Catholics appear to be unaware of the official teachings of their own Church—even those who attend Mass regularly. A study by the Public Religion Institute (2011) found that compared with the general church-going public, Catholics are less likely than other churchgoers to hear about the issue of homosexuality. Compared with other religious groups, Catholics are significantly more likely to give their Church poor marks for how it is handling the issue of homosexuality. A majority of Catholics (56%) believe that sexual relations between two adults of the same gender is not a sin, compared with the only 46% from the general population who believe it is not a sin.

The fact that the majority of self-identified Catholics believe that same sex behavior is not sinful suggests that these Catholics may be more influenced by the popular culture and the "selling" of new definitions of deviance rather than the teachings of the Church itself. In addition, there are some Catholic theologians who have attempted to dispute the Catholic social teachings contained in the *Catechism*. This has caused confusion for Catholics—but the bishops are mindful of this and have recently begun to challenge some of these theologians. On September 15, 2010, the United States Conference of Catholic Bishops' Committee on Doctrine released a 24-page critique of a book published in 2008 by two Catholic theology professors, which attempts to "define down" the immorality of homosexual acts (Committee on Doctrine 2010). The Bishops issued their critique of *The Sexual Person: Toward a Renewed Catholic Anthropology* by Creighton University Theology professors, Todd A. Salzman and Michael G. Lawler, because they allege that the book proposes ways of living a Christian life that do not accord with the teaching of the Church and the Christian tradition. The bishops' primary claim is that "much of the book is devoted to demonstrating the supposed inadequacy of magisterial statements and the moral theology that underlies them" (Committee on Doctrine 2010, 5). Concluding that "rather than setting moral limits," the bishops allege that "the chief concern of the authors of *The Sexual Person* appears to be to provide a moral justification for sexual behaviors that are common in contemporary culture but rejected as immoral by the Church" (18).

Like most redefinitions of deviance, *The Sexual Person* appeals to historical consciousness in an attempt to discredit norms based on scriptural texts, natural law, or Church statements. The authors acknowledge that some scriptural texts condemn homosexual behavior because it is a perversion of the natural hetero-sexual condition. Yet, they argue that these biblical condemnations are based on a "false assumption, shaped by the socio-historical conditions of the times in which they were written" (Salzman and Lawler 2008, 217). They maintain that there can be no perversion of the heterosexual condition by homosexuals since their natural orientation is not heterosexual, but homosexual.

The bishops charge that there are two major flaws in Salzman and Lawler's argument. First, an examination of the structure of the argument reveals that it is circular, for it depends on the authors' prior assumption that homosexual activity is "natural" for those with a homosexual inclination: "Salzman and Lawler argue that the fact that the scriptural writers condemn homosexual behavior as unnatu-ral without making an exception for those with a homosexual inclination shows their ignorance of the supposedly established fact that homosexual behavior is natural for those with a homosexual inclination. This alleged ignorance makes what the scriptural writers say about homosexuality irrelevant to the contempo-rary discussion." The second flaw in the argument presented in *The Sexual Per-son* depends on the equivocal use of the term "natural." The bishops maintain that from the perspective of the writers of Scripture: "natural refers to what is consistent with the natural order established by God, in which man and woman were made for each other and the intrinsic purpose of human sexuality is ful-filled only in the marriage bond of man and woman. Salzman and Lawler's cri-tique of the scriptural writers' position presumes a different meaning of 'natu-ral'" (Committee on Doctrine 2010, 9).

The argument over what is "natural" is an important one for our discussion of Catholic perspectives of the sociology of deviance. While the authors of *The Sexual Person* maintain that "nature" is a socially constructed category, the Catholic Church teaches that natural law is a human participation in the divine law. Departing from Catholic teachings on natural law, the authors object to the proposition that the divine law is "accessible to our minds." They claim this proposition raises "serious hermeneutical questions" (Salzman and Lawler 2008, 227). This dismissal of natural law by Salzman and Lawler brings the strongest criticism from the bishops' Committee on Doctrine as they maintain that in *The Sexual Person* "there is virtually nothing left of natural law apart from the name." And, they continue that "without the divine law being accessible to our minds, there is no human participation in the divine law and hence, no natural law" (Committee on Doctrine 2010, 9). The bishops conclude that "the Cate-chism goes on to insist that the historicity of the natural law does not negate its universality…the natural law remains as a rule that binds men among them-selves and imposes on them, beyond the inevitable differences, common princi-ples" (13).

The Absolutist Perspective of Deviance

The Committee on Doctrine is so concerned about the dismissal of natural law by the authors of *The Sexual Person* because from Catholic social teaching, natural law includes an acknowledgment that we are not the ultimate creators of the moral order—that there is a moral order prior to all human creation. In fact, "The capacity to distinguish the natural order from what is a matter of human convention, whether custom or law, presupposes a grasp of the fundamental order of creation which in turn points to the fact that human reason participates in the eternal law governing that order" (Committee on Doctrine 2010, 13).

Pope John Paul II's (1993) *Veritatis Splendor* provides the foundation for the bishops' argument on natural law when he writes that "The moral law has its origin in God and always finds it source in him…Indeed, as we have seen, the natural law is nothing other than the light of understanding infused in us by God, whereby we understand what must be done and what must be avoided. God gave this light and this law to man at creation" (#40).

From a sociological perspective, drawing upon natural law as Professor George suggests, is described as an "absolutist perspective" of deviance. Most contemporary sociology texts are critical of applying this approach. In fact, the authors of *Social Deviance and Crime: An Organizational and Theoretical Approach* describe the absolutist approach as "impossible." Claiming that "deciding what is good for society is largely arbitrary and subjective. Furthermore, concepts like justice, goodness, or exploitation depend completely on the definer's values. One person's justice is another person's exploitation, and good and evil are necessarily in the eyes of a beholder" (Tittle and Paternoster 2000, 8).

Still, most Marxist sociologists, as well as some radical feminist and gay and lesbian sociologists maintain that an absolute moral standard must be applied to some behaviors. For them, any behavior that results in the exploitation of one person or a category of persons for the benefit of another or threatens the dignity and quality of life for specific people and humanity as a whole is inherently evil, and thereby deviant. Marxists point to the exploitative nature of economic relations in capitalistic societies and regard this inherent exploitation as a form of deviance (Simon and Eitzen 1993). Pro-abortion feminists regard any restrictions on a woman's right to choose as deviant because they deprive women of equal rights and human dignity. Some define "social justice" so broadly to include the right to marriage by same sex couples and the right to an abortion even in the last months of pregnancy. These are all absolutist perspectives of deviance—yet because they support causes that many sociologists support, few define the Marxist or the radical gay and feminist perspectives in that way.

For example, in a book entitled *Love the Sin: Sexual Regulation and the Limits of Religious Tolerance,* authors Janet Jakobsen and Ann Pellegrini (2003, ix) take an absolutist approach "to argue for the production of new values through various forms of intimacy. These intimacies and the values they enable do not come from nowhere, but emerge in part out of social movements." In the Introduction to their book, the authors write that they "owe a special debt to the Queer Faculty Group at New York University," and they decry "how it has come to pass that Christian theological pronouncements have become so institutionalized in the official life of the nation that they can be taken for just good old American values" (3). Asking how it is that religion provides the backbone for much of state policy and law around sex, the authors argue for making religion "the ground for sexual freedom, rather than the justification for sexual regulation" (16). Changing Church teachings on homosexuality is the real goal for such criticisms. For Jakobsen and Pellegrini, the Church's tolerance of "love the sinner, hate the sin" is "antidemocratic" (149). They assert that democracy has to mean more than coercive homogeneity, and their solution is to encourage others to think about religion differently. Jakobsen and Pellegrini are encouraging the social movement within the Church to change Church teachings on homosexuality. No longer content with tolerance, these authors want to remove the "sinfulness" from the sin of homosexual behavior so that Catholics can not only love the sinner but will also love what used to be the sin of engaging in same sex acts.

Indeed, there is already a social movement within the Catholic Church itself to change the Church's teachings on homosexuality. Reflecting the social movement beyond the Church, gay and lesbian advocates from organizations like the Rainbow Sash, Dignity, the American Catholic Council, and others have staged demonstrations and held protests—sometimes disrupting the celebration of the Mass in their attempt to force the Church to change its stance on the sinfulness of homosexual acts. These gay rights advocacy groups know that the Catholic Church is the last line in the defense of teachings on the deviance of homosexual acts. In order to achieve full acceptance and equality—including marriage equality—they must, as Jakobsen and Pellegrini advocate, change the Church's stance from loving the sinner and hating the sin to loving the sin as well as the sinner.

Some of the progress made by the homosexual advocacy community in gaining full acceptance for homosexual acts has employed social movement strategies used by the civil rights movement. But, the success of the strategies implemented by the civil rights movement of the 1960s was due also to the moral authority that religious leaders brought to it. Under the leadership of Martin Luther King Jr., the movement became ecumenical with representatives from diverse faith traditions, all of them contributing resources and volunteers to assist in the progress toward equal rights. Stamping discrimination and racism as deviant was greatly facilitated by an appeal from the religious sources of moral authority. This has been a challenge for the gay rights movement as the Catholic Church remains steadfast in its teaching on the immorality of homosexual acts.

While there has been an attempt by theologians and others to move the Church to change her teachings on homosexuality, this attempt continues to be stymied by the teachings themselves. The Magisterium has resisted every attempt—including this latest attempt by Salzman and Lawler. And, despite the savvy marketing campaign run by professional propagandists like Kirk and Madsen, Catholics remain conflicted about homosexual behavior. Unfortunately, some Catholic institutions—including most prominently Catholic colleges and universities—have added to the confusion. While support groups for gay and lesbian students are laudable attempts to provide a welcoming environment for those students experiencing same-sex attraction, dances like those at the University of San Diego, "coming out weeks" like those on many campuses like Notre Dame, and events like the "Queer Kiss-In" at DePaul only cause confusion.

Social Order and Sacred Order

More than fifty years ago, the poet, T.S. Eliot wrote about the sense of alienation that occurs when social regulators begin to splinter and the controlling moral authority of a society is no longer effective. In his play, *The Cocktail Party*, a troubled young protagonist visits a psychiatrist and confides that she feels a "sense of sin" because of her relationship with a married man. She is distressed not so much by the illicit relationship, but rather by the strange feeling of sinfulness. Eliot (1950, 156) writes, "Having a sense of sin seems abnormal to her—she had never noticed before that such behaviour might be seen in those terms. She believed that she had become ill."

When Eliot writes of his protagonist's feeling unease or uncertainty about her behavior, he is really speaking of the sense of normlessness that has traditionally been a focus of sociology. In many ways, Eliot's play is about anomie—the state that sociologists identify as resulting when one is caught between the loosening moral norms regulating behavior and one's own moral misgivings. Eliot's play echoes the scholarship of Durkheim. Both men saw that the identification and stigmatization of deviant behavior is functional for society because it can produce certainty for individuals and solidarity for the group. And, both recognized that dramatic social change through rapid redefinition of deviance can be dysfunctional for society. Strong cultural values and clear concepts of good and evil integrate members into the group and provide meaning. When traditional cultural attachments are disrupted, or when behavior is no longer regulated by these common norms and values, individuals are left without a moral compass (Anderson and Taylor 2000, 504–6).

Durkheim knew that social facts like crime statistics, abortion rates, and poll data on support for gay marriage can be explained only by analyzing the unique social conditions that evolve when norms break down. The resulting anomic state leads to deviant behavior as the individual's attachment to social bonds is weakened. According to this view, people internalize social norms because of their attachments to others. People care what others think of them and attempt to conform to expectations because they accept what others expect (Hirschi 1969). However, when these same people are unsure about the norms, or when the norms are changing rapidly—as they have for the past few decades—there is a growing unwillingness to make moral judgments about behavior.

This value-free ideology was predicted forty years ago by sociologist Philip Rieff (1966), who warned in his now-classic book, *The Triumph of the Therapeutic* that "psychological man" was beginning to replace "Christian man" as the dominant character type in our society. Unlike traditional Christianity, which made moral demands on believers, the secular world of psychological man rejected both the idea of sin and the need for salvation. Replacing the concept of sin with the concept of sickness was predicted by Eliot's *Cocktail Party*, but documented by Rieff who wrote in 1966 that the authority that had been vested in Christian culture had been all but shattered. Nothing had succeeded it. What worried him was that the institutions of morality—especially the Church—lacked authority and could no longer persuade others to follow them. Further, Rieff (2006) believed that this failure of authority was no accident, but rather the program of "the modern cultural revolution" which was conducted "not in the name of any new order of communal purpose, but rather for the permanent disestablishment of any deeply internalized moral demands" (205).

Once this religious authority is gone, Rieff believed that a kind of anti-culture emerged. It is a culture in which religion is privatized—completely removed from the public square and used only as a type of therapy for individuals. For Rieff (1966, 20), "Psychological man becomes a hedger against his own bets, a user of any faith that lends itself to therapeutic use." In a later book, *Fellow Teachers,* Rieff (1973, 39) goes even further to say that: "At the end of this tremendous cultural development, we moderns shall arrive at barbarism. Barbarians are people without historical memory. Barbarism is the real meaning of radical contemporaneity. Released from all authoritative pasts, we progress towards barbarism, not away from it."

In *Sacred Order/Social Order: My Life among the Deathworks*, Rieff (2006) further relates society's attempt to "level all of the verticals in authority." Published in 2006, shortly after his death, Rieff asserted that one of the reasons that we have such problems with social order is that "moral constraints are now read as social constructions that have no status in being beyond what is given by those who have constructed these constraints" (xxii). While defining down the deviance of homosexuality has occurred within the culture—even within the Catholic community, the reality remains that it is simply a symptom of a much bigger problem. The real problem is the failure to recognize that there are indeed rules—and a natural law basis for such rules—that for centuries have led to sacred orders, or what Rieff calls "interdicts." Following Durkheim, Rieff points out that the challenge to social order is the growing inability of the culture to translate sacred order into social order. In the past, the faithful knew that their identity as Catholics came from what Rieff calls the "vertical axis in authority." Believers looked to authority figures like priests and bishops for guidance as these clergymen were willing to do the hard work of translating sacred order— helping others to understand the scriptural and natural law basis for the inter- dicts. The United States Catholic Conference of Bishops' Committee on Doc- trine has courageously claimed that role. The criticism and correction the bish- ops issued to Salzman and Lawler was really meant to be a teaching document for all Catholics. It was intended to show that there are indeed what Rieff calls "verticals in authority" within the Catholic Church. The Magisterium is the teaching authority of the Church and it reflects the truth of these teachings.

The basis for the culture war we are currently experiencing both within the Church and within the greater society is really one that is waged between those who assert that there are no truths, and those who remain dedicated to the propo- sition that the truths have been revealed and require constant rereading and ap- plication. James Davison Hunter (1994), author of *Culture Wars; The Death of Character; and Before the Shooting Begins*, writes that "Culture is nothing if it is not first and foremost, a normative order by which we comprehend ourselves, others, and the larger world and through which we order our experience" (200). A sociologist, Hunter reminds readers that at the heart of culture is a system of norms and values: "These norms and values are better understood as *command- ing truths* so deeply embedded in our consciousness and in the habits of our lives that to question them is to question reality itself." These commanding truths—like the commandments Catholics know well—define the "shoulds" and the "should nots" of our experience and accordingly, the good and the evil, the right and the wrong, the appropriate and inappropriate, the honorable and the shameful (201).

Against these commanding truths is a multicultural approach to culture in which all cultures are equal and even the definition of marriage can be redefined as an individual choice. Charles Taylor (1992), a postmodern Catholic philoso- pher, rejects traditional categories of moral virtue, good and evil, right and wrong and replaces them with what he calls the contemporary "culture of au- thenticity" (39). This eliminates any type of significance to our lives. In some ways, Taylor and the other postmodernists are promoting a return to the individ- ualism and privatization that the earliest sociologists rejected. It is the same kind of privatization of religious faith that today's pro-choice Catholic legislators hold. Claiming to be "personally opposed" to abortion, these Catholic lawmak- ers say that they refuse to impose their personal religious beliefs on others and continue to pass laws which will expand abortion here and abroad. But, some Catholic bishops are beginning to publicly challenge these Catholic lawmakers.

The faithful know that teachings on life issues and marriage and the family cannot be changed. For Catholics, these teachings comprise Rieff's "interdicts." And, although there are some issues—including some liturgical changes and devotional practices—that are constantly being redefined and strengthened within the Church, there remain the enduring truths, those that Philip Rieff calls "commanding truths," that cannot be changed: "Commanding truths will not be mocked, except to the destruction of everything sacred" (Rieff 2006, 59). Of the family as a commanding truth, Rieff wrote, "the destruction of the family is the key regimen of technological innovation and moral deviance" (Rieff 1973, 107). And, of life itself, Rieff wrote: "We must stand against the re-creation of life in the laboratory and the taking of life in the abortion clinic" (42). Rieff knew, as the sociologists of the past knew, that culture survives by faith in the highest absolute authority and its interdicts. For Catholics, there can be no Catholic culture and no true Catholic Church without such commanding truths.

The recent decision by lawmakers—including Catholic lawmakers—in New York State to legalize same-sex marriage was made despite New York Archbishop Timothy Dolan's (2011) warnings about the "undeniable truth that marriage is one man, one woman, united in lifelong love and fidelity, hoping for children." This statement by the Archbishop is what Hunter and Rieff would call a "commanding truth" and was rejected by New York's Catholic governor and the majority of the state's Catholic legislators. Understanding well the power of the advocates to redefine deviance, Archbishop Dolan used his archdiocesan blog to criticize the lawmakers for "dictating what the very definition of family and marriage means," and he added that "not every chic cause deserves to be called a right." But, in the current social constructionist model of defining deviance, the legislature has reinvented what Catholics and other Christians have always believed was the God-given institution of marriage.

The Sociology of Deviance provides a useful framework to help us understand the tremendous success that the gay and lesbian community has achieved in defining down what had long been viewed as the deviance of homosexuality. Beyond redefining homosexuality, the continued refinement of theory on deviance is probably one of the greatest contributions that Sociology can make to understanding social change. Yet, it is difficult to predict whether the study of deviance will become again a vibrant sub-discipline within Sociology. In an effort to avoid alienating those with diverse lifestyles and values, even sociologists have become hesitant to make judgments on the behavior of others. Citing privacy concerns, most sociologists are unwilling to speak of behavior that may or may not be "functional" for society—unless it involves the liberation of all oppressed groups, including gays, women, and other minority group members. And, in their place, a powerful advocacy community—representing these oppressed groups—stands ready, willing, and able to redefine deviance for the rest of us.

In the aftermath of September 11, 2001, President George W. Bush repeatedly called the terrorist acts "evil" and those who perpetrated them "evildoers." This language drew only a minor protest from those who on September 10th would have excoriated the president for such inflammatory language. Reassessing the politics and culture after the terrorists declared war on America, we were reminded again that evil exists. We again realized that there are those who are capable of doing monstrous acts. And, to achieve social order, we must be willing to identify and defend ourselves against those who want to do us harm. Perhaps the re-moralization of our public discourse that occurred after September 11th was the only good to come out of the terrorist attacks. Most of us were reminded again that evil exists and that good people must recognize this fact. Perhaps, in time, sociologists will again be willing to recognize that a society that continues to define down the deviant acts our common sense tells us are destructive is a society that has lost the capacity to confront evil.

Bibliography

Anderson, Margaret, and Howard Taylor. 2000. *Sociology.* Belmont, CA: Wadsworth.

Bawer, Bruce. 1993. *A Place at the Table.* New York: Touchstone Books.

Becker, Howard S. 1963. *The Outsiders.* New York: Free Press of Glencoe.

Bryjak, George J., and Michael Soroka. 2001. *Sociology: Changing Societies in a Diverse World.* Boston: Allyn and Bacon.

Committee on Doctrine of the United States Conference of Catholic Bishops. 2010. "Inadequacies in the Theological Methodology and Conclusions of *The Sexual Person: Toward a Renewed Catholic Anthropology.*"

Dolan, Most Rev. Timothy. 2011. "The True Meaning of Marriage." Published in the Archbishop's online blog. June 14, http://blog.archny.org/.

Durkheim, Émile. (1895) 1964. *Rules of Sociological Method.* New York: Free Press.

Eliot, T. S. 1950. *The Cocktail Party.* Orlando, FL: Harcourt Brace Jovanovich.

Erikson, Kai. 1966. *Wayward Puritans: A Study in the Sociology of Deviance.* New York: Macmillan.

Foucault, Michael. 1967. *Madness and Civilization: A History of Insanity in the Age of Reason.* London: Tavistock.

Gans, Herbert. 1971. Quote for back cover of *Blaming the Victim*, by William Ryan. New York: Pantheon.

George, Robert. 2002. *Clash of Orthodoxies: Law, Religion, and Morality in Crisis.* Wilmington, DE: Intercollegiate Studies Institute.

Hendershott, Anne. 2002. *Politics of Deviance.* San Francisco: Encounter Books.

Hirschi, Travis. 1969. *Causes of Delinquency.* Berkeley: University of California Press.

Hunter, James Davison. 1994. *Before the Shooting Begins: Searching for Democracy in America's Culture Wars.* New York: Free Press.

Jakobsen, Janet and Ann Pellegrini. 2003. *Love the Sin: Sexual Regulation and the Limits of Religious Tolerance.* New York: New York University Press.

Jenness, Valerie. 1993. *Making It Work: The Prostitutes Rights Movement in Perspective.* New York: Aldine DeGruyter.

Jones, Robert P. 2011. "Study: Strong Catholic Support for Gay Rights." *Washington Post*, March 24. Accessed from http://www.washingtonpost.com/blogs/guest-voices/post/why-do-catholics-support-gay-rights-when-the-hierarchydoes-not/2011/03/24/AFqObxVB_blog.html

Jones, Robert P., and Daniel Cox. 2010. "Old Alignments, Emerging Fault Lines: Religion in the 2010 Election and Beyond." *American Values Survey*, Public Religion Research Institute, November.

Kirk, Marshall, and Hunter Madsen. 1989. *After the Ball*. New York: Plume.

Lawrence v. Texas. Supreme Court Ruling. 539 U.S. 558 (2003). Accessed December 29, 2011, http://www.law.cornell.edu/supct/html/02-102.ZS.html.

Mills, C. Wright. 1956. *The Power Elite*. New York: Oxford University Press.

Moynihan, Daniel Patrick. 1965. *The Negro Family: The Case for National Action*. Washington, DC: U.S. Department of Labor, Office of Policy, Planning and Research.

——. 1996. *Miles to Go*. Cambridge, MA: Harvard University Press.

John Paul II, Pope. 1993. *Veritatis Splendor. Encyclical Letter Regarding Certain Fundamental Questions of Church's Moral Teaching*. Rome: The Vatican.

Public Religion Research Institute. 2011. "Majority of Americans Say They Support Same-Sex Marriage, Adoption by Gay and Lesbian Couples."

Rieff, Philip. 1966. *The Triumph of the Therapeutic: The Uses of Faith after Freud*. New York: Harper and Row. (Wilmington, DE: ISI Books, 2006 re-release)

——. 1973. *Fellow Teachers*. New York: Faber and Faber.

——. 2006. *Sacred Order/Social Order: My Life among the Deathworks*. Charlottesville: University of Virginia Press.

Salzman, Todd A., and Michael G. Lawler. 2008. *The Sexual Person: Toward a Renewed Catholic Anthropology*. Washington, DC: Georgetown University Press.

Satinover, Jeffrey. 1996. *Homosexuality and the Politics of Truth*. Grand Rapids, MI: Baker Books.

Simon, David, and Stanley Eitzen. 1993. *Elite Deviance*, 4th edition. Boston: Allyn and Bacon.

Sullins, D. Paul. 2010. "American Catholics and Same-sex Marriage." *Catholic Social Science Review*, 15: 97–123.

Sullivan, Andrew. 1996. *Virtually Normal*. New York: Vintage Books.

Sumner, Colin. 1994. *The Sociology of Deviance: An Obituary*. New York: Continuum Press.

Taylor, Charles. 1992. *The Ethics of Authenticity*. Cambridge, MA: Harvard University Press.

Tittle, Charles, and Raymond Paternoster. 2000. *Social Deviance and Crime: An Organizational and Theoretical Approach*. Los Angeles: Roxbury Publishing.

United States Conference of Catholic Bishops (USCCB). 2003. *Catechism of the Catholic Church*, 2nd Edition. New York: Doubleday.

Wilson, James Q. 2011. "Hard Times Fewer Crimes." *Wall Street Journal*, May 28: C1.

5

How a Catholic Grounding Can Contribute to the Empirical Social Sciences

Patrick Fagan

Belief in Objective Reality

The scientific project is a community of scholars intent on understanding reality to its fullest, in which the different disciplines take a particular part of reality to study, knowing they are limited by that constraint but that each has its own appropriate unique ways of observing and measuring its object of study. They know they are bound by the object of study, the limits this imposes and the methods appropriate, all resulting in each discipline's canons. The Catholic social scientist fits easily herein and becomes the friend and sometimes the guardian of science for his faith gives him an intellectual reverence for all of nature, knowing it comes from and is sustained continuously by God. All data point toward His underlying order. Both the functioning and malfunctioning are a manifestation of the same laws of nature, and even great disorder pays indirect homage to the order that should reign in its place.

It bears constant repetition that any and all of the following suggestions can come from social science practitioners of any religion or of no religion, though I suspect that social scientists who are practicing orthodox Jews would also more speedily, easily, and naturally come up with these or related suggestions, because they also have the same deep tradition of awareness of the unity between Creator and creation and have a long history of the cultivation of reason without ever suspecting it, in itself, to be an offense against Revelation. To them also may be applied the agenda that Catholics often refer to: faith seeking understanding.

This is but another way of pointing toward Natural Law: the acquired insight into the laws of physical and human nature and the deduction of binding rules of the physical, biological, or social orders. Thus the aphorism for the social scientist: "The social sciences well done cannot but illustrate the way God made man."

Yet the Catholic also brings another disposition that serves the social sciences well: he knows he cannot get a final fix on all truth, and especially is this so when only the insights of one discipline are under discussion. Though, as explained below, there is no such thing as a Catholic sociology, psychology, or social science, the Catholicism of any of its practitioners should make the discipline advance quicker and deeper, because the philosophical insights they bring to their study (in turn enriched by the philosophical implications of Christian theology) stimulate them to frequently propose unique hypotheses that arise from the rich philosophical grounding of Catholicism.

By contrast, other philosophical influences, especially those which can be bundled under the postmodernist label, frequently undermine the disciplines of the social sciences, especially because they foster the doubt, if not outright rejection, of the know-ability of reality. Such doubt or skepticism in a social scientist raises the question of what such a scientist is doing with his social science. If he does not believe in reality how can he measure it and how can he teach about it? If reality does not anchor his science what does? And if he has an anchor does it have a valid relationship to the social sciences? Or stated differently, can any ideology (the default replacement of philosophy) have a beneficent relationship to the social sciences? I contend it cannot, for ultimately it seeks power not truth.

This ideological default position, wherein the objective pursuit of truth is laid aside, is that such a search will be replaced with a pursuit of ideologically desired research findings. If the exercise of truth-seeking ceases to be the object of the discipline, in practice its place is taken by power-seeking to create the practitioner's unique view of "reality." (Catholics, however, can also fall into a similar ideological use of the social sciences if they pursue them only to confirm their conception of the Catholic faith. To do this is, at base, an abuse of both the discipline and of the Faith.)

Ideologues of either stripe will dismiss data and insights therefrom, which do not advance their ideological position. Thus the husbanding of "the data that does not fit" is the hallmark of the good social scientist, for therein are found the paths to advances in social sciences (and all other sciences), while the dismissal of "contrary data," merely because it is contrary, is the hallmark of the ideologue posing as social scientist.

Ideological Manipulation rather than Unbiased Truth Seeking

One of the greatest illustrations of the avoidance of reality in the social sciences, by denial or minimization, is most clearly to be seen in the phenomenon of abortion research.

The twentieth century rise in rates of abortion, as well as contraception, are two of the greatest changes ever in the history of human behavior, changes that occurred during a period of massive growth of the empirical social sciences. Given this co-occurrence one would expect social scientists to have been heavily engaged in studying these new phenomena. However that was not the case, intimating that major issues other than scientific inquiry may have been in play.

A major illustration of this phenomenon is the American Psychological Association's (APA) handling of its report on the state of knowledge of the psychological effects of abortion. It stands accused of not being a truly scholarly body on this issue by one who is not morally opposed to abortion, the much-published David Fergusson of New Zealand, director of the Christchurch Health and Development Longitudinal Survey, in his review of the literature review for his team's first research report on the effects of abortion (Fergusson, Horwood, and Ridder 2006). The Christchurch team had available to them what may well be the most intensely measured histories of men and women available in the social sciences, starting at birth and still continuing as they enter mid-adulthood. This team could, and did, control for all the potentially confounding variables in studying the effects of abortion on women at age 25. Fergusson's review of the literature on the effects of abortion was a maiden voyage for him, because he was, at that time, new to that subject.[1] In the discussion section of his team's article (after describing the results of the effects they found in young women who had abortion) the authors note:

> In particular, in its 2005 statement on abortion, the American Psychological Association concluded that "well-designed studies of psychological responses following abortion have consistently shown that risk of psychological harm is low...the percentage of women who experience clinically relevant distress is small and appears to be no greater than in general samples of women of reproductive age." This relatively strong conclusion about the absence of harm from abortion was based on a relatively small number of studies which had one or more of the following limitations: a) absence of comprehensive assessment of mental disorders; b) lack of comparison groups; and c) limited statistical controls. Furthermore the statement appears to disregard the findings of a number of studies that had claimed to show negative effects for abortion. (Fergusson, Horwood, and Ridder 2006, 22–23)

For a second illustration, the National Cancer Institute (NCI) stands similarly accused by a different scholar for its treatment of the research into the link between abortion and breast cancer. Joel Brind (2005), professor of biology and endocrinology at Baruch College, New York, delineates the scientific malfeasance of a government institute of science in his 25 page critique of their handling of their abortion-breast cancer research. Having recently edited a forthcoming paper on the issue of abortion and breast cancer (Lanfranchi, forthcoming), I became particularly familiar with the variables in play in the research questions delineated by Brind. What is notable in the history of that research is that for one side at least, it seems to be a battle, not a pursuit of clear knowledge.

In both these instances the APA and the NCI seemed bent on confounding, not parsing, the potentially active variables and their differential rates of impact. It seemed to this lay reader of the abortion-breast cancer literature that there were clear circumstances that *decreased* the risk of breast cancer for women who had abortions, other circumstances that *increased* the risk and, potentially, even a very few that may *almost certainly lead* to breast cancer.

With a scientific insistence on knowing reality as objectively as possible, a Catholic in this controversy would be as clear on what *decreases* the risk as much as he is clear on what *increases* the risk, gradually disaggregating the variables in play. It seems that the "pro-abortion NCI" is loath to draw attention to factors that may decrease breast cancer for women who have abortions for to do so would also bring attention to increasing rates of breast cancer for women with different abortion histories and backgrounds, thus opening up the comparison of variables and their differential rates of cancer occurrence.

The Elusive Study of Cause and Effect in Matters Individual and Social

The social sciences have a particular difficulty as a body of science: the cause-effect relationship is not always direct, and is often teleological (and this form of causation is often unrecognized in the social sciences). These sciences must also grapple with the issue of the free choice of human beings. Free choice often baffles the social sciences, always upsets its predictive validity models, and thus poses the constant challenge of delineating where choice begins and social conditioning ends or better and more complex still, how they overlap and interplay. However the work of the critical realists—especially Margaret Archer's (2003) *Structure, Agency, and Internal Dialogue* is forging a way through this morass for sociologists, psychologists, and public policy idealists. She links the three in a most needed way, while laying the intellectual rationale for the Catholic (or any) social scientist at odds with his professional colleagues, not necessarily on the personal level, but on the definition of the canons and mission of the social sciences themselves as they seek to participate in building "the good society."

A Social Science of the Immeasurable?

A social science of religion is not possible but a social science of religious behavior is. At the heart of religion is the person's relationship to God who cannot be observed, much less measured. Thus the relationship between God and man cannot be observed nor measured. It lies outside the canons of the discipline. However what can be observed and measured is the person's behavior while engaged in religious acts and his behavior after such acts. Measures of such behavior can include subjective reports on internal dialogue during religious behaviors. Though these present their own methodological difficulties, such difficulties can be dealt with within the science. Thus there can be a social science of religious behaviors, even intimate religious behaviors, and their correlates.

For those who do not believe in reality at all a social scientist of religious behavior must present severe difficulties and may even result in injustice, as has happened to some. In the first chapter of his recent book *More God, Less Crime*, Byron Johnson (2011) recounts his early days, on track for tenure at the University of Memphis, ironically as it turn out, in the Criminal Justice Department. After stellar work, publications, student reviews, and research grant awards he was fired without cause or comment a few months before his tenure review by the department head, backed by the dean. The dean told him he could fire him for the color of his eyes. But as his "friend" the provost told him he was let go because of his interest in religion and his religious work on campus. It turned out to be a blessing in disguise for Johnson as well as for the universities that subsequently hired him: determined to make his way in academia, he went on to become a heavyweight in religion research and now is co-director of the Institute for Studies of Religion at Baylor University. To date, during his career he has brought in $24 million in research grants. I suspect the University of Memphis belatedly regrets its call. But the main lesson is not the injustice but the anti-scientism of the department head and the dean. Neither were men of true science, yet they posed as such.

The Great Relationships, the Great Objects of Study

Leaving what must seem ethereal because much of it may be a long way off, to return to the more easily studied, a vast sea of research already opened up beckons yet more—namely, the domains of the great relationships: marriage, prayer, worship, and all the other social relationships embodied in the Ten Commandments. The probable interrelatedness of these findings adds yet another agenda, as does their connection to the flourishing or debilitation of the human condition. Much is underway in marital, sexual, and religious behavior research but the potential agenda is vast.

Grace Builds on Nature

The Thomistic aphorism that grace builds on nature opens a whole avenue of application of the social sciences to the work of the Church. In my own studies in the area of marriage, I see most powerfully how grace builds on nature—or stated in the negative, how one cannot expect grace to substitute what nature is meant to provide as a foundation. Or yet differently again, one cannot expect grace to substitute when nature is violated.

In marriage, Christian marriage needs to be built on sound natural marriage. And the study of marriage, of what makes it work well for non-believers as much as for believers, leads to basic insights on sexuality, communications, child-raising, finances, education, work and workplace issues, and the whole realm of self-control. In all of these, modern psychology and sociology have much to give, making for a better-rounded, full man or woman. Such a man and such a woman uniting in marriage will have a much better marriage and family than a man and woman without these cultivated gifts, strengths, or virtues.

When grace is added to all of this (through faith, prayer, and worship and even more with penance, fasting, and almsgiving) then we should expect to see marriage and family life thrive even more. The parsing out of these differences by sociologists and psychologists—a vast agenda in itself—will help the religiously-believing young man or woman to see nature at play in marriage more clearly. This will be especially helpful today as young couples seek the path to happiness and truth in our less institutionally-oriented modern culture. In our type of much more person-centered culture, it is even more imperative that the couple see and understand the good of nature (as well as the good of faith). Otherwise the person-centered goodness that could be theirs, of the kind developed by John Paul II, may instead become a debased self-centered relativism with all modern sufferings that come with the rejection or distancing of the other, rather than the growth that comes with the sacrifice of belonging to the other.

The social sciences have the potential to cast much light on the observable consequences of self-giving in marriage compared to those of self-seeking. It will not be a social science of the cross but nonetheless it will be an exciting parallel.

Catholic Sensibilities

Catholics, because they are realists, can live with the fact of man's constant tendency to undo the good already achieved and man's constant need to get along with others for his own benefit and happiness. Two pistons drive the social project: integration and disintegration. Both happen constantly at all levels of human functioning: that of the individual, of the married couple (parents), of the family, of the community with its local institutions (where we gather in group/role arrangements to carry out complex tasks, be they for profit or for a common non-profit good), right up to the provincial and national levels.

In most cases there is the desire to go forward to something better (fulfilling our goals) while contending with our tendencies, even habits, of undermining our own best efforts and seeing the same struggles in others. In other cases we see a dedication to destruction, such as in the habitual liar, thief, womanizer, criminal, corrupt factotum, or the power-seeking individual or group. Habits pile up at all these levels and can lead to either "golden ages" or to hells such as Nazi Germany or Leninist Russia. Our own society may be at a crossroads, in the danger Douglas Porpora (1990) presents in his critical realist study *How Holocausts Happen*: the danger of a society gradually accommodating to patterns of powerful evils. Cardinal George of Chicago seems to think so in his oft quoted "I expect to die in bed, my successor will die in prison and his successor will die a martyr in the public square."

Catholics can understand these patterns of evil in either smaller or bigger manifestations, given their sense of their own faults and personal evils (constantly brought home to them in the regular confession of their sins). There is the difficulty of breaking free from these patterns so as to be able to move forward, or the slow pace at which this seems to happen even with the best of efforts (again, brought home in confessing the same sins repeatedly for decades on end, even if in different forms or levels of severity). Further, they readily understand and empathize with the social nature of man: how we are influenced by our peers, by the example of others, by what we read (the ideas of others), and what conversations we partake of. Confession constantly teaches us about ourselves and our social nature.

The sociology of divorce and out of wedlock births and sex outside of marriage all drive this home. For instance, in my estimation, the single most powerful finding in the social sciences is the correlation between the number of sexual partners before marriage and the subsequent probability of divorce. We know from the National Survey of Family Growth (Fagan 2010) that the rates of intactness of the marriages of women between ages 30 to 44 are strongly related to this issue. For those whose first sexual partner was their husband (even without knowing anything about the men they married), 80 percent were still in that marriage. If they had one sexual partner outside of marriage (normally before the marriage) the rate dropped to 54 percent, and with two sexual partners before marriage it dropped to 44 percent. In turn this compounds through the generations because children of divorced parents are much more inclined to become sexually active with multiple partners, thus perpetuating and widening the destructive cycle (Fagan and Churchill 2012).

Thus Catholics can make sense of both good and evil. We can empathize with patterns of evil becoming entrenched because we experience the same in ourselves at our own levels, and we can see the need for building and preserving patterns and habits of good. These strengths are acquired with effort. We see we are blessed when we have others who invest their time and energy in helping us acquire these strengths, such as parents, teachers, pastors, religious, and other kind folk who so dedicate their lives. Catholics are aware that all this going upwards toward good and toward increased strength is a constant struggle and investment of time and effort. We know (again from experience) that we can let go and slide backwards; and both in ourselves and in others we are close to or have been close to, we can see that backsliding can become habitual and lead to very different levels of living out our lives. "There but for the grace of God go I."

Thus Catholics bring a sense of realism to our psychological and sociological research. We know the relationship between grace, effort, prayer, and the good works of others toward us to the outcomes in our lives. And we know the difference between what is observable and what is not, with much of what is most important, most idiosyncratic and therefore most personal being beyond what we can observe with our senses, much less measure with our science. Yet we know that what we see and measure is very important for it shapes the perception of realities upon which we act. Knowledge begins with the senses. In that we are grounded.

Two Main Projects

There are two projects that seem most needed yet also seem to fly in the face of contemporary postmodern social science. First is a grand synthesis of the empirical findings of the social sciences, for by definition they can offer no organizing principle that holds all together. The second is the construction of a social science model of how society works or falls apart—again because they can offer no organizing principle of how people can work together for the common good, nor do they seem inclined to catalog patterns of evil and their consequences.

The author was blessed to know John Boyd, designer of the F-15 and F-16 jets, author of the OODA loop insight and many other major military accomplishments and breakthroughs. One of his favorite sayings was "To call me an analyst is to insult me as a half-wit: analysis is only half the game, the other half is synthesis." Every time a new analytic insight is uncovered a new integration (synthesis) of the impacts of that analytic insight beckons and is needed. We synthesize even as we analyze.

In the physical sciences, because new discoveries are so often applied almost immediately, there is a lot of ongoing integration of new analytic insights into the corpus of knowledge of the physical world. Not so in the social sciences. Man himself (at the individual and social levels) is the ever-ongoing synthesis, thus perhaps this reality obfuscates the challenge of such synthesis projects. Maybe the complexity of man and society flag the immensity of the challenge and undermine the motivation and practice of such syntheses. Nevertheless it must be done.

The first great synthesis is that of the already published literature where Catholics ought to be to the fore in trying to synthesize the analytic findings because, as these are integrated they ought to come together in a way which illustrates human nature as moral philosophy and moral theology would have us expect things to be. Thus the moral sciences would be one natural source to provide a hypothetical framework for this synthesis of the empirical, social science findings.

However, as those who disagree with realism in philosophy will be quick to point out (to us but seemingly rarely to themselves) there is a big danger of bias in such synthesis. This is where the Catholic will be quick to seek both contrary data as well as the critique of those who disagree with the hypothesis in the first place. Contrary data is uniquely important to the realist because it is that most "social science based" correction available to him in keeping him honest and unbiased. Like a miser hoarding his gold, the Catholic social scientist will hoard "contrary data" until the conflict is reconciled through new insight and exploration and the data is able to be integrated into the synthesis. This can happen either through the rejection of the data through repeated experiments or observations, or through the rearranging of the synthesis, which is especially necessary if the contrary data is repeatedly found to be true. When this happens the contrary data will have been the royal road to the new insights as well as being significantly corrective of the prior more limited form the synthesis had.

The second project that beckons is the building of a different form of synthesis: a dynamic synthesis model of how society works. In this project we attempt to approximate the bigger social changes given differences in major social variables. For instance, given the levels of intactness of marriage can social scientists inform those who lead society on the differential impacts these have on the many different tasks of society? Here we would consider impacts on fertility and the next generation, levels of education, of income, of savings, of health and longevity, of crime, of mental health or diseases. Can we parse this still further when we posit different family configurations in levels of divorce, out of wedlock births, abortions, and cohabitations (stable or serial)? Can we approximate the changes in society in such variables if the levels of weekly worship of God rise or fall? Can we approximate the changes throughout society if education levels truly rise or fall, or if income levels truly rise or fall? Given the five fundamental institutions of society—namely, family, religion, education, marketplace, and government—what are the changes in all the other four if there are significant changes in just one of these five?

To answer these questions may seem a monumental task but it can be made much simpler than it seems. We have two great data resources in the United States, unmatched anywhere else in the world. We have a very detailed decennial census and we have many longitudinal surveys, which means we can track the life course of many individuals and families and the impact that changes in the five basic institutions (tasks) on that life course. And finally we have even more, nationally representative special-topic, cross-sectional surveys. All of these can gradually be knit together to form a large data pool in which to detect the inter-relationships we want to address: namely, those that ought to illuminate natural law in action, or in other words, virtuous behavior leading to thriving and vices leading to dysfunction.

In many ways the impact of change at the family level is more important than the impact of change at the national level because people live out their lives at the family level, not the national. They feel more capable and indeed are more capable of controlling their own family life than of affecting national life. However in terms of public discourse about modeling the impacts on society, the story is much the same, because the impact on the family writ millions of times will likely be the impact on the nation.

An accurate modeling of how society works will, in theory, be no different whether done by Catholics or non-Catholics. However in reality the final product may be quite different. For instance, who but Catholics will model the impact of contraception on the behaviors related to family, religious practice, education performance, income and savings, or levels of crime? Who else will be motivated to learn how to measure the impact of abortion combined with contraception, or even simpler still: the impact of contraception on rates of abortion?

The compounding complexity of merging the impacts is a great statistical (modeling) challenge. But man did not land on the moon without a plan to get there and even before man set about the plan the challenge had first to be conceived, issued, and accepted.

Both these projects will prompt frequent discourses with philosophy, or even theology. This is a natural and significant interdisciplinary contribution from the Catholic habit of seeing all of creation as coming from the Creator, whether it be empirical social or natural sciences, the insights of philosophy gained by human reason, the insights of theology gained by the application of reason to Revelation, or of Revelation itself. For the Catholic there is ultimately no conflict between these disparate realms of knowledge, and when conflict seems to exist we delight in it because in identifying the sources of the conflict and in harnessing the intellect to reconcile them we make great strides in learning.

One particular realm of moral philosophy that urgently beckons the social scientist today is the social scientific study of the virtues and vices: their modes of acquisition and loss, and the optimum conditions for the acquisition of virtues and the shedding of vices. Cognitive behavioral psychology is making rapid advances in this field. Sociology has yet to follow apace.

Projects that Beckon

I think several big tasks beckon for Catholics who are social scientists: the integration of the constantly growing corpus of empirical research into an emergent synthesis, plus a constantly changing encyclopedia of the findings of the social sciences. These can be broken down into a number of more specific activities in the empirical social sciences that might not be undertaken if Catholic social scientists do not lead therein:

1. Clarifying anew the canons of the empirical social sciences;
2. Developing a philosophical-cum-statistical curriculum for social scientists that covers all forms of causation, exploring their metaphysical nature as well as their statistical implications and limitations;
3. Cultivating a discourse with moral philosophy on the implications for moral philosophy of the findings of the social sciences, and in turn the clarifying of hypotheses to be explored empirically by the quantitative social sciences, where these are empirically feasible;
4. Compiling an empirical research agenda that stems from a Catholic sensitivity (but is not Catholic) on social science issues being neglected by the mainstream of the social sciences;
5. Encouraging the parallel development of a social science of spiritual behavior as well as religious behavior;
6. Broadening the scope of the social science of the spiritual to include the major human relationships identified above;
7. Compiling an ongoing list of good empirical data that seems contrary to Catholic moral teaching, so that it may serve as a stimulus to further exploration both empirically as well as philosophically, especially should that contrariness persist in the data;
8. In collaboration with all social scientists of goodwill, building a grand ongoing synthesis of the empirical findings of the social sciences;
9. In collaboration with all social scientists of goodwill, building a model of how society works;
10. Identifying and cultivating the brightest students so inclined to take on the course of studies necessary to become an expert social scientist, so that they may influence the discipline for good, and so that they in turn will come in contact with students they can similarly cultivate for the very same ends of good social science in the service of all humanity.

A Catholic Social Science?

Is all this a Catholic social science?

The term "Catholic sociology" as used in the introduction is employed to facilitate discourse. Functionally, "Catholic sociology" is simply sociology stimulated by hypotheses that are likely generated only by Catholics, given their unique sensitivities. The social science part is not Catholic because its solid findings will be universal and repeatable by any competent social scientist. However, such social science is catholic in a different way: it is universal. It holds for all men.

Thus it is that a Catholic social scientist is naturally a catholic social scientist. He seeks the universals, while knowing that culture and social conditions modify behaviors and attitudes. He is at home with all data as long as it is methodologically robust, and he has a predilection for contrary data. Assuming he is as accomplished in knowledge and skills as they are such dispositions make of him a good peer of the best in his field.

Notes

1. Personal communication by phone, shortly after publication of his first study.

Bibliography

Archer, Margaret. 2003. *Structure, Agency, and Internal Dialogue*. Cambridge, UK: Cambridge University Press.
Brind, Joel. 2005. "The Abortion-Breast Cancer Connection." *The National Bioethics Quarterly*, Summer: 303–29.
Fagan, Patrick. 2010. "Chastity and How Society Works." Presentation at Georgetown University. Accessed January 16, 2012, http://marri.us/research/powerpoints.
Fagan, Patrick F., and Aaron Churchill. 2012. "The Effects of Divorce on Children." Washington, DC: Marriage & Religion Research Institute. Accessed January 11, 2012, http://marri.us/effects-divorce-children.
Fergusson, David M., L. John Horwood, and Elizabeth M. Ridder. 2006. "Abortion in Young Women and Subsequent Mental Health." *Journal of Child Psychology and Psychiatry*, 47 (1): 16–24.
Johnson, Byron. 2011. *More God, Less Crime: Why Faith Matters and How It Could Matter More*. West Conshohocken, PA: Templeton Press.
Lanfranchi, Angela, M.D. forthcoming. "Advances in Human Biology and Continued Epidemiological Studies Prove a Link between Abortion and Breast Cancer." Washington, DC: Marriage and Religion Research Institute.
Porpora, Douglas. 1990. *How Holocausts Happen: The United States in Central America*. Philadelphia: Temple University Press.

6

A Cohort Analysis of Happiness among Young Adults

G. Alexander Ross and Michael C. Wagner

Although the renewal of an explicitly Catholic approach to sociology is well under way, the phrase, "Catholic sociology," is puzzling to many. As we hope the present chapter will illustrate, such an approach does not involve distinct logical or methodological tools. Careful logical reasoning and competent application of statistical and methodological techniques are important whether one approaches social questions from a Catholic or a secular framework. Rather, it is in the theological and philosophical assumptions about the nature of man and his social reality that a Catholic approach will display its uniqueness. A sociologist who approaches his craft from an authentically Catholic framework will recognize that we are created in the image and likeness of God, a likeness that includes an inherently social nature that draws us into relationship with our fellow men and with God. He will recognize also the reality of original sin, that we have fallen from grace and cannot reach true happiness by our own power alone but are in need of the sanctifying grace of our Redeemer, Jesus Christ. A Catholic sociologist will, therefore, be skeptical of approaches to social theory that treat the moral realm as a mere social construction, that underestimate our inherent attraction to and need for human relationships, or that put no limits on our power to reshape our social reality.

It is within this Catholic orientation that we were drawn to examine for this volume significant changes that have been observed among young adults in American society. Recent popular accounts have noted a growing reluctance in this age group to embrace the status of adulthood (Henig 2010; Koganzon 2010). Common sociological indicators of adult status are economic and residential independence, termination of schooling, marriage, and parenthood. Changes in two of these indicators have been especially striking over the past few decades. For example, the percentage of 18- to 24-year-olds currently enrolled in college increased from 26 percent in 1970 to 41 percent in 2009 (U.S. Census Bureau 2009). During this same period marriage among young adults declined steeply; the percentage of 18- to 24-year-olds currently married dropped from 42 percent in 1970 to 13 percent in 2009 (U.S. Census Bureau 1971; 2011).

The economic and demographic changes over the past half century that have heightened the influence of the young in developed societies may explain much of this tendency to postpone adulthood. Market forces that have responded to the concentration of large cohorts of affluent young adults in institutional (educational) settings have given rise to a youth culture that has altered much of modern life. Patterns of thought, speech, and dress, tastes in music, media and popular culture, have all been heavily influenced by the preferences of young people (West 2007). It is possible that this greater esteem for youth has enabled young adults to remain in their favored status.

The influence of youth culture has been manifested particularly in challenges to normative expectations regarding sexual relationships (Regnerus and Uecker 2010). Traditional sexual norms have in the past encouraged young adults to assume the adult responsibilities of forming families and settling into occupations that can financially support them. However, the normalization of premarital sex, abetted by the widespread acceptance and availability of contraception and abortion, has divorced sexual behavior from the permanent and exclusive commitments of marriage. For example, among many current college students, conventional patterns of dating in which over time young people develop a relationship that may later lead to sexual intimacy have been replaced by sexual encounters between two previously unacquainted people (Hendershott and Dunn 2011, 6). These "hook-ups" involve no expectation of a future relationship.

Even more widespread is the practice of cohabitation, particularly among those with less than a college education (Popenoe 2008; Wilcox 2010). In 1970, the Census Bureau estimated the number of unmarried opposite-sex couples to be approximately one-half million; by 2010, that estimate had grown to more than 7.5 million unmarried couples, of which 24 percent contained a female partner between the ages of 15 and 24 years (U.S. Census Bureau 2010). By their nature, cohabitation and "hooking-up" evade the permanent commitments traditionally associated with sexual relationships. These behaviors exemplify the increasingly common patterns by which many young people avoid the commitments associated with adult life.

This tendency to extend the adolescent or pre-adult stage has even given rise to the claim of a newly discovered developmental stage called "emerging adulthood" (Arnett 2000). The psychologist Jeffrey Arnett finds that in recent years, for those living in economically developed societies, the ages 18 to 25 have become "a time of exploration and instability" (4). He characterizes this new stage by specifying five patterns exhibited by the most recent cohorts of 18- to 25-year-olds: identity explorations, instability, self-focus, feeling in-between, and perceiving possibilities. His evaluation of this new developmental stage is strongly positive; he writes that "it is the age of possibilities, when optimism is high and people have an unparalleled opportunity to transform their lives" (7). "More than ever before," he states, "coming of age in the 21st century means learning to stand alone as a self-sufficient person, capable of making choices and decisions independently from among a wide range of possibilities" (4).

Though we are unconvinced that emerging adulthood should be considered a new developmental stage, our focus in this chapter is on the presumption that an extended period of self-discovery and exploration prior to the commitments of adulthood is beneficial for the age group Arnett describes. Our Catholic perspective leads us to question this presumption, because we believe it exaggerates the importance of autonomy for the human person and it neglects the moral content of the behaviors exhibited. But we can let these young adults speak for themselves about this question by asking them to evaluate for themselves the state of their lives. Do the self-reports of well-being and happiness of the cohorts who most exhibit the emerging-adult patterns of self-focus and extended exploration indicate that they are happier and more satisfied with their lives than earlier cohorts?

Methods

To examine this question we have turned to the comprehensive data file of the General Social Survey (GSS) for the years 1972–2010 (T. Smith, et al 2011) and constructed a series of four birth cohorts of 18- to 25-year-olds. Each of the cohorts comprises eight consecutive birth years, roughly approximating the decades of the '50s, '60s, '70s, and '80s. Our intention is to compare the self-reported happiness of young adults born in each of these four decades.

In constructing the cohorts, it was important that each cohort contain a full complement of the relevant ages (18 to 25) so as to avoid artificially modifying the age structures of the cohorts constructed. Because the first GSS was conducted in 1972, the birth cohort of 1954 is the earliest birth year for which the GSS includes all the ages from 18 to 25. At the other end of the time spectrum, 1985 is the last cohort that can be included because for 2010, the latest year of the GSS, 1985 is the last birth cohort for which the GSS includes all the ages from 18 to 25. This span of time from 1954 to 1985 includes 32 birth years, conveniently divisible by 8 into four cohort groups. The resulting four cohort groups are specified in table 6.1 along with counts of the number of respondents by age in each cohort.

Table 6.1. Frequency counts of respondents by birth cohort and age, GSS 1972–2010

Age of respondent	Birth cohort			
	1954–1961	1962–1969	1970–1977	1978–1985
18	49	30	29	24
19	201	163	129	138
20	182	178	134	140
21	182	216	176	167
22	192	239	129	193
23	237	209	218	215
24	228	195	206	203
25	247	265	230	203
Total	1,518	1,495	1,251	1,283

To measure happiness we utilized a conventional self-report measure. In comparisons with a variety of non-self-report measures, Sandvik, Diener, and Seidlitz (1993) have demonstrated that self-reports—even single-item measures—can provide valid assessments of subjective well-being. Since its inception, the GSS has employed a simple three-category self-report of trait happiness under the variable name HAPPY. This question was worded identically in all years of the GSS: "Taken all together, how would you say things are these days—would you say that you are very happy, pretty happy, or not too happy?" In this study, we reversed the original codes given to the answers—we coded very happy as 3, pretty happy as 2, and not too happy as 1—resulting in a simple ordinal measure for which higher values indicate greater self-reported happiness.

When examining change over time, one must guard against variation in the measuring instrument. In the case of the variable HAPPY, Smith reports that some inadvertent measurement variation did occur in the GSS (Smith 1985; 1990). In all years other than 1972, a question on marital happiness (HAPMAR) preceded HAPPY. Furthermore, in every year other than 1972 and 1985, HAPPY was preceded by a five-item satisfaction scale. Testing at the GSS found evidence that scores on personal happiness are higher for married people when preceded by an item on marital happiness and significantly lower for all respondents when not preceded by the five-item satisfaction scale (Smith 1990). By modifying the GSS sampling weights in the data set with a procedure developed by Stevenson and Wolfers (2008), we adjusted the data for these variations. We also modified the data set by eliminating the 1982 and 1987 GSS over-samples of the black population and dropping the 2006 and 2008 interviews that would have been excluded as a language problem had Spanish not been offered in those two years.

Description of the Cohorts

Before examining any variation in happiness among the four cohorts, it is important to test whether the most recent cohorts did in fact exhibit a greater tendency to postpone entrance into adult roles as claimed in the literature cited above. In tables 6.2 and 6.3 below we compare the four cohorts we have constructed on several indicators related to adult status.

Table 6.2 displays the marital and parental status of the four cohorts. The percent married reported in the table declines noticeably and consistently from the earliest to the most recent cohort. For the '50s cohort (1954–1961), 33 percent of the respondents were married, while the cohorts of the '60s (1962–1969), '70s (1970–1977), and '80s (1978–1985), contained declining percentages of 24 percent, 20 percent, and 15 percent married, respectively. The percent married in the most recent cohort, therefore, was less than half the percentage reported for the earliest of the cohorts. As a test of the statistical significance of the pattern displayed by the data, a probit regression of marital status on birth cohort found that the marital status of the '80s cohort was significantly lower than all three of the earlier cohorts ($p < .01$).

Table 6.2. Marital and parental status in percent, by cohort, ages 18 to 25, GSS 1972–2010

Birth cohort	% Married	% Who Are Parents	% Who Are Married Parents
1954–1961	33.0%	25.8%	18.7%
	1477	*1463*	*1477*
1962–1969	23.6%	20.6%	12.1%
	1425	*1421*	*1425*
1970–1977	19.6%	24.1%	11.6%
	1251	*1248*	*1251*
1978–1985	15.3%	24.5%	8.9%
	1266	*1264*	*1266*

Note: Weighted samples, cell frequencies in italics

Table 6.2 also provides information regarding parental status of the four cohorts. No clear pattern of change is visible when examining the percentage of respondents in the four cohorts who were parents. For three of the cohorts, approximately one-quarter of the respondents were parents, while the '60s cohort had an only slightly lower percentage (21 percent) of parents. The percentage of the cohorts who were *married* parents, however, does display a noticeable pattern, and it is one that is consistent with the observation of a tendency to postpone the adoption of the adult role that grows with each cohort. While 19 percent of the '50s cohort had assumed the adult role of married parent, only 9 perpercent of the '80s cohort had done so. In other words, the four cohorts display no marked difference between the likelihood of having children, but they do exhibit an increasing reluctance both to marry and to have children. As a means to confirm the statistical significance of this pattern, a probit regression of married-parent status on birth cohort found that the married-parent status of the '80s cohort was significantly lower than all three of the earlier cohorts ($p < .05$).

Contrasts between the cohorts in employment and educational status are displayed in table 6.3. No statistically significant difference is visible between the cohorts in the percentage working full time, but the table does exhibit an increasing tendency among the cohorts to stay in school longer. Among the 18- to 25-year-old members of the '50s cohort, 15 percent reported to the GSS that they were currently in school, while the comparable percentage for the '60s and '70s cohorts was just short of 18 percent, and for the '80s cohort, nearly 20 percent. A probit regression of current school attendance on cohort found that only the difference between the '50s and the '80s cohorts was statistically significant ($p > .01$).

Table 6.3. Employment and educational status, by cohort, ages 18 to 25, GSS 1972–2010

Birth cohort	% Working full time	% Currently in School	% with Degree beyond High School
1954–1961	46.6%	15.0%	11.7%
	1477	*1477*	*1472*
1962–1969	42.9%	17.6%	12.1%
	1425	*1425*	*1419*
1970–1977	45.8%	17.7%	14.3%
	1251	*1251*	*1246*
1978–1985	43.2%	19.8%	18.2%
	1265	*1265*	*1258*

Note: Weighted samples, cell frequencies in italics

Table 6.3 also demonstrates that the percentage reporting an educational degree beyond high school increased from earlier to later cohorts. Among the 18- to 25-year-olds in both the '50s and '60s cohorts, about 12 percent received a degree beyond high school, among the '70s cohort a little more than 14 percent did, and among the '80s cohort, just above 18 percent reported receiving an educational degree greater than a high school diploma. A probit regression of reception of a degree beyond high school on cohort found that the educational attainment of the '80s cohort was significantly greater than all three of the earlier cohorts (p < .05).

Summarizing these findings, we can say that they confirm a pattern consistent with the observations made in the literature regarding the tendency of the most recent cohorts of young adults to take longer to leave the statuses associated with youth and enter those associated with adulthood. Particularly with respect to marital commitments and duration in school, the most recent cohort—what we are calling here the '80s cohort, born within the years 1978 to 1985—displays the greatest tendency to postpone entrance into a fully adult role.

Assuming Arnett's claim that the age period of 18 to 25 years of age that he labels emerging adulthood is one of "possibilities" and "high optimism," one would expect to find that the cohort that most closely approximates this pattern of extended role exploration and self-focus would report greater satisfaction with their lives. Given that the '80s cohort—the most recent cohort analyzable with our data—most closely meets Arnett's criteria, we propose to test the hypothesis that this cohort will exhibit greater self-reported happiness than the three earlier cohorts.

Results

To compare the levels of self-reported happiness for the four cohorts of 18- to 25-year-olds, we constructed ordered probit regressions of self-reported happiness on cohort. We employed the technique of probit regression because the measurement characteristics of the dependent variable did not conform to the requirements of OLS regression. A probit coefficient can be interpreted as an estimate of the change in the z-score of the cumulative normal probability distribution of the dependent variable resulting from a change of one unit in the independent or predictor variable.

We entered the independent variable into the regression as three indicator variables for the '50s, '60s, and '70s cohorts, with the '80s cohort (1978–1985) serving as the base. By specifying the '80s cohort as the base, we are able to treat the coefficient reported for each cohort indicator as a measure of the difference between that cohort's happiness and the happiness of the '80s cohort. A negative coefficient for a particular cohort signifies lower happiness for that cohort relative to the '80s cohort. Table 6.4 reports the coefficients for two ordered probit models, one without controls for exogenous variables and one with controls.

Although our hypothesis based on Arnett's presumption was that the '80s cohort would report greater happiness, none of the three uncontrolled coefficients in the first model of table 6.4 is negative. The coefficients are small, from 0.062 to 0.136, and only one of them reaches statistical significance; but being positive, they do not support the hypothesis that the '80s cohort reports greater happiness than the three earlier cohorts.

Model 2 in table 6.4 includes a series of exogenous control variables. These were added to establish more comparability between the cohorts by statistically controlling for factors external and temporally prior to the theoretical model. For example, race and sex are usually significantly associated with happiness, yet we do not want differences in the race or sex composition of the cohorts to influence our results. The exogenous variables included in the second model are sex (female indicator), age, race (black indicator), foreign childhood (an indicator of foreign residence at 16 years of age),[1] and two indicators of mother's education (respondent's mother earned a high school degree and respondent's mother earned a college degree).

Table 6.4. Ordered probit regression models of self-reported happiness on cohort, 18- to 25-year-olds, GSS 1972–2010

Dependent variable: "Taken all together, how would you say things are these days—would you say that you are very happy, pretty happy, or not too happy?"						
	(1)			(2)		
Regression coefficients	Ordered probit	Stand. Error	Prob.	Ordered probit	Stand. Error	Prob.
Cohort indicators **(80s cohort is base)**						
'50s cohort (1954–62)	0.062	0.055	0.266	0.133*	0.058	0.022
'60s cohort (1963–69)	0.136*	0.055	0.013	0.172***	0.057	0.002
'70s cohort (1970–77)	0.075	0.056	0.183	0.096	0.058	0.102
Exogenous control **variables**						
Female				0.143***	0.037	0.000
Age				0.014	0.009	0.109
Black				−0.378***	0.060	0.000
Foreign resident @16				−0.081	0.127	0.521
Mother has h.s. degree				0.179***	0.046	0.000
Mother has college degree				0.374***	0.063	0.000

Note: Weighted samples. Probabilities reported as 0.000 should be understood as indicating a probability of less than .0005. n for model 1 = 4993; n for model 2 = 4618. * p < 0.05, ** p < 0.01, *** p < 0.005

For the model including the exogenous controls for sex, age, race, foreign status, and mother's education, the probit coefficients not only remain positive, but increase in size and significance. The coefficients in model 2 in table 6.4 indicate that both the '50s and '60s cohorts report significantly higher self-reported happiness than the '80s cohort. The coefficient for the '70s cohort also displays a positive sign, though it is not statistically significant. However, a post-estimation test of the overall effect of the three cohort indicators was statistically significant ($\chi^2(3) = 9.68$, p = 0.022).

The greater size and significance of the positive coefficients displayed by model 2 compared to model 1 can be explained by a more careful examination of the exogenous controls. Specifically, it appears that it is especially mother's education that acts to suppress the model 1 differences between the cohorts in self-reported happiness. One can see from the coefficients reported in table 6.4 (0.179 and 0.374, for "mother has high school degree" and "mother has college degree," respectively) that mother's education is a factor that displays a positive association with respondent's self-reported happiness. In an analysis not shown here, we found that mother's education increased in value from the '50s to the '80s cohort. This resulted in an artificially higher level of happiness among the '80s cohort. By controlling for this variable, as we do in model 2, the true differences in happiness between the cohorts become more visible.

In summary, contrary to the hypothesis that the most recent cohort would display higher levels of self-reported happiness than the earlier cohorts, the results point us in the opposite direction. All reported cohort coefficients are positive, and three of the six are statistically significant. These data lend no support to the hypothesis that those in the most recent cohort of 18- to 25-year-olds are happier than earlier cohorts.

Exploration of Mediating Variables

To observe that the most recent cohort is less happy than the earlier cohorts does not, however, explain precisely why this is the case. The two sets of factors examined above in tables 6.2 and 6.3—the family status variables of marriage and parenthood and the education/occupation variables—display striking contrasts between the cohorts. These are likely candidates to explain the diminished happiness among the '80s cohort, but further analysis is necessary in order to demonstrate this. To test how these factors may account for the difference in happiness displayed by the four cohorts, we added them to the regression models in order to observe their impact on the original cohort coefficients.

Table 6.5 displays two ordered probit regression models of self-reported happiness on cohort with different sets of mediating variables. Both models contain the same cohort indicators and exogenous control variables specified in table 6.4 (model 2). Model 3 in table 6.5 also includes two mediating variables serving as indicators of marital and family status: whether the respondent is currently married or is a parent of at least one child. Model 4 contains a different set of mediating variables. In this latter model, we include three indicators of educational and employment status: whether the respondent is employed full time, is currently in school, or has earned a degree beyond high school. What we want to test with these two models is whether the original coefficients for the cohort indicators decrease in value upon the introduction of the set of mediating variables. The decline of a statistical association when one controls for a mediating variable usually indicates that the mediating variable provides an explanation or interpretation of the original relationship (Rosenberg 1968).

Table 6.5. Ordered probit regression models of self-reported happiness on cohort, with mediating variables, 18- to 25-year-olds, GSS 1972–2010

Dependent variable: "Taken all together, how would you say things are these days—would you say that you are very happy, pretty happy, or not too happy?"						
	(3)			(4)		
Regression coefficients	Ordered probit	Stand. Error	Prob.	Ordered probit	Stand. Error	Prob.
Cohort indicators (80s cohort is base)						
'50s cohort (1954–62)	0.065	0.059	0.273	0.140*	0.058	0.016
'60s cohort (1963–69)	0.131*	0.058	0.024	0.189***	0.057	0.001
'70s cohort (1970–77)	0.080	0.059	0.174	0.107	0.059	0.068
Exogenous control variables						
Female	0.126***	0.038	0.001	0.162***	0.038	0.000
Age	0.006	0.009	0.513	−0.007	0.010	0.478
Black	−0.273***	0.062	0.000	−0.349***	0.060	0.000
Foreign resident @16	−0.114	0.127	0.367	−0.115	0.126	0.363
Mother has h.s. degree	0.171***	0.047	0.000	0.141***	0.047	0.003
Mother has college degree	0.380***	0.066	0.000	0.289***	0.066	0.000
Mediating variables						
Married	0.444***	0.051	0.000			
Parent	−0.318***	0.050	0.000			
Works full time				0.241***	0.043	0.000
In school				0.284***	0.055	0.000
Degree beyond high school				0.326***	0.058	0.000

Note: Weighted samples. Probabilities reported as 0.000 should be understood as indicating a probability of less than .0005. n for model 3 = 4597; n for model 4 = 4601. * p < 0.05, ** p < 0.01, *** p < 0.005

Examining model 3 in table 6.5, we find that both of our family status indicators are highly significant. The strongest association is between marriage and self-reported happiness; this relationship is positive (0.444), indicating that 18- to 25-year-olds who are married report significantly higher happiness than those who are not married. Nearly as strong is the association between parental status and happiness; however, the sign of this coefficient is reversed (−0.318). Being a parent is negatively associated with self-reported happiness, most likely because of the greater stresses in a household with small children. Although not shown here, we examined the interaction between the married and parent indicators and found it not to be statistically significant.

Our principal interest in the model, however, is the effect of the addition of the mediating variables on the cohort coefficients. Comparing model 3 in table 6.5 to model 2 in table 6.4, we find that all three associations have decreased in strength. With the inclusion of the family status variables, the coefficient for the '50s cohort declined from 0.133 to 0.065; for the '60s cohort, from 0.172 to 0.131; and for the '70s cohort, from 0.096 to 0.080. A post-estimation test found that the overall effect of the three cohort indicators was no longer significant ($\chi^2(3) = 5.30$, p = 0.151). This statistical effect provides evidence that these family status variables explain in part the difference in self-reported happiness between the four cohorts.

Model 4 in table 6.5 examines the impact of the addition as mediating variables of the indicators of educational and employment status. We see, first of all, that all three coefficients are positive and highly significant. Working full time, being currently in school, and earning a degree beyond high school are all associated with higher levels of happiness. Note, however, that with the addition of these three mediating variables, the cohort coefficients measuring the differences between the cohorts in self-reported happiness maintain their strength. When comparing these coefficients in model 4 of table 6.5 to those in model 2 of table 6.4, we see that all three coefficients rose slightly with the inclusion of educational and employment status mediators. For the '50s cohort, the value of the coefficient changed from 0.133 to 0.140; for the '60s cohort, from 0.172 to 0.189; and for the '70s cohort, from 0.096 to 0.107. We applied a post-estimation test to the overall effect of the three cohort indicators in this model and found it to be statistically significant ($\chi^2(3) = 11.28$, p = 0.010). Thus, unlike the effect produced by the family status mediators, the educational and employment status variables do not appear to account for the observed difference in happiness between the cohorts.

In summary, while variables measuring educational and employment status of the respondents do not appear to account for the differences in self-reported happiness between the cohorts, the family status variables of marriage and parenthood do offer us a partial interpretation. However, although the cohort indicators taken together dropped from significance when the family status variables were entered into the regression, it should be noted that the coefficient for the '60s cohort did remain statistically significant, though at reduced strength. In other words, differences in family status do not entirely explain the lower level of happiness displayed by the '80s cohort. Nevertheless, of two major patterns of change experienced especially by the most recent cohort, it appears likely that it is the decline in marriage rather than the prolonging of education that accounts in part for the reduced happiness experienced by the '80s cohort.

Discussion

Our results indicate that, in contrast to Arnett's positive evaluation of the pattern of extended role exploration and self-focus characterizing the most recent cohort of young adults, these young people themselves do not appear to share his appraisal of this period of their lives. Controlling for a variety of exogenous factors that might otherwise act to distort the comparisons made, our regression model (model 2, table 6.4) showed that the most recent cohort of young adults reported the lowest level of subjective well-being among the cohorts studied. We then entered into our models two sets of mediating variables in an attempt to specify an explanation for the lower happiness reported by the '80s cohort (table 6.5). The results of these additional models suggested that changes in family status—particularly, lower levels of marriage—appeared to account in part for the differences displayed; however, a full explanation of the variation in happiness among the cohorts was not provided by our data.

In short, we have good evidence that young adults in the most recent cohort report lower happiness than earlier cohorts; yet, other than pointing to the negative impact from a change in family status for the most recent cohorts, our data are not able to specify fully the reasons that young people are less sanguine about this period of their lives than Arnett's positive appraisal of the emerging-adult pattern would predict. We can, however, suggest some likely explanations consistent with our analysis.

We would note, first of all, that Arnett's (2006) theoretical perspective entails a highly individualistic conception of the human person. In his description of emerging adulthood, he celebrates the exploration of self-identity and the personal choices to be made among a range of possibilities. "Emerging adults are self-focused in the sense that they have little in the way of social obligations, little in the way of duties and commitments to others, which leaves them with a great deal of autonomy in running their own lives" (10). Although this may sound attractive, this focus on self results in considerable time spent alone. Citing a study by Larson (1990), Arnett (2006, 10) states that "according to time-use studies across the life span, emerging adults aged 19 to 29 spend more of their leisure time alone than any other persons except the elderly, and more of their time in productive activities (school and work) alone than any age group under 40."

However, both the social psychological literature on happiness as well as Catholic teachings on the inherently social nature of man show that one of the most important factors fostering happiness is the presence of close and enduring social relationships (Baumeister and Leary 1995; Diener and Oishi 2005; Pontifical Council for Justice and Peace 2005, #149). These works suggest that focusing on self rather than forming the enduring relationships characteristic of adult life is not likely to increase one's sense of well-being.

We would also suggest that major changes in the lives of young people over the past four decades may also have contributed to the lower happiness in the '80s cohort. Earlier in this chapter we commented on the dramatic rise of cohabitation and the normalization of anonymous sexual encounters. Mainstream sociology tends to be indifferent to the morality of such behaviors. But a Catholic sociological framework will recognize that while morality can be shaped remarkably by social and cultural practices, its fundamental source transcends the social context and is embedded in the created nature of man. In other words, behaviors may be normalized, but they are not thereby made benign. Particularly apt illustrations of this truth can be seen in the effect of fatherlessness on children (Gallagher and Baker 2004) or of abortion on the mother (Coleman 2011; Vitz and Vitz 2010). Regardless of how common or normative these patterns are, they produce great harm. It is not difficult to visualize how the progressive degradation of our culture brought by these and other changes would lower the well-being of its members.

Recent work by Christian Smith supports our concern regarding the deterioration in the moral climate of young people and its effect on their happiness and well-being (C. Smith, et al. 2011). From in-depth personal interviews of young adults between the ages of 18 and 23, he finds ample evidence of a "dark side" to emerging adulthood: moral shallowness, uncritical attraction to consumer society, lack of civic involvement, and indifference to a transcendent purpose in life. Smith places the blame for these flaws on adult American society for having failed "to convey what any good society needs to pass on to its children" (238).

Our suggested explanations above present significant points of divergence with mainstream sociology. A sociology that recognizes that man is created in the image and likeness of God understands that, though man may have considerable freedom in shaping his world, he finds himself in a universe that he himself did not create. In that universe, there is an order—natural, logical, and moral— that he must abide by if he is to live happily (Schall 2007, 23–27). In contrast, mainstream sociology posits man as the creator of his own reality, a reality that is socially constructed in conformity to man's will. Within this framework, individual expression and freedom are the greatest goods and expected to bring happiness. Arnett's theoretical emphasis on self-expression and exploration illustrates well this latter orientation.

It is an orientation that is rooted in the philosophical assumptions embraced by much of modern science. In his introduction to his translation of the *Theology of the Body of John Paul II*, Michael Waldstein (2006) sketches the philosophical foundations of modern science promoted by figures such as Francis Bacon and René Descartes (34–44). He explains that Bacon's mechanistic account of nature, stripping it of its own inherent meaning, interior principles, and ends, was part of his program to reorient scientific reason toward the goal of exercising complete power over nature. In this program, the meaning and purpose of natural beings is determined by human consciousness, not by their Creator. Man assumes power over reality itself.

Descartes proposed that free will was the greatest and noblest human good, making man "in a certain manner equal to God" (Waldstein 2006, 41). Not bound by any inherent purpose in nature, the human being is free to exercise his will over all of nature, including his own body. The Baconian/Cartesian program, therefore, directs man to remake his world—including his social world—according to his own desires, regardless of any purpose or end that transcends those desires.

While the Church teaches that freedom is necessary to the dignity of man, it does not make it an absolute (Paul VI 1965, #17). A greater good than freedom is love, and love calls us to limit our freedom in the gift of self. "Man longs for love more than for freedom—freedom is the means and love the end" (Wojtyla 1981, 136; Waldstein 2006, 41). While freedom certainly promotes happiness, man achieves his greatest happiness through the gift of self that is love. As a passage of *Gaudium et Spes* so often quoted by John Paul II states: "man…cannot fully find himself except through a sincere gift of himself" (Paul VI 1965, #24).

A Catholic theoretical perspective will therefore lead one to predict that an orientation to life that concentrates on self-exploration and self-fulfillment will ultimately be unsatisfying. Such behaviors may promise happiness, but a Catholic understanding of man tells us that true happiness requires that we look beyond ourselves to others and be willing to give as well as receive love. Young adults find themselves approaching a stage of life that calls them to engage with others at a more mature level and to assume new responsibilities and form new relationships that may last for the remainder of their lives. The results of the present study suggest that postponing this new stage of life to concentrate on oneself is not likely to bring greater happiness.

Notes

1. Foreign residence at age 16 was used as the indicator rather than foreign birth because in the GSS the latter measure was omitted prior to 1977.

Bibliography

Arnett, Jeffrey Jensen. 2000. "Emerging Adulthood: A Theory of Development from the Teens through the Twenties." *American Psychologist*, 55: 469–80.

Arnett, Jeffrey Jensen. 2006. "Emerging Adulthood: Understanding the New Way of Coming of Age." In *Emerging Adults in America: Coming of Age in the 21st Century*, edited by J.J. Arnett & J.L. Tanner, 3–19. Washington, DC: American Psychological Association.

Baumeister, Roy F., and Mark R. Leary. 1995. "The Need to Belong: Desire for Interpersonal Attachments as a Fundamental Human Motivation." *Psychological Bulletin* 117 (3): 497–529.

Coleman, Priscilla K. 2011. "Abortion and Mental Health: Quantitative Synthesis and Analysis of Research Published 1995–2009." *The British Journal of Psychiatry* 199 (3): 180–86.

Diener, Ed, and Shigehiro Oishi. 2005. "The Nonobvious Social Psychology of Happiness." *Psychological Inquiry* 16 (4): 162–67.

Gallagher, Maggie, and Joshua K. Baker. 2004. "Do Moms and Dads Matter?" *Margins Law Journal* 4: 161–80, http://www.marriagedebate.com/pdf/Do_Moms_Dads_Matter.pdf

Hendershott, Anne, and Nicholas Dunn. 2011. "The 'Hook-Up' Culture on Catholic Campuses: A Review of the Literature." *Studies in Catholic Higher Education.* http://www.catholichighered.org/

Henig, Robin Marantz. 2010. "What Is It about 20-Somethings?" *New York Times Magazine* August 18, http://www.nytimes.com/2010/08/22/magazine/22Adulthood-t.html

Koganzon, Rita. 2010. "Slacking as Self-Discovery: The Rebranding of Indolence as 'Emerging Adulthood.'" *The New Atlantis* Fall: 146–52, http://www.thenewatlantis.com/publications/slacking-as-self-discovery

Larson, Reed. 1990. "The Solitary Side of Life: An Examination of the Time People Spend Alone from Childhood to Old Age." *Developmental Review* 10: 155–83.

Paul VI. 1965. *Pastoral Constitution on the Church in the Modern World, Gaudium et Spes.*

Pontifical Council for Justice and Peace. 2005. *Compendium of the Social Doctrine of the Church.* Washington, DC: United States Conference of Catholic Bishops.

Popenoe, David. 2008. *Cohabitation, Marriage, and Child Well-being: A Cross-National Perspective.* Piscataway, NJ: The National Marriage Project.

Regnerus, Mark, and Jeremy Uecker. 2010. *Premarital Sex in America: How Young Americans Meet, Mate, and Think about Marrying.* New York: Oxford University Press.

Rosenberg, Morris. 1968. *The Logic of Survey Analysis.* New York: Basic Books.

Sandvik, Ed, Ed Diener, and Larry Seidlitz. 1993. "Subjective Well-Being: The Convergence and Stability of Self-Report and Non-Self-Report Measures." *Journal of Personality* 61: 3.

Schall, James. 2007. *The Order of Things.* San Francisco: Ignatius Press.

Smith, Christian, with Kari Christoffersen, Hilary Davidson, and Patricia S. Herzog. 2011. *Lost in Transition: The Dark Side of Emerging Adulthood.* New York: Oxford University Press.

Smith, Tom W. 1985. "Unhappiness on the 1985 GSS: Confounding Change and Context." GSS Methodological Report No. 34. Chicago: National Opinion Research Center, University of Chicago. Accessed from http://publicdata.norc.org:41000/gss/DOCUMENTS/REPORTS/Methodological_Reports/MR034.pdf.

Smith, Tom W. 1990. "Timely Artifacts: A Review of Measurement Variation in the 1972–1989 GSS." Methodological Report No. 56. Chicago: National Opinion Research Center, University of Chicago. Accessed from http://publicdata.norc.org:41000/gss/DOCUMENTS/REPORTS/Methodological_Reports/MR056.pdf.

Smith, Tom, Peter Marsden, Michael Hout, and Jibum Kim. 2011. *General Social Surveys, 1972–2010.* Chicago: National Opinion Research Center [producer]; Storrs, CT: The Roper Center for Public Opinion Research, University of Connecticut [distributor].

Stevenson, Betsey, and Justin Wolfers. 2008. "Happiness Inequality in the United States." *Journal of Legal Studies*, 37 (S2): S33–S79.

U.S. Census Bureau. 1971. "Table 1. Marital Status, by Race, Age, Farm-Non Farm Residence and Sex, March 1970." Population Characteristics: Current Population Survey. Series P-20, No. 212, February 1.

———. 2009. "Table A-5a. The Population 14 to 24 Years Old by High School Graduate Status, College Enrollment, Attainment, Sex, Race, and Hispanic Origin: October 1967 to 2009." Accessed from http://www.census.gov/population/www/socdemo/school.html.

———. 2010. "Table UC-1. Unmarried Partners of the Opposite Sex, by Presence of Children, America's Families and Living Arrangements: 2010." Accessed from http://www.census.gov/population/www/socdemo/hh-fam/cps2010.html.

U.S. Census Bureau. 2011. *Statistical Abstract of the United States: 2011* (130th edition) Washington, DC. Accessed from http://www.census.gov/statab/www/.

Vitz, Evelyn Birge, and Paul C. Vitz. 2010. "Women, Abortion, and the Brain." *Public Discourse: Ethics, Law, and the Common Good* September 20, http://www.thepublicdiscourse.com/2010/09/1657

Waldstein, Michael. 2006. "Introduction." In John Paul II, *Man and Woman He Created Them: A Theology of the Body*, translated by Michael Waldstein, 1–128. Boston: Pauline Books and Media.

West, Diana. 2007. *The Death of the Grown-up*. New York: St. Martin's Press.

Wilcox, W. Bradford. 2010. "When Marriage Disappears: The Retreat from Marriage in Middle America." In *The State of Our Unions: 2010*, edited by W. Bradford Wilcox, 13–60. Charlottesville, VA: The National Marriage Project. Accessed from http://www.stateofourunions.org.

Wojtyla, Karol. 1981. *Love and Responsibility*, translated by H.T. Willetts. New York: Farrar, Straus and Giroux.

7

Responding to the Challenge of Postmodernism: Potential Grounds for Future Collaboration between Sociology and Catholic Social Thought

Stephen R. Sharkey

In this concluding paper for Part One of the anthology, I want to bring the discussions taken up in my own introductory essay and the other articles back around to focusing on what a Catholic sociological imagination, resting on the historical work of Catholic sociologists to shape society and Catholic social teaching in diverse ways, might do to address some of today's overarching problems. In each era Catholic sociologists were confronting key problems of the society of their time and discerning best ways to build up a Catholic intellectual culture for their situation. We should expect no less of ourselves today. I also want to anticipate some material that will be taken up by the authors later, in Part Two.

As I noted in my first essay, I believe one of the major socio-cultural problems facing us at this time is *how to effectively convince others, in a relativist postmodern culture, that Catholic social teachings grounded in transcendent and absolute principles are valid and worthy of use as an infrastructure for addressing our social questions.* Is it possible for us to transcend the anomie of a culture that one of its popular apologists, Richard Rorty (1989; see also Lundin 1993), characterized as fascinatingly replete with "irony" and "contingency," and in which any semblance of solidarity comes from a temporary, optional, and utilitarian collusion of individuals occupying a particular social location for a pragmatic purpose? Our first step is to consider the texture of this anomie: its origins, major features, and possible soft spots that could provide openings to change.

Features of the Postmodern Social Landscape

The notion of a crisis in the modernist mentality and culture has been around in nascent form since the Romantics challenged the rationalism of industrializing society in the 1800s, but it came to a more social scientific point, for example, with Weber's angst over the emergence of an iron cage of bureaucratic rationality at the turn of the twentieth century. To draw a portrait of postmodernism I want to start with a very broad analysis then narrow things down to a more specifically sociological perspective.

To develop the broad analysis I want to employ the ideas of a perhaps unusual figure to introduce into a sociology paper: Fr. Romano Guardini, a major influence on many intellectuals but perhaps most importantly for us here on Benedict XVI. Guardini was able to observe what we now call postmodernism's first hint at itself, then ever more forcefully take shape in society over the full arc of the first two-thirds of that twentieth century, from its nascent emergence in positivism, secularism, and Neitzschean nihilism, through the horrors of totalitarianism, and into the anomie and uncertainty of materialist existentialism and the 1960s. He passed away in 1968. He was a man of the Church known by theologians and Church historians as a major force in the liturgical reform movement and "precursor of Vatican II." Yet he can speak also to the social sciences in general and us in particular, because he had the difficult but grand opportunity to start something new in the German university system, and he made the most of it in a way that can teach us helpful lessons about analyzing society from a Catholic point of view.

For a variety of circumstances, at the age of only thirty-seven he was appointed to an inaugural chair of something called the "Philosophy of Religion and the Catholic Worldview" at the University of Berlin, in 1923. He was given the task of defining what the Catholic worldview actually meant in a Protestant and secular academic context, and to demonstrate its plausibility to colleagues and students in the very heart of specialized scientific university life. His approach to developing the idea was thoroughly multidisciplinary. He was being asked to formulate a scholarly Catholic outlook on society and religion, drawing on both the history of the arts and humanities but also contemporary observations on culture, politics, and how young people understood their futures. His mandate was to try to re-affirm the value of Catholicism in a German society that had abandoned that faith by and large for several generations. To the extent that this scenario sounds rather familiar to us today, he can thus be a worthy initial guide.

Guardini's opus is enormous but we can helpfully focus on three works that are perhaps the most "sociological": *Letters from Lake Como, The End of the Modern World,* and *Power and Responsibility,* published originally in 1923, 1950, and 1953, respectively (Guardini 1994; 1998). I characterize these works as proto-sociological and they blend sociological observation, philosophy, and theology into a comprehensive philosophical reflection and social analysis. Across this set of texts his main thesis—set forth with bold precision yet also with a strong current of apprehension and melancholy—was that we were losing our organic place in the divinely created world as we assumed the role of God ourselves and sought to create our own circumstances through a triumphal, Gnostic application of reason. Initially, in the period of modernism fueled by the Enlightenment, such power to change conditions through greater knowledge and technology could be and was often used for good, to overcome social ills and human limitations. But as the negative side of industrialization and urbanization became painfully obvious, early faith in Progress and the promises of the Enlightenment collapsed: the modernist moment gave way to a post- or late modern period of radical uncertainty, cultural decadence, and systemic aggression. A new definition of the person arose emphasizing the pursuit of individual self-interest and normative relativism: with God dead or dying and Progress no longer offering a siren song of utopia, people lost a sense of overarching direction and meaning, made up their own rules, and lived by them in a condition of fearful expediency. Without the natural check of transcendent values and norms on the inherent sinful predilections of human nature, and with the diminishing of a Church capable of mounting a real challenge to these trends, the door was opened tragically not only to individualism and utilitarianism at the micro level, but also to totalitarian manipulation of people in entire societies. Such societies used the new social and behavioral sciences to propose false gods to fill the hole at the center of human experience left by the displacement of God—a fact that needs no demonstration here. Perhaps more dangerously, some of the basic processes that characterized overtly totalitarian states like Germany and Italy were gradually emerging, in softer and less overt forms, in a wider range of late capitalist settings. Grace and the soul at the heart of our human identities, our personhoods, were replaced with a scientifically-framed matrix of manipulable factors. Everything about life, both our external and internal terrains, was open to analysis and manipulation, and all thought and behavior patterns, value sets and norms were seen as mere products of particular historical and material conditions—including religious ideas and experiences. People indeed saw themselves not as created in the image of God, but as a composite of scientifically ascertainable factors and characteristics open to rearrangement and improvement.

To use sociological language, society and human nature became complex sets of analytic variables, and truth only the results of studies that the new priesthoods of scientists and pundits could agree on based on their empirical observations about the relationships between these abstract variables. Guardini foresaw a world in which people saw themselves and their own life course the way the new behavioral scientists saw them: as systems of interrelated material factors and conditions. Guardini knew that life in such a climate would ultimately be marked by a profound sense of alienation and despair, as well as a hopelessness about the future, insofar as any larger understandings of direction or purpose—what postmodernists like to call "master narratives"—seem impossible to take seriously. Anxiety prevails in a world without solid moorings and where personal choices and individual subjectivities become the only available measure of value. Will to power, to rearrange life to meet goals, replaces authentic spiritual discovery as the justification of "truth"—a term now in permanent quotation marks, uncannily echoing Pontius Pilate.

Guardini argued that only a life re-grounded thoroughly in Christ—a firmly formed understanding of reason and freedom in Christ and in the doctrines of His Church—can counter such powerful forces and rescue society. And such a life, registered as absurd and even dangerous to others by postmodern standards because of its audacity in declaring the existence of a universal truth, will most likely be lived by a smaller but more resolute group of believers capable of withstanding the social pressures to surrender or transmogrify their faith to accommodate the surrounding culture.

Guardini was influenced by Bergson, Simmel, and others who valued the ordering power of tradition and roots, but he was no romantic rhapsodizing about returning to a lost Christendom. He was more focused on the imbalances in human experience and culture wrought by the collapse of a healthy tension between roots and creative change. Modern life *was* in this way unbalanced, pointing in all sectors, toward unfettered change. Yet at the same time the Church of his era was not well positioned to present a serious challenge or offer a more balanced vision: it was pointing mostly in the opposite direction toward stagnant traditionalism. Thus Guardini worked hard for a critique of contemporary modernism in the wider society while at the same time helped forge the renewal of the liturgy and theology that could enable Catholicism to better respond to contemporary cultural needs and challenges, based upon a comprehensive *ressourcement*. Guardini's original analysis has been powerfully taken up and developed within the Church, especially by Benedict XVI who encountered him and his works as a student in Germany and has regularly cited him in his writings (Sharkey 2011; Benedict XVI 2010; Magister 2008). Benedict's whole concept of the dictatorship of relativism has important roots in Guardini's framework, as does his view that the Church of the future may be smaller but stronger and fed by its wet and dry martyrs, a kind of new "creative minority."

Narrowing our purview now to more traditionally sociological boundaries, prophetic analyses like Guardini's were often taken up by those students of culture for whom the loss of meaning, disenchantment of the world, alienation, the predominance of practical atheism, and anomie were bellwether signals of a society in big trouble, even as that society celebrated itself as more modern and full of possibilities for autonomous self-definition than ever.[1]

Just to cite a few recent examples from the history of sociological thought, Philip Rieff's (1966) notion of the triumph of the therapeutic emphasized the rise of psychology and therapy techniques as pathways to meaning, through the manipulation of aspects of personality and contextual factors to produce states of immediate well-being and contentment. Scientific psychological reductionism dissolves the historical Christian search for meaning and purpose into the analysis of prior material factors that explain current conditions and feelings and offer practical maps for altering those conditions and feelings. Feeling better is the mark of human success. In effect Psychology is a transmogrified religion, a means for flattening out human experience into one-dimensionality.

Daniel Bell (1977) wrote about this a-religious flattening as well, describing the "profanation" of a society in which individual experience now assumes the place of divine revelation as the source of wisdom and meaning. Many sociologists, from Robert Bellah to Amitai Etzioni to Robert Putnam, have written extensively about the damaging effects of hyper-individualism and the loss of community in late capitalism. Edward Shils (1981) carefully analyzed what we are losing when we define a society in terms of rejection of all traditions and past understandings, and the impoverishment resulting from a loss of worthwhile values and norms, criteria for meaning and action that can transcend our immediate social situation. We become ever more temperocentric at the same time we believe we are being more universalistic. Berger, Berger, and Kellner (1973) wrote about the "homeless mind" in which each person has no interior or exterior home, only a plurality of life worlds that challenge our capacity for creating a coherent and grounded identity and undercut even the possibility of a traditionally rooted religious view of the world.

Much contemporary sociology on this pattern of social change has only confirmed and amplified the details of Guardini's analyses, spelling out details of its cultural and structural dynamics and how they impact the person. Current scholars often focus on the essentially paradoxical and contradictory quality of our society, rather much like the critical theory tradition did in the twentieth century—as for example with Marcuse's (1969) notion of "repressive tolerance," whereby being apparently free to think and believe what we want in effect depletes our capacity to identify and act on an objectively oppressive and limiting capitalist society where all choices are merely market choices. Thus, to give some illustrations, consider the hoopla about the benefits of life online. We seem to live in a world of apparent abundance of rich personal relationships; but these are actually impersonal and often inauthentic, what Eva Illouz (2007) called the "cold intimacies" of Facebook "friending," speed dating, impersonal pseudo-communities, and creations of fictional personae for online match websites and virtual social spaces. We translate ourselves into terms defined by desirable market characteristics and scales, and airbrush out our parts that score a bit too low to be attractive to others. Participants often create multiple fictional personae for different contexts and purposes, inviting fragmentation. Or consider our literal computing power. We have an incredible technical capacity for productivity, connectivity, and knowledge acquisition, but in fact, as Maggie Jackson (2009) has explored, our minds are not meant to proceed at the pace and complexity demanded of our computers and networks. We are simply becoming less and less capable of focused attention and concentration; we inefficiently multitask while deluding ourselves that we are more efficient, and distract ourselves to death in compulsive ways. Especially younger generations are literally addicted to cell phones and messaging, and cannot find the way or the time to meditate on larger meanings and purposes. We are becoming more like machines as our machines are designed to be more like us.

Given this backdrop and buildup, what are current social scientists and cultural analysts saying about postmodernism in detail? According to a recent summary by Swift (2007), "The term postmodernism refers to both a culture and a way of thinking—an often contradictory set of sentiments and notions that are both a reaction to modernism and sometimes its outgrowth. Both postmodern culture and thought are characterized by skepticism, atomism, and a profound distrust of humanism, history, universal concepts, authority, and institutions. For postmodernists, meaning is ephemeral and fragmentary. Social fragmentation, self-indulgence and boredom mark postmodernity." An outgrowth of the counterculture and its challenges to given accounts of reality, postmodernism is "built on the premise that 'everything that is received must be suspected, even if it is a day old.'" Authoritative explanations, accounts, and declarations, in science, religion, politics, and art, are seen not as objective or universal truths but rather only *myths* propagated by individuals or groups seeking influence and power. Claims of ultimate truth are deceptive, cloaking particular standpoints and interests. "Society" consists of the constant jostle of efforts of individuals or groups to assert and impose their perceptions on others, and individuals seeking some sort of protective (yet shifting and temporary) group identity and affiliation. Conversation and interaction thus become not mutual search for truth but interesting, more or less amusing exchanges of perspectives that cannot effectively challenge each other on rational grounds, since even reason is merely assertion of a perspective disguised in universal language.

Swift continues that while postmodernism's roots are in the political left, its core relativism undermines the possibility of a clear moral stance on injustice, since morals are suspect and it is hard to say what justice is besides what one group does or does not like being done. This results in postmodernism being very appealing, ironically, to right-wing libertarians. Solidarity does not really exist in the humanist or Christian sense, because whatever mutual cooperation exists is present essentially and only because of temporary convergences of pragmatic interests.

Furthermore, given the flux of the broader culture, personal identity and identity politics become very prominent, as seen in economic and social phenomena like niche marketing and population segmentation. What Swift meant above by "boredom" becomes clearer: without meaning, life becomes a search for the next curiosity, the next cool thing to be part of that might relieve identity anxiety. The phrase "1-Phone" takes on a whole new meaning. "Cool hunters" working for marketing firms spread out across the country searching for what the hippest people are doing, saying, and wearing, feeding this information back to corporations so that they can manufacture the next new kind of earrings, music, and jeans that everyone wanting to be cool must have.[2]

Thomas Storck (2001) shares much of this general definition of postmodernism but focuses more on the "de's" we hear so much about. The overarching "de" is deconstruction of *ultimate truths*, which means a kind of anti-humanist attacking of apparently universal claims and meanings as deceptive instruments of power. When Foucault says that ideas are surveillance, he means that ideas are systems meant to control what we think. When gender-bending radical feminists or LGBTQ activists claim that there is no such thing as given human nature, that sexuality is just what we want to say it is or wish it to become, they are challenging the inherited binary account of bodies as "natural" to be a trick of heterosexists. "What is really behind this statement or claim?" becomes the operant and indeed often only method of research.

Storck's second feature is deconstruction of *authors*, sometimes called "decentering." We may think of an author as the one whose ideas we are learning, and the originator of ideas. But this is not so from a postmodern perspective, not only because generating ideas today is hardly ever solitary given collaborations and working from the Internet, but also because of the fact that the meaning of a text is shifting, not stable. It is as much what I the reader make of it as what the author thought or pretended she intended at some point of time in the past. The reader is as much the "author" of the text as the one whose name is on the title page or screen credits (or bible, for that matter). Hidden and unacknowledged authors occupy the landscape, including the landscape of our own interior responses. What we think of as the "author" is but a false god which we envision out of our need for security, put up on a pedestal and erroneously singled out. The text we think we are reading contains all sorts of conscious and unconscious bracketing and exclusions we are not meant to notice.

Thus postmodernists look as much at who is *not* apparently the author, and what is *not* said, as what is presented in the delivered package. This is sometimes called "working at the margins" of cultural products and systems. It is rather like catching fleeting images of others' voices and ideas hiding behind the pages in a book. Thus the author as authoritatively owning the text and commanding meaning is shoved to the side to make room for all the others who participate in making a text or cultural artifact seem authoritative. At a certain point there is no longer an author or an authoritative rendering of anything, only inter-

pretations and interpretations of interpretations, etc. All efforts to define a
Meaning are provisional and multiple. This is as true for regular individuals as
for elites of artists and scholars. But there is a political edge to this: finding and
giving voice to a marginal character in the story or a hidden author can realign
the story itself, giving it new or multiple possible endings made up by a collage
of authors implicit and explicit.

Third is the deconstruction of *texts*. Texts are not just cultural artifacts like
books and art, but all of life, since all aspects of culture, material and non-
material, are framed semiotically as assemblages of signs and symbols that acquire an appearance of stable meaning for sociological reasons. This is why in
radical feminist and LGBTQ discourse, for example, much attention is paid to
calling human bodies "sites" upon which are written or inscribed societal norms,
roles, and meanings. Bodies are texts upon which are written meanings that can
also be unwritten or rewritten. There is an analogy between the postmodernist
philosophical and communicative position on this and the actual translation of
all cultural products into digital information that can be assembled, disassem-
bled, and modified at will with the right technology. Postmodernists use phrases
like "interrogating a cultural scene" and "decentering the dominant discourse" as
a way of saying that what we have before us is nothing more than a social construction of reality that hides and suppresses other truths that could be there if
we looked differently—or can be made to look different with the right tools and
force of will. It is as if we can photoshop our selves, just like we do our pictures
of ourselves. Culture and human experience are therefore like play, like thea-
ter—but also like war, because they are about a huge power to change "reality"
and impose the new image on others. They are made up, though we may not be
aware of it, and can be edited just to see what happens; but the changes can also
be deadly serious and meant to upend a social order.

What of reason and argument? What of evidence and counterevidence to
debate the merits of claims made about life and reality? Radical Postmodernists
reject argument as rigid, and rationality as impossible, since there is no certain
floor for epistemology and ontology to stand upon. If their own truth claims thus
implode as just another imposition, postmodernists are amused, not taken aback.
Thus cynicism and irony dominate the emotional palette. Postmodernism never
overcomes the old paradox that says A: the statement below is false; B: the
statement above is true. But the looping of one's sensibilities in circles in this
paradox is not framed as a signal of some error in thinking, but instead as a
heady freedom from linearity (a major sin of the patriarchy). The disconcerted
spinning is considered liberation.

It is easy to see how consonant some of this position, though not all, is with
the mainstream sociological imagination and disciplinary politics, as I explored
in the introductory paper. Mills has been our contemporary "things are not what
they seem" mentor, whose definitive empirical research was in fact on power
elites and their manipulations. And what informed sociologist could disagree

with the idea that culture and society usually contain hidden power structures, or that widespread norms and values may reflect the interests of dominant groups? Who would not agree that marginalized and outcast groups like women and other minorities may need to be brought into the center of analysis and cultural attention, whom our master narratives previously hid or pushed aside? Who would not recognize that issues of authenticity and truth are raised in any social process involving impression management and the presentation of self? In a highly pluralist social environment, what sociologist cannot recognize that there are probably multiple views of a given situation or reality?

The rub is here: in that word "reality." Some sociologists have lost heart in the notion that sociology is about reality, and can only muster itself as a form of fascinating narrative. Even Mills hardly went that far in his deconstruction of power dynamics and unmasking of hidden elites, because he believed ultimately in the truth of Marxism and a scientific materialism needed to get to it. But today many in our field are well beyond that. As sociologist Zygmunt Bauman (1991) describes, the idea that sociology is a form of universal knowledge about reality has failed in the face of the utter contingency and culture-boundedness of its understandings; what we are left with is only the courage to embrace that contingency through tolerating ambiguities and sticking to whatever personal convictions about truth we opt for. In the same vein Laura Bovone (2005)[3] has tried to argue, for example, that at this point in time sociology as a discipline can really be no more than an "account of accounts," a systematized way of setting stories people tell next to each other for pondering, essentially an exercise in Habermasian communication. Sociology is a set of stories collected and recounted with some clarity and fairness, plus reactions to those narratives. She argues we cannot claim any higher authority for sociological arguments about what is more true or less: there is no higher authority for our claims as scientists. Sociology is just one of the many narratives we create, perhaps told persuasively, and we had better be careful not to impose our story line on others. There is a grain of truth in Bovone's position: traditional sociology tends to reduce people to abstract categories and explain away their lifeworlds and experiences— including spiritual experiences—in a reductionist manner, suggesting we know more about "what's really causing things" than they do. But the Bovone position implies that sociology can't be in touch with objective realities in any deep way, it can only tell stories; and the disciplinary norms for call and response are primarily about Baumanian tolerance of ambiguity.

The narrative and reflexive turn in sociology has led us to this pointless point. But can the quite valid awareness of the necessity for reflexivity in our sociology, and the absurdity of the positivist claims about truth, also lead us to another point? Sociologists need to believe that reality *can* be discovered and observed; otherwise the whole discipline collapses like just another text in the wind. Sociologists such as Rosenau (1992) and Smith (2010) have taken this danger very seriously and tried to confront it. They argue that while there may be full-blooded postmodernists scampering around in humanities and cultural studies departments, where the notions of irony, playfulness, and the *jouissance* of deconstruction can be fascinating (and get you tenure), the concrete human impact of such notions is relatively low there: novels and philosophical tracts can be important especially for shaping students' worldviews but they are not social policies with actual costs and benefits. Sociology needs to argue that findings are possible, that some theoretical and empirical arguments are better than others. I think this underlying reality may be why those interested in actual policy changes with roots in postmodernist deconstruction, such as advocates of same sex marriage, realize they are better positioned to influence public discussion if they perform as social scientists than as English professors. In this sense sociology still has a foot resting on the realist foundations of the modern worldview, which assumes the ontological possibility of finding truth and claims authoritative epistemological rules for doing so. The field can't exist as a social science without these premises.

It is true that sometimes the hipster sociology teacher facing drowsy students in required courses can use postmodern shock talk to wake up the audience: "Your most cherished beliefs and ways of life are nothing but a social construction!" can sound profound and scary, something important to think about and pursue further.[4] Beyond the classroom, sociology's angry use of deconstructionist frameworks to attack various enemies on and off campus can certainly result in political correctness and, paradoxically, a demand that deconstructed victims respond to such attacks with only tolerance and acceptance, following an academic paradigm first set most prominently in motion in the realm of the Modern Language Association during the 1980s (Lundin 1993). But most sociology today is *not* so strongly tilted that way: it is still looking for some good balance between the arrogant assertions of the positivist project and the overblown and hopelessly paradoxical insights of radical deconstructionism.

We can do a sociology of the postmodern landscape to help us sort this out. Rosenau and Smith each explain that postmodernism is really *multiple*: there are "skeptical" and "affirmative," "strong" and "weak" versions of the relativism and social constructionism lying at the heart of postmodern culture and operating in academia. To be sure these are ideal typical categories with ranges in between. Scanning the discipline, these two scholars are quite sure that most practicing sociologists really fall into the "weak" and "affirmative" camp, even though there are occasional rhetorical efflorescences of the other sort, especially in specialty areas whose cutting edges depend on postmodernist postures and ideas, such as the sociology of sexuality and gender. What does this mean?

Let me first quote at length from Rosenau (for the sake of convenience omitting the extensive scholarly documentation she provides on the sources of ideas and data). Rosenau (1992) emphasizes the *tone, affect, and political implications* of the two approaches:

Within th[e] diversity of post-modern pronouncements, as far as the social sciences are concerned, two broad general orientations, the *skeptical* postmodernists and the *affirmative* postmodernists, can be delineated.

The skeptical post-modernists (or merely skeptics), offering a pessimistic, negative, and gloomy assessment, argue that the modern age is one of fragmentation, disintegration, malaise, meaninglessness, a vagueness or even absence of moral parameters and societal chaos....Inspired by Continental European philosophies, especially Heidegger and Nietzsche, this is the dark side of postmodernism, the post-modernism of despair, the post-modernism that speaks of the immediacy of death, the demise of the subject, the end of the author, the impossibility of truth, and the abrogation of the Order of Representation. Postmodernists of this orientation adopt a blasé attitude, as if "they have seen it all" and concluded that nothing really new is possible....They argue that the destructive character of modernity makes the post-modern age one of "radical, unsurpassable uncertainty"...characterized by all that is grim, cruel, alienating, hopeless, tired, and ambiguous. In this period no social or political "project" is worthy of commitment....Even where there is room for happiness, farce, pleasure, "joyous affirmation"...these are only temporary, empty, meaningless forms of gaiety that merely mark a period of waiting for catastrophe....If, as the skeptics claim, there is no truth, then all that is left is to play, the play of words and meaning.

Although the affirmative post-modernists, also referred to as simply the affirmatives, agree with the skeptical post-modernists' critique of modernity, they have a more hopeful, optimistic view of the post-modern age. More indigenous to Anglo-North American culture than to the Continent, the generally optimistic affirmatives are oriented toward process. They are either open to positive political action (struggle and resistance) or content with the recognition of visionary, celebratory personal non-dogmatic projects that range from New Age religion to New Wave lifestyles and include a whole spectrum of postmodern social movements. Most affirmatives seek a philosophical and ontological intellectual practice that is non-dogmatic, tentative, and non-ideological. These post-modernists do not, however, shy away from affirming an ethic, making normative choices, and striving to build issue-specific political coalitions. Most affirmatives argue that certain value choices are superior to others, a line of reasoning that would incur the disapproval of the skeptical postmodernists. (15–16)

In this account Rosenau highlights a common experience in sociology of hearing postmodern critics rail against universal principles as disguised forms of oppression, yet advocate a universal principle of their own: namely, non-dogmatic openness to alternative culture and lifestyles.

Using a slightly different approach, Smith (2010) tends to foreground the issues of *ontology and epistemology* embedded in the postmodern position:

The weak version—which I am going to propose below to call a "realist" version—sounds something like this: All human knowledge is conceptually mediated and can be and usually is influenced by particular and contingent sociocultural factors such as material interests, group structures, linguistic categories, technological development, and the like—such that what people believe to be real is significantly shaped not only by objective reality but also by their sociocultural contexts. Furthermore, there is a dimension of reality that humans socially construct, what I will refer to…as institutional facts, that is, those aspects of the real that humans think, speak and act into existence. This weak or realist version is an essential sociological insight crucial for understanding human persons and social reality.

The strong version, by comparison, claims something like this: Reality itself for human is a human, social construction, constituted by human mental categories, discursive practices, definitions of situations, and symbolic exchanges that are sustained as "real" through ongoing interactions that are in turn shaped by particular interests, perspectives, and, usually, imbalances of power....[O]ur knowledge about reality is therefore entirely culturally relative, since no human has access to reality "as it really is" (if such a thing exists or can be talked about intelligibly) because we can never escape our human epistemological and linguistic limits to verify whether our beliefs about reality correspond with externally objective reality. (121–22)

Smith goes on to say that as sociologists we must reject the strong version because of serious faults with its idealism, subjectivism, and conflation of epistemology and ontology.

Responding to This Landscape in a Catholic Way

I present these sociologies of the situation in order to provide some greater texture to the understanding of the term postmodernism in social science, but also to portray what sociologists interested in helping the Church are up against within their own intellectual/academic climate as we try to make a case for the truth and plausibility of Catholic social thought and teaching. For me two features of the situation stand out.

First, what we are usually up against is not the strong or skeptical version of postmodernism—though in the heat of attacks against Catholic ideas and in our own frustration it may seem otherwise—but rather the other. This means that we are facing not a despairing relativism and bottomless social constructionism, but one that is using relativistic and deconstructionist ideas to supplant one vision of the social good with another, highly utopian, individualistic and subjective vision, based on a will to power or a more new age conviction about the wheel of time turning away from Christianity toward secular, at best deistic culture. The implication for our work is that we need a sociology that is clearly, overtly based on an ontology and epistemology visibly and powerfully different from those that weak social constructionism rests on—and in particular on a different and actually more accurate model *of man* than postmodernism allows. The Catholic position is that there exists an objective moral order discernible across cultural diversity and operant in social life, in one way or another; within this order persons who are neither totally free nor totally malleable seek to find and express their deepest being and know the world through the good use of reason endowed by their creator. The best society is the one that makes it easiest for persons to do this. This is a very different model of the person in society than the "body site" inscribed on and swallowed up by social forces, or the self-affirming individualist in Hobbsean competition with other atomistic beings, that even weak constructionism deploys.

Second, the postmodernism we mostly encounter moves from an apparently diverse but nevertheless quite uniform vision of the social and personal good, where the good is defined as the fulfillment of personal choices and the credibility of personally-constructed moralities. It is not aimless, but committed to social and political projects of liberation of a certain relativist kind, only seemingly tolerant of opposition. These strive to build concrete social structures and institutional arrangements to bring that vision about through a process that at bottom transgresses long-held traditions and any sense of the "vertical-in-authority," to use a concept from Philip Rieff (2006). As Smith (2003) argued convincingly in an earlier empirical and historical work on the secular revolution, the postmodern era is not merely a matter of playing with ideas in faculty meetings but about control of organizations, institutions, and resources: secularism is a *social movement,* involving recruitment, mobilization, political engagement, formal organizations and informal networks, and the rest, attempting to infiltrate all social institutions from religion to education to politics to law. Thus Catholic sociologists need to stand in the public arena confident that they can challenge this movement ideationally and politically—optimally, with our own countermovement—in a way that can get past its easy dismissal as "mere ideology" or, with greater vitriol, an imposition of irrational religion on a supposedly neutral and objectively rational public square of science and policy.

I think there are two current trends within secular sociology focusing precisely on these issues: trends that we can draw on, learn from, and adapt for our Catholic purposes and thus keep open lines of communication between sociology and Catholic thinking. The first is the emerging theoretical and empirical school called *personalist critical realism,* of which Smith happens to be a fairly recent advocate and champion. It is a major response to the historical problems of positivism as well as the weaknesses of postmodern sociology. Our anthology happens to include an article by one of its major international representatives, Margaret Archer. Personalist critical realism is very consistent with much of the Catholic vision of the person and of the nature of reason and science; it also poses a research agenda concerning life experiences in postmodern society that Catholic social thought can effectively draw on.

The second is the movement toward *public sociology,* which for about a decade now has been trying to support the importance of sociologists becoming researchers for and advocates of value positions in the broader society, in civil society and politics. Public sociology requires a more depthful and articulate excavation of the value premises of sociological work so that they can be examined for consistency with sociological theory and research. The movement to build it is about the culture of the discipline: surpassing its tradition of supposed neutrality standing aside from society, rearranging its criteria for prestige and influence in scholarship and academic life, opening the door to a wider variety of value positions and political opinions among sociologists, not always parroting the progressive line. Public sociology argues that work done in connection with social movements can be considered as legitimate sociological practice and should be rewarded thusly. But in order for this to be framed as social science, it must not be seen as less noble and pristine than "pure" scholarship, but rather as another form of scholarship, with its own perhaps distinct but still high standards. This cuts two ways: for example, working sociologically to bring about feminist socialism may be as legitimate as working for Christian democracy. But from a public sociological view at least the possibility of working for Christian democracy must be acknowledged as a legitimate genre of sociological inquiry and application.

In the next section I will briefly consider each of these potential disciplinary resources.

Some Highlights of Personalist Critical Realism

There are many excellent accounts of this emerging sociological approach and so in this brief section I must limit myself to identifying some of its key themes and do so in a way that cuts to the chase, emphasizing some of its striking compatibilities with Catholic social thought.[5] Not all critical realists care about religion and theology, but when they do they say interesting sociological things and open the door of a secular discipline to a much wider territory and set of concerns.

One thing we know about sociology is that its *models of man*, of the person, tend to be quite confining, with an emphasis on materialist social determinism and/or social constructionism. As Catholics we work from a model of man that assumes the presence of transcendent dimensions and motives in human experience, focuses on freedom and responsibility, and distinguishes between what truly exists and what we have directly measured or observed. Critical realism got its start in the last decades of the twentieth century as a critique of positivism and a reply to postmodernism. It accuses much contemporary sociology, including both positivist and strong constructionist versions, of making a number of crucial errors at the level of philosophy of science, and of resting on fundamentally inadequate models of man and society. The postmodernist critique has been helpful to sociology insofar as it helped kick the struts out from under the pretensions of modernist, positivist discourse, and also revealed the power dynamics behind much of what was portrayed as objective knowledge—all of which we as Catholics can already agree with. But it failed because, ironically like its positivist forbearer, it commits the *epistemic fallacy*, conflating the real in its totality with what we can measure or experience. There is simply more to reality than what we think we know; that as yet unobserved reality produces effects which can eventually come into our view. As Smith (2010) puts it (building on a range of works including those of sociologists Andrew Collier, Andrew Sayer, Douglas Popora, and Margaret Archer),

> Critical realism's central organizing thought is that much of reality exists inde-
> pendently of human consciousness of it; that reality itself is complex, open, and
> stratified in multiple dimensions or levels, some of which come to exist through
> the crucial process of emergence; that humans can acquire a truthful though fal-
> lible knowledge and understanding of reality through various forms of disci-
> plined conceptualization, inquiry, and theoretical reflection; that (social) sci-
> ence is rightly concerned with what is real and, second, understanding real
> causal capacities mechanisms and processes that operate in reality to produce
> various events and outcomes of interest (rather than discovering allegedly law-
> governed regularities among observable events or, for social scientists, merely
> interpreting the meanings that actions have for actors); and finally, that
> knowledge and understanding of the truths about reality position knowers to
> critically engage the world in normative, prescriptive, and even moral terms in
> ways that may overcome the traditional fact-value divide and intentionally try
> to shape the world for the better. (92–93)

Critical realists begin with a distinction between the *real*, the *actual*, and *empirical*, because on the one hand, positivist sociology has tended to conflate what is empirically measurable with what is real, and on the other hand, con-structionists have mistaken what they actually feel and experience with all that is real. In other words *both depend on a mistaken conflation of epistemology with ontology*. For critical realists the real is the totality of what actually exists: mate-rial and non-material, social entities like structures and institutions as well as the brute facts of physical existence. This reality exists whether we know or under-stand it or not, apart from our awareness. The actual is what we could detect in the world that comes about through the causal activity of aspects of the real. Then the empirical is what we actually experience and measure, directly or indi-rectly, a sub-portion of the real. These distinctions are important for several rea-sons. One, they open us to a wider world of possible reality to study, including things we don't now see or believe. Two, they invite humility in our science that has not been particularly evident in the strict empiricism characteristic of much scientistic sociology. And three, they contradict the overstated nominalism and subjectivism lurking in social constructionism. The upshot here is that critical realism beckons us to study reality in a more open way, aware of the tentative nature of our understanding and perception but also convinced that there are true realities out there for us to discover.

A further distinction critical realists make is between levels of reality, that relate to each other through processes of *emergence*. This is as true of physical reality as social reality, and also of the person, who may be defined non-reductionistically as having emergent properties and qualities from the level of physical functioning and existence up through capacities for perception and experience, through capacities for creation and decision making, completed by higher order capacities for moral judgment, love, and interpersonal bonding. All these levels can in turn exert some downward causal activity as well: for example, our minds and consciousness emerge from the workings of our bodily structures but then our minds and consciousness influence how our bodily structures operate and with what they interact in the world. Critical realism thus broaches into the territory of *personalism* in its effort to map who the complex people are that social science studies, as well as who the complex people are that are doing the social scientific studying. This personalist critical realism thus embraces the kind of reflexivity which postmodernism's critique of the positivist and materialist sociology advanced, without falling into the tendency toward strong constructionist nihilism that reflexivity without the possibility of discovering truth engenders.

Finally, personalist critical realism focuses our attention on the human processes of people in social systems: at the level of social order, while institutional arrangements emerge out of the interactions and relationships of people, people exert some upward causal pressure on how the order operates. There is no structure without people to "do" it with some agency, even if that agency is impaired or denied: people have causal efficacy, "in relation to the social beings they become and the powers of transformative reflection and action which they bring to their social context—powers that are independent of social mediation" as Smith puts it. This gets us to a useful critique of the methodological individualism or abstract structuralism so often embedded in variables sociology, reminding us that while statistical analyses of data sets helps us see patterns, it is actually scientifically incorrect to say something like "race causes social income differences." As a shorthand we might use such language, but the reality is that people acting in a certain way—and certainly often acting within constraints created by emergent social systems like opportunity structures—cause other people to be treated in certain ways that result in income differences. Personalist *agency*, the capacity for choice and a more careful view of the limits to freedom, comes to the foreground. This is highly consistent with a Catholic understanding of how social systems operate, inclusive of human freedom and responsibility within the constraints of opportunity structures.

Smith's already cited 2010 work develops these topics in considerable detail, but it is interesting to note that Margaret Archer developed much of the groundwork for the personalism in critical realism earlier, for example in a paper she presented to the 2005 meetings of the Pontifical Academy of Social Sciences with the theme *Conceptualization of the Person in Social Sciences*.[6] In that paper, offered to the Church for consideration, she summarized her arguments about an appropriate sociological model of the person as follows (Archer 2005):

> The sociological problem of conceptualizing the person is how to capture someone who is partly formed by their sociality, but also has the capacity to transform their society in some part. The difficulty is that social theorizing has oscillated between these two extremes. On the one hand, Enlightenment thought promoted an "undersocialised" view of man, one whose human constitution owed nothing to society and was thus a self-sufficient "outsider" who simply operated in a social environment. On the other hand, there is a later but pervasive "oversocialised" view of man, whose every feature, beyond his biology, is shaped and moulded by his social context. He thus becomes such a dependent "insider" that he has no capacity to transform his social environment.
>
> Instead, if we are to understand and model the human being as *both* "child" and "parent" of society there are two requirements. Firstly, social theory needs a concept of man whose sociality does make a vital contribution to the realization of his potential *qua* human being. Secondly, however, it requires a concept of man who does possess sufficient relatively autonomous properties that he can reflect and act upon his social context, along with others like him, in order to transform it.
>
> It is argued that both the "undersocialised" and the "oversocialised" models of humankind are inadequate foundations for social theory because they present us with either a self-sufficient *maker* of society, or a supine social product who is *made*. (261–62)

Archer then goes on to historically analyze how each of these models came to dominate in the social sciences, and cumulatively created a curious and distorting situation regarding how "self" is understood and discussed in those sciences. Archer argues that one of the primal and absolutely necessary conditions for the very existence of social life at all is the awareness among people that they exist as entities with some continuity over time: they are there as themselves today, were also there yesterday, and probably will be there tomorrow. This personal "I am-ness" is a *universal* property of humans in society, and exists *prior* to the possibility of social life: Archer goes so far as to say that this line of thinking is a *transcendental* argument for the necessity of a *sense of self* to the existence of society. This *sense* of self is different from the *concept* of self, and what the self is supposed to be like in a given society: concepts of self differ by culture, and are thus empirically relative, but the sense of self is not.

Such a distinction is necessary to sustain in order to be able to differentiate between the universal and the culturally specific aspects of the person. But, says Archer, "there has been a persistent tendency in the social sciences to absorb the *sense of self* into the *concept of self* and thus to credit what is universal to the cultural balance sheet whose territory is claimed by social science." Archer's challenge of this disciplinary colonialism, her personalist critical realism, is thus built on the necessary distinction between sense and concept of self—a distinction also central to the Church's definition of personhood as in part universal and in part cultural that would be at the base of any sociology in service to Catholic social teaching.

This kind of personalist critical realism results in sociological research directions of great interest to Catholic social thought, and entirely compatible with Catholic ontology and social principles. Of major importance are studies of the role of freedom and responsibility within the parameters of social structure. Such work combines quantitative examination of trends and patterns in thought and behavior with qualitative analysis of the *agency* of people in their situations: their experience and inner thought processes that serve as the foundation for their actions that result ultimately in larger patterns. This is a strong tradition in the best sociology, that personalist critical realism picks up and amplifies. Two recent examples of such research would be the National Study of Youth and Religion by Smith and colleagues, already referred to; and some very interesting work by Margaret Archer on how people navigate and act in social stratification systems to locate themselves in a lifeworld, in effect "making" the stratification system reproduce itself or morph. A recent summary of this ongoing research is contained in her book *Making Our Way through the World: Human Reflexivity and Social Mobility* (Archer 2007). This is a study of students and townspeople in Warwick, England, which tracks how their internal conversations are of different types which result in different stances toward their class point of origin and differences in their class destination. Agency is thus linked to the structure of social mobility.

A second direction is implied by the focus on reflexivity: how do people anchor themselves and come to be socialized in a world where almost permanent change is the order of the day—what Archer has called "morphogenetic" society? This is a type of social system in which yesterday's patterns of thinking and acting are of little use, and the notion of socialization as learning about what you are supposed to do from traditions and from those who have trodden the path of growing up before seems tenuous if not fatally problematic. Archer has articulated the theoretical issues involved here through a consistent critique of Bourdieu's concept of *habitus*, which is a mindset people develop over time in relationship to a fairly stable set of social structures that provide social location. Archer (2010) argues that the concept works or applies only in social structures unchanging enough over time to acquire a meaningful sense of certainty or predictability.

I suggest that sociologists interested in repairing the shaky plausibility structures of the Church should consider the implications of Archer's approach for our vision of what we are praying and working toward. I think that our present model for a return to a vibrant Catholicism tends to rely too much on creating a society where *habitus* is in effect: fairly traditional family units living in stable social contexts like neighborhoods and parishes, where "socialization" means learning the traditions and holding to them in the *sturm und drang* of the broader turbulent society. There is a bit of nostalgia here, maybe, but more importantly a model of society and social change that may be lagging behind the actual morphogenetic reality sociologists readily document. If Archer is right, socializing our next Catholic generation is not what it used to be: they need to be constantly self-reflexive and adaptive, constantly making judgments with a kind of metacognition even people used to rapid social change might find daunting. I am not saying we always want to return to the ethnic neighborhoods of the days of the Catholic ghettos and *Going My Way*, but I think we need to ask what lingers in us about this world that we must admit is sociologically impossible, and why. Given our actual sociological perspective, what do we think socialization to a Catholic worldview means today, and what can we learn about how to make it effective in a constantly changing social landscape where the old anchors for Catholic identity and sense of self are either gone or hard to discern? This is a crucial domain for research, where new theories of socialization can converge directly with what we are learning about the post-parish social organization of the Church.

Archer comes to the concern for *internal conversation* as a way of integrating the personalist dynamism of agency with the emergent realities of social structures, seeking to challenge both the overly deterministic model of the person of much structuralist sociology and the flatness of rational choice models of the person which exaggerate the calculative nature of thinking, assuming all thinking is "nothing but" interest-maximizing market thinking. In fact Archer has done a lot of work on the role of human agency in social structure, which she often elaborates as a part of her theory of "morphogenetic" society, in which routine habitual thought, the kind most associated (often stereotypically) with traditional societies, no longer dominates as a form of consciousness because we live in a world where social change, often dramatic social change, is normal. In effect reflexivity is essential to contemporary social life and a sociology that insists on social deterministic models of the person or downplays the role of internal reflexivity in the functioning of society is defective. Sociology today, to understand today's types of society, must include the analysis of patterns of reflexivity in its research priorities.

Thus a significant aspect of critical realism becomes the exploration of the contents and workings of reflexivity: what we think about and feel and how those in turn shape our actions that result in individual and social patterns. Given their concern for the emergent properties of persons and society and their openness to levels of reality that while not for the moment empirically measurable are no less of major importance in personal and social life, it is not surprising that a number of scholars in this school, including Smith and Archer themselves, end up interrogating the role and functioning of religion and the transcendent in the mix of reflexive processes that forge the agency of individuals and groups.

(Recall the discussion of an opening to this that comes from a reframing of the sociological imagination in my introductory essay to this volume.)

However, their interrogation is not meant to sociologistically "explain away" religion as merely a product of ideological manipulation (the Marxian view) or an internalized symbolic image of the social collective (the Durkheimian view), but rather to own religious thinking and experiences as a domain of people's reflexivity and agency which must be taken seriously as part of human reality. Religion is more than a dependent variable: it is a signal of a level of reality that sociologists must put into their mix to truly understand people and social systems. It is, as was put earlier, a sociology that acts as if the transcendent is real,[7] something that neither positivism nor postmodernism can allow is admissible to meaningful debate. A good recent example of this is a work called *Transcendence: Critical Realism and God* (Archer, Collier, and Porpora 2004). In an essay from this book, Archer recounts that

> Throughout their history the social sciences have privileged atheism. They are an extended example of the general asymmetry between the need to justify faith and the assumption that atheism supposedly requires no such justification. Indeed, social science bears much responsibility for enabling atheism to be presented as an epistemologically neutral position, instead of what it is, a commitment to a belief in the absence of religious phenomena. In part, this is derived from the personal irreligiosity of the founding fathers; Durkheim and Marx were prominent "masters of suspicion," whilst Weber declared himself "religiously unmusical." In equal part it can be attributed to the pervasive methodological endorsement of empiricism, which illegitimately confines investigation to observables. At best, empiricists confined consigned nonobservables to the metaphysical realm; at worst, the non-observable was deemed "nonsense" in logical positivism. In sum empiricism confirmed the hegemony of sense data over everything that can be known. (Archer 2004, 65)

Atheism flows naturally from this framework: religion and religious experience are framed as an ever smaller category of human experience where the empiricists have not yet quite been able to exercise their explanatory powers—yet. Behaviorism and psychoanalysis are two poignant examples, but so are sociologistic determinism and rational choice theory, which strip away the obvious capacity of humans to experience reality in all its levels of complexity, including the level of the transcendent. This level must be included because the very nature of our lives as persons requires us to root what we do in judgments we make about what is most important for us to do, and this in fact is often not what would by "rational" standards be best for us. We do things for others, we sacrifice, we love selflessly, we contribute beyond our means. Archer then explains that from a realist position a person is one who must interact with the complex levels of reality in three ways: with nature and the physical environment, with the practical order of acquiring competencies for making a living, and with the social system in which we relate to others. A realist model of the person is about one who *practices* living in all three of these domains at the same time. Religious practices have always been a part of this multilayered living, also, and in fact are connected to our species need to decide what is most important to us, what concerns us.

Archer argues that our personal identities are in fact derived from our ultimate concerns: we are what we value and what we care most about. And for many (certainly not all, though they too must have a higher set of values to practice their lives), reflecting on all this from a religious perspective, responding to God or a higher power in some quite conscious way, is part of the reality of their lives. We may judge wrong, err, fail to meet a standard we ascribe to, but that does not make the fact that we engage higher or ultimate realities any less real or powerful. There are, as Archer concludes, "certain ways-of-being-in-the-world which are simply incomprehensible without the admission of transcendence." There are simply no good theoretical and empirical reasons to keeping religious practice bracketed out of human being; the primacy attached to practice in realism's model of man makes it thoroughly amenable to letting religion in.

To be sure this is a very sketchy overview of a highly elaborated emerging paradigm in sociology. What I hope it can accomplish is to whet the appetite of readers to explore this territory further, with confidence that personalist critical realism shares considerable foundational premises with Catholic social thought in terms of the model of the person it rests upon and the model of society it employs. Future Catholic sociologies would do well to incorporate its insights.

The Public Sociology Movement

The second recent development in sociology that offers potential for a bridge between Catholic social thought and the discipline has been the movement to redraw the map of legitimate sociological *practice* and expand the repertoire of legitimate professional *identities* of scholars by affirming territories that existed previously in the field, but were undervalued or were not clearly in focus. This is a movement about what counts as doing real sociology and what counts as being a real sociologist. There is some paradox here, as I mentioned earlier: this movement has its origins in a radical call for sociology to return to its authentic roots as a moral force in public life, primarily understood in liberationist terms, yet within this call space is nevertheless opened up for many values critical of society to enter the conversation. These include those amenable to much of Catholicism's social vision and teaching. This movement emerged within the discipline particularly in the early 2000s, as a way to comprehensively understand and address long-standing tensions and conflicts among various types and purposes of—as well as audiences for—sociology.

Movement advocates examine sociology as a terrain of power and prestige (something Catholics can readily affirm since those power dynamics have been part of the reason earlier Catholic sociologies could never get a leg up), and seek to give voice and credibility to parts of sociological work not acknowledged or justly rewarded by the mainstream. Much has been written recently about this movement pro and con, laudatory and critical, and the initial ideas of this sociology of sociology have been elaborated and refined over the last half-decade: it is a major theme of disciplinary *reflexivity* at this time. For present purposes I can simply outline its central arguments to stimulate further interest, and will do so sticking quite closely to its initial articulation by ASA past-president Michael Burawoy in 2004 (Burawoy 2005). Then, given our interest in how public sociology can offer a bridge to Catholic social thought, I will describe one way in which Catholic sociologists have used the public sociology platform to build arguments for a sociology that can include a transcendent dimension.

It is hardly a new idea that what should count as legitimate scholarly sociology should include more than doing quantitative or qualitative research published in one of the prestigious journals. Most sociologists with doctorates actually teach for a living: about 70% work on campuses, about 30% work elsewhere primarily in research or policy settings. Yet the reward structure for academic tenure and scholarly reputation typically hardly recognizes this fact— or ruefully acknowledges the reality of especially undergraduate teaching as a price to pay on the way to getting to the real stuff of disciplinary fame and fortune. This incongruity is maddening and unjust, and in fact has served as one of the significant drivers of the emergence of the public sociology movement.

Those who value teaching in sociology have fought long and hard for recognition that, for example, pedagogical inquiry and curricular design should "count" toward tenure and promotion, and that journals like *Teaching Sociology* were not low powered sideshows but central to the operation of the discipline. Starting especially in the late 1970s sociology as a discipline developed a feisty internal movement about teaching and learning, which inevitably conflicted with the power structure of the discipline for which funded original research, especially if enhancing the success of a graduate program and spawning more grants, was the gold standard of professional activity and identity. Despite this conflict, today the field enjoys a successful ASA section on teaching and learning, reaches out effectively to new faculty, sustains its journal, and can defend the teaching movement in terms of the support sociologists, of all people, owe in justice to both undergraduates as an oppressed group and sociologists with high teaching loads as marginalized in the discipline.

Members of this internal teaching movement were early active contributors to the multidisciplinary national higher education efforts to advocate for improved undergraduate education, defend the liberal arts, connect assessment to student learning, and resist the corporatization of campuses with its relentless drives for efficiency measured in terms of larger classes and expanded use of contingent faculty. They piggybacked on a national counteroffensive fostered by various higher education associations against the increasing bureaucratization of academic work and the rewarding only one type of professional scholarly activity. A major theme in this pushback was articulated around the concept of "the scholarship of teaching and learning." This phrase came from a framework for organizing faculty roles and rewards set forth by the Carnegie Foundation for the Advancement of Teaching and Learning in a famous report on what academics actually spent their time on and valued, called *Scholarship Reconsidered: Priorities of the Professoriate,* by Ernest Boyer (1990).

Boyer had argued that legitimate academic work, scholarship, was more than simply original disciplinary research, which he called the "scholarship of discovery." Faculty also did, and should be rewarded for, three other forms of scholarship: "application," that is the use of disciplinary research to address public issues; "integration," that is the drawing together of trends and patterns in a field for non-specialists, or creating a synthesis of a complex area, as in a textbook; and "teaching," that is the analysis of teaching and learning patterns and structures to better understand how people acquired the intellectual tools of their field. Boyer and others, especially at Carnegie, clarified a definition of scholarly quality that could apply to all four forms. Boyer's model sparked a decade long national discussion in higher education about how faculty roles and rewards were biased against three of the four types of the actual scholarship that faculty in many disciplines did, and what could be done about such bias on campuses. In effect, the "scholarship" argument became a terrain upon which the politics of the professoriate and their prestige structures was on the table for critical analysis. Sociologists like R. Eugene Rice and William Sullivan, with their expertise in fields such as occupations and professions and the nature of professional education and identity, became significant players in the debates.

The movement for public sociology within our discipline drew significant energy from this intramural and national debate about how power, status, and prestige systems created unlevel playing fields for faculty interests, roles, and rewards, and in effect smothered many a faculty member's career aspirations and original intellectual passions.[8] It also drew from the need for sociology as a field to come to terms with its diminishing influence overall on campuses and in the broader society after the heady days of the 1960s and '70s, when enrollments were high and sociology played an important role in national political discourse. Burawoy calls this a "scissors" hypothesis: as the country moved center and then right during the next two decades by some measures, sociology, already predominantly left, tended to keep moving left and teetered near the left edge of the broader ideological map.

Could this emargination change, and if so, could it change without sociology either selling out to corporate conservative values and practices or becoming simply a soapbox for leftist ideology and haven for political correctness? To explore this would demand a new sociology of sociology—in particular a sociology of the multiple publics sociology engages with, and why, and how. Such a sociology came to be articulated in a high profile, high stakes way at the 2004 ASA convention by Michael Burawoy in his presidential address.

I think it is important for us to understand Burawoy's arguments, even though he expresses them in the critical language of his own leftist leanings, even if we disagree with the dominant paradigm he draws on and which we have amply criticized. For Burawoy may be Marxist and a bearer of all the biases of the field that make it hard for us to seek common ground with the discipline, but he is no strong social constructionist: he maps sociology as an institution in terms we can sociologically recognize and in language whose moral fervor and accuracy about systems of academic and political power are hard for Catholic sociologists to simply dismiss. He reminds his audience that sociology defines its very self as one that uncovers hidden realities and gives voice to the marginal, and that sociological research and policy advice have figured strongly, for example, in most chapters of the movements for social justice and liberation not only in the U.S. but around the world. As Catholics we may have seen the deleterious effects of this sociology's influence on contemporary CST, but that does not mean that sociologies of other types should not help shape CST in principle. If we can bracket some of Burawoy's particular politics, prototypical though they may be, we can discern some opening to a larger vision of the field through which we may walk.

Burawoy begins by calling his audience back to the foundational moral mission of the discipline—sidetracked for a while, to be sure, by the occasionally powerful addictions to Comtean visions of pure science and social engineering among sociology's elites—but reborn since the 1960s through sociology's often direct role on campuses where protests turned into movements and its later institutionalized adoption of critical stances toward society:

> In the beginning sociology aspired to be...searching for order in the broken fragments of modernity, seeking to salvage the promise of progress. Thus Karl Marx recovered socialism from alienation; Emile Durkheim redeemed organic solidarity from anomie and egoism. Max Weber, despite premonitions of a "polar night of icy darkness," could discover freedom in rationalization, and extract meaning from disenchantment. On this side of the Atlantic W.E.B. Dubois pioneered pan-Africanism in reaction to racism and imperialism, while Jane Addams tried to snatch peace and internationalism from the jaws of war. (Burawoy 2005, 5)

Burawoy calls sociology to continue this heroic tradition, but there are problems now that need clearing away. Original passions for social justice and liberation that drew people into sociology in the first place become over time the pursuit of careers and credentials. "Progress" is measured no longer in terms of freedom and overcoming of unjust power structures but instead by the acquisition of professional prestige and the successful pursuit of power and status within inherently conservative, hierarchical, and competitive institutions: "standardized courses, validated reading lists, bureaucratic rankings, intensive examinations, literature reviews, tailored dissertations, refereed publications, the all-mighty CV, the job search, the tenure file, and then policing one's colleagues and successors to make sure we all march in step."

Burawoy then calls his colleagues to take a good look in the mirror and ask themselves if this is all there is or should be to sociology today. He points out that the discipline experienced a sort of schizophrenia about whether "advocacy" work was really sociology or something else and lesser; squatting on a legacy of the positivist epistemological heritage and intellectual prestige system, deciders framed advocacy work as less scientific and neutral than true sociological science should be, and thus of lesser value in the professional reward structure. Yet ironically, some of the best research, the most evocative, that reaches wider audiences and interests them in what sociologists have to say, is often rooted in a passionate concern for justice and aimed at shedding light on and eventually helping to solve social problems. It could seem, too, that mainstream sociology's preoccupation with neutrality and distance and the construction of abstract covering laws of social organization was also in itself a politics of safety, distasteful to those seeking just acknowledgment of the many ways in which one could be a sociologist engaged in civil and political society.

In the mid 2000s some of these critical thrusts within sociology's professional culture began to synergize, especially since postmodernist critiques of positivism and its legacy were now consolidated and sociologists were seeking new grounds upon which to base their claims of sociological expertise and meaning making. Burawoy began talking with colleagues about a kind of sociology of sociology that could highlight the discipline's underlying structure and culture and give new voice and honor to the full varieties of sociological work actually being done on the ground. This appealed strongly to the educators of the field, as we have already noted, but also those whose careers were pursued through community-based action research, in non-academic settings, in high schools, or in smaller departments where the luxury of managing a large funded research project was highly unlikely.

Buroway indicates how public much sociology actually has been, in different ways: how often sociologists engage people outside the formal discipline either colloquially or as expert commentators or advisors, to address general social issues or a specific social problem. In fact *students* not yet inside the field are public number one, it is easy to forget. But many examples of audiences that are not other academic specialists could be identified, from sociologists supporting and talking to social movements to supplying information for court decisions to addressing the press with new research about upcoming legislation.

A key aspect of this broadly public nature of the field, for us as sociologists with Catholic concerns, is his following premise:

> The multiplicity of public sociologies reflects not only different publics but different value commitments on the part of sociologists. Public sociology has no intrinsic normative valence, other than commitment to dialogue around issues raised in and by sociology. It can as well support Christian Fundamentalism as it can Liberation Sociology or Communitarianism. If sociology supports more liberal or critical public sociologies that is a consequence of the evolving ethos of the sociological community. (Burawoy 2005, 8–9)

One can just imagine the groans in the audience, but there it is: sociology in its public works is not inherently radical or leftist, it is so because most sociologists think that way, and a true public sociology movement must be seen as open to more than this one normative valence. This is the first opening through which we can walk. Sociology's two great classic self-reflexive questions are crucial for all to explore: *sociology for whom*, and *sociology for what*; and there is no reason apart from powerful peer pressures for us as Catholics not to be able to join that discussion.

In the course of his speech Burawoy then develops more fully a four-fold typology of sociology's division of labor, which I summarize as follows:

Professional sociology: at its core the creation and elaboration of true and tested methods, accumulated bodies of knowledge, orienting questions, and conceptual frameworks. It is elaborated through diverse research programs across the field and within its subspecialties. It is the *sine qua non* of all other forms of sociology, the core knowledge used with various publics for various purposes. It is also what most deciders think of as "real" sociology often funded by major research grants.

Public sociology: strikes up dialogic relationships between sociologists and one or more publics in which the agenda of each is brought to the table, in which each adjusts to the other. There can be differences and disagreements, but dialogue and communicative action are the goals in order, for example, to contribute to the construction of social problems or public issues out of private troubles, and building movements to address them. The works of C. W. Mills and Barbara Ehrenreich come to mind.

Policy sociology: especially in contrast to public sociology, where goals emerge in dialogue or argument, policy sociology is sociology in the service of a particular goal already defined by a client, and its *raison d'etre* is to provide solutions to problems presented to us or to legitimate solutions already formulated. Experts testifying for one side in court cases would be an example, or contributing expertise to government hearings on a problem like terrorism or poverty. Consider for example family sociologist Steven Nock testifying before the Attorney General of Canada about scientific flaws of studies on same-sex parenting.

Critical sociology: examines the implicit and explicit foundations, both normative and descriptive, of the research programs and theorizing of professional sociology. Works like those of Alvin Gouldner come to mind, or Robert

Lynd before him, or feminist sociology today. Critical sociology focuses on the two classical questions noted earlier: sociology for what and for whom.

Each of these overlap to some extent with the other in terms of people and activities, though since professional sociology is the most mainstream and highly articulated, it has what Burawoy calls "faces" of the other three embedded in its practices already. A key point for him is that for sociology to be truly healthy, authentic to its original calling, and vital to society, *all four types of sociology should interact in a dynamic ecology*. A first step in this is to openly admit to the prevalent disciplinary hierarchy which has valued professional and policy sociology much more than public and critical sociology in its roles and rewards. The public sociology movement is being institutionalized in the discipline, for example through a recently formed Section on Sociological Practice and Public Sociology.

Finally, Burawoy elaborates in considerable depth the types and features of the dominant ways of thinking of each of the types. The vertical axis delineates dimensions of knowledge, while the horizontal axis delineates the primary audience to which each type turns. Here is Burawoy's synthesizing graphic:

	Academic audience	Extra-academic audience
Instrumental knowledge	*Professional sociology*	*Policy sociology*
Knowledge	Theoretical/empirical	Concrete
Truth	Correspondence	Pragmatic
Legitimacy	Scientific norms	Effective
Accountability	Peers	Clients
Politics	Professional self-interest	Policy intervention
Pathology	Self-referentiality	Servility
Reflexive knowledge	*Critical sociology*	*Public sociology*
Knowledge	Foundational	Communicative
Truth	Normative	Consensus
Legitimacy	Moral vision	Relevance
Accountability	Critical intellectuals	Designated publics
Politics	Internal debate	Public dialogue
Pathology	Dogmatism	Faddishness

The framework can of course be criticized for stereotypes and false dichotomies, and has been, but it is certainly an interesting heuristic, and may be evocative for considering where a sociology aimed at helping advance CST might fit into the sociological territory as Burawoy defines it. For example, we could say that our sociology in service to the quality and promulgation of CST contains elements from all four types, i.e., has four faces. Like any sociology we draw on a core of sociological data and theory from professional sociology. With critical sociology we share the questioning of mainstream sociology's paradigmatic foundations and political purposes, the development of sociologies based on a moral vision pegged to a set of fairly clear normative truths, and are certainly thereby accused by many of dogmatism! With policy sociology we share an interest in getting a Catholic perspective resting on sociological data to the table of policy formation and debate at all levels of government. And with public sociology we share an aspiration to engage in ever wider conversation with many audiences on the general direction of society and culture and in influencing the parameters of that conversation to respect, or revalue, a Christian social vision.

Sorokin's Integralism as a Larger Frame for Public Sociology

Finally, one very interesting development in the public sociology movement has been the influence of holistic sociology, meant to give a larger theoretical frame to the understanding of the division of labor enunciated by Burawoy and elaborated thereafter by others, in terms not entirely dependent upon the Marxist bent underpinning Burawoy's original formulation. This holistic sociology is being articulated especially by Vincent Jeffries and Lawrence Nichols, for example, and is based on a renewed interest in the work of Pitirim Sorokin's "integral sociology." Resurgence of interest in Sorokin came to light in the pages of *The Catholic Social Science Review* in the early 2000s (e.g., Jeffries 2005) and that this perspective has found its way into the mainstream's debates over public sociology is itself remarkable. In 2009 Jeffries then edited a very recent and comprehensive reader on public sociology, which included materials comparing Sorokin and the sociology of sociology underpinning the public sociology movement (Jeffries 2009).

What is so valuable about Sorokin? In the first place it is helpful to recall that Sorokin was involved in a major struggle with Talcott Parsons over control of the prestigious sociology program at Harvard for what we might call the soul of American sociology. Parsons won, and in Burawoy's terms Parsons holds some major responsibility for establishing the hierarchical dominance of professional and policy sociology, in terms of control of roles and rewards, over critical and public sociology in our time. It is widely acknowledged that the champion of the positivist paradigm in sociology was Talcott Parsons: Benton Johnson (1987) goes so far as to say Parsons was the primary architect of the uneasy détente between sociology and religion that dominated the field. But how did he become top dog? We can look for some insight about this from the contest between Pitirim Sorokin and Talcott Parsons over whether prophetic wisdom or bureaucratic professionalization would triumph in the Sociology Department at Harvard during and after World War II. How it came to be that the functionalism and naturalism of Talcott Parsons rose to such a powerful position—so powerful that even today, after decades of criticism by critical theorists and others, it is still identified as a major disciplinary approach that defines the field and spawns new versions—is an archetypal chapter in the contemporary process of distancing sociology from wider publics and moral discourse, and which Burawoy is now trying to overcome.

One of the stepping stones of Parsons' rise to near hegemonic dominance involved his victory in an academic power struggle during the 1940s with another, truly opposite titan in the field, Pitirim Sorokin, over the future direction of the discipline. Commentators recall that Sorokin's macro and comparative sociology was premised on *discerning the moral trajectories of different types of societies*, and raising alarms about the empiricist tendencies of our own contemporary civilization that threatened dehumanization. Sorokin was warning that what was held to be "progress" might in fact be a tragedy in the making. His "integral" sociology was built around an assumption of the ontological role of the supernatural and transcendent in cultural and social dynamics, the epistemological validity of blending social science and moral analysis, and the crucial power of the ethics of altruism in maintaining a decent society—a crucial glue in societies coming undone because of increasing specialization, institutional differentiation, and cultural fragmentation. Two of his major works, *Social and Cultural Dynamics* and *Crisis of Our Age*, were written in a prophetic mode, and especially the latter is startling in its perspicacity even today; but at the time they were rejected by American sociologists as not meeting their research standards for objective scientific discourse, and also because they had the wrong "tone."

Parsons' kind of sociology, on the other hand, at once modeled the modernist, professional vision of social science and also *fit better with the emerging professionalization* of academic activity that Burawoy has brought into focus. As Buxton (1997, 367) cogently observed in a review of recent work on Sorokin,

> Arguably, Sorokin's work of the late 1930s and early 1940s was rejected not simply because it failed to meet the standards of scientific sociology but because it challenged the notions of progress, modernity, and expert intervention that were becoming central tenets of an increasingly professionalized sociology. Sorokin's decline was bound up with a shift away from the sociologist as a public figure toward the sociologist as expert, whose main point of reference was the emergent sociological profession, along with foundations and government bureaucrats. And Sorokin's fall from favor was not an isolated case: Harry Elmer Barnes, Charles Ellwood, Robert Lynd, and Jerome Davis, among others, were all prominent figures before the late 1930s; and their careers, too, declined thereafter. Indeed, it could be argued that the rise of Talcott Parsons at Harvard (the mirror image of Sorokin's decline) was due not to the superior power and attractiveness of his theoretical system...but to the fact that his views on the need for the social sciences to model themselves along the analytic/interventionist lines of the medical profession were congruent with those of the elite network at Harvard as well as of those of influential foundation officials. It was primarily for this reason that Parsons was given a free hand to de-

velop what was to become the Department of Social Relations, while Sorokin
was forced to spend much of his latter career in academic exile.

Sorokin had founded the Department of Sociology at Harvard around 1930,
but by the time the struggle with Parsons was over, Parsons had built a new interdisciplinary Department of Social Relations in 1946 which blended sociology,
psychology, and anthropology (these are now separated out again) and carried
forward the Parsonian empirical and experimental research agenda. Personalities
certainly played a role, as Parsons was said to be a smoother operator and better
administrator, less cantankerous and belligerent. But the paradigmatic difference
was certainly in play. In his comparative research Sorokin was concerned most
about how features of culture, in particular how a society "reckoned ultimate
truth and reality," gave shape to a given social order; and how the most vital
cultures were multidimensional, "in which reality was many-sided and human
needs were both spiritual and material, with the former dominating....The
known world, and knowledge of it, resulted from the dominating interplay of
spiritual with empirical truths" (Johnston 2007). Sorokin's sociology thus allowed in the reality of the transcendent. Parsons' sociology recognized the so-
cio-empirical reality of religion as a motive for human action, but would hesitate
to give ontological status to such reality. Parsonian functionalism framed faith
and religion as not ontological but rather subjective realities: factors of the human experience in society that must be considered naturalistically, as social
facts, in both explanatory models of social change and policy positions regarding how to solve social problems.

I think it is no accident that Parsons' approach led much more readily to
success in acquiring the almighty scientific research grants upon which the
emerging academic prestige of sociology depended, and upon which successful
department chairmanships are won.[9] Sorokin remained a force within sociology
and even became ASA president in 1963, honored as a senior scholar. Nevertheless he focused much of his later intellectual and moral energies on the margins,
working to build up a Harvard-based Center for Creative Altruism, conceptually
based on his vision of the Good Society, and died in 1968.

Recalling Sorokin to the sociological stage at this time thus represents an
opportunity to revise the disciplinary history and recapture something the field
had lost with the rise of the professional model. This is why editor Vincent Jeffries chooses to include discussions of Sorokin's work in the 2009 public sociology anthology.[10] In his introduction to that volume Jeffries points out that Bu-
rowoy's essential call is for the interdependence of different kinds of
sociological knowledge, an "organic solidarity [Burawoy's term] in which each
type draws energy, meaning, and imagination from its connection to the others."
This means that each type needs to give central attention to the concerns and
agendas of the others, lest it lose its own effectiveness. It may seem a grand or
grandiose vision of the discipline, but its holism is clear. Then, in an article enti-

tled "Burawoy's Holistic Sociology and Sorokin's 'Integralism': A Conversation of Ideas" by Nichols, and in another article called "The Scientific System of Public Sociology: The Exemplar of Pitirim A. Sorokin's Social Thought" by Jeffries, the authors lay out how Sorokin's sociology maps into the conceptual space provided by Burawoy, finds considerable fit, and yet offers a healthy counterpoint.

On the side of fit, Sorokin is proposed as an exemplar: he published major works of all four types, and personally attempted to keep the various parts and types of sociology playing in harmony. Sorokin was an integral sociologist, and very importantly, his capacity to work in that manner was in large measure due to his commitment to bringing religious and spiritual values into the heart of his own work and in his cyclical model of society. The problems of our age, he had argued, came in significant measure because we have lost this lodestar. It happens that Sorokin was dubious about policy sociology because of his criticism of large-scale social engineering of the Stalinist type, but in general he practiced all forms of sociology in the division of labor, and he did not reject policy sociology in principle.

And on the critique side, Nichols (2009) points out that while Burawoy is correct in his call for a reform of the discipline in holistic terms, Sorokin would certainly argue that Burawoy is wrong about the nature of the crisis both within sociology and in the larger society. Burawoy emphasizes the political scissors movement of society moving too far right while sociology, correctly, is moving left, and the role of capitalist and other elites in suppressing freedoms. On the contrary, from a Sorokinian perspective and paraphrasing many of Sorokin's writings, Nichols thinks

> The contemporary crisis is not primarily economic in nature, nor is it even economic and political. Rather, it is an extraordinary crisis of the type that occurs only once in many centuries, and it involves every fundamental compartment of the dominant sensate culture [a term Sorokin employed to characterize cultures whose epistemology is entirely, flatly materialistic and naturalistic, *editor's note*]: its art, literature, law, system of truth, economics, politics, science, religion, and system of social relationships (contractual and compulsory). To diagnose the crisis as primarily economic, or as economic and political, is to mistake the part for the whole, the symptom for the disease.
>
> None of the types of sociological work identified by Burawoy can be completely successful if they remain grounded in the obsolescent assumptions of a dying sensate culture. The premises of the sensate mentality are partly true, but they are incomplete, and the more they are treated as the total truth, the more they mislead humanity. Sociologists must begin by realizing that, in addition to the sensory and rational aspects of the total reality, there is also a super-sensory and super-rational dimension that has been recognized for countless centuries in the philosophies and religions. Without this understanding, it is not possible for sociologists to develop and adequate view of human personality, which must include a super-sensory, super-rational dimension. The assumption

of this aspect of human reality is also necessary for a new ethics of absolute values, grounded in love and asserting the spiritual unity of all human persons and the sacred value of all human life. (Nichols 2009, 39–40)

So from Nichols' point of view Burawoy is right about the need for a new integration of sociological work, but partial and thus fatally flawed in his understanding of how to accomplish it: his materialist power analysis will eventually only reproduce the conflicts and splits we live with now because no higher values can come into play to help groups transcend their interests. Nichols also points out that Sorokin would say Burawoy is strong on some values but weak on others that must exist at the same time: strong on freedom and liberation, but weak on self-control and responsibility; strong on justice, but quite weak on articulating the compassion and mutuality that must operate to keep struggles for justice from becoming just more episodes of violent confrontation. Finally, Burawoy is wrong if he believes, despite his admitted disclaimer about value-neutrality quoted earlier, that his new sociology depends on liberal and radical-left attitudes, which Burawoy clearly glorifies. There is in the first place no such thing as a science defined in terms of the political values of its practitioners—something argued in the present volume about why confessional sociological science is not correct; and in the second place it clearly violates the value of diversity the discipline claims to uphold.

Nichols then lists some ways Burawoy might respond to a Sorokinian criticism, a primary one being that the sort of *gemeinschaft* Sorokin would prefer to see is not really possible in our kind of pluralist and fractioned society any longer except on small local scales, so that the vision of a decent society can't be so much about universal love as humane tolerance. Nevertheless, the Sorokinian contribution to the public sociology movement is powerful and appealing, and ever so consonant with the values and social analysis typically expressed in Catholic social teaching.

Concluding Comments

We have covered a wide arc here, beginning with an effort to comprehensively define the postmodern territory in which sociology and Catholic sociologists now think and create, and then examining possible bases for contemporary dialogue between sociology and Catholicism by reviewing two major developments in the usually ambivalent discipline that offer such promise. I hope the discussion has provided a ray of hope and sense of possibility, whereby we can overcome some major intellectual and spiritual barriers that have impeded the fruitful exchange of ideas between the discipline and the Church. I think developing sociologies in the service of Catholic Social Teaching has never had more potential than it does today. I also think that it is more possible and plausible now than in the past to forge a scholarly identity as a sociologist working with and for the Church. This scholarly identity has power and must be institutionally leveraged now, through greater activity across all the four types of sociology Burawoy has outlined, to heal the societal maladies we as Catholics know so well. This entire book is essentially an invitation to Catholics to pursue sociology in a new key, to explore what the field can offer the Church to help in its mission to refine and propagate CST in our time.

We can only hope such work can help rebuild the plausibility structures the Church has lost in a better, stronger way. But there is a creative irony here: while potential grows for collaboration between sociology and Catholic social thought, the wider culture may be even more difficult to challenge. In a work I have drawn from several times here, Gay (1998) has argued that we are in a time that is not only postmodern, but also *post-Christian*. By this he means that "modern society and culture have, in effect, been inoculated against the transforming impact of the Gospel due to the immanentization of Christian truth." Such "Truth" as there is resides entirely on the worldly plane. So when we proclaim something to be powerful because it is grounded in the Gospel, it is not so much argued with as met with vacant stares. We think the Gospel ought to scandalize or give offense to the world, but the world gazes back not scandalized but, really, indifferent, especially insofar as the age old questions of truth and salvation we seek to introduce point to reality outside the social construction of self and reality. Since that fact is itself obscured, our sociology must reflexively relativize that cultural situation. This is what it would mean to begin to rebuild the plausibility structure of Catholic social thought and teachings.

Notes

1. Craig Gay (1998), whose work I cited in my opening paper in this anthology, provides an excellent synthesis of how Guardinian themes emerged in sociology from Weber forward, in a chapter focusing on "The Worldly Self at the Heart of Modern Culture."

2. See the PBS Frontline video documentary *Merchants of Cool*, available at www.pbs.org/wgbh/pages/frontline/shows/cool.

3. See Laura Bovone (2005), "Sociology as an Account of Accounts." Her article's publication venue is somewhat ironic, appearing as it does in an anthology dedicated to exploring the work of Fr. Paul Hanley Furfey, the noted and foundational Catholic sociologist!

4. On pp. 123 ff. Smith offers a wryly amusing but also disturbing critique of the use of overblown and logically erroneous social constructionism in one popular contemporary introductory sociology textbook, well worth a look.

5. As I say, the literature on critical realism is growing rapidly, and represented within sociology per se by such figures as Christian Smith (cited earlier), Margaret Archer (whose work appears later in the anthology), Douglas Porpora, and Andrew Collier.

6. Available at http://www.vatican.va/roman_curia/pontifical_academies/acdsoc/.

7. Of interest here is a recent report by the Social Science Research Council (Smilde and May, 2010) on trends in how religion is treated empirically in prestigious sociology journal articles between 1978 and 2007. It suggests there is some turnaround in this, where religion is increasingly treated as an independent variable, thus acknowledging that religion can impact society and people as well as be impacted, thus opening a door to religion per se as "something important" in a broad way. But whichever way the model is working, sociology tends to reduce religion to something to be accounted for by other sociological variables. See Jaschik (2010) for a wry account of the report.

8. For further discussion of the connection between the national debate about the meaning of scholarship and the specific movement for public sociology within the discipline, see Kleidman (2009).

9. On the contest between Parsons and Sorokin over influence in the discipline, see for example Ford, et al (1995) and Johnston (1995).

10. It is significant that Jeffries also has been centrally involved in a very recently formed ASA section on Altruism, Morality, and Social Solidarity, which takes as its main concern the moral and spiritual aspects of social life, and whose research agenda has been helpfully supported at times by the Templeton Foundation. The language of this section's title rings very familiar to Catholic sociologists, I expect, and may be surprising to those who are not aware of how the reflexive turn in the discipline is having some surprising results.

Bibliography

Archer, Margaret. 2004. "Models of Man: The Admission of Transcendence." In *Transcendence: Critical Realism and God*, by Margaret Archer, Andrew Collier, and Douglas Porpora, 63–81. New York: Routledge.

———. 2005. "Persons and Ultimate Concerns: Who We Are in What We Care About." Proceedings of the 11th Plenary Session of the Pontifical Academy of Social Sciences. Available online at www.vatican.va/roman_curia/pontifical_academies/acd soc.

———. 2007. *Making Our Way through the World: Human Reflexivity and Social Mobility*. New York: Cambridge University Press.

———. 2010. "Routine, Reflexivity, and Realism." *Sociological Theory* 28 (3): 272–303.

Archer, Margaret, Andrew Collier, and Douglas Porpora. 2004. *Transcendence: Critical Realism and God*. New York: Routledge.

Bauman, Zygmunt. 1991. "Postmodernity, or Living with Ambivalence." In *Social Theory: Roots and Branches*, 200, edited by Peter Kivisto, 396–402. Los Angeles: Roxbury Press.

Bell, Daniel. 1977. "The Return of the Sacred? The Argument on the Future of Religion." *British Journal of Sociology* 28 (4): 419–49.

Benedict XVI. 2010. "He Aspired to the Truth of God and to the Truth About Man." Address to the Romano Guardini Foundation. Accessed at http://www.zenit.org/rssenglish-31063.

Berger, Peter, Brigitte Berger, and Hans Kellner. 1973. *The Homeless Mind: Modernization and Consciousness*. New York: Vintage Books.

Bovone, Laura. 2005. "Sociology as an Account of Accounts." In *Paul Hanley Furfey's Quest for the Good Society,* edited by Bronislaw Misztal, Francesco Villa, and Eric Williams. Washington, DC: The Council for Research in Values and Philosophy, Catholic University of America.

Boyer, Ernest. 1990. *Scholarship Reconsidered: Priorities of the Professoriate.* Princeton, NJ: Carnegie Foundation for the Advancement of Teaching.

Burawoy, Michael. 2005. "2004 ASA Presidential Address: For Public Sociology." *American Sociological Review* 70 (1): 4–28.

Buxton, William. 1997. Review of Barry V. Johnston, *Pitirim A. Sorokin: An Intellectual Biography. Isis* 88 (2): 366–67.

Ford, Joseph, Michel Richard, Palmer Talbutt, and Roger Wescott, eds. 1995. *Sorokin and Civilization: A Centennial Assessment.* New York: Transaction.

Gay, Craig M. 1998. *The Way of the (Modern) World Or, Why It's Tempting to Live as if God Doesn't Exist.* Grand Rapids, MI: Eerdmans.

Guardini, Romano. (1923) 1994. *Letters from Lake Como: Explorations in Technology and the Human Race.* Grand Rapids, MI: Eerdmans.

———. 1998. *The End of the Modern World.* Wilmington, DE: ISI Books. Contains *The End of the Modern World,* originally published 1950, and *Power and Responsibility,* originally published 1953.

Illouz, Eva. 2007. *Cold Intimacies: The Making of Emotional Capitalism.* Malden, MA: Polity Books.

Jackson, Maggie. 2009. *Distracted: The Erosion of Attention and the Coming Dark Age.* New York: Prometheus Books.

Jaschik, Scott. 2010. "Sociologists Get Religion." *Inside Higher Education.* Accessed online at http://www.insidehighered.com/layout/set/print/news/2010/02/09/soc.

Jeffries, Vincent. 2005. "Symposium on Integralism and the Forms of Social Science." *The Catholic Social Science Review* 10: 9–106.

———, ed. 2009. *Handbook of Public Sociology.* Lanham, MD: Rowman and Littlefield.

Johnson, Benton. 1987. "Faith, Facts, and Values in the Sociology of Religion." In *Religious Sociology: Interfaces and Boundaries,* edited by William Swatos, 3–14. New York: Greenwood Press.

Johnston, Barry. 1995. *Pitirim Sorokin: An Intellectual Biography.* Lawrence: University of Kansas Press.

———. 2007. "Sorokin, Pitirim Alexandrovitch." In *Encyclopedia of Catholic Social Thought, Social Science, and Social Policy,* edited by Michael Coulter, Stephen Krason, Richard Myers, and Joseph Varacalli, 1015–17. Lanham, MD: Scarecrow Press.

Kleidman, Robert. 2009. "Engaged Social Movement Scholarship." In *Handbook of Public Sociology,* edited by Vincent Jeffries, 341–56. New York: Rowman and Littlefield.

Lundin, Roger. 1993. *The Culture of Interpretation: Christian Faith and the Postmodern World.* Grand Rapids, MI: Eerdmans.

Magister, Sandro. 2008. "Benedict XVI Has a Father, Romano Guardini." Accessed at www.chiesa.espressonline.it.

Marcuse, Herbert. 1969. "Repressive Tolerance." In *A Critique of Pure Tolerance,* by Robert Wolff, Barrington Moore, Jr., and Herbert Marcuse, 95–137. Boston: Beacon Press.

Nichols, Lawrence. 2009. "Burawoy's Holistic Sociology and Sorokin's 'Integralism': A Conversation of Ideas." In *Handbook of Public Sociology*, edited by Vincent Jeffries, 27–46. Lanham, MD: Rowman and Littlefield.

Rieff, Philip. 1966. *The Triumph of the Therapeutic: Uses of Faith after Freud.* Chicago: University of Chicago Press.

————. 2006. *My Life among the Deathworks: Illustrations of the Aesthetics of Authority.* Charlottesville: University of Virginia Press.

Rorty, Richard. 1989. *Contingency, Irony, and Solidarity.* Cambridge: Cambridge University Press.

Rosenau, Pauline. 1992. *Post-Modernism and the Social Sciences.* Princeton: Princeton University Press.

Sharkey, Stephen. 2011. "Guardini, Romano." In *Encyclopedia of Catholic Social Thought, Social Science, and Social Policy.* Vol. III, edited by Michael Coulter, Stephen Krason, Richard Myers, and Joseph Varacalli, 132–34. Lanham, MD: Scarecrow Press.

Shils, Edward. 1981. *Tradition.* Chicago: University of Chicago Press.

Smilde, David, and Matthew May. 2010. "The Emerging Strong Program in the Sociology of Religion." In *Social Science Research Council Working Papers.* Brooklyn, NY: Social Science Research Council.

Smith, Christian. 2003. "Introduction: Rethinking the Secularization of American Public Life." In *The Secular Revolution: Power, Interests, and Conflict in the Secularization of American Public Life,* edited by Christian Smith, 1–96. Berkeley: University of California Press.

————. 2010. *What Is a Person? Rethinking Humanity, Social Life, and the Moral Good from the Person Up.* Chicago: University of Chicago Press.

Storck, Thomas. 2001. "Postmodernism: Catastrophe or Opportunity—Or Both?" *Homiletic and Pastoral Review,* January. Accessed April 24, 2011 from http://www.catholicculture.org/culture/library.

Swift, Donald. 2007. "Postmodernism." In *Encyclopedia of Catholic Social Thought, Social Science, and Social Policy,* edited by Michael Coulter, Stephen Krason, Richard Myers, and Joseph Varacalli, 868–70. Lanham, MD: Scarecrow Press.

PART TWO

Contributions from the
Pontifical Academy of Social Scientists

Selections from the
Proceedings of the 14th Annual Meeting of the
Academy entitled "Pursuing the Common Good: How
Solidarity and Subsidiarity Can Work Together,"
Rome, 2008

8

Address of His Holiness Benedict XVI
to the Participants in the 14th Session
of the Pontifical Academy of Social Sciences

The Vatican, Consistory Hall • Saturday, 3 May 2008

Dear Brothers in the Episcopate and the Priesthood,
Distinguished Ladies and Gentlemen,

I am pleased to have this occasion to meet with you as you gather for the four-teenth Plenary Session of the Pontifical Academy of Social Sciences. Over the last two decades, the Academy has offered a valuable contribution to the deep-ening and development of the Church's social doctrine and its application in the areas of law, economics, politics, and the various other social sciences. I thank Professor Margaret Archer for her kind words of greeting, and I express my sin-cere appreciation to all of you for your commitment to research, dialogue, and teaching, so that the Gospel of Jesus Christ may continue to shed light on the complex situations arising in a rapidly changing world.

In choosing the theme *Pursuing the Common Good: How Solidarity and Subsidiarity Can Work Together,* you have decided to examine the interrelation-ships between four fundamental principles of Catholic social teaching: the digni-ty of the human person, the common good, subsidiarity, and solidarity (*Compendium of the Social Doctrine of the Church,* #160–63). These key realities, which emerge from the living contact between the Gospel and concrete social circumstances, offer a framework for viewing and addressing the imperatives facing mankind at the dawn of the twenty-first century, such as reducing inequalities in the distribution of goods, expanding opportunities for education, fostering sustainable growth and development, and protecting the environment.

How can solidarity and subsidiarity work together in the pursuit of the common good in a way that not only respects human dignity, but allows it to flourish? This is the heart of the matter which concerns you. As your preliminary discussions have already revealed, a satisfactory answer can only surface after careful examination of the meaning of the terms (cf. *Compendium of the Social Doctrine of the Church,* chapter 4). *Human dignity* is the intrinsic value of a person created in the image and likeness of God and redeemed by Christ. The totality of social conditions allowing persons to achieve their communal and individual fulfilment is known as the *common good. Solidarity* refers to the virtue enabling the human family to share fully the treasure of material and spiritual goods, and *subsidiarity* is the coordination of society's activities in a way that supports the internal life of the local communities.

Yet definitions are only the beginning. What is more, these definitions are adequately grasped only when linked organically to one another and seen as mutually supportive of one another. We can initially sketch the interconnections between these four principles by placing the dignity of the person at the intersection of two axes: one horizontal, representing "solidarity" and "subsidiarity," and one vertical, representing the "common good." This creates a field upon which we can plot the various points of Catholic social teaching that give shape to the common good.

Though this graphic analogy gives us a rudimentary picture of how these fundamental principles imply one another and are necessarily interwoven, we know that the reality is much more complex. Indeed, the unfathomable depths of the human person and mankind's marvelous capacity for spiritual communion— realities which are fully disclosed only through divine revelation—far exceed the capacity of schematic representation. The solidarity that binds the human family, and the subsidiary levels reinforcing it from within, must however always be placed within the horizon of the mysterious life of the Triune God (cf. Jn 5:26; 6:57), in whom we perceive an ineffable love shared by equal, though nonetheless distinct, persons (cf. *Summa Theologiae,* I, q. 42).

My friends, I invite you to allow this fundamental truth to permeate your reflections: not only in the sense that the principles of solidarity and subsidiarity are undoubtedly enriched by our belief in the Trinity, but particularly in the sense that these principles have the potential to place men and women on the path to discovering their definitive, supernatural destiny. The natural human inclination to live in community is confirmed and transformed by the "oneness of Spirit" which God has bestowed upon his adopted sons and daughters (cf. Eph 4:3; 1 Pet 3:8). Consequently, the responsibility of Christians to work for peace and justice, their irrevocable commitment to build up the common good, is inseparable from their mission to proclaim the gift of eternal life to which God has called every man.

9

Address to the Holy Father

Margaret S. Archer

The Vatican, Consistory Hall • Saturday, 3 May 2008

Your Holiness,

It is a privilege for the members of the Pontifical Academy of Social Sciences and their invited experts to be granted this audience. As you know, for this fourteenth Plenary Session the Academy is focusing on the topic *Pursuing the Common Good: How Solidarity and Subsidiarity Can Work Together*. I would like to thank the Dean-President Prof. Belisario Betancur for inviting me to give this address as one of the coordinators of this meeting, together with Professor Pierpaolo Donati.

Above all, the Academy wants to explore the radical implications of the Church's social doctrine for civil society. We are convinced that were the dignity of the human person and the common good, promoted by solidarity and subsidiarity, to be effectively recognized and upheld in practice, this would be capable of regenerating civil society. We think, in short, that it is possible to achieve a future global social system that is not based solely on the market or dependent upon states that do not pursue the common good of civil society. In making its contribution, the Academy re-emphasises that the central principles of the social doctrine are indivisible and therefore must be implemented together.

Secondly, given that in the social sciences theory must not be separated from practice, this meeting has taken the innovative approach of examining current exemplars of "good practice"—ones which seek to generate common goods through new combinations of subsidiarity and solidarity. In this globalised world there are novel practices that can stimulate free-giving and foster those relations of reciprocity which recognize the dignity of the human person. Examples of such good practices are now emerging that could prove to be forerunners of an authentic civil society, based upon human rights and duties: the "economy of communion," the "Food Bank" and micro-credit; the new "Local Alliances for the Family," originating in Germany but spreading throughout Europe; shared access to informational goods through the Internet; and educational activities based on innovatory forms of subsidiarity in developing countries.

In conclusion, given that a recurrent feature of modernity has been a lack of solidarity and subsidiarity at all levels, our challenge is to detect and suggest how these principles could be applied to generate common goods in abundance—thus holding out the promise of transforming global society into a "civilization of the common good." Our hope, in conformity with our Statutes, is that our deliberations will offer the Church elements which can be of use in the development of her social doctrine.

Your Holiness, we would like to thank you for your enlightened Magisterium. Your words will encourage us in our research and discussions.

10

Pursuing the Common Good: How Solidarity and Subsidiarity Can Work Together
Conference Introduction

Margaret S. Archer and Pierpaolo Donati

1. In the *Compendium of the Social Doctrine of the Church* (#160–63) we read that the principles of *the dignity of the human person, the common good, subsidiarity,* and *solidarity* are the permanent principles of the Church's social doctrine. They constitute the very heart of Catholic social teaching. "These principles, the expression of the whole truth about man known by reason and faith, are born of 'the encounter of the Gospel message and of its demands summarized in the supreme commandment of love of God and neighbour in justice with the problems emanating from the life of society.'"

In the course of history and with the light of the Spirit, the Church has wisely reflected within her own tradition of faith and has been able to provide an ever more accurate foundation and shape to these principles, progressively explaining them in the attempt to respond coherently to the demands of the times and to the continuous developments of social life. *These are principles of a general and fundamental character, since they concern the reality of society in its entirety*: from close and immediate relationships to those mediated by politics, economics, and law; from relationships among communities and groups to relations between peoples and nations. Because of their *permanence in time* and their *universality of meaning*, the Church presents them as the primary and fundamental parameters of reference for interpreting and evaluating social phenomena, which is the necessary source for working out the criteria for the discernment and orientation of social interactions in every area (#160–61).

2. On the other hand, as we observe social phenomena in contemporary societies, we see that these principles are largely misunderstood. Quite often they are interpreted in ways which are very far from the meaning and intentions proper to the social doctrine. As a matter of fact, reductionist and biased interpretations prevail almost everywhere. For instance: the common good is identified with material goods, like water, a healthy environment, or similar things; solidarity is identified with feelings of love, or philanthropy, or public charity; subsidiarity is defined as leaving decisions to the lower levels of the political system (see art. 3/B of the EU Maastricht Treaty).

These misinterpretations lead to serious consequences. Take, for example, the case of the family: the common good of the family is identified with its assets, family *solidarity* with sentiments of love, *subsidiarity* with leaving each actor to define the family as he/she likes. At the macro level of the national state, *solidarity* is defined in terms of political control over resources, the pursuit of equal opportunities, redistribution via the welfare state (*lab* side); and *subsidiarity* is identified with devolution or privatization (*lib* side). These examples are only a few of the general misunderstandings surrounding key concepts—the common good, solidarity, and subsidiarity.

3. The 2008 Plenary Meeting is based upon taking the present situation as a challenge to the social doctrine, which is requested to reflect anew on how society can achieve a configuration that is able to implement its principles. We must look for a proper vision of a truly human society by taking into consideration the cultural, social, economic, and political changes of our times in the light of the Christian perspective. In sum, the aims of this Plenary can be synthesized in three points:

(i) first, it is necessary to examine in-depth the current uses of these concepts in order to clarify their correct meaning; such a clarification should be undertaken with reference both to the historical aspects of the concepts and to the way they are put into practice today;

(ii) second, it is particularly important to try to look at social reality and see if there are both theoretical developments and practical exemplars of the correct use of these principles, showing how subsidiarity and solidarity can work together in order to produce the common good in an effective way;

(iii) third, if the two above aims are achieved, we can expect that new ideas and practical orientations will be put at our disposal in order to think of a new configuration of society, one that leaves behind the Hobbesian and Hegelian heritages which still impinge upon contemporary societies and impede the sound working of the four basic principles of the social doctrine.

4. In seeking to accomplish these aims, special attention will be given to the issue of the interdependence among the four principles, and how they can and should work together. As the *Compendium of the Social Doctrine* reminds us,

The principles of the Church's social doctrine must be appreciated in their unity, interrelatedness and articulation. This requirement is rooted in the meaning that the Church herself attributes to her social doctrine, as a unified doctrinal corpus that interprets modern social realities in a systematic manner. Examining each of these principles individually must not lead to using them only in part or in an erroneous manner, which would be the case if they were to be invoked in a disjointed and unconnected way with respect to each of the others. A deep theoretical understanding and the actual application of even just one of these social principles clearly shows the reciprocity, complementarities and interconnectedness that is part of their structure. These fundamental principles of the Church's social doctrine, moreover, represent much more than a permanent legacy of reflection, which is also an essential part of the Christian message, since they indicate the paths possible for building a good, authentic and renewed social life.

The principles of the social doctrine, in their entirety, constitute that primary articulation of the truth of society by which every conscience is challenged and invited to interact with every other conscience in truth, in responsibility shared fully with all people and also regarding all people. In fact, man cannot avoid the *question of freedom and of the meaning of life in society*, since society is a reality that is neither external nor foreign to his being. *These principles have a profoundly moral significance because they refer to the ultimate and organizational foundations of life in society.* To understand them completely it is necessary to act in accordance with them, following the path of development that they indicate for a life worthy of man. The ethical requirement inherent in these pre-eminent social principles concerns both the personal behavior of individuals—in that they are the first and indispensable responsible subjects of social life at every level—and at the same time institutions represented by laws, customary norms and civil constructs, because of their capacity to influence and condition the choices of many people over a long period of time. In fact, these principles remind us that the origins of a society existing in history are found in the interconnectedness of the freedoms of all the persons who interact within it, contributing by means of their choices either to build it up or to impoverish it (#162–63).

5. In the social teaching of the Church, *solidarity* and *subsidiarity* are viewed as linked, mutually reinforcing and necessary to realizing the *common good.* Ideally, this is the case. Indeed, it being the case is what makes for a robust civil society—one serving the common good and respecting the dignity of each and every person. However, the relationship between *solidarity* and *subsidiarity* is more complex than implied above. Moreover, circumstances have changed so radically that by the third millennium the desired relationship between *solidarity* and *subsidiarity* is badly out of alignment. Therefore, what we have to examine during the 2008 Plenary Meeting are the possibilities for aligning these two features of society in a newly transformed social context in which the common good has become more and more problematic.

(a) Firstly, it is necessary to acknowledge that the relationship between *solidarity* and *subsidiarity* can never be taken for granted because their relations are not symmetrical. It is possible for *solidarity* to be high and for *subsidiarity* to be low. This was the case during early Modernity. Throughout Europe the *solidarity* of the Working Class *community* was at its peak. Yet, early capitalism was precisely where Market control was at its (unrestrained) highest and commodification reduced the value of working people to the wage form. Certainly, a thrust toward *subsidiarity* developed in the attempt to found Trade Unions, but it was deflected into wage bargaining and away from control over the work process, working conditions, and work relations, let alone production and productivity. In short, Unions were incorporated into market relations and into the government of the liberal state.

(b) Equally, *subsidiarity* cannot work without *solidarity*. If such a combination is tried, then the organs of *subsidiarity* distance themselves still further from *solidarity*. These agencies are either commandeered from below, by parties claiming to speak for their "community," and/or they are invaded from above, by the commanding powers of the state bureaucracy. For example, the relative autonomy of the Academy in Europe has seen both autonomy and collegiality reduced by the imposition of government performance indicators and accountability. Subsidiarity has been forfeited largely because there has been insufficient solidarity between academics to defend it.

(c) The conjunction between these two social forms—*solidarity* and *subsidiarity*—and thus their contribution to achieving the common good is therefore contingent and not axiomatic. This is the case despite their mutual reinforcement *when* they do happen to co-exist. Moreover, it also seems indubitable that much contemporary social change militates against their co-existence. Specifically, what has changed that makes the conjunction between *solidarity* and *subsidiarity* ever more problematic?

(d) There is a diminishing supply of community-based *solidarity*, of shared values, and thus, of social cement. Everywhere, a variety of changes undermine the stable, geo-local, and face-to-face community. Certainly, *elective* communities (and virtual communities and imagined communities) are on the increase, but without making any significant contribution to the overall *social solidarity* necessary to sustain *subsidiarity*, since, at best, it remains extremely restricted in kind (e.g., football and FIFA).

(e) Conversely, the invasion of everyday life by market forces (advertising, easy credit facilities, and money as the sole currency) and by bureaucratic regulations (national and transnational) jointly accentuate increased materialism within an enlarged iron cage of bureaucracy. Can this infelicitous cycle be broken? Here we have to consider the role of reciprocity.

6. To do so, it is necessary to be able to point to some process whose workings amplify *solidarity* and *subsidiarity* simultaneously, thus enabling the common

good to be augmented. We find the key linking the two in the concept and practice of *reciprocity*. *Reciprocity* comes into its own as a "starting mechanism." In so doing, it solves a problem encountered in studies of participation in voluntary associations. It is regularly found that membership of them increases trust of fellow members and in general, and trust is the common denominator of *solidarity*. Yet, where does the impetus come from to develop voluntary associations in the first place? The role of *reciprocity* as a "starter motor" has long been recognized. Cicero wrote that "There is no duty more indispensable than that of returning a kindness" and added that "All men distrust one forgetful of a benefit." However, *homo reciprocus* has often been and often is subject to a one-sided accentuation (actually a distortion) of his contributions and their consequences.

For example, Marcel Mauss saw reciprocal gifts as underwriting exchange relationships and, thus, inexorably leading to the Market and its inhuman principles. Conversely, Alvin Gouldner viewed *reciprocity* as a generalized social norm, stabilized by a "mutuality of gratifications" (a *do ut des* relationship) and socially stabilizing in its turn. However, such "mutuality" was always at the mercy of force which, in turn, undermined *reciprocity* and replaced it by relations of coercion. Note, that neither view can sustain an active view of *justice* (law working for the common good), for in the two cases Law would serve respectively to reinforce market relations and power relations.

Some notions, seemingly cognate to or substituting for *reciprocity*, actually break away in the same two directions—toward market relations or toward power relations. Thus, the economic and political theory of "social capital" tends to assume that even the most *Gemeinschaft*-like groups are based upon "interest," whose advancement (or defense) involves exchanges with other forms of capital and thus entails a commodification of persons which is antithetic to *solidarity* and *subsidiarity* alike.

Conversely, Communitarianism, as its liberal critics suggest, seeks to combine the virtues of fraternity with the vices of intolerance. Reciprocity is linked to free-giving. *Reciprocity* can only be the key link between *solidarity* and *subsidiarity* provided that it retains its own linkage to free-giving—based upon affect, concern, and involvement in the lives and well-being of others. There appears to be sufficient impetus toward free-giving in our populations (for example, organ donors or blood donors) that fuels *reciprocity* as a process that is independent of legal injunctions or reinforcement and expansionary rather than degenerative. Crucially, for our times, the free-giving, without search for material benefit or control, evidenced on the Internet—a neutral medium, also exploited for both other purposes—is a practical exemplification of (virtual) *solidarity* and effective *subsidiarity* that works *because* of *reciprocity* and could not work without it.

It is *reciprocity* that also results in an upward spiral, which reinforces *solidarity* because more and more of the human person, rather than just their labour power and intellectual skills, is invested in such agencies as voluntary associations—rendering their contributions ones that cannot be commodified or commandeered (e.g., dedicated child care, care of the aged, or living in an eco-friendly manner). It is an upward spiral because: (a) there is a development of mutual obligations and practices of mutual support; (b) there is an extension of "friendship" (in the Aristotelian sense); (c) there is a tendency for social identity increasingly to be invested in such associations.

Hence, the seeming paradox of the third millennium that *Gemeinschaft* can develop from *Gesellschaft*—as the solution to the problem Modernity could never solve—"the problem of solidarity."

7. Justice should promote the common good. *Subsidiarity* requires both legal protection and mechanisms for just correction. Otherwise, and regardless of being buttressed by internal *solidarity*, it can be taken over by other forms of control and guiding principles or fragment through the crystallization of sectional interests.

Thus, on the one hand, there is a need for protection by a form of justice differentiated for different spheres of society, according to criteria appropriate to them. Most obviously, the "Third Sector" requires protection from incursions from the state, beyond those measures ensuring probity in the conduct of their affairs. On the other hand, *subsidiarity* entails allocation, but of itself neither the "Third Sector" nor classical definitions of justice give sufficient guidance about what is due to each social subject or human group. Without the articulation of such a theory, grievances can accumulate and hierarchies with distinct material interests become differentiated, such that no common good can really be achieved.

8. That's why this Plenary Meeting will give serious attention to "practical exemplars" of *solidarity* and *subsidiarity* in action, to prevent this from being an arid, though necessary, academic exercise. Between the theory and the practice, what we will effectively be examining are the building blocks of a new civil society able to reach new frontiers in the advancement of the common good. The following topics will be illustrated: new forms of solidary and subsidiary economy; educational initiatives in developing countries; state-family relationships; access to information goods (the Internet); and micro-credit and the third sector.

11

Discovering the Relational Character of the Common Good

Pierpaolo Donati

1. The Common Good as a Relational Good

In ordinary language, as well as in most empirical sciences, the common good generally refers to a "something," an entity belonging to everyone by virtue of their being part of a community. The community can be big or small, from a family, to a local or national community, to the whole of humankind. In any case, the common good is seen and treated as an *asset* or an opportunity to be preserved and enhanced, if possible, for the benefit of the individuals involved.

That "something" which the common good consists of generally refers to a tangible reality, but it may also be an intangible good. Tangible goods are, for instance, the natural resources that must be at everyone's disposal (such as air and water), spaces usable by everyone (such as streets and squares, though today we would include the web and Internet as well), and artistic monuments that must be maintained without being commercialized. Examples of intangible goods include peace, social cohesion, international solidarity along with the appropriate institutions for safeguarding and promoting them.

Modern thought has increasingly identified the common good with a collective, materialistic, and utilitarian good, which must be available to all members of the community. The notions of affluence, development, and progress conform to the above when they are considered "common goods." Thus, modern thought is always in danger of reducing the sense and value of the common good to a possession (literally, a property), whose holders are conceived of as shareholders or stakeholders; hence, the supremacy and prevalence today of economic and/or political conceptions which reduce the common good to a sum of individual goods.

Most current economic theories define the common good as "*the greatest possible good for the greatest possible number of individuals.*" In their best case scenario, the "greatest possible number of individuals" would include *all* sentient beings (even animals as well as humans). This definition of the common good presents it as an entity that is convertible, or reducible to the sum total of all the private interests of the individual members of a given society, and interchangeable with them.

In the prevailing definitions given by the social, economic, and political sciences, the common good is *an allocation of resources from which everyone derives advantage.* Of course, this means that such an allocation can be also unequal and even unfair. Hence, the common good is cut off from justice. Instead, what is relevant is that everyone may derive *some* benefit from the allocation of the resources. Difficulties are not considered to relate so much to the definition of common good as to the rules for its implementation.

Such implementation may take place on the basis of one of four criteria, ranging from consent to the use of force. The first criterion is *familiarity*; so, for example, within the family the allocation of resources consists in giving something to each member and the distribution is accepted by *consent*. The second is *merit* or *credit*, as dictated by individual moral conscience, where each person accepts the allocation received because he/she believes himself or herself to deserve it. The third is *mutual benefit*. Here the allocation is accepted because it is based on the expectation of *cooperation that leaves everyone better off,* and if some do not cooperate in creating a common good they will be punished by exclusion from future cooperation because the principle of reciprocity is invoked. Finally, in case any of the former criteria do not work, the common good is produced by a fourth criterion, namely *enforcement*, involving the use of force by a third party, generally the State. Economists hold that the common good is produced only if there are sanctions against those who shirk their responsibilities. Such sanctions are different in the above four cases: the family takes one's consent for granted; individuals who did not deserve the benefits they received from the common good will experience inner guilt; in the third case, the possibility of future cooperation is forfeited (someone can no longer draw upon common goods); and in the fourth case, sanctions take the form of external penalties like graduated fines, as in the case of tax evasion.

From the point of view of political studies, the common good is often defined as the central and essential aim of the State. It consists in granting fundamental rights to those entering society, especially the rights of all to have the opportunity to freely shape their own lives through acting responsibly and in accordance with the moral law. In that case, the common good is defined as the sum total of the conditions of social life that enable people more easily and readily to act in this manner. The object of State sovereignty is to provide the means for creating these conditions. Others, in particular John Rawls, make the distinction between the Good, which actively creates a better world (however that may be defined) and the Just, which creates a fair, liberal, social infrastructure—one that allows the pursuit of virtue, without prescribing what the common good actually is.

Such ideas of the common good are typically institutionalized in one of two main contemporary structures which may be called "*lib*" and "*lab.*" These are social, economic, and political systems based on two complementary principles: on the one hand, the individuals' freedom in the market (the classic liberal or *lib* side); and on the other hand, the equality of individual opportunities brought about by the political power (the labour or *lab* side). Both such structures appear to be *limited and misleading* as regards a deeper and more inclusive notion of the common good. This is because, from the moral point of view, they obscure the social conditions transforming an object into something common and also into a good. A better definition of the common good can be offered, however.

Toward a More Relational Definition

If the good is a *common* object, it is because the individuals who share it also have certain relations among themselves. If it is a *good* (in a moral sense), this is because people relate *in a certain way* to such an object and also to one another. In short, a good is a common good because *only together* can it be recognized and acted upon (generated and regenerated) as such, by all those who have a *concern* about it. At the same time, it must be produced and enjoyed together by all those who have a stake in it. For this reason, *the good resides within the relations that connect the subjects.* Ultimately, it is from such relations that the common good is generated. The single fruits that every single subject may obtain derive from each being in such a relationship. The relational definition of the common good highlights those fundamental qualities that are obscured by proprietary definitions, previously mentioned.

To understand such qualities, let us start from a basic consideration. If we state that the common good is an asset belonging to the whole community, we must also admit that the good we are talking about is such because those belonging to that community recognize it as something both preceding and outlasting them. It is a good of which they cannot freely dispose. They can and must use it, but only under particular conditions, ones excluding its divisibility and commodification. Should they divide or alienate it, they themselves would not be able to enjoy its fruits.

What makes the common good indivisible and non-commodificable? Is it perhaps an inner quality or power of that object (be it tangible as is water or intangible as are social cohesion and peace)?

In general, the answer is negative. The object in itself is always *potentially* divisible and marketable. For instance, both water and social peace, although common goods, are susceptible of being divided and marketed.[1] The reason why the common good cannot and must not be divided and marketed lies in the fact that, if it is divided or commodified, the relations among the members of that community would become estranged or even broken. The common good is, before and above anything else, the guarantee of their social link.

The quality making an entity a common good lies neither in that thing as an indivisible and inalienable "whole" in itself, nor in the will of the members of a community. It does not depend on their opinions, tastes, preferences, individual and aggregate choices. People generate and regenerate it, but the good has its own (emergent) reality that does not depend on people desiring or benefitting from it. They contribute toward generating it, but they do not create it by themselves. Rather, they can destroy it by themselves. If they do so, they break the social links connecting them to the other people in question.

We realize that the common good has its own inalienable nature, resting upon the relations existing among those sharing it, because it preserves the foundations of the social bond. But the *sharing* must be, and is, indeed, voluntary. It has not, and cannot have, a character reliant upon force. Precisely because the common good has a relational character, it resides in the mutual actions of those who contribute to generating and regenerating it. Should the social link break, there would be a collapse of the qualities of the people sharing it, since human qualities depend on the link itself. Only if we see the common good as a relational good, can we understand its inner connection with the human person.

That is exactly what is stated by the Catholic social doctrine.

A Catholic, Relational Vision of the Common Good

As a matter of fact, the social doctrine of the Church proposes a concept of the common good that is quite different from mainstream economic and political versions of it. In the *Catechism of the Catholic Church* (CCC, #1905–12) and in the *Compendium of the Social Doctrine of the Church* (Pontifical Council for Justice and Peace 2005, #164–70) a vision of the common good is outlined, according to which the common good is the social link joining people together, on which both the material and non-material goods of individuals depend as the *Compendium* states:

The human person cannot find fulfilment in himself, that is, apart from the fact that he exists "with" others and "for" others. This truth does not simply require that he live with others at various levels of social life, but that he seek unceasingly—in actual practice and not merely at the level of ideas—the good, that is, the meaning and truth, found in existing forms of social life. No expression of social life—from the family to intermediate social groups, associations, enterprises of an economic nature, cities, regions, States, up to the community of peoples and nations—can escape the issue of its own common good, in that this is a constitutive element of its significance and the authentic reason for its very existence. (#165)

Further, the common good does not consist either in a state of things, or in a sum of single goods, or in a prearranged reality, but it is "the whole *conditions* of social life that allow groups, as well as the single members, to completely and quickly reach their own perfection" (*Gaudium et Spes*, #26). In particular, it consists in the conditions and exercise of natural liberties, which are essential for the full development of the human potential of people (e.g., the right to act according to the promptings of one's conscience, the right to the freedom of religion, etc.).

In other words, the common good represents the social and community dimension of the moral good; the common good is the moral good of any social or community relations. Again in the words of the *Compendium*,

The common good does not consist in the simple sum of the particular goods of each subject of a social entity. Belonging to everyone and to each person, it is and remains "common," because it is indivisible and because only together is it possible to attain it, increase it and safeguard its effectiveness, with regard to the future. Just as the moral actions of an individual are accomplished in doing what is good, so too the actions of a society attain their full stature when they bring about the common good. The common good, in fact, can be understood as the social and community dimension of the moral good. (#164)

Therefore, the social doctrine of the Church is critical toward materialist, positivist, and utilitarian objectifications (reifications) of the common good. Its picture of the common good openly clashes with the "proprietary and utilitarian" picture given by the ideas prevailing today. It appeals to reasons based on the fundamental *sociability* of human beings.

From this sociability, it draws conclusions that mean the common good cannot be confused with concepts whose similarity is only apparent, such as concepts of the *collective* good, of *aggregate* good, the good of the totality, vested interests, *general interest*, and so forth. With that, the social doctrine preserves a potential for critique and for the advancement of human emancipation that modern and postmodern thought seem to have lost or relegated to the fringe of society.

Nonetheless, the concrete application of the Catholic social doctrine does not yet appear to be living up to its potential. In fact, the concept of the common good—rather than being developed in a relational way—is often, in practice, traced back to an organic and vertically stratified picture of the society. This image is based on two mainstays: (a) the assertion of the primacy of politics as "synthesis" of the common good ("Each human community possesses a common good which permits it to be recognized as such; it is in the *political community* that its most complete realization is found." CCC #1910); and (b) the consequent granting to the State of the privileged role of being the apex of society, which protects, rules, and creates its civil society ("It is the role of the state to defend and promote the common good of civil society, its citizens and intermediate bodies." CCC #1910).

In presenting these "Prospects" to the XIV Plenary of the Pontifical Academy of Social Sciences, I wish to push the social doctrine forward by claiming that, today, it can and must enlarge its horizons on the common good through an adequate *widening of its relational vision*. That is, it can develop its potential for illuminating and supporting new politics and social practices, only insofar as it widens the relational basis of the common good and derives the necessary consequences from it in terms of applications and operative principles in the new context of globalization.

In fact, this context underlines certain problems that can no longer be bound by the political configuration to which the social doctrine still refers when it claims:

> *The responsibility for attaining the common good, besides falling to individual persons, belongs also to the State, since the common good is the reason that political authority exists.* The State, in fact, must guarantee the coherency, unity and organization of the civil society of which it is its expression, in order that the common good may be attained with the contribution of every citizen. The individual person, the family or intermediate groups are not able to achieve their full development by themselves for living a truly human life. Hence the necessity of political institutions, the purpose of which is to make available to persons the necessary material, cultural, moral and spiritual goods. (*Compendium*, #168)

Certainly, "The goal of life in society is in fact the historically attainable common good" (*Compendium*, #168), but the State is *not* the exclusive bearer of such a task. The task of ensuring participation, social inclusion, security, and justice is certainly what justifies the existence and the action of the State, but the State must accomplish those tasks in a subsidiary way as regards the civil society, local, national, and international, and in any case it is not the one and only and supremely responsible body involved.

A development of the social doctrine is required that takes into account globalized society's great differentiation into spheres, which are more and more distinct and articulated among themselves, both at an infra-state and at a supra-state level. The common good becomes a responsibility not only of individuals and of the State, but also—in a completely new way—of the intermediate social bodies ("*civil societarian* networks")[2] now playing a fundamental role in mediating the processes by which the common good is created. These are no longer solely *bottom-up* (realization of the common good though movements that come from below) and *top-down* (the creation of the common good by the State and then spreading downwards to the grassroots), but are also horizontal and lateral processes that depend upon neither the State nor the Market.

Summing up what has been said so far, the common good is not the result or the sum of the individuals' actions, because it is a reality exceeding individuals and their products. On the other hand, neither is it an "already given whole," possessing inner properties and powers, making it indivisible and non-commodifiable. It has an ontological status by virtue of its fruits because, without the common good, those fruits could not exist. But people can always make it divisible and commodifiable. When they do so, they destroy the common good and consequently the community ceases to exist.

Instead, the common good belongs to that reality which is *relational* in character: "Life in its true sense…is a relationship," affirms Benedict XVI in his encyclical *Spe Salvi* (#27).

Social dynamics continuously both create and destroy common goods. Within modernity, those processes which have become detached from social relations have made the destructive forces more powerful than the creative ones. But, at the end of Western modernity, in what I call an *after*-modern society (or "relational society,"[3] which Margaret Archer would prefer to call a "morphogenetic society"[4]), the opposite may occur: society can make inalienable what was actually divisible and marketable, namely, it can generate a new and novel common good.

Empirical processes are always reversible, at least in principle if not as a matter of fact (this is what sociology means when it says that society is becoming more and more complex along with higher-order cybernetic processes). In any case and in concrete terms (i.e., ones not restricted to a metaphysical notion of common good), it can be seen that in human society there are a variety of common goods: there are non-negotiable common goods and others that, under some circumstances, may be subject to considerations of utility or convenience.

How is it possible to trace these distinctions?

To trace the distinction between the common goods which *can* be made negotiable (e.g., some natural resources) and those which are *not* negotiable in any way (e.g., human dignity and peace) is the task of a relational vision of the common good. Let us make this claim clearer by introducing a basic argument.

The first common good is the dignity of the human person, which is—at the same time—also the basis of any further common good. In this apparent circularity lies the solution of self-paradoxes of the postmodern thought (for instance, in the works of Jacques Derrida or Niklas Luhmann), according to which the common good is a paradox based on unsolvable paradoxes. It is a fact that the human dignity of a single person cannot be violated without all the surrounding community suffering because of this. To violate human dignity means to wound the possibility of pursuing the common good from the start.

But what is human dignity? What can be or cannot be negotiated within it?

Human dignity is not a quality that individuals may individually own and upon which they can individually decide. On the other hand, neither is it the sum (the aggregate) of a quality pertaining to all members of a community. It is something coming before them and going beyond them. It is something that they enjoy without being able either to divide or to alienate it.

From the Catholic point of view, human dignity is rooted in the filial relation with God. Such a relation is therefore the first, originary (*fontalis*) and decisive common good of and among human persons. It is so for all the great world religions. If we deny the existence of such a relation, as do non-believers, atheists or agnostics, human dignity is hardly justifiable as a common good: in fact, from where else can it spring?

From the above, we can define that which *can* be negotiated in the common good. It is that which does not touch its vital root, namely, the divine filiation of the human person and its implications for interpersonal relations. The remainder can be discussed, modified, made the object of agreements or circumstances, with the purpose of achieving further good.

Without its religious basis, human dignity, being the first among common goods, must find some source of justification, yet those proffered are always seemingly insufficient. All the criteria advanced by the contemporary social sciences are insufficient. They appeal to human reason, but scientific reason is not enough. They appeal to the individual's abilities, but such a criterion results in discrimination between those who are able to perform functionally and those who are not. They appeal to an abstract concept of humanity, but this appears to be a purely artificial and contingent construction.

That is why a certain "secularized reason" of our time appeals to "a religion without God" (as claimed, for instance, by Gunther Teubner). Postmodern thought needs religion to solve its paradoxes, but it does not accept the divine filiation, where the solution to those paradoxes lies.

Nonetheless, Catholic thought also needs to take some steps forward. In fact, in the field of Catholic thinking, the "metaphysics of the common good," as formulated in past centuries, needs considerable revision. Such a metaphysics has defined the common good of humankind as consisting in God, and—as a consequence—the relation of each individual with Him. Such a perspective is certainly not wrong, it is undoubtedly right, but not completely adequate. To take it in a simplistic way is to obscure the common good existing *among* human persons (if this is not viewed as a reflex of their fundamental individual filiation and as an expression of the Mystical Body). Today, such metaphysics should be considered necessary but not sufficient. They require revision starting from the premise that the dignity of the human person is neither an individualistic (inherent to the individual *qua talis*) nor an holistic property (emanating from the Mystical Body). This is because human dignity is both inherent in each human person but also in their connections with other persons. It is supplied both by the relation of filiation with God, but also by the interpersonal relations that constitute it. The dignity of the human person, if considered as a common good, shows us that such a quality is not an individual one, but it is connected to and inherent in the relations of the person with the whole creation, with God and with other human persons.

Prior to all else, the good is common thanks to its dignity. And dignity is a quality that cannot be circumscribed and limited to a single individual (*qua* isolated monad), but spreads to the relations in which the individual expresses him/herself, where it is preserved and where it flourishes. The family, for instance, is a common good if and because it is seen as a specific relation realizing the dignity of the human person.

So we come to see the moral dimensions of the common good, ones which extend beyond those which are concretely expressible, whether material or nonmaterial. The moral dimensions signal that the common good is a relational good, which is legitimated by the foundational criterion of human dignity.

To briefly sum up: the common good is neither a "collective heritage" that may be expressed concretely in an entity separate from the human person, nor an aggregate of individual goods (in that case, we call it the collective good or the good of the totality). It is something that belongs, at the same time, *to all the members of a community and to each of them, as it resides in the quality of relations amongst them.* It is here that the principles of subsidiarity and solidarity come social scientifically into their own. In fact, only a relational theory can represent the common good as an emergent consequence of the combined actions of subsidiarity and solidarity, on the part of subjects (individuals or social groups) as conceived of from within the framework of a relational anthropology. From such a relational vision it is possible to differentiate the negotiable from the non-negotiable common goods. The task of discovering and understanding the relational character of the common good has just started and must be further and more thoroughly analyzed in the future.

2. Consequences for the Definitions of Subsidiarity and Solidarity

There are varieties of definitions of subsidiarity as well as of solidarity. The lists are very long and there is no need to itemise them fully now. Just to give some examples, subsidiarity has been defined as entailing proximity to the subjects concerned or, according to the organizational dimension, as devolution, privatization, articulation of citizenship rights, multilevel governance, and so forth. Many different types of subsidiarity have also been delineated: vertical and horizontal subsidiarity, defensive and promotional subsidiarity, reflexive subsidiarity, strengthened subsidiarity, and so on. Solidarity, in its turn, has been conceived of as: redistribution, beneficence, charity, social welfare benefits, interdependency, etc.

What we want to point out here is that to conceptualize these two terms (subsidiarity and solidarity) properly, we need not only to employ them together, but also to *define them in relation to one another*. That is exactly what the relational approach does. It claims that, considered in their social phenomenology, *common goods are the products of those action systems that have human dignity as their value model* (referring not only to the individual as such, but also to his or her social relations) *and which operate through social forms that are both solidary and subsidiary among the subjects concerned.*

The relational definition of the common good leads to a relational vision of the principles of subsidiarity and solidarity, meaning that subsidiarity and solidarity are seen as two ways of relating to others, both of which acknowledge the dignity of the Other.

Solidarity is a relation of Ego with Alter, in which both do what they can in relation to the responsibility that everyone has toward the common good. Solidarity means that all play their own part, according to their capabilities. Subsidiarity means to relate to the Other in a manner that assists the Other to do what he or she should, according to a relational guidance system of action.[5]

These two principles should generally operate *together* (co-operate) because, if they do not, no common good will be generated. At the same time, it is clear how one is defined in terms of its relationship with the other. If Ego wants to help Alter without oppressing him or her, then *subsidiary and solidary* must co-exist between them. Subsidiarity (the very fact that Ego wishes to help Alter to do what Alter has to do) requires an act of solidarity. In this case, solidarity is neither (unilateral) beneficence nor charity, but the assumption and practice of the joint responsibility that both Ego and Alter must have toward the common good (this is also the meaning of solidarity as interdependence, which is still valid when one party cannot give anything material to the other party).

The common good is therefore the fruit—the emergent effect—of *reciprocity between solidarity and subsidiarity*, as implemented by Ego and Alter in their mutual interaction.

At this point, one can now appreciate the importance of the claim that the common good is the fruit of reciprocity understood as the rule of action, which stems from the spirit of free giving. Reciprocity exists in society as an irreducible phenomenon, since it is neither a sharing of utilities (*do ut des*: such a form is appropriate to contracts and the sharing of equivalents, as Alvin Gouldner maintains), nor a sharing for sharing's sake (as Mark Anspach argues), namely, reciprocal giving, serving to underline the sense of belonging to a common tribal entity (the *Hau* as interpreted by Marcel Mauss). *Instead, reciprocity is a mutual helping, performed in a certain way. In other words, reciprocity is help concretely given by Ego to Alter in a context of solidarity. This context is one of common responsibility and recognized interdependency, such that Ego is aware or recognizes that Alter would do the same when required: Alter would assume his/her responsibility within the limits he or she can afford when Ego needs it.*

Reciprocity is upheld and is effective as long as it is firmly grounded upon a recognition of the dignity of the Other. The common good takes root in the human person precisely because it exists and derives its meaning from serving the other person in his/her dignity.

Upon these premises, we can understand the specific configuration of the action system generating a common good, adapting Talcott Parsons' general framework for social action, which is schematically represented in figure 11.1.[6] The relation between the human person and the common good is the vertical, referential axis, which is needed to link that which has an inalienable dignity in itself with the situated, particular relational good in a given context (the axis L-G). To become operative, an action system oriented toward the common good also needs means and rules (the horizontal, adaptive axis A-I), which must complement the value of human dignity. Only such an action system can avoid both the holism and individualism critiqued earlier. What enables the action system to work effectively for the *situated* common good—namely, to produce a concrete common good here and now, context after context, situation after situation—are the two principles of subsidiarity and solidarity. They have the task of specifying the means and rules of the acting "system." Without them, the common good could not actually be generated.

Thus, it may be stated that *the common good is the emergent effect of an action system operating under the "combined provisions" of subsidiarity and solidarity to increase the value of the dignity of the human person.*

The principle of subsidiarity is an operating instrument. It is not to be confused with the principle of competence attribution (the distribution of *munera*—as is clearly stated by Russell Hittinger). The distribution of tasks lies on the axis that connects the dignity of the human person to the common good. Subsidiarity is a way to supply the means, it is a way to move resources to support and help the Other without making him/her passive. Subsidiarity allows the Other to accomplish his/her tasks, namely, to do what he/she should do, what is up to him/her and not to others (*munus proprium*). On the other hand, solidarity is a sharing of responsibility, operating according to the rule of reciprocity.

In fact, providing means, resources, aid, and benefits to Alter could have the consequence of making him dependent on Ego, or of exploiting him for some other purpose. *That is why subsidiarity cannot work without the principle of solidarity.* Through it, Ego recognizes that when helping Alter, there is a responsibility (shared with Alter): Ego and Alter are linked by their interdependence on one another, and interdependency is viewed as a moral category according to the encyclical *Centesimus Annus*.

Figure 11.1. The Configuration of an Action System for the Common Good

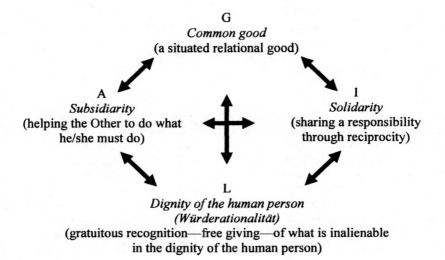

G
Common good
(a situated relational good)

A
Subsidiarity
(helping the Other to do what
he/she must do)

I
Solidarity
(sharing a responsibility
through reciprocity)

L
Dignity of the human person
(Würderationalität)
(gratuitous recognition—free giving—of what is inalienable
in the dignity of the human person)

The Relationship between the Common Good and Justice

The above framework serves to explain why the common good does not coincide with justice. Certainly, the common good is a "just" good. Justice is a means to reach the common good, being its aim. However, by itself justice runs the risk of being purely legal. What makes it "substantial" or "fully adequate" is that its constitutive criterion (*suum cuique tribuere*) works through the connection between subsidiarity and solidarity.

For instance, the person committing a crime must be sanctioned because he/she has violated the common responsibility (solidarity), but the sanction must not have a merely punitive or revengeful aim. Its objective should be to assist the guilty person to do what he/she has to, namely, to re-establish the circuit of reciprocity. If an act of solidarity toward those who commit a crime is not subsidiary to them, in order to have them re-enter the circuits of social reciprocity, it would not be a right action. Solidarity by itself does not produce the common good: quite often, it becomes pure charity or the kind of egalitarianism that does not take real differences and diversities into account, not to speak of cases where solidarity can lead to real "bads" or evils.

On the other hand, neither does subsidiarity alone produce the common good. In itself, subsidiarity may easily be interpreted in a reductive way as *devolution*, as a system of balancing powers (*check-power-check*) or, at worst, as *laissez-faire*.

Justice generates the common good only if it works through an active complementarity or interaction between solidarity and subsidiarity, as shown in figure 11.2. We must remember that, according to the CCC (#1905), "In keeping with the social nature of man, the good of each individual is necessarily related to the common good, which in turn can be defined only in reference to the human person: Do not live entirely isolated, having retreated into yourselves, as if you were already justified, but gather instead to seek the common good together."

Figure 11.2. Justice Produces Common Good Only If It Passes through the Combined Work of Solidarity and Subsidiarity

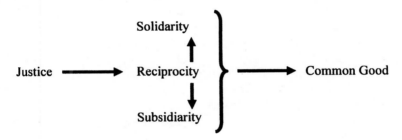

In short: the common good is that relational good stemming from the fact that Ego freely recognizes the dignity of what is human in Alter and he/she moves through actions which jointly invoke solidarity and subsidiarity toward Alter. The common good of a plurality of subjects is generated on the assumption of the equal moral dignity of persons as an emergent effect of actions combining reciprocity (incident to the principle of solidarity) with the empowerment of the Other (incident to the principle of subsidiarity). Several important consequences follow from all that for the configuration of society.

3. Implications for the Relationships between the State and Civil Society

The relational understanding of common good leads to various implications for society's organization, beyond the *lib-lab* configuration typical of the 20th century.[7]

First, we see that *the common good coincides neither with the State, nor with the State-Market* compromise, but it is the product of a system of social action, involving a plurality of subjects orienting themselves to one another on the basis of reciprocal solidarity and subsidiarity.

Second, we see that *subsidiarity does not concern only the vertical relations* existing in a society, but also a set of *horizontal* relations. That is, subsidiarity can only partially be conceived of as a pyramid sloping downwards from the supranational to the national level (State, regions, municipalities), to the family, and finally to the human person. Such a version of subsidiarity is quite limited and is fit only for the internal hierarchic relations of the political-administrative system. That is why it is called "*vertical* subsidiarity." When we affirm that subsidiarity means that responsibility is taken closer to the citizens (*subsidiarity means having responsibility at the actual level of actions*), generally we refer to that kind of subsidiarity defined by Pius XI in *Quadragesimo Anno* (#80). But not all instances are of this particular kind, because the idea of closeness to citizens implies other ways in which subsidiarity may operate. Thus there is a principle of subsidiarity between State and organizations of civil society (for instance, municipalities and voluntary organizations), termed "*horizontal* subsidiarity." And, there is a principle of subsidiarity among the subjects of civil society (for instance, family and school, or between an enterprise and the employees' and clients' families) which may be called "*lateral* subsidiarity." Only by having a generalized idea of subsidiarity is it possible to differentiate its different modalities (vertical, horizontal, and lateral). This general concept is that of *relational* subsidiarity, which consists in helping the Other to do what he/she should. Such a generalized concept is then developed vertically, horizontally, and laterally, according to the nature of problems and subjects at issue.

Third, as was the case with subsidiarity, solidarity too can take various shapes. There is solidarity generated through redistribution, but also through free giving; through solidarity contracts, or through reciprocity. Solidarity in its more generalized meaning is a sharing of responsibility within interdependency. As such it is a value and a model but may be defined in different ways according to subjects and circumstances.

In brief, the relational approach leads to an understanding of what is meant by saying that global society can and must *extend* and *enlarge* the concepts of subsidiarity and solidarity. To extend those two principles of social action means to be able to generalize and differentiate them at the same time, though always treating them in combination.

Hence, for instance, to extend subsidiarity means having a generalized concept (relational subsidiarity) structured in its different modalities (vertical, horizontal, and lateral) and applied at different times and places, according to the performative exigencies of the various social spheres involved and of their actors. Exactly the same goes for solidarity. Thus, we can conceptualize a generalized system for the creation of common good through the extension of the solidary-subsidiary relationship (see figure 11.3 below).[8]

The norm of reciprocity nourishes recourse to the complementary subsidiary-solidary relation among distinct, varied and differentiated spheres, such as an enterprise and the employees' families, or the local political-administrative institutions, a volunteers' organization, and the beneficiaries of the voluntary work. Nonetheless, reciprocity needs a reason to be activated (who gives first?). In fact, the "structural coupling" of the various spheres being distant and different from one another, and probably scarcely disposed to create subsidiary-solidary relations with each other (i.e., a local government and an organization for mutual aid, an enterprise and the employees' families, etc.), means that there is a need for a free act of recognition (a "gift") to kick-start the mobilization of solidarity and to direct it toward subsidiarity. A symbolic, though rare, case is that of an enterprise not only activating *family friendly* services for employees, but conceiving more widely of professional work as being subsidiary to the family rather than the contrary (it is called "corporate family responsibility").

Figure 11.3. Elaboration of the Solidary-Subsidiary Relation in Its Various Articulations

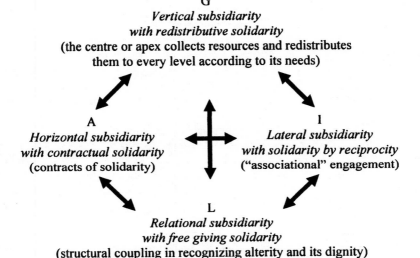

G
Vertical subsidiarity
with redistributive solidarity
(the centre or apex collects resources and redistributes
them to every level according to its needs)

A
Horizontal subsidiarity
with contractual solidarity
(contracts of solidarity)

I
Lateral subsidiarity
with solidarity by reciprocity
("associational" engagement)

L
Relational subsidiarity
with free giving solidarity
(structural coupling in recognizing alterity and its dignity)

A society that, because of its organization, is inspired by the common good must extend its subsidiary-solidary relations throughout all spheres of life—inside them and between them.

It is clear how such a configuration differs from all those theorized in the modern age, starting from Thomas Hobbes to Friedrich Hegel, Karl Marx and the great theorists of the welfare state of the twentieth-century, to the current *lib-lab* structures. The *lib-lab* welfare systems do not take their inspiration from the model of systems oriented toward the production of common good through the principle of subsidiarity combined with that of solidarity. Instead, they are based on the compromise between Market and State (profit and political power). They stand on two legs: the one, individual liberties to compete in the market, the other, state interventions to ensure equality of opportunities for all.

It should be underlined that the relational model of common good is necessary today not only to solve the failures of the combination "State + Market." It is not a model understandable simply in terms of better evolutionary adaptation. It stems from a new "relational anthropology of civil society," that is, from a new way to practise human reflexivity in civil relations (those which are not "political" because they *do not* refer to the political-administrative system, though not excluding it, but even less are they reacting against it).

After these considerations, we may be in a better position to point out the implications of the relational theory of the common good for configuring the relations between State and civil society in a new way. The discontinuity with the past does not imply any need to revise the key concepts (person, subsidiarity, solidarity, and the common good). Instead, the discontinuity affects the interpretation and implementation of such concepts, which is *no longer functionalist in kind.*

In the context of the functionalist approach, the common good is a state of affairs that, other things being equal, improves the position of at least one participant. It does not require solidarity, not to mention reciprocity. It says nothing about human dignity. Subsidiarity is used to refer to a kind of *smooth functioning.* Solidarity is understood as resulting from social compensation (redistribution, charity), necessary in order to make the system work.

In the context of the relational interpretation, everything is very different. The common good is *a quality of relations* on which the concrete *goods* (in the plural) of the participants in a given situation depend, that is, the goods of everyone and of all those belonging to a community, according to their different needs. Referring back to figure 11.3 and using the language of action systems theory, the State (or the political-administrative system, from the supranational to the local one) has four ways to relate to the civil society:

G) a vertical modality, maintaining solidarity through re-distributional measures;

A) a horizontal modality, supporting the organizations of civil society through a type of relational contract, called "contracts of social solidarity," not dependent upon political command and not oriented to mere profit, but operating on the basis of mutual subsidiarity;

I) a lateral modality, generating subsidiarity among subjects of civil society, without any intervention (or only a residual one) by the State, so that the basic social norm followed by actors is reciprocity (reciprocal subsidiarity) instead of (political, legal) command or monetary equivalence (for profit);

L) a generalized relational modality simply recognizing the dignity of the Other and giving him/her the gift of such recognition, thus establishing the free credit that sets reciprocity in motion.

Such a relational configuration seems to be able to produce common goods far beyond that of current typical configurations, where for example the State relates to civil society as an absolute power (Thomas Hobbes' *Leviathan*), or as an ethical State (Georg Friedrich Hegel), or as an expression of the hegemonic forces of civil society (Antonio Gramsci), or as the political representation of the Market (Robert Dahl). In such a "relational" configuration, the Third sector and the Fourth sector (constituted by informal networks and families) play a central role, precisely because they are moved by free giving and reciprocity. These two sectors are put in a position from which to express their potentialities (namely, to develop their own *munera*) precisely because they are not treated as residual subjects, as if they needed only aid, rules, and control by the complex of the State + Market.

Third sector organizations and family associations become social actors with their own powers, independent from State and Market. Concrete instances are: the *community foundations* widespread in many countries, the *charter schools* in the USA, or the Forums of *family associations* in Italy, Spain, and other countries.

4. A New Sociocultural Order Suited to Globalized Society

Is it possible that these new actors, generating common good through the conjoint work of subsidiarity and solidarity, can indicate a generalized model of action for the governance of globalizing society?

On the whole, this seems to be the case. In fact, in the 21st century, society is no longer pyramidal or hierarchical, but reticular and autopoietic in its structures and in its morphogenetic processes. Given such structures and processes, common goods are produced more effectively, efficiently, and fairly through modalities based on subsidiarity and solidarity, rather than all outcomes depending upon the primacy of command and/or profit (as in *lib-lab* systems). Concrete instances are: fair trade, NGOs for health assistance in developing countries, and the novel "epistemic communities" that transfer knowledge and learning outside commercial circuits.

The main problem is represented by the political system, which is now incapable of representing and governing civil society. The latter enhances its developmental potentials far beyond the ruling and controlling abilities of political systems, be they local, national, or supranational ones. In some cases, in fact, political systems are seen to be perverting civil society, because they introduce ideological and interest divisions characteristic of the political parties, rather than directing civil actors toward the promotion of the common good.

The principles of Catholic social doctrine—as regards the common good, subsidiarity, and solidarity—were originally expressed in the context of the *political constitutions* of Nation States, with supranational political systems such as the European Union on the horizon. But the age dominated by the political constitutions of Nation States is disappearing (it survives only in those areas which have yet to pass through it, such as the former Yugoslavia, the Balkans, and some geopolitical areas of Africa and Asia). Nation States cannot govern the global social context. Nor can we think of the United Nations as a supranational State. To cope with globalization, new political configurations are necessary on a supranational and infra-national level, and it can be useful to draw on the principles of subsidiarity and solidarity in order to envisage them. These principles must be interpreted from a new perspective—no longer that of just Nation States, but rather of an emergent global civil society, which is no longer limited or bound to the frontiers of the Nation States.

The idea is growing that these principles can form the basis of action systems able to generate common goods and elaborate and promote the rights/duties of persons through the networks of civil society, which are now emerging from the processes summarized as globalization. This is the theme of *civil constitutions*. It has to do with *charters* or *statutes* drawn up by civil bodies, rather than by the political apparatuses of Nation States, ones which regulate the actions of the civil subjects who operate in a certain sector of activity. These activities may be economic, social, and cultural ones, including the mass media. Some examples are found in the statutes of the UN's International Labor Organization and World Trade Organization, internationally proscribing child labour, or in the charters of international organizations approved by journalists, forbidding the exploitation of children in TV advertising.

Civil constitutions are normatively binding and have the following features. First, they are "constitutional" because they concern the fundamental rights of the human person: for example, in the areas of bioethics, labour, and consumption. Second, they are "civil" because the social subjects to whom these constitutions are addressed in order to define a complex of rights and duties, have a civil, rather than a political character: they are not the expression of political parties or political coalitions, but of the associational world in the economy and in the non-profit sector such as trade organizations and non-governmental organizations. Third, they give shape to *deliberative* rather than representative forms of democracy: the social subjects to whom civil constitutions are addressed (and applied) are at the same time the subjects who have to promote them through forms of societary rather than political governance. In other words the subjects of such constitutions are at the same time the bearers (*träger*) of rights and duties and the actors responsible for their implementation.

These civil constitutions are quite independent from territorial boundaries because they are elaborated and implemented by global networks, often international ones, made up of civil subjects. Thus, they place themselves alongside, not against, the classical political relation of citizenship, namely, the relation between the individual citizen and the Nation State, by assuming certain functions. In particular these functions concern the advocacy and empowerment of the rights/duties of persons and of social bodies.

This is the new scenario that renders obsolete the old *lib-lab* configuration of society, and the social sciences have coined several terms to capture this new reality. They talk of "connectivity," of a "society of networks" or "network society" (Manuel Castells), of "project-cities" (Luc Boltansky and Eve Chiapello), of "atopia" (that which does exist anywhere geo-locally), instead of utopia (that which exists nowhere) (Helmut Willke). We talk here of a "relational society."

All those expressions point to the advent of a society that is a plural whole made up of different spheres, which are all now de-territorialized, where different criteria of justice (and ultimately of justification) are valid. The "pluralization of spheres of justice" spreads without solving the problem of how to put the more and more differentiated spheres of justice in relation with one another (a problem actually left unsolved by Michael Walzer [1983]). To confront that problem requires a "relational reasoning" such as I have expounded elsewhere in more detail (Donati 2008), that is capable of exercising "meta-reflexivity" in the sense intended by Margaret Archer (2007).

From that relational and meta-reflexive point of view, the principles of Catholic social doctrine that would configure a social system capable of generating the common good appear to be exactly what is needed in order to meet the new demands of a society that is "relational" in new ways. The mix of subsidiarity and solidarity (the axis A-I of figure 11.1) may lead to building up social practices that, on the one hand, are sensitive to basic human rights, and on the other, are able to generate those common goods that neither political command nor the economic profit motive can truly realize. There are many examples of social practices reflecting—or acting as pointers to—such a new spirit of the millennium: the *économie solidaire*, the economy of communion, the local Alliances for the family (*Lokale Bündnisse für die Familie*), the Food Bank, electronic giving and sharing, NGOs like *Médecins sans Frontières*, microcredit run by non-profit entrepreneurs, ethical banks, and so forth.

It is essential to initiate a new process of empirical reflection to examine whether, how far, and in what ways those initiatives are sensitive to human rights and foster the emergence of new common goods through the conjoint operation of solidarity and subsidiarity—each of these operating within its proper "sphere of justice." This would involve analyzing the concrete examples mentioned above in the light of the theory summarized here and represented visually in the three figures employed above. Such an analysis should show under which conditions these instances of seemingly "good practice" actually do produce new common goods or not. At the moment, it seems that good practices need a more precise and shared theoretical-practical framework that underlines how subsidiarity and solidarity cannot currently produce common goods if they do not operate as forms of recognition of the dignity and rights-duties (*munera*) of the human person, in the respective social spheres in which they work.

Furthermore, to pursue the common good in a generalized way, we need to widen the scope of our reasoning to be better able to embrace and to handle the properties of those action systems generating the common good. In such systems, the subsidiarity-solidarity relationship certainly has to play a central role. Nonetheless, there is no doubt that the most delicate and critical dimension of our reasoning concerns the recognition of human rights, because there is the ever-present risk of ideological or reductive distortions of human dignity.

Contemporary Western culture urgently needs to elaborate a theory of the recognition of human rights, one that does not lose, forfeit, or sacrifice the peculiar quality of the human being. Certainly, modernity expressed strong ethical tensions when elaborating the different forms of recognition based on love (friendship), rights (legal relations), and solidarity (community normativity). Nevertheless, current exemplifications of de-humanization go far beyond the expectations of modernity. There is talk today of the coming of a post-human, trans-human, in-human, or cyber-human era. There is also talk of the hybridization and metamorphosis of humankind. Those phenomena present such radical challenges as to require a new vision of human rights: we have to re-configure them from the point of view of the common good, that is, to *conceive of human rights as common goods*.

A society wanting to pursue the common good in a progressive rather than a regressive (not to say ideological) way must reformulate the criteria of what is human through good practices, i.e., practices which can be called "good" insofar as they combine four elements: *the gift of dignity conferred upon the human person, interdependency among people, acting so as to empower the Other, and caring for the relations among persons as goods in themselves.* The common good is a relational good: these elements are relational in themselves and relational to one another.

Each element is a relation endowed with its own "value"[9] and at the same time has to realize itself in relations with others. Each has value in relation to the others, not according to a sequence of "dialectic overcoming" between a thesis and an antithesis that should "unite them while preserving their inner truth without any contradiction with each other" in a utopian "synthesis" (*Aufhebung*). The common good is not like this. Rather, it is constituted by and constitutes relations (reciprocal actions!) that combine to generate the common good in the various social spheres—which now endorse more and more differentiated and plural criteria of justice and worth.

Notes

1. It may seem strange to think of "marketing peace," but this is precisely what occurs when "good industrial relations" are advanced as a reason for the location of a factory or a "safe and secure environment" is given as the reason for higher house prices.

2. M.S. Archer (personal communication March 20, 2008) has rightly pointed out that a network, per se, is not necessarily relational, as in the case of a distribution list. She suggests that "perhaps, the key is the distinction between relational and non-relational networks (say, the difference between kinship and genealogy)." I agree with that. I must signal, however, that, in my language (see my *Relational Theory of Society*, Donati 1991), networks are always intended to be networks of relations (and not networks of material objects or simply "nodes") and, therefore, since a social relation implies a reciprocal action, what I call networks, are to be understood as "relational networks" (for instance, from the sociological point of view, "a gift" must be understood not as "a [material or non-material] thing" freely given to somebody which links two or more persons, but as a social relation inscribed within a network of free giving-receiving-reciprocating actions which relate a complex chain of actors to each other). That's what distinguishes my critical (and relational) realism from others, viz. Dave Elder-Vass', to whom social relations are understood as "real" structures (as in the relation between two atoms of hydrogen and one of oxygen in a molecule of water). Social reality is ontologically different from material (physical, chemical, biological) reality. And therefore relations are made up of a different stuff (which implies a different concept of "structure"). The term *civil societarian* can be explained in the following way. A *civil societarian* strongly supports the institutions of civil society. These include families, corporations, religious groups, private schools, charities, trade associations, and the other peaceful, voluntary collective organizations that promote our individual and collective well-being insofar as they are relational networks. These are the civil societarian networks to which I am referring. The stereotypical libertarian might cite Ayn Rand and exalt the independent individual. Instead, a civil societarian would cite Alexis de Tocqueville, and his observation that democracy is based upon people who, whatever their age, social conditions, and personal beliefs, constantly form associations. These voluntary associations are what a civil societarian sees as the key to civilization. Government may contribute to civil society, but it also intrudes on it. The means of avoiding colonization is precisely to appeal to the principle of subsidiarity. Jean-Jacques Rousseau's theory of the General Will serves as a good contrast to the civil societarian's view.

3. I have introduced the term *relational society* since 1986 (Donati 1986).

4. See Archer (forthcoming), *The Reflexive Imperative*.

5. A relational guidance system of action is needed in order to avoid the fallacy that subsidiarity presupposes a "normative approach" governing the giving of assistance. When I say that subsidiarity means that Ego helps the Other to do what s/he has to (or must) do as a *suum munus*, I do not imply that Ego dictates the norms of conduct to Alter, by providing him or her with a sort of Decalogue. In that case Alter's internal and external reflexivity would be impeded. On the contrary, relational guidance means that Ego

acts as a stimulus to the internal and external reflexivity of the Alter, since all the needs, desires, and projects of Alter should be met by supporting him or her to develop their own capabilities, aspirations, concerns, etc. through an evolving relational setting in which Ego is charged with the task of ensuring that the goals selected are ethically good and that the means chosen are adequate to the pursuit of these goals. The goals themselves are primarily defined by Alter, or, when Alter is a child or a handicapped person, jointly by Alter and her/his in/formal helper (see the "relational guidance scheme" discussed in *Teoria relazionale della società*, Donati 1991). In parent-child situations, relational guidance is not a directive command or impulse (it is not directly normative), but is a prompt to activate those relationships which lead the child toward the good things he desires. Ego is helping insofar as s/he assesses the goodness of the goals adopted by the child and makes sure that appropriate reflexive relations are activated and established in order for those goals to be attained.

6. *Editor's note:* The following discussion of the dimensions and features of a social action system is based on the original general theory of social action systems developed by Talcott Parsons, as for example in Parsons' (1970) classic work *The Social System*. Very briefly Parsons argued that any cybernetic system, such as a social system, had four "functional imperatives" it had to address and meet in order to survive and evolve. They are **A: Adaptation,** the problem of acquiring sufficient resources; **G: Goal Attainment,** the problem of setting and implementing goals; **I: Integration,** the problem of maintaining solidarity or coordination among the subunits of the system; and **L: Latency,** the problem of creating, preserving, and transmitting the system's distinctive culture and values over generations.

7. *Editor's Note:* The terminology "lib/lab" refers to earlier work of both Donati and Margaret Archer in which they portray typical policy approaches to solving social problems in one of two ways, that tend to flip back and forth over time with political changes of regime in Western democracies, or blend uneasily in some sort of compromise. "Lib" refers to classical liberal economics, market-driven approaches often favored by smaller central government conservatives in Europe and Republicans in the U.S.; while "lab" is shorthand for "labour" in Europe or Democratic Party policy in the U.S., which favors large government intervention and spending on social issues, jobs, and income redistribution.

8. One might query if this is a typology of subsidiarity rather than an action system. From a theoretical point of view this question goes back to the meaning of the Parsonian AGIL scheme, whose formulation was intended to be both in a very ambiguous and misleading way. In the relational version, the AGIL scheme is never a pure typology, but is a compass to orient observations of the structure and dynamic of an action which is supposed to be reciprocal (in the sense of being an action in response to another action). This is where reflexivity comes in. The paper by M.S. Archer (2008; see chapter 12 in this volume) on "Education, Subsidiarity, and Solidarity; Past, Present and Future" is a fine example of how the scheme can work when applied to the field of education. The four dimensions of subsidiarity must, and in fact do interact and work together, if we want to get out of the Modern System which is now producing a deficit, instead of an increase, of common goods (as relational goods) in education (for an empirical investigation, see Donati and Colozzi 2006). The same holds true of health care and many kinds of social services (particularly family services: Donati and Prandini 2006).

9. Value here means its own criterion of assessment according to its own directive distinction, which is contained in the latency (L) dimension of the social relation (in my relational version of AGIL).

Bibliography

Archer, Margaret S. 2007. *Making Our Way through the World: Human Reflexivity and Social Mobility*. Cambridge: Cambridge University Press.

————. 2008. "Education, Subsidiarity, and Solidarity; Past, Present and Future." Plenary Session at the 14th Session of the Pontifical Academy of Social Sciences.

————. Forthcoming. *The Reflexive Imperative*. Cambridge: Cambridge University Press.

Donati, Pierpaolo. 1986. *La famiglia nella società relazionale. Nuove reti e nuove regole*. Milano: FrancoAngeli.

————. 1991. *Teoria relazionale della società*, Milano: FrancoAngeli.

————. 2008. *Oltre il multiculturalismo. La ragione relazionale per un mondo comune* (*Beyond Multiculturalism. The Relational Reason for a Common World*). Roma-Bari: Laterza.

Donati, Pierpaolo, and Ivo Colozzi. 2006. (a cura di) *Capitale sociale delle famiglie e processi di socializzazione. Un confronto fra scuole statali e di privato sociale*. Milano: FrancoAngeli.

Donati, Pierpaolo, and Riccardo Prandini, eds. 2006. *Buone pratiche e servizi innovativi per la famiglia*. Milano: FrancoAngeli.

Parsons, Talcott. 1970. *The Social System*. New York: Routledge and Kegan Paul.

Pontifical Council for Justice and Peace. 2005. *Compendium of the Social Doctrine of the Church*. Washington, DC: USCCB Publishing.

Walzer, Michael. 1983. *Spheres of Justice: A Defence of Pluralism and Equality*. New York: Basic Books.

12

Education, Subsidiarity, and Solidarity: Past, Present, and Future

Margaret S. Archer

Introduction

The development of education throughout Modernity presents a paradox. To be educated gradually became considered an indisputably good thing, like health. Yet, nothing in the historical emergence and subsequent development of educational systems meant that they were orientated towards the *common good.* Instead, the "good" that was sought was the promotion of sectional interests, increasingly organised to contest the control of education and thus the definition of instruction. Of course, every group involved in these struggles presented the achievement of its educational ambitions as being for the "general good," but such self-interested rhetoric says nothing about the *common good.* In relation to the idea of *munus regale,*[1] interest groups placed much less stress upon the first term, *munus,* as free-giving or rendering service, than upon *regale,* (mis)interpreted as the domination of education.

Indeed, the fact that all known educational systems emerged from struggles to control education also meant that the recognition of each contending party as having gifts to contribute was overshadowed by the *competitive conflict* in which they were engaged. Such conflict made any idea of co-operation, let alone relations of reciprocity, between these contestants a contradiction in terms. Simultaneously, social solidarity was a victim of these struggles for control. Since the interest groups involved (throughout Europe) represented particular sections of the stratification system (whether Estates or Classes) as well as sectional interests (the new industrialists or the various religious denominations etc.), the educational advancement of one was to the detriment of others. *Competitive conflict* is hostile to solidarity because its tendency is to foster social cleavage(s).

In other words, the components and relationships that Donati (2008; see figure 11.1 in this volume) outlines as constituting "The Configuration of an action system for the common good," where *subsidiarity* and *solidarity* are based upon recognition of the *dignity of all human beings* and mutually reinforce one another for the *common good,* were entirely lacking in the interactions resulting in the emergence of State Educational Systems in Europe. The reasons for this are embedded in the *competitive conflict* out of which State Educational Systems emerged, from roughly the end of the eighteenth century to the end of the nineteenth.[2] *Competitive conflict* is zero-sum and thus the antithesis of interaction for the common good, which is an emergent benefit for all and thus, in principle, constitutes a win-win situation for all (especially children and the young in this context). It is important not to see the Catholic Church as a bystander or disinterested observer of the interaction resulting in the emergence of State Educational Systems. Prior to those events it had enjoyed an unopposed monopoly over the provision, control, and definition of such formal instruction[3] as existed in most of Europe, with the Post-Reformation Churches occupying a similar unchallenged position in Protestant countries. In short, the Churches supplied the buildings, the teachers, and the texts. Formal education has always been particularly expensive in terms of physical and human resources, which is one important reason why the ecclesiastical position was unassailed for so long—that and the relative indifference of other social groups toward formal education.

As Hittinger importantly points out, it was precisely the French Revolution, whose educational effects involved confiscating Church schools and prohibiting religious orders and secular clergy from teaching that prompted Catholic social doctrine into being. "[T]he post-1789 church-state crisis is what gave the Church real incentive to develop a body of social doctrine. On this score it is important to understand that the social doctrine did not begin with the industrial revolution and the problems of benighted and dislocated workers. It began with the need to defend the institutions of the Church" (Hittinger 2008, 106).

Precisely because the Church's defence of its right-and-duty to teach was part and parcel of the conflictual interaction leading to the formation and development of State Educational Systems, this is where I will begin in Part I of this paper. A State Educational System is defined as "a nationwide and differentiated collection of institutions devoted to formal education, whose overall control and supervision is at least partly governmental, and whose component parts and processes are related to one another" (Archer 1979, 5). This definition stresses that both the political and the systemic aspects should be present together for a State System of Education to exist. The appearance of either characteristic alone was not uncommon in European history. I begin here because the emergence of State Educational Systems, at different times in different countries, marks a new boundary between the State and civil society as far as education is concerned. Yet, such State systems were structured in very different ways within Europe—the most important distinction being between those that were centralised and those that were decentralised. The main question examined here is whether centralisation and decentralisation made a significant difference to the role that other parts of civil society could play in education. That is, did the structuring of the new State Educational Systems influence their responsiveness to the principle that later became known as *subsidiarity*? It is equally important to ask if either type of structure was more closely associated than the other with promoting the social *solidarity* that needs to accompany *subsidiarity* if the common good is to be generated in and from education.

Part II moves on to consider much the same issues during "late" Modernity, in other words during the twentieth century and especially its final quarter. Throughout Europe (which increasingly included Central and Eastern Europe), State Educational Systems now operated in the context of representative democracy, which was far from being the case at their origins. Moreover, in the last couple of decades many State systems in Europe and other parts of the world have come to endorse certain forms of "devolution" at the level of individual educational establishments—schools, colleges, and universities. This policy raises exactly the same issues as those examined in connection with centralisation and decentralisation. Does such managerial devolution promote *subsidiarity* and *solidarity* and are they promoted conjointly, as needs to be the case?

Finally, Part III examines the new millennium and asks whether the structural and cultural transformations, whose most obvious effect has been to generate globalisation, are more propitious to education working for the common good? Much of this is sketchy and tentative. Any conviction that it carries is predicated upon the assumption that it is now possible to discern the first signs of Modernity being superseded—a prospect with considerable implications for education in relation to the common good.

Part I: The Emergence of State Educational Systems

In those countries where State Educational Systems developed endogenously[4] their consolidation followed one of two basic patterns. Either new political elites used the command they had recently gained over the central State apparatus to *restrict* existing educational provisions and their suppliers and then to *replace* these—through public and no longer private funding—under their own *étatiste* control. This is a politically directed "top down" process, explicitly designed to serve the State and its (often new) governing elite. However, problems over mobilising the novel but requisite public funding and of marshaling support and minimising opposition usually meant that certain educational concessions had to be made to powerful elements in civil society in order to consolidate the system.

Conversely, where educational discontent with existing provisions lay amongst interest groups with little influence upon government—even to the point of their lacking enfranchisement—a different process led to the emergence of State systems. Basically, it consisted in market competition where independent networks of schools and colleges were *substituted;* ones designed to serve the parties whose requirements were obstructed by the status quo in education and in the hope of undermining the latter if its own network of establishments could prove more popular. However, since such competing networks were usually plural and because the existing suppliers fought back, market competition resulted in deadlock. Such "middle up" *substitution* both invited and allowed State intervention to consolidate a State System of Education through the *incorporation* of these diverse networks, sponsored by different parts of civil society and with divergent definitions of instruction, under a single governmental authority for education.[5]

State Educational Systems originating from *restriction* are invariably *centralised* ones because their predominant characteristics are strong *unification* (tight State control) and principled *systematisation* (such that certain educational institutions lead from one level to another, whilst others are designed as terminal, according to the perceived requirements of the governing elite). Conversely, the other pair of characteristics, common to all emerging State Educational Systems, are weak: *differentiation,* requiring relative autonomy from central control, was kept as low as possible and resulted in limited *specialisation* to provide those particular educational services sought by different parts of civil society.

On the other hand, the reverse characteristics preponderated in State Educational Systems originating from *substitution.* Their relatively strong *differentiation* and *specialisation* resulted from the incorporated networks retaining sufficient control to continue supplying many of the distinctive services for which they had been formed. Correspondingly, *unification* remained weak because governing elites had to work with what was there, as functioning establishments whose practices were defended by their founders and suppliers. *Systematisation* was exceedingly difficult to impose on these chaotic, overlapping and still adversarial networks. In short, these invariably become *decentralised* systems.

The structural differences between centralised and decentralised State Educational Systems are crucially important for explaining many processes in the decades following their consolidation: how public instruction is defined and by whom; which portions of the general population have access to which parts of education; by what means educational change can be introduced; and the patterns of change themselves—local, incremental, and slowly additive or central, dramatic, and uniform. Despite the fact that the above processes are far from being irrelevant, what will be accentuated in this paper are the implications of centralisation and decentralisation for the four intertwined[6] principles of Social

Doctrine: the *dignity of the human person, subsidiarity, solidarity,* and the promotion of the *common good.*

Centralised State Educational Systems

France, after 1789,[7] will be used as the exemplar here because so many other European educational systems owe their origins to the imposition of the *Université impériale* model in the wake of Napoleonic conquests—just as their legal systems still owe much to the *Code Napoléon.* In Hittinger's (2008) terms, the Imperial University was a particularly "mean" exemplar of the "concessionary model" because the very concessions made to civil society were intended to buttress State power and priorities in education.

Whilst all of the revolutionary Assemblies[8] had sought to promote national unity and to replace religious teaching by secular enlightenment, had also envisaged a State monopoly of public instruction (with the exception of Lepelltier's plan), and had endorsed gratuity, female equality, and universal enrolment, one key element was the central importance they attached to primary education as a means for enhancing social *solidarity.* This was a joint function of the "generous" republican conception of citizenship and of political awareness that popular support was indispensable to the survival of the new regime.

Successive laws were too short-lived to shape a new system, quite apart from the constraints represented by a complete lack of trained lay teachers and an absence of funds with which to carry out *replacement* of the now debarred Church schools. Only under the Empire of Napoleon I did the new State system finally take shape. By then, *étatisme* and its requirements had obliterated any concern for educational egalitarianism, even in order to promote *solidarity* in the interests of political stability.

It is helpful that the Emperor was not reticent about publicly stating his aims and rationale for State education. His own words[9] can be used to present his outlook toward the spirit of the four key principles of Social Teaching. Of course, these latter had yet to be articulated but they were to owe much to the resistance invoked by Napoleon's view of Church-State relations and its practical embodiment in his *Université impériale.*

As far as the cardinal principle of the *dignity of the human person* was concerned and the role that education could play in realising the potential of each and every one—to which the Revolutionary Assemblies had been far from deaf—Napoleon counterposed his conviction that "to instruct is secondary, the main thing to do is to train and to do so according to the pattern which suits the State" (Liard 1888, 69). That pattern meant that if the State had no need of mass instruction, the people had no right to it. Consequently, "no special allocation of funds was ever made in the budget of the Empire for primary education" (Delfau 1902, 40–41). Instead, the cost and task were passed back to the Church. Responsibility for this level was restored to the *Frères de la doctrine chrétienne,* provided they swore their oath of allegiance to the Emperor, taught the *Caté-chisme impérial* and underwent inspection to ensure that teaching did not exceed literacy and religious instruction. This policy in primary schooling had a double aim: to control the Church in the State and the people in society.

In relation to both *subsidiarity* and *solidarity* the Emperor became gradually convinced that only a State monopoly over education (Aulard 1911, 363ff) could lead to the integration he sought—between education and State service and between citizenship and nationalism.

> Teaching is a function of the State, because this is a need of the nation. In consequence, schools should be State establishments and not establishments in the State. They depend on the State and have no resort but it; they exist by it and for it. They hold their right to exist and their very substance from it; they ought to receive from it their task and their rule. Then again, as the State is one, its schools ought to be the same everywhere. (Liard 1888, 35)

Not only was *subsidiarity* explicitly prohibited by the decree of 1808, which forbade any private school without State authorization, but was exacerbated by the central standardisation of national curricula, of qualifications, and of teacher training—the latter reinforced by making teachers Civil Servants.

Solidarity was deliberately set aside. The new educational system was intentionally bifurcated into (terminal) primary schooling for the masses, whereas for the bourgeoisie, *lycées* led to the *baccalauréat* and from there into higher education and on to the professions, the military officer corps, and the higher reaches of the civil service. Hence, the bourgeoisie became a "diploma elite." In terms of *solidarity* the ephemeral unity of the Third Estate had been riven in two. As Goblot (1930, 126) commented, "It is not completely true that the bourgeoisie exists only in culture but not in law. The *lycée* made it a legal institution. It even has official certificates, with a ministerial signature….The *baccalauréat* is the real barrier guaranteed by the State, which is a protection against invasion."

Napoleon's defence of his State system depended upon the linkage he forged between his definition of State requirements and the general good of society. The efficiency of governmental administration and the stability of civil society could be presented—if only in contrast with the disorder of the revolutionary years—as synonymous with the interests of society. And the *common good?* That was for the State to define, to generate, and to arbitrate upon. The one thing it was not, was a good emergent from *human dignity, subsidiarity,* and *solidarity,* [10] all of which had been categorically nullified during the consolidation of the Imperial University. Napoleon had declared that "Public education is the future and the duration of my work after me." The structure of this centralised educational system proved durable but, like all social institutions, not everlasting. Since this is not the place for a potted history of education, suffice it to say that despite the political turbulence of the 19th century, the possession of central control over instruction proved irresistible to successive regimes and governments. Differences in political support-bases were dealt with by making additional, selective concessions to the relevant sectors of civil society: demands from the burgeoning industrial economy were propitiated by various adaptations to existing schools from the July Monarchy onwards; *liberté de l'enseignement* (conceded under the Loi Falloux in 1850) restored the Church's right to open private Secondary schools—albeit with stringent controls hedging their independence.

However, the endurance of centralisation throughout the 19th century simply re-confirmed its "concessionary" nature. Demands for educational change from civil society were strongly constrained to work through one process of interaction alone if they were to stand any chance of success, namely, "political manipulation." This is illustrated in figure 12.1 (below). To obtain any further concession entailed aggregating such demands with entirely different groups in order to put effective pressure on central government. Yet, the aggregation of demands spelt their dilution, if various interest groups were to work together. In turn, dilution meant that, even when "successful," the changes gained were always insufficiently specific to satisfy the original demands.

Figure 12.1. Educational Interaction in the Centralised System

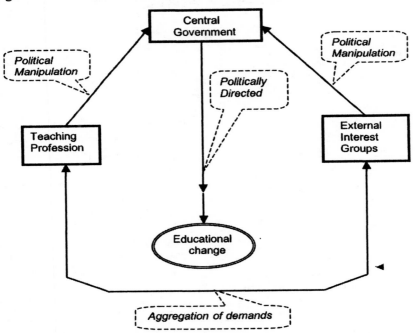

There was no alternative. The teaching profession itself (denied the right to become a professional association until 1924) was equally powerless to respond directly to any wishes teachers might have countenanced from local civil society as they were to engage in the "internal initiation" of pedagogical change in line with their professional values. Similarly, interest groups could not engage in direct "external transactions" with any part of the State Educational System. Instead, they had to go outside education and find allies with whom to exert joint pressure on the political centre. The alternative resort of the re-buffed, namely, to use and to extend the private sector, was of little use to them because it lacked the independence to offer anything significantly different from provisions defined by the State.

In short, the centralised State Educational System typically had vitriolic critics and, at most, tepid supporters from within civil society. This is why it was prone to periodic outbursts of direct action, usually followed by panic legislation and then by administrative clawing-back of the new concessions obtained.[11] In conclusion, the "concessionary" centralised model of education continuously frustrates large sections of civil society and militates against realisation of the key principles of Social Doctrine.

The Decentralised Educational System

Sometimes *subsidiarity* is interpreted as being equivalent to decentralisation. To confound or conflate the two is a mistake. Although a limitation of central powers is necessary for the actualisation and maintenance of *subsidiarity,* decentralisation alone is not co-existent with its realisation. The reason for this is rooted in the need for *subsidiarity* and *solidarity* to be mutually reinforcing, to work in tandem if they are to promote the *common good.*

On the contrary, decentralisation *tout simple* is simply a free market model in education. Bluntly, it may indeed be responsive to the educational demands of the wealthier parts of civil society, but its precise effect in satisfying these is to reduce social *solidarity* by widening the gap between those served by the educational system and poorer groups who lack the resources "to have a say." Indeed, as a market model, decentralised education may (and usually does) increase the educational "wealth" of all over time, whilst maintaining marked social differentials in its distribution.

Using Hittinger's terms, the (protracted) consolidation of England's decentralised State System of Education conforms more closely to his "power-check" model. However, in the beginning, the main groups involved were rather more concerned with checking one another's progress in the foundation of competitive educational networks—hoping to be able to declare checkmate eventually—than as parts of civil society attempting to limit the power of the State. Only when central government began to intervene seriously in the educational market did all network suppliers seek to repel those political incursions damaging to their particular interests.

Between the Reformation and the late eighteenth century, the Established Church of England continued to run and to develop Cathedral schools, endowed schools, colleges (which had become Oxford and Cambridge Universities), all of which had been confiscated from the Catholic Church. By the start of the nineteenth century both Tory and Whig parties considered themselves as beneficiaries of Anglican education on two counts. The social exclusivity of secondary and higher education complemented that of the two political parties; the production of churchmen was in no way seen as incompatible with the instruction of statesmen. Secondly, growing working class unrest made the contribution of religious instruction to social quietism increasingly valued. Both parties supported the National Society for Promoting the Education of the Poor in the Principles of the Established Church, which funded elementary schools through voluntary subscription.

Conversely, two groups felt particularly impeded by the Anglicans' acquired right to define instruction and from these came market-based *substitution*—the form taken by *competitive conflict* over education in England. On the one hand, there were the industrial entrepreneurs for whom Anglican education's confirmation of hereditary privilege and whose concentration on classicism and pure mathematics were irrelevant to the spirit of capitalism. On the other, there were the Dissenters (members of the Free Churches), disbarred on religious grounds from attending many endowed schools and from University graduation because of the Test Acts[12] and also from entering the teaching profession.

Because there was a significant overlap between these two groups—the entrepreneurs and the Nonconformists—this enabled the British and Foreign School Society to challenge the Anglican control over primary instruction in the marketplace. However, the control of the former by Nonconformists effectively alienated the working class leadership who strongly endorsed secular rationalism. With the latter, we now have the three networks that were to struggle for educational control throughout the 19th century: the Established Church, the entrepreneurial-Dissenter alliance, and the secularist aristocracy of labour. Given that neither of the latter two groups was enfranchised,[13] their use of *substitution* is readily understood.

Relations between the competing parties resulted in the partitioning of elementary instruction amongst those engaged in market competition. Given distrust of State intervention on the part of Anglicans and Dissenters alike, coupled with Tory reluctance to pursue it (no education being viewed as the best instruction for the poorer classes) yet Whig commitment to extending literacy, these stances represented a parallelogram of forces whose outcome was the "Voluntary System"—meaning that schools received government subventions but that such finance was funneled through the two Voluntary societies.

However, by the mid-nineteenth century, market competition "did not produce a surplus of schools and cheap education, as some educational 'free-traders' expected, but tended to paralyse the activities of all parties, so that schools were built that could not be maintained and children were educated for such short periods that they could benefit very little from the instruction given" (Rich 1970, 63). Increasingly, *competitive conflict* for educational control reached deadlock between the promotive networks. To extricate themselves from this stalemate each protagonist sought Political Party support for the advancement, finance, and protection of its network. Since all did the same, the unintended consequence—at the end of the century—was their *incorporation* into a State Educational System.

The (Tory) 1902 Act created a single central authority for English Education (see Bishop 1971) and linked the networks together for the first time to form a system. Undoubtedly, it was the working class definition of instruction that lost out. Given minimal political sponsorship in the absence of a "labour party," it was virtually eliminated. Compared with the ferocity of elementary school politics, secondary and higher education were settled by give and take between the political elites. The Anglicans maintained their traditional definition of instruction in the independent Public Schools and ancient Universities; middle class technical instruction was accommodated and came under the aegis of the new Local Educational Authorities in 1902, whilst the University extension colleges, serving business and commerce, received their Royal Charters.

When the social origins of an educational system are based upon market competition, then "checks and balances" undoubtedly generate weaker educational powers for the State because of the much lower degrees of *unification* and *systematisation* that are politically possible. However, are the four principles of Social Doctrine better realised in State educational systems such as the English, the Danish, and those of the component states of the USA?

When *competitive conflict* takes the form of *substitution,* the active participants funding and fostering any given network are interest groups defending or promoting their particularistic concerns. These interests may be material (the entrepreneurs) or ideal (both the Anglicans and the Nonconformists) but they are specific to the group, despite every attempt being made by them to generalise their ideology or values for purposes of legitimation. Examination of these ideas shows scant recognition of *human dignity* and a greater concern—sometimes mystificatory and manipulative—to use education to generate a compliant workforce or congregation.

Political sponsorship of the networks showed the same motivation. Sectional interests had motivated the struggle over education and the relative political strength of these interest groups determined the prominence of their networks in the resulting State system. In the nineteenth century debate on the motion "to educate or not to educate the people" concerns about public order were ever-present whilst mention of the *common good* scarcely featured.

In close parallel, the priority given to public order consistently prevailed over any concern for social *solidarity*. The low *systematisation* achieved under the 1902 Act, which did nothing whatsoever to connect the elementary and secondary levels of schooling, effectively meant that they were for different classes, thus still reflecting Disraeli's "Two Nations." The furthest the Act went was the loose injunction that "post-elementary" provisions must be considered by the new Local Educational Authorities in relation to the needs of their areas.

Given the need for *solidarity* and *subsidiarity* to work in reciprocity with one another, it is paradoxical that the structure of a decentralised State Educational System, such as that to emerge in England, should sometimes be viewed as synonymous with strong *subsidiarity*. To view it in this way is to accentuate isolated features at the turn of the twentieth century: that the freedom of instruction (liberté *d'enseignement*) was not in question; that the Churches (plural) could open any educational establishment they wished[14]—as could any other body; that there was a large and flourishing independent sector, to which anyone could add; that numerous forms of technical and commercial schooling could flourish; and that entrepreneurial groups could sponsor the majority of Universities in England (Sanderson 1972) (those receiving their Charters in 1902 and now known as "the redbricks").

However, each of these instances carries the caveat "for those who could pay"—either to found them or to attend them. Thus, for example, the largest portion of the independent sector has always been dominated by the Public Schools (which, despite their confusing nomenclature, are entirely private and very expensive). From 1869 their governing body, the Headmasters' Conference, had withdrawn from the nascent State System to ensure that these schools "should be free from any form of external guidance and control" (Simon 1965, 103).

Decentralisation is not *subsidiarity*. Nevertheless, the *variety* of processes through which educational change can be introduced in a *decentralised* system (see figure 12.2 below)—Internal Initiation, External Transactions, as well as through Political Manipulation—clearly makes it more responsive to demands from the social environment than is the case for the *centralised* system (figure 12.1 earlier). In the latter, all pressures for change have to be politically adopted, passed up to the central decision-making arena, before, if successful, being passed back down to educational institutions in the form of laws and decrees— that is, as uniform, politically directed changes.

Decentralisation is not *equivalent* to subsidiarity, but it is not a structural barrier to it. In principle, it is structurally propitious, provided that there is sufficient *solidarity* in society for its three processes of educational negotiation to be used for the *common good*. Another way of putting this is that this form of "system integration" (decentralisation) presents no obstacle to *subsidiarity* in education. However, the actualisation of *subsidiarity* also depends upon a high degree of "social integration," such that the impulses to express *munera* educationally are generous and that the support for *subsidia* is socially generalized.

Figure 12.2. Educational Interaction in the Decentralised System

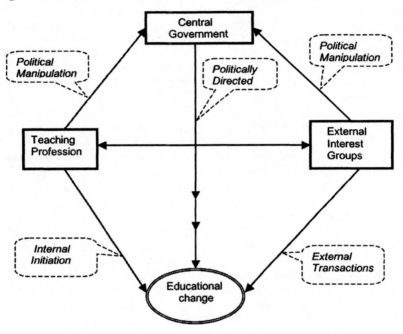

Fundamentally, what we find in twentieth century England is that a society deeply stratified on lines of social class does not possess the requisite degree of social *solidarity* to furnish the sufficient condition for the realisation of *subsidiarity*. On the contrary, to cite the two most important examples, although the primary school teachers sought to devote their *munus* to the development of "child-centred learning" (Selleck 1972)—a model and method structurally available, thanks to the wholly independent Progressive school movement (Stewart 1968)—this was undermined as the task of primary schooling was first linked to preparation for selective entry to different types of secondary schools (1944) and later eliminated by the imposition of national "performance indicators" at primary level (1988). Secondly and similarly, when certain of the Local Educational Authorities (LEAs) used their considerable autonomy to spearhead the movement toward Comprehensive secondary schooling (Rubenstein and Simon 1969)—and indeed to win over the Labour Party to adopt the policy nationally (1964)—this too was undermined by various class pressures to restore selectivity and culminated in the steady erosion of the LEAs.

In short, the structural enablements of decentralisation, which allowed the processes of Internal Initiation and External Transaction to pioneer radical educational changes, arguably representing nascent *subsidiarity*, also indicates that each time the relevant parties pressed forward towards robust transformations in education, they broke up on the rocks of divergent middle-class interests in defending their privileges against the *common good*. And they were increasingly abetted in this by what became middle-class Political Parties. At the hands of the latter, the *munera* representing free educational giving were repressed and denied institutional expression and the *subsidia* themselves were legally withdrawn.

Part II: Educational Systems in a Vice Between State and Market

As these centralised or decentralised educational systems entered the twentieth century, we can broadly characterise their relations with society's sub-systems as follows. In stark and simplified terms, centralised educational systems remained servants of the State, just as they had been founded, and consistently failed to be sufficiently responsive to Market demands, even whilst seeking to accommodate them. Conversely, decentralised systems, generated from market competition, retained their responsiveness to market forces but, in so doing, consistently frustrated the State in its attempts to use education as an instrument for societal guidance. Such were the major effects of subsequent reforms produced through the different processes for negotiating educational change in these different types of system (as portrayed in figures 12.1 and 12.2 earlier) and to be examined more closely in a moment.

Yet as Modernity moved towards its climacteric, before the end of the twentieth century, neither of these kinds of State Educational Systems was suited to meeting *simultaneously* the new requirements of central government and of the modernising economy. The attempt to satisfy both is the main story line of educational changes in the twentieth century. But, we must first explain what made giving *simultaneous satisfaction to the State and to the Market* a new imperative for education in Europe.

On the one hand, nearly every State in Western Europe had moved (or was swiftly moving) toward some version of representative democracy based upon universal suffrage. They were consequently under increasing pressure, usually from their equally new Parties of the Left, to rectify the abysmally low state of social *solidarity* and to extend political concern for civil society beyond the maintenance of "social order." Thus, democratic governments experienced relentless pressures to reduce the great divide between social classes—viewed as dangerous or iniquitous, depending upon ideological standpoint—by an equali-sation of life-chances through enhancing the equality of educational opportunity.

On the other hand, as industrial competition intensified within Europe and Germany took over the lead in the late nineteenth century (thanks, it was gener-ally accepted, to its advanced Technical High Schools, crowned by Charlotten-burg); as the applications of science to production were stimulated by the two world wars; and as Fordist production techniques in the United States were adopted as the key to industrial reconstruction, these all enhanced the economic role assigned to education in national economic competition. However, for it to play this role well, many of its protagonists were effectively advocating some-thing close to techno-educational *subsidiarity*.

Thus, at the most macroscopic level, it is being argued that the central prob-lem for educational systems in Europe was how to align these two very specific forms of *solidarity and subsidiarity* within the structures of education inherited from the nineteenth century—ones imperfect for either purpose and undoubtedly even more unsuited to realising the two simultaneously.

"Late" Modernity, reached before the end of the twentieth century, will be briefly reviewed as a period during which the reforms of State Educational Sys-tems operated in zero-sum fashion. The more reform sought to promote *solidari-ty* (through educational egalitarianism as the third part of the Welfare State + Representative Democracy formula), the less well it served techno-educational or any other form of *subsidiarity*. In short, these two elements, ones that must necessarily stand in a relationship of mutual reinforcement if they are to recog-nise the *dignity of all* and foster the emergence of the *common good,* in fact stood in precisely the opposite relationship.

For over twenty years, Donati (2006)[15] has analysed the manifestations of this opposition between them as the oscillation between *lib/lab* policies. Politi-cally directed "lib" changes favoured market competition, whilst "lab" egalitari-anism favoured the stability of society. I am in full accord with this analysis. Indeed, it was precisely because of this alternation that most European educa-tional systems managed to stagger toward the end of the twentieth century.

However, I would add that the final fling of this approach, in which "half a loaf of bread" was handed out alternately in "lib" or "lab" interests, revealed the generic antinomy between the two, precisely when attempts were made in the last quarter of the century to run *lib* + *lab* in tandem. At exactly that point, the consequences of their truly zero-sum relationship became apparent—one that could be only partially concealed by making education bigger, longer, and still more expensive for all concerned.

Their fundamental antinomy has deeper roots, in the very nature of Moder-nity itself, because based upon the situational logic of *competitive contradic-tions,* where the dynamics of conflict are unrestrained by the mutual interde-pendence of groups.[16] All competitive situations are "game like" with their outcomes approximating to the zero-sum formula. That itself explains why more and more are "mobilized" into active competition (Archer 1995, chapter 8). Either a group competes, in the hope of winning, or necessarily loses through non-participation, which allows others to win more easily. Formally, Modernity's "games" are very similar for all institutions in civil society. Generically, they are about "having, gaining, or retaining a say" in order to obtain or to secure benefits for the contending groups.

For all social groups, the zero-sum nature of outcomes served to place a premium upon strategic thinking of the means-end variety. In turn, instrumental rationality is fundamentally antipathetic to the voluntary creation of common goods through free-giving—which is exactly what *solidarity and subsidiarity* themselves depend upon. Thus, when the benefits of *subsidiarity and solidarity* are sought for self-interested ends and against others, that is, as matters of advancing objective group interests or defending vested interests, we should not be surprised by their mutual antipathy.

Lib/Lab Antinomies in Centralised State Educational Systems

"Political manipulation" still being the main process through which educational reform could be introduced in the twentieth century meant that substantive changes in education remained consistently *centripetal* in kind. These formal continuities in educational control and co-ordination (strong *unification and systematisation*) continuously generated a problematic relationship between education and civil society. In the centralised system there is a perpetual state of tension between education and its *external environment,* because politically directed educational change produces an endless series of mismatches in its attempts to meet (irresistible) demands from outside the system because of the inflexibility of the system.

Both of the main pressures for change emanating from civil society—for vocational modernisation and for equality of opportunity—required a significant reduction in the two main structural characteristics of the centralised system. On the one hand, to have conceded vocational specialisation at all levels in order to modernise the definition of instruction would have entailed a significant reduction in *unification.* On the other hand, to have responded to organised demand for egalitarianism—as expressed by the *école unique* movement in France after the First World War—would have meant just that, the creation of a new single, self-standing school for all, entailing a complete revision of the bifurcation between primary and secondary schooling.

Yet, a serious reduction in central control (unification) for *subsidiary* modernisation would have deprived central government of the powers requisite for egalitarian reform. Conversely, a genuine weakening of the traditional bifurcated principle of *systematisation,* in the interests of integrative *solidarity,* would have deprived industrial interests of the very different forms of vocational training sought for workers and managers, which fitted well with bifurcation. Consequently, the reforms needed to realise modernisation and egalitarianism were incongruent with one another, reflecting the antimony between realising increased *subsidiarity* simultaneously with increased *solidarity* in the structural context of a centralised State Educational System. The result was that both modernisation and equality of opportunity each received "half a loaf of bread" when centre-right ("lib") and centre-left ("lab") were in office.

In France, the Imperial University was a heritage that had neglected to provide educational services for the (largely) pre-industrial economy, in preference to privileging State requirements. It had also, through the various regimes up to and including the Third and Fourth Republics, perpetuated a structure subdivided into two levels, unlinked to one another, fulfilling totally different functions and enrolling very different social strata. Why did the endurance of strong central control (unification) militate against reforms producing a satisfactory degree of vocational specialisation? The policy of developing modern technical training failed largely because the political centre would cede no authority to local industrialists, enabling them to adjust it to their diverse requirements.

Instead, successive attempts were made at the primary level to introduce more differentiated and specialised courses of vocational or pre-vocational instruction, but only rarely succeeded when these courses broke away from the Ministry of Education altogether. Otherwise, their practical orientation steadily gave way to general education the longer they remained part of the system.

At the secondary level, "special education" was the vehicle for introducing higher-level vocational specialisation under the Third Republic but, popular as it had been, it soon lost its distinctiveness, disappearing altogether in 1902. A further assault was made on the problem by introducing "modern studies" as a section of the *baccalauréat,* but these lost their distinctive character between pressures to imitate the prestige branches and to prepare for University entry. An identical sequence was repeated with the creation of the technical *baccalauréat* in 1946 (Anderson 1975, 218).

As Antoine Prost (1968) summed up the situation in 1967, "French schooling disdains to train the producer. Its rationalism turns into intellectualism" (340). Again, in Bourdieu's words, students were treated "as apprentice professors and not as professional apprentices" (Bourdieu and Passeron 1964). This is explained by reluctance to weaken central unified control: teachers and Professors remained civil servants trained by the State and for the State. The diminution of *unification,* necessary to have allowed industrialists any role in public instruction and to have adapted the national curriculum to their specialised, practical and applied needs, was held too valuable to *étatisme* to be ceded by any government assuming office. Meanwhile, the economy had not received "half a loaf," but only a couple of slices of bread.

From early in the twentieth century, demands for educational democratisation bombarded the National Assembly, but produced only grudging and tentative moves toward the fundamental structural change sought—the linking of the primary and secondary sub-systems.

By the start of the Fifth Republic, all that had been introduced was a "harmonization" of programmes at the end of the first *degré* and the beginning of the second; the orientation of pupils, at least in principle, to different types of further instruction on the basis of their performance; and the establishment of *classes passerelles* for the transfer later on of those who had taken the wrong route. Thus, there was no audacious structural change and the differentiation of no self-standing institution committed to overthrowing a century and a half of socio-educational discrimination (Decaunes and Cavalier 1962, 154ff).

Continued pressures led to the eventual foundation of the *Collèges d'Enseignement Secondaires*. However, this was accomplished by the regrouping of existing components (the final class of primary, the first cycle of secondary and of the old *Collèges*)—elements which resisted reintegration and often refused to collaborate. Overcoming the bifurcation of primary and secondary instruction needed a separate and forceful institution committed to equality in education, as in the original conception of *école unique*. Instead, the task was given to this weak and warring amalgam of existing elements of the system.

Just as the "lib" concessions to vocationalism had been miserly, so were the "lab" concessions to democratisation. The reasons for both were identical: an unwillingness to cede any significant degree of unified, central political control of education or radically to transform the inherited, negative, or bifurcated principle of systematisation. In sum, the effects of these politically directed concessions—the results of more than half a century of "lib/lab" compromises—had done nothing to increase either *subsidiarity or solidarity*.

Lib/Lab Antinomies in Decentralised State Educational Systems

In a very different manner, the inheritance of a decentralised system with three distinct processes responsible for the negotiation of reform, also served to weaken any strong and coherent response to the same two demands: for equality of educational opportunity and vocational relevance. Here, it was the weakness of *unification and systematisation* that was considered responsible: the teaching profession, especially primary school teachers, promoting "child-centred" instruction, were held to jeopardise standards in *both* academic and vocational branches of secondary schooling; equally, the LEAs, consistently countenancing the proliferation of technical instruction, were considered to vitiate any notion of a national policy for education.

Again and again these burgeoning forms of technical schooling were accommodated by central government by confining them to lower or inferior and generally terminal levels, branches, or tracks of instruction. Thus, the price for the accommodation of manifest "lib" demands was their sub-ordination within national education. This is simply a different way of doling out "half a loaf."

Thus, the 1902 settlement, elaborating the decentralised system in England, had officially endorsed the spread of the (terminal) Higher Elementary School and promoted the academic Grammar School at secondary level. However, with the approval of the new LEAs, a range of diverse but practical institutions continued to develop alongside: science schools, technical day schools, pupil-teacher centres, trade schools, vocational schools, etc.

The 1918 Act, which confirmed the structural and cultural hegemony of the academic Grammar School, intended to crowd most of these other developments into "continuation schools," which would be allowed some practical orientation but would remain firmly elementary. The Depression weakened the thrust of the Act, many of whose provisions were suspended. Yet, despite austerity, a variety of intermediary institutions again proliferated and these central, senior, and technical schools represented a real challenge since they enrolled two-thirds as many pupils as the "official" Grammar Schools before the outbreak of the Second World War. The 1944 Act trained them into line with its policy of selection by ability through now cramming them into the inferior part of the secondary level. Hence, the loss of a strong practical, real, or technical definition of instruction in England was the trade-off for having a national policy for education in a system that was weak in *unification*.

Did "lib" or "lab" concerns fare better in the post-war period, when the Labour Party was regularly returned to office? It is important to underline that the impetus for a single "Comprehensive" secondary school came from outside central government and that certain "progressive" Local Educational Authorities (Leicestershire being the pioneer) had become fully comprehensive before the Labour government endorsed the policy in 1966. When it did so, its weak *unification* once more served to reinforce its weak *systematisation*, such that six different organizational models were centrally recommended as being in conformity with comprehensivization. In other words, the question "What is an English comprehensive school like?" remained unanswerable.

Although the legislation consolidating the comprehensive policy was the furthest reaching in terms of democratising educational opportunity, it was far from being a radical "lab" policy, as sociologists of education continued to highlight (Benn and Simon 1970). Not only were there the six different models, but many of these new secondary schools practised intensive "streaming" of pupils by ability, thus reproducing social selection within them. More generally, the residential quality of catchment areas produced "good comps" and "bad comps," with the term "inner-city comprehensive" becoming one of abuse. Finally, a handful of LEAs simply refused to implement the policy at all.

The period from the end of the war until 1979 is generally regarded as the high-water mark of educational democratisation, a "lab" period in which equality of opportunity in education formed a crucial plank of the welfare society.

That seems incontestable. However, it is also important to note that this high tide had also been accompanied by a significant lack of concern for vocational training, work preparation, or the regeneration of industry. In other words, "lib" and "lab" policies had alternated rather than complemented one another.

In entrenched centralised systems, such as French education, only once—in the aftermath of the May events of 1968—was the idea of devolution or of reducing *unification* seriously voiced. However, De Gaulle's "recovery" served to make *unification* appear as indispensable as ever to any effective policy for national education. Conversely, the secular failure to incorporate techno-educational provisions satisfactorily did result in a gradual willingness to recognise that the exceptionally weak *differentiation and specialisation* of institutions within the system would continue to frustrate the economy—and should be allowed to increase to meet "lib" demands.

In the sixties, this was tackled by the progressive segregation of different cycles within existing levels. A short and a long secondary schooling, each with its own diploma; a division of the *baccalauréat* into numerous sub-sections, related to different occupational outlets and higher educational inlets; at the higher level, the differentiation of *Instituts Universitaires de Technologie* again replicated the segregation of short and long alternatives. The long alternative remained University education "proper," but now itself divided into three cycles, each with specialist options and a specific diploma at the end of it. In brief, the meeting of "lib" and "lab" demands was orchestrated by the State, thus serving to augment its power *vis-à-vis* civil society, whilst the former purported to be serving the latter.

In entrenched decentralised systems, such as the English one, the same lesson was learned from its very different starting point. Weak *unification and systematisation* were increasingly viewed as obstructions to the effective implementation of national educational policy—either "lab" or "lib." The autonomy of Local Educational Authorities to pioneer or to resist, the ability of the teaching profession to pursue its own pedagogical agenda, and the freedom of the private sector to follow its own concerns, all these inherited powers of intermediary bodies were gradually perceived as impediments to State policy and Market needs alike. The result was to undermine them in the last quarter of the twentieth century.

Those twenty-five years were thus ones of structural convergence, during which centralised systems, by definition strongly unified, retained this *unification* in the interests of central political guidance of educational policy. On the other hand, decentralised systems increased their *unification* precisely in order to achieve such State guidance. Conversely, where *differentiation* of parts within the system was concerned, decentralised systems sought to weaken them and centralised systems to strengthen them.

Such convergence—marked toward the end of the twentieth century compared with its absence in 1900—appealed because it seemed to hold the key to servicing "lib" and "lab" concerns simultaneously, to becoming responsive toward both Market and State. It remains to be seen what implications such convergence held for *subsidiarity and solidarity*.

Central Control, "Lib + Lab" and the Zenith of Educational Competitiveness

Another of the terms with which *subsidiarity* is often confounded is "devolution." In the last two decades of the twentieth century much educational play was made of it—in Europe as in other parts of the world (Whitty, Power, and Halpin 1998)[17]—in the form of increased "parental choice," a perennially popular "lib" theme. Much did need to be made of it politically in order to deflect attention from the unprecedented incursion of central control in all aspects of education. In England, the form of this political "straightjacket" for every level and type of instruction also meant that independent school providers of many kinds could be welcomed on board, without fear of their disrupting the central guidance of educational policy. Thus, for example, Catholic schools (indeed, Faith schools in general) could be *incorporated* without a qualm.[18] Their gradual incorporation in France, under "contracts of association" in the sixties contrasts tellingly with Sarkozy's recent hints about throwing the door wider if not wide open. This further "lib" concession has also muddied the waters. Enduring Catholic interest in the protection of their institutions (see above) was served by this "advancement" and only recently has the legal threat (in Britain) that these must include a "quota" of non-Catholic children brought home the terms of this deal. Catholic schools are there, not on sufferance as in the past, but to increase the diversity of parental choice for all—the truly modern "lib" policy.

On the "lab" front, politically directed changes fundamentally embraced Ulrich Beck's ([1986] 1992) contention that social class had now become a "zombie category." Indeed, with Anthony Giddens (1998) as mentor, it was this that enabled the old Labour Party to become New Labour under Tony Blair. However, even "old Labour" and its finest spokesman in the sociology of education, acknowledged that traditional "lab" policies, stressing equality of access, had to be updated. "In 1900 the vast majority of Britons were educational proletarians....By the end of the century millions of children of manual workers had risen into non-manual jobs and many thousands had become the graduate children of butchers, bakers, and candle-stick makers, following professional careers" (Halsey 2000, 17). What then was New Labour going to offer them in the nineties? The answer was competitive excellence, high standards, and qualifications which could be upgraded through life-long learning. The terms in which this was couched in Ministry papers are even more revealing: *Excellence for Everyone* (1995), *Excellence in Schools* (1997), *Qualifying for Success* (1997), and *Learning to Succeed* (1999).

If the above titles did not differ significantly from those issued by the Conservatives during their seventeen years in office (1979–96), this is not surprising. Most of Europe was now fully given over to political "centrism," appearing earlier in some countries than in others. In this connection, Maurice Duverger (1971) had presciently analysed "The Eternal Morass: French Centrism," which he refused to attribute to the electoral system or multi-party politics. The swing back and forth from centre-right to centre-left governments (or governing coalitions between parts of both) was undoubtedly general, and its educational implications were common ones. If it was hard to distinguish their distinctive policies, that did nothing to preclude their combined onslaught on education—now no longer a pillar of the welfare society and increasingly a prop for the global market economy (Tomlinson 2001, 166).

It is the emphasis placed upon "Choice and Diversity"[19] that convinced some that the "lib" reforms taking place represented a genuine devolution of powers to the grass roots level—to parents, their children, and the individual school they attended. To accept this is an acceptance of the governmental rhetoric in which it was presented. Tony Blair's clarion-call, "standards, not structures," helped to deflect attention away from the radical structural changes introduced. Perhaps imperturbability was an understandable reaction in countries with a long history of a centralised State Educational System. In them, there was mainly a growing diversity of provisions to attract attention, whilst central powers were established custom and practice. Even in such countries, "devolution" (more properly, State controlled differentiation and diversification) being entirely concessionary, had nothing in common with *subsidiarity*.

However, in what had historically been a decentralised system, the arrogation of new educational powers to the State in England was shocking in its speed, thoroughness, and systematic nature. The number of Educational Acts (previously rare) increased to almost one a year under the Tories (1988–96) and the Secretary of State for Education gained over a thousand new powers in the same period. This entirely novel accumulation of educational powers at the centre had clear objectives. "While individual freedom, market choice and power for consumers rather than 'producers' of education were extolled, the central state took tighter control of finance, curriculum and examinations, teachers' practice and training. Part of what became a continuing agenda was to remove power from institutions and groups, which were bases for dissent, criticism or independent advice" (Tomlinson 2001, 35).

In fact, they were more than this. The two main institutions and groups targeted by this spate of legislation were exactly those which had promoted a nascent *subsidiarity* from the emergence of the English State Educational System onwards: the Local Educational Authorities and the teaching profession. That was the reason for pausing so long in Part II above over "External Transactions" and "Internal Initiation."

Through "External Transactions," LEAs in different areas had been able to sponsor a variety of technical schools in partnership with local users and to give financial support to almost exactly what was sought, without dilution. Furthermore, they had won over the Labour Party to the audaciously democratic policy of national comprehensivization, through successfully piloting local schemes with parental backing. In short, they had been forces for both *subsidiarity and solidarity*. Now, it made no difference which party was in office; almost every year saw a statutory diminution in LEA powers and responsibilities.

Equally, the teaching profession, despite its protracted struggle to gain this status (Archer 1979, 718–38), had used "Internal Initiation" to introduce a wealth of pedagogical innovations: child-centred methods, activity-based learning, groupwork, project-based assessment, open classrooms, etc. Most of these were now anathematised as the causes for "low standards." In the interest of "high standards," the English system acquired for the first time a National Curriculum, programmes of study, attainment targets for each subject, and Standard Assessment Tasks (SATs) at the ages of 7, 11, 14, and 16. Teachers suddenly became the most alienated group in the educational "enterprise." Although their protests (and problems of recruitment) achieved a slight modification of SATs in 1993, New Labour took over the baton and minutely prescribed its "Literacy hour" in defence of the standards that teachers were supposedly not producing.

Performance on the new National Curriculum became the main plank of both the "lab" appeal to "high standards for all" and the "lib" appeal to "parental choice." In 1992, National Curriculum test results appeared publicly and these "League Tables" were published in national newspapers, as they have been every year since, ranking schools of every kind, complete with the naming and shaming of "failing schools." Since financial management had been devolved to the level of the individual school, praise or blame, repute or disrepute for their results could be considered the responsibility of the particular Head (now a heavy managerial role) and the school's staff. Neither the fact that they had very little scope for manoeuvre, given the detailed nature of central curricular prescriptions and fierce inspection, nor the fact that so many studies showed that school attainment reflected the social composition of the pupil body, diminished the fact that parents were induced to follow the League Tables when making their choice of schools.

Thus, "[A]s many of the responsibilities adopted by the state in the post Second World War period begin to be devolved to a marketized version of civil society, consumer rights increasingly come to prevail over citizen rights" (Whitty, Power, and Halpin 1998, 46). Marketization of schooling had turned parents into the educational bargain-hunters of Rational Choice Theory, whose main concern was to become better off in terms of educational "utiles" by gaining a place in the highest ranked schools. Such educational consumerism was diametrically opposed to parental *solidarity* and sedulously served to undermine it. Under New Labour's legislation (1997–1998), there were now thirteen (statutorily) different types of school (Tomlinson 2001, 98) to choose between, thanks to the welcome given to both traditional religious establishments and specialised schools, partly financed by private (mainly business) sponsors.

Solidarity between parents was fragmented as they became individualistic "shoppers" for personal educational advantage. As competitive clients for entry to "the best" schools, the desire to seek the best for their children was perverted into a divisive and sometimes dishonest instrumental rationality, whose strategies were entirely self-interested. Thus, parish priests often reported an influx of regular attenders at Mass amongst those with three-year-old children, ones whose devotions plummeted once the child had been admitted to a Catholic school. Today, whilst writing this section, I picked up the local newspaper because of its headline: "PARENTS CHEAT TO WIN SCHOOL PLACES." The story recounts twenty detected cases of Coventry parents lying about their addresses "in an attempt to get places at some of the city's most popular state schools....The figures highlight a problem throughout the city and Warwickshire where parents in catchment areas with poorly regarded schools are desperate to get their children into top performing schools."[20]

What these central governmental interventions have done is not only to undermine both *subsidiarity and solidarity*, in the ways just described, and not only to substitute for the *common good*, a definition of the "general good" (of Britain in a global society) furnished by the political centre, they have done more radical damage. In effect, they have paralysed free-giving—the source of energy initiating and sustaining all other components necessary to the *common good* (Donati 2003). The straightjacket of central control has cut the roots of free-giving both motivationally and organizationally.

In terms of motivation, the two main parties involved at ground level— teachers and parents—are structurally discouraged from acknowledging and promoting the *human dignity* of each (potential) pupil. At the point of admission, teachers are constrained to consider children not as bearers of a *munus in potentia* but only under the guise of their potential contribution to the future ranking of the school. Similarly, parents are induced to commodify their children into objects for placement, involving strategic parental exertions but not ones where the first consideration is the well-being and needs of the unique child in question.

In parallel, what could parents do organizationally to make matters otherwise? Some optimism has attached to the enablements embedded in the official promotion of diversity and the development of Charter Schools in the USA. In California these involve contracts stipulating active parental participation in the school (Dianda and Corwin 1994). However, a number of school prospectuses reveal parental "participation" being defined in terms of direct debit financial contributions.[21]

In short, if we return to Donati's basic diagram of the components and the relationships between them that are required to realise the *common good*, we find them all to be even more lacking around the world in the period of "late" Modernity than often in the past, particularly in decentralised State Educational Systems. Caught in a vice between the State and the Market, with parents and teachers condemned to the roles of customers and managers, does education have the autonomy to do anything or are other parts of civil society able to do anything to re-direct education? I believe the answer to be negative to both questions. However, *grosso modo*, this vice in which education finds itself derived from politically directed changes intended to align State Educational Systems adaptively to the new challenges of global society.

Conversely, if we view globalisation as the effect of underlying structural processes and their generative mechanisms, rather than as the (primary) cause of anything, it is possible to see "late" Modernity as an important but passing phase in social morphogenesis. In other words, it is part of a process which will supersede itself—and with it comes the possibility of a truly "New Deal" for education.

Part III. "Morphogenesis Unbound"[22] and the Reconstruction of Education

All social formations are only relatively durable. What prolonged them in the past was morphostasis, that is, processes of negative feedback in both the structural and cultural domains, whose simultaneity maintained the status quo. Morphostasis dominated in early societies; that is what made them "traditional." The successive stages of Modernity were ones in which negative, restorative feedback loops intertwined with positive and deviation amplifying feedback processes. This meant that social transformation was slow, partial, and hesitating because "old" vested interests resisted change and "new" ones had time to consolidate themselves. What is, as yet, unprecedented and un-conceptualised is a world of untrammelled morphogenesis.

This has not yet arrived and nor has Modernity reached its last gasp. Nevertheless, structure, culture, and agency have begun to be governed by positive feedback and are less and less restrained by the simultaneous circulation of negative and restorative feedback loops that was characteristic of Modernity.

Vertiginously, the generative mechanism of morphogenesis—for variety to stimulate yet greater variety—has begun to engage and to manifest its tendential effects, of which globalisation and global connectivity are amongst the first instances. Of equal importance is the fact that whilst Modernity generated a "situational logic of *competition*" for action (because of the resistance, re-creation and reproduction of vested interests), action in Morphogenetic society follows a much looser "situational logic of *opportunity*" (an inducement to innovate and produce further variety through synthesis, syncretism, and synergy).

We are in a transitional phase, but there are already sufficient substantive manifestations of morphogenetic changes in the structural, cultural, and agential domains for this transformation to be more than pure speculation. Thus, it is possible to consider the implications of the unbinding of morphogenesis for education in the near future, without remaining entirely hypothetical.

In these last few pages, I would like to put together two considerations and then briefly to discuss their implications for one another. The first consideration concerns the very different effects produced by the new "situational logic of opportunity" compared with the zero-sum outcomes and conditional influences of Modernity's "situational logic of competition." The fundamental novelty about the "logic of opportunity" is that for the first time since the earliest societies, the relationship between Ego and Alter (who are not necessarily individual persons) is not governed by *cui bono* or by their conjoint ability to benefit in some way by outdoing (beating, exploiting, or coercing) third parties. Both or all parties can become beneficiaries by pooling and sharing resources. This is reinforced by the fact that the main resource in question is knowledge, whose value is not reduced by it being shared.

The second consideration is that all the educational struggles examined in this paper—competitions about gaining, maintaining, and exercising educational control—were predicated upon formal education having expensive physical and human resource requirements. Indeed, these have become even greater in "late" Modernity[23] as university education has been extended to approximately 40% of the age cohort in Europe. Because of this, the main value of a first degree, in most developed countries, is to avoid the penalty of not having one. In turn, the demand for further postgraduate degrees becomes inflated (see Archer 1982). Hence, the universities, competing in terms of State imposed performance indicators (of research as well as teaching) and corporately raiding the global market for registration fees, continue to increase dramatically in numbers and to decline in quality. Such is the payoff for all those competitive exertions on the part of parents to get their children into the best schools earlier on!

If these two considerations are put together, it becomes possible to conceive of an alternative future for education, one which reduces the academic obesity of young people, bids to escape State control and confronts Market forces with a process outside the cash nexus. In concrete terms, we can begin to contemplate some "de-institutionalisation of education." Another way of putting this is that in its global cyber version, "de-schooling," as it used to be known, has become a real possibility—although that does not make it desirable at all stages of the educational process. However, it is already in train. What is of particular interest is its potential for helping to actualise the four key principles of Social Doctrine in the area of education. What follows is a quick sketch of the relationships between each of these, based equally upon my current study of young people's reflexivity in relation to employment and Donati's formalisation of "the solidarity-subsidiarity relation in its various articulations" (Donati 2008; see figure 11.3 in this volume).

Relational Subsidiarity

Free-giving is not only the "starter-motor" of reciprocal relations it is also needed to fuel their continuation—rather than their degenerating into exchange relationships, as in one interpretation of Marcel Mauss' original analysis of the gift (Schrift 1997). Other than *caritas*, secular versions of altruism (usually distorting it into delayed self-interest to advantage one's "inclusive kin" [Trigg 1982]) show that the social sciences have been at a loss about what could turn people into free-givers.

The "situational logic of opportunity" appears to provide a new sociological perspective on free-giving. Let me illustrate this in relation to "intellectual property." Amongst multinational companies, the "Assurance game" may continue to be played with industrial patents, which enable the innovator to be the sole beneficiary for a set number of years and buy enough time for the company to come up with another profit-maker—but it generalises very badly beyond industry proper. The antics of the music "industry" to assure musical performance rights through law are defeated daily by the "playground pirates."

More pertinently, many writers, academics, performers, and "geeks" in general have motives which are contrary to placing restrictions upon their "intellectual property." Like most academic colleagues, when Eastern Europe produced "unauthorized" versions of my works in the bad old days, my reaction was not that of a (futile) contumacious litigant. On the contrary, since we do not write for profit, we delight in free diffusion. Now we have greater opportunities of the latter. The motives are not necessarily entirely altruistic, but the actions are tantamount to free-giving and their consequences are beneficial.

"Peer to peer" givers on the Internet are better exemplars because their relations entail both the diffusion *and* the infusion of new ideas. This is a key example of reciprocity, since there are neither controls nor guarantees of direct or indirect, short-term or long-term exchanges—let alone of exchange relationships—being established. Continued interchange cannot be enforced; its continuation is voluntary and based upon interest in one another's ideas and mutual respect for each other as their source. It recognises the dignity of alterity because it acknowledges the intrinsic value of the *munus* that the other has freely supplied. Certainly, this is not synonymous with full recognition of the dignity of a *human person,* but secular society is not going to be moved by the argument of divine filiation. Nevertheless, the *intrinsic* value accorded to the Other greatly surpasses the exchange value assigned to social relations in Modernity.[24]

Vertical Subsidiarity

How do the practices just described relate to the *common good?* In educational terms, the answer might simply be by means of the hand-cranked $100 laptop and the non-profit organization aiming to supply one to every child on the planet (Negroponte 2007). Between the two lie other requirements, some of which will be examined in a moment. However, in terms of direct vertical links, there are many who will freely write programmes of instruction in literacy, numeracy, and any other topic in any language. There are e-books and enough authors who are ashamed to collect $5 for someone xeroxing their articles in Nairobi. There is Wikipedia, which is our own students' first resort today, and if we find some of its entries could be improved upon, the invitation is there.[25] Already the educational costs are spiraling downwards; we simply do not need a library per campus or a per capita textbook allocation per school child. This is vertical subsidiarity coming into play. Already, to work with the Internet is not co-action, as in early societies, nor is it interaction, as in Modernity, it is transaction with the global database, which collects and redistributes knowledge through usage.

Of course, simply to reduce educational costs and to increase access is only one element in reconstructing education. Yet, the cost-barrier hugely privileged the educational hegemony of the State in the past. Nevertheless, there remain the two perennial problems. How to prevent socio-economic differences in pupils' family backgrounds from being reproduced through education, thus perpetuating socially divisive inequalities? How to deal with the fact that the school, college, or university should be more than a combination of an educational production line and a childcare-cum-recreational facility? This is where both the lateral and horizontal aspects of *subsidiarity* and *solidarity* are essential. Nevertheless, the change toward Morphogenetic society makes its own contributions to both of them.

Lateral Subsidiarity

Let us take the problem of "reproduction" first. What the accelerating tendency of variety to generate further variety in knowledge means is that parental background increasingly possesses no corpus of *cultural capital* whose durable value can be transmitted to their children, as opposed to cultural transmission *tout simple.* Parental culture is rapidly ceasing to be a capital good, negotiable on the job market and counting as a significant element in the patrimony of offspring. *Les Héritiers* are being impoverished by more than death duties. Culture is still their inheritance but is swiftly becoming an internal good—valued at the estimate of its recipients, like the family crystal and silver—rather than an external good with a high value on the open market.

Consequently, strategies for ensuring the inter-generational transmission of cultural capital start to peter out, partly because such "capital" has been devalued almost overnight and partly because rapidly diminishing calculability makes old forms of strategic action increasingly inapplicable. Those middle class and higher class parents who stuck to past routines, which had served their own parents well, of "buying advantage" through private schooling began to face offspring who felt they had had an albatross tied round their necks. Confronting the incongruity between their background and their foreground, an increasing number of Public School leavers began to blur their accents, abuse their past participles, make out they had never met Latin, etc., in subjective recognition of the "contextual incongruity" in which they were now placed.

Of course it will be objected that such an education still gains a disproportionate number of entrants to the oldest universities in England, but some of the sharpest Public School leavers have no desire to go there and, in any case, both establishments are now besieged by egalitarian-cum-meritocratic pressures which somewhat undercut their social point.[26] Equally, it will be objected that their graduates still have preferential access to careers in the Civil Service, in diplomacy, and in the traditional professions. But that is quite compatible with the fact that by the end of the twentieth century some of the kids from privileged backgrounds began to discount these openings. The fast learners had got the message: the Stock Exchange wanted the "barrow-boy" mentality on the floor. Effectively, their possession of old-style cultural capital was a disadvantage *vis-à-vis* new openings and opportunities, although it retains lingering value for the more traditional occupational outlets.

In a very different way, working class parents found themselves in much the same position of literally having nothing of market value to reproduce among their children. With the rapid decline of manufacturing and frequent joblessness, their previous ability to recommend high wages and to "speak for" their sons also disappeared. With the computerisation of secretarial, reception, and much work in retail, mothers found their daughters already more proficient in keyboard skills, than they were themselves. With involuntary redundancies, makeshift jobs and frequent visits to the Job Centre, there are less and less remnants of working class culture to be reproduced—especially the old attractions of a lasting group of convivial workmates—and decreasing incentives toward reproductory practices in employment among both parents and offspring. The latter, in any case, are now mostly "at College," for varying amounts of time, but long enough for many to come to think that courses such as IT, Design, and Media Studies present a blue beyond of opportunity. Meanwhile, many of their parents retreat into a non-directive goodwill toward their children's futures, usually expressed as "We'll support them whatever they want to do."

In other words, the very notion of *transferable cultural capital* is being outdated by morphogenesis and simultaneously all those intricate manoeuvres of substituting between different kinds of capital are becoming obsolete. However, this growing contribution of social morphogenesis to overcoming the biggest problem of social discrimination in twentieth century education is both partial and negative. It is partial because there are both older and newer forms of poverty which still impact seriously upon equality of educational opportunity and outcome—thus reducing social integration. It is negative because even if the influence of socio-economic background—which subtracted massively from social solidarity—were to be removed entirely, this does not mean that solidarity would spring back into being, as if it were a natural force which had been dammed up.

On the contrary, developed societies suffer from a huge deficit in sources of solidarity. This, in turn, undermines "lateral subsidiarity" and, in consequence, weakens the support available to "horizontal" agencies seeking to actualise subsidiary establishments for schooling in the Third Sector. Indeed, some of the forms of "associational engagement" that have succeeded the now moribund forms of geo-local community—and in particular virtual communities, which are very real—tend to direct their energies upwards, toward vertical sources of subsidiarity by enriching the resources available (in principle, to all) within the world's cyber-bank. This is good in itself, but it rarely contributes to the solidary support required by novel forms of schooling which by definition are geographically localised.

What is much more positive is that educated young people (at least) are starting to become "associationally engaged" with localized (or glocalized) endeavours: voluntary work, restoration of public amenities, ecological initiatives, inner-city regeneration projects, and, importantly, in mentoring and auxiliary work in schools. In short, the deficit in social solidarity is actively being reduced by our recent cohorts of undergraduates.

Horizontal Subsidiarity

This leads to the second question, namely, that real alternative schools are really needed in determinate locations and as more than nodal points for information-transfer. De-schooling can only go so far and I venture that it can go furthest at the higher levels. After all, the e-university only goes one step further than the Open University in England, which works by distance-learning and has played a major role in the voluntary re-skilling of teachers, without reference to the national curriculum. Its Summer Schools satisfy, at least partially, the relational requirements of learning—especially for mature students with family responsibilities—which prevent the degree from becoming merely a certificate in having absorbed so many videos and displayed mastery with e-resources. Equally, the "Education in Europe" initiative[27] was popular in the participating schools, but its purpose and function was the furtherance of European understanding, rather than supplying alternative education.

Quite apart from parents being accustomed to outsourcing education and needing to outsource in the growing number of dual career families (and in the professional interests of women), children also need schools. Since having only one child is already the norm in some European countries, where else are these children to gain companionship and social skills?

Who is to teach them is probably the least of the problems, given the alienation of many of the teaching profession from State education and their collective tendency to avoid privileged forms of Private education.[28] But how is the responsibility, shared by teachers and parents, to be generated for creating an environment in which the potentials of children can be better realised than when sandwiched between State directives and market requirements?

Contracts of "support + participation" are all very well, but the pre-contractual rules of contract are needed to breathe life into what otherwise can degenerate into "minimalist participants." Such alternative schools cannot thrive on minimalism. Indeed, they need to be very robust because they can easily slide in one of two directions: into becoming "just another" private school of privilege in the educational Market or into colonization by the State. These tendencies within the Third sector have been thoroughly registered and discussed in Italy (Donati and Colozzi 2004). They have attracted less attention in Britain, and it is salutary that the Government now has its own Ministry of the Third Sector, which promotes contracts of association that are almost the obverse of subsidiarity.

Conclusion

In his paper on "Prospects," Donati (2008; see chapter 11 in this volume) signals the underlying need for all manifestations of *subsidiarity* (in conjunction with the necessary *solidarity*) to be nourished by "a new 'relational anthropology of civil society,' that is from a new way to practise human reflexivity in civil relations" (13). Here, my current research on modes of reflexivity shows this not to be an empty exhortation.

As the Morphogenetic society gathers momentum, it appears that it fosters a Meta-reflexivity amongst young, educated people—which is as socially critical as it is self-critical—revealing a profound disassociation from Party politics and an equally strong aversion to personal occupational association with the corporate Market. The preference of young Meta-reflexives is for employment in the Third Sector, to escape the *étatisme* that now seriously infects the social services and traditional professions and to avoid the consumerism, eco-indifference, and competitiveness that they see as integral to corporations in the global market (Archer 2007, chapters 6 and 7). Thus, they pin their hopes upon developing civil relations within civil society. What they want, above all, from their future work is "to make a difference" and, as some add, "even if only to the life of one person."

It is premature to do more than venture the congruity and complementarity between Meta-reflexivity and an orientation toward civil society that would show associational solidarity with the nascent institutions constitutive of subsidiary. Yet if such a reflexive orientation toward civil society does not become more general, it is hard to see how education can be reconstructed in this new millennium.

Notes

1. See Russell Hittinger (2002) for an exceptionally clear discussion of the relationship between *munera* and subsidiarity, in "Social Roles and Ruling Virtues in Catholic Social Doctrine."

2. The material and arguments advanced in Part 1 of this paper are covered in detail in Margaret S. Archer (1979), *Social Origins of Educational Systems*.

3. In the years preceding 1789 in France there had been criticism from the provincial *parlements* (especially by Rolland and La Chalotais) and the *ancien régime* only became an unambiguous supporter of Catholic-run education once the ultramontaine Jesuits had been expelled (1762) and the more Gallican and modernist Oratorians had become the leading teaching order.

4. Worldwide, these are probably in a minority because of territorial conquest (for example, Napoleon's European conquests) and imperialism, where the external power imposed the domestic model (for example, the French in North Africa) or one suited to their version of colonial rule (as throughout the British Empire).

5. These two paragraphs greatly overcompress the intricacies of the interactions involved. They are treated at length in the 800 pages of *Social Origins of Educational Systems* (Archer 1979), which analyses the emergence of four endogenously developed State Educational Systems in France and Russia (centralised) and England and Denmark (decentralised).

6. It is extremely important, as Roland Minnerath stresses, to see the interconnections between these principles rather than viewing them in isolation. See "Les principes fondamentaux de la doctrine sociale. La question de leur interprétation" (Minnerath 2008, 45–56).

7. This very compressed account can be found in extended form in Michalina Vaughan and Margaret S. Archer (1971), *Social Conflict and Educational Change in England and France 1789–1848.*

8. Cf. C. Hippeau (1883), *La Révolution et l'éducation nationale* for a detailed discussion of the educational plans presented to the three Revolutionary Assemblies.

9. These, as all other translations from French sources, are my own.

10. See Pierpaolo Donati, "Prospects: Discovering the Relational Character of the Common Good." (2008, 659–66; reprinted as chapter 11 in this volume).

11. I have analysed the "May events" of 1968 in these terms. See "France," in *Students, University and Society* (Archer 1972).

•

12. Finally abolished in 1870, these tested knowledge of the "Thirty-Nine Articles" of the Church of England and thus conformity to the teachings of the Established Church.

13. Most of the former, as property owners or rent-holders gained the vote in 1832. Because of this property qualification most of the (male) working class did not (until 1866 or even 1884). Their disillusionment at their exclusion in 1832 was a major factor in persuading the Chartist movement to go it alone in the educational struggle, despite their poverty of economic resources, and to found their own Halls of Science and Mechanics Institutes. See M. Tylecote (1957), *The Mechanics' Institutes of Lancashire and Yorkshire before 1851*.

14. For the uses made of this, see James Murphy (1971), *Church, State, and Schools in Britain, 1800–1970*.

15. This received systematic formulation in *La cittadinanza societaria*, Roma: Laterza, 1993. Recently he has defined "lib/lab" as the symbolic code of late Modernity. See Pierpaolo Donati (2006), "Introduzione," (38, see also 110–13).

16. I do not have the space to enter into this analysis here, which forms part of my current book, *The Reflexive Imperative* (Archer, forthcoming).

17. The countries covered are Australia, England and Wales, New Zealand, Sweden, and the United States (Whitty, Power, and Halpin 1998).

18. Anglican, Catholic, and Jewish schools educated some 23% of pupils in the late eighties.

19. The title of a White Paper produced for the Conservative government in 1992.

20. *Warwickshire Telegraph*, March 25, 2008, p. 1.

21. For example, the Palisades school in Los Angeles has a ranked nomenclature for parents as financiers, according to the amount they contract to donate regularly.

22. A term first coined by Walter Buckley (1967), *Sociology and Modern Systems Theory*. Morphogenesis refers "to those processes which tend to elaborate or change a system's given form, structure or state" (58). It is contrasted to Morphostasis which refers to those processes in a complex system that tend to preserve the above unchanged.

23. This is not registered in many national budgets because costs have been passed to parent/student consumers and to a variety of sponsors in civil society.

24. It may be objected that cyber-interchange of the Facebook variety is both degrading and prone to dishonesty, which is often the case, but no epoch or practice is proof against voluntary self-debasement; the best we can do is to protect against its coercive and exploitative social imposition.

25. Granted, my inept attempts failed to reveal who manages Wikipedia, just as the Elders of the Internet remain faceless and their means of appointment opaque, but a bored 13-year-old in Manila could probably help out.

26. The government has recently established an Office of Fair Access for universities.

27. Directed by Alberto Martinelli, Dean of Milan University, it interviewed a group of academics from different European countries and then encouraged Secondary School pupils to e-mail their questions.

28. For an illustrative vignette of such a teacher, see "Bernadette," in Margaret S. Archer (2007).

Bibliography

Anderson, R.D. 1975. *Education in France 1848–1870.* Oxford: Clarendon Press.

Archer, Margaret S. 1972. "France." In *Students, University, and Society,* edited by Margaret S. Archer. London: Heinemann.

———. 1979. *Social Origins of Educational Systems.* London: Sage.

———, ed. 1982. *The Sociology of Educational Expansion: Take-off, Growth, and Inflation in Educational Systems.* London: Sage.

———. 1995. *Realist Social Theory.* Cambridge: Cambridge University Press.

———. 2007. "Bernadette." In *Making our Way through the World,* by Margeret S. Archer (133–41). Cambridge: Cambridge University Press.

———. Forthcoming. *The Reflexive Imperative.* Cambridge: Cambridge University Press.

Aulard, A. 1911. *Napoléon Ier et le monopole universitaire.* Paris: Colin.

Beck, Ulrich. [1986] 1992. *Risk Society: Towards a New Modernity.* London: Sage.

Benn, C., and B. Simon, 1970. *Half Way There.* London: McGraw-Hill.

Bishop, A.S. 1971. *The Rise of a Central Authority for English Education,* Cambridge: Cambridge University Press.

Bourdieu, Pierre, and Jean-Claude Passeron. 1964. *Les Héritiers, les étudiants et la culture.* Paris: Minuit.

Buckley, Walter. 1967. *Sociology and Modern Systems Theory.* Englewood Cliffs, NJ: Prentice Hall.

Decaunes, Luc, and Marie Louise Cavalier. 1962. *Réformes et projets de réformes de l'enseignement français de la révolution à nos jours.* Paris: Publication de l'Institut Pédagogique National.

Delfau, Albert. 1902. *Napoléon Ier et l'instruction publique,* Paris: A. Fontemoing.

Dianda, M.C., and R.G. Corwin. 1994. *Vision and Reality: A First Year Look at California's Charter Schools.* Los Alamitos, CA: Southwest Regional Laboratory.

Donati, Pierpaolo. 2003. "Giving and Social Relations: The Culture of Free Giving and its Differentiation Today." *International Review of Sociology* 13: 2.

———. 2006. "Introduzione." In *Il paradigma relazionale nelle scienze sociali: le prospettive sociologiche,* edited by Pierpaolo Donati and Ivo Colozzi. Bologna: Il Mulino.

———. 2008. "Prospects: Discovering the Relational Character of the Common Good." Plenary Session at the 14th Session of the Pontifical Academy of Social Sciences.

Donati, Pierpaolo, and Ivo Colozzi, eds. 2004. *Il privato sociale che emerge: realtà e dilemma.* Bologna: Il Mulino.

Duverger, Maurice. 1971. "The Eternal Morass: French Centrism." In *European Politics,* edited by Mattei Dogan and Richard Rose. London: Macmillan.

Giddens, Anthony. 1998. *The Third Way.* Cambridge: Polity.

Goblot, Edmond. 1930. *La Barrière et le Niveau,* Paris: Presses Universitaires de France.

Halsey, A.H. 2000. *Social Trends,* 30: 17.

Hippeau, C. 1883. *La Révolution Française et l'éducation nationale.* Paris: Charavay frères.

Hittinger, Russell. 2002. "Social Roles and Ruling Virtues in Catholic Social Doctrine." *Annales theologici* 16: 385–408.

————. 2008. "The Coherence of the Four Basic Principles of Catholic Social Doctrine—An Interpretation." Plenary Session at the 14th Session of the Pontifical Academy of Social Sciences.

Liard, L. 1888. *L'Enseignement supérieur en France, 1789–1889* (2 vols.). Paris: Colin et cie.

Minnerath, Roland. 2008. "Les principes fondamentaux de la doctrine sociale. La question de leur interpretation." Plenary Session at the 14th Session of the Pontifical Academy of Social Sciences.

Murphy, James. 1971. *Church, State, and Schools in Britain, 1800–1970.* London: Routledge and Kegan Paul.

Negroponte, Nicholas. 2007. "The $100 Laptop." In *Globalization and Education,* edited by Marcelo Sánchez Sorondo, Edmond Malinvaud, and Pierre Léna. Berlin: de Gruyter.

Prost, Antoine. 1968. *L'Enseignement en France 1800–1967.* Paris: Armand Colin.

Rich, Eric E. 1970. *The Educational Act, 1870.* London: Longmans.

Rubinstein, David, and Brian Simon. 1969. *The Evolution of the Comprehensive School.* London: Routledge and Kegan Paul.

Sanderson, Michael. 1972. *The Universities and British Industry, 1850–1970.* London: Routledge and Kegan Paul.

Schrift, Alan D., ed. 1997. *The Logic of the Gift: Toward an Ethic of Generosity.* London: Routledge.

Selleck, R.J.W. 1972. *English Primary Education and the Progressives, 1914–1939.* London: Routledge and Kegan Paul.

Simon, Brian. 1965. *Education and the Labour Movement, 1870–1920,* London: Lawrence and Wishart.

Stewart, W.A.C. 1968. *The Educational Innovators* (2 vols.). London: Macmillan.

Tomlinson, Sally. 2001. *Education in a Post-welfare Society.* Buckingham: Open University Press.

Trigg, Roger. 1982. *The Shaping of Man: Philosophical Aspects of Sociobiology.* Oxford: Basil Blackwell.

Tylecote, Mabel. 1957. *The Mechanics' Institutes of Lancashire and Yorkshire before 1851.* Manchester: Manchester University Press.

Vaughan, Michalina, and Margaret S. Archer. 1971. *Social Conflict and Educational Change in England and France 1789–1848.* Cambridge: Cambridge University Press.

Whitty, Geoff, Sally Power, and David Halpin. 1998. *Devolution and Choice in Education: The School, the State, and the Market.* Buckingham: Open University Press.

PART THREE

About the Authors:
Personal and Professional Reflections on
Doing Sociology to Serve the Church

13

Margaret S. Archer

Margaret Archer took her first degree and PhD in Sociology at the London School of Economics. Afterwards she registered for post-doctoral study at L'Ecole Pratique des Hautes Etudes (Sorbonne, Paris); worked with the re-search équipe of Pierre Bourdieu, and was in Paris during les événements of 1968. On returning to Britain she took up posts at the Universities of Cam-bridge, London School of Economics, Reading, and the new University of War-wick, becoming Reader (1973) and full Professor (1979). She was elected Presi-dent of the International Sociological Association (1986–90); helped found the Centre for Critical Realism (1990); and in 1994 was appointed a Councillor and founding member of the Pontifical Academy of Social Sciences.

I have always held that the term "Catholic Sociology" is a category mistake. There is simply good social theory and research and the better it is the more useful it will be to the Church. However, over the years, I did come to recognize that certain theoretical tendencies in the social sciences were incompatible with (most kinds of) faith and wrote accordingly against relativism, social construc-tionism, and postmodernism. My 1986 Presidential address to the International Sociological Association (at New Delhi) on "Sociology for One World" was a transcendental argument for what needed to be the case in order for there to be one discipline in a global social order.

After 1990, a number of factors combined to make me less of a Catholic-who-was-more-active-as-a-sociologist. Firstly, I was rather alarmed at the anti-intellectualism I encountered on retreats and began a series of critiques of the Enneagram, etc., thus beginning my sporadic journalism for *The Tablet*. Second-ly, I became involved with the Sisters of Mercy and tried to help them reorgan-ize their ministry in Britain. This involved a survey of all Mercy Union Sisters, visiting 32 convents, writing 14 reports, and making some lasting friends. Third-ly, through teaching at Warwick I became increasingly aware that believing students lived a double life, keeping their faith and academic work completely compartmentalized. Thus began a long involvement with the Catholic Chaplaincy on campus and sharing the RCIA programme with our Chaplains. This was the big push leading me to develop a detailed involvement with Catholic Social Teaching in order to "bridge" the Church and the (secular) University, particularly for social science students.

What was important for me during this period (roughly the 1990s) was coming to recognize two things. Firstly, many of the categories in classical philosophy—the basis of most clerical formation—simply could not deal with central issues in social theory. Specifically, it was impossible for the former to conceptualize "social relations and relationality" as real and irreducible and, equally, to theorize about "emergent properties and powers." Secondly, given secularization (including "believing without belonging") it seemed to me imperative to continue to produce social theory that could be defended in wholly secular terms. The better it was, the more useful it would be to the Church. This I have consistently maintained and do object to being described as a "Catholic sociologist." Used adjectivally, "Catholic" is not a descriptor in the same family as "tall" or "British"—as one author claimed in self-justification. It is used intentionally as an undermining concept and intended to do its job!

However, with the militancy of the "Dawkins" corpus of anti-religious books (on sale in the supermarkets), some of us felt that despite not being theologians we should present the counter argument for our students and fellow academics. Hence, with my good friends Andrew Collier (Quaker) and Doug Porpora we ventured to write *Transcendence: Critical Realism and God* (2004). The book is an argument for a level playing field in which, as William Alston had argued, religion is unfairly expected to pass two tests: its own "insider" criteria, based upon religious experience; plus the "outsider" criteria of positivism that mathematics and logic would also fail. The book's reception was interesting. The book provoked antagonism and attack from some (certainly not all) critical realists, whose animus remains just as puzzling as why a recognized biologist like Dawkins would take time out to write against a faith he believes is intellectually disreputable and doomed to decline.

When the Pontifical Academy of Social Sciences was founded by Pope John Paul II in 1994, this signalled a deep involvement for me in collaborating with the Church to elaborate her Social Teaching (this is Clause 1 of our Constitution). I organized the first three annual Plenary sessions on the *Rerum Novarum* theme of "work," and became more and more interested in conceptualizing Civil Society and a Civil Economy working for the Common Good (itself an emergent, relational good). With Pierpaolo Donati we organized the 2008 Plenary meeting from which we published *Pursuing the Common Good: How Solidarity and Subsidiarity Can Work Together*. It is from this meeting that my papers in the present volume are taken. Perhaps we are entirely wrong in detecting some resonances within *Caritas in Veritate*: working in the Vatican always feels as if we are posting letters into limbo.

A year ago I moved to L'Ecole Polytechnique Fédérale de Lausanne, to start up the Centre d'Ontologie Sociale as Directrice and Professor of Social Theory. The main research project is "From Modernity to Morphogenetic Society?" Our international workshops explore whether, indeed, modernity is being left behind as global social change intensifies, and how the lineaments of the social order that is coming into being might better serve the common good. If you want to know more, please visit our website http://cdh.epfl.ch/ontology. Meanwhile, I live in France, as a *frontalier* (commuter by ferry boat across the lake) and continue to be an advisor to the British Conference of Bishops.

14

Pierpaolo Donati

Pierpaolo Donati is Professor of Advanced Sociology and Chair of the BA and PhD programs in Sociology at the University of Bologna (Italy). Past-President of the Italian Sociological Association, he has served as Executive Committee Member of the International Institute of Sociology. Since 1997 he has been a member of the Pontifical Academy of Social Sciences, and currently serves as the Director of the National Observatory on the Family of the Italian Government. He has received awards from the U.N. and U.N.E.S.C.O., and in 2009 the Doctorate Honoris causa from the John Paul II Pontifical Institute for Studies on Marriage and the Family, at the Pontifical Lateran University. He has published more than 700 works, including 92 books, in particular on social theory, social policy, family sociology, sociology of the Third Sector, and welfare issues. He is known as the founder of an original "relational sociology" or "relational theory of society." Among his more recent publications: Repensar la sociedad, El enfoque relacional, *Madrid: EIU, 2006; "Building a Relational Theory of Society: A Sociological Journey." in M. Deflem (Ed.),* Sociologists in a Global Age, *Aldershot: Ashgate, 2007*; Manual de Sociología de la Familia, *Pamplona: Eunsa, 2007;* La matrice teologica della società, *Soveria Manelli: Rubbettino, 2010; and* Relational Sociology. A New Paradigm for the Social Sciences, *New York: Routledge, 2010. Email: pierpaolo.donati@unibo.it*

Two great passions have been dominant in my life: sociological studies and an interest in the human person. Each of these passions demanded a connection with the other. I found this connection in the Church's social doctrine, which provides their referential, ideal, and practical frame. I maintain that the synergy between the social sciences and Christian social thought is absolutely necessary if we wish to produce a process of real civilization. This synergy, however, is arduous and cannot be taken for granted. It requires a *totally new* scientific paradigm for the social sciences, which makes dialogue possible between the empirical analysis of social facts and a reading of them inspired by Christianity. It is to the theoretical and empirical formulation of this new paradigm that I have dedicated most of my efforts.

I began my studies reflecting and doing empirical research on Western symbolic and cultural systems. My attention was marked, from the beginning, by interest in the crisis of modernity and ways to overcome it. I believe that the Catholic theological matrix is the one that, better than any other, can allow us to overcome the errors of the modern social sciences. I have applied this general thought in many fields.

I have dedicated considerable energy to the theme of the family in order to understand the sociological reasons for the existence of this social form, as an originating and original reality (*"fontalis,"* as John Paul II expresses it). I then opened new avenues for the construction of a sociology of health/illness that analyzes and seeks to overcome current processes of degeneration, in a technocratic, medicalizing, and iatrogenic sense.

I formulated a sociological theory of the "social private sector" (the nonprofit sector) using a framework of new processes of societal differentiation. And, in this connection, I have elaborated an original theory of *relational goods* within a theory of "societal citizenship." I have tried to offer new explanations for the crisis of the social State and new paths to overcome it. I have investigated the structures of civil society from a new angle, that of the sociology of civic relations.

The development of my research has gone hand in hand with the formulation of a paradigm I have named "the relational theory of society." I believe that this theory is absolutely necessary as an interface between the social sciences and Catholic social thought if a fruitful dialogue is to take place between these two disciplines.

When I began my career in the 1970s, sociological studies were dominated by two major currents: Marxism and structural-functionalism. I rejected these dominant theories and looked for another way to understand society. This search gave rise to my "relational sociology," based on an epistemology of critical, analytical, and relational realism.

The sense of this sociology lies in showing that the social world is a construction of relations that are always and contemporaneously references of meaning (*refero*) and connections that bind (*religo*), which give life to emergent phenomena of a morphogenetic nature. Society is the product of concrete human persons, but they play a role that is only a part of the larger reality of Divine

Creation. The central concept of "relation" points us to Trinitarian theology. It is in light of this *relational vision* that we can interpret the society produced by men and women as a reality expressing continual tension between the human and the divine.

The idea constantly facing me is that modernity has produced an inevitable differentiation or divide between the social and the human. If we wish to have a society suited to the dignity of the human person, we must produce it through new cultural mediations whose meanings are concretely reflected in the political, economic, and social arenas. It is here that relational sociology can contribute to the formulation of new concepts and good practices in the area of social doctrine, which otherwise runs the risk of remaining too abstract.

I think that the sociology of the 21st century will succeed in being truly and fully relational only if it is able to leave behind the myths and idols of modernity, and to continue in the development of those values—even modern ones—that have roots in Christian civilization. Only in this way will mankind be able to successfully overcome the great challenges of the Third Millennium, such as the battles against poverty, war, and terrorism, in favor of justice, a worthy human ecology, and peace.

15

Patrick Fagan

Patrick Fagan trained as a clinical psychologist in Ireland and then worked for five years in Canada at the General Hospital, Sault Ste. Marie, then at the Jewish General Hospital, Montreal, where he trained McGill Medical School family physicians in family issues. He completed his clinical psychology doctoral studies at American University in 1976. After transitioning into family public policy in 1983, he eventually completed a second doctorate in sociology at University College Dublin in 2006. He worked in the U.S. Senate as a staff member for Senator Dan Coates, and served in the U.S. Department of Health and Human Services as Deputy Assistant Secretary for Social Services Policy. Then followed 13 years at The Heritage Foundation as Senior Research Fellow in Family and Religion. Since 2007 Patrick serves as a Senior Fellow at the Washington-based Family Research Council; there he founded and now directs the Marriage and Religion Research Institute. At FRC he has published many reports and monographs which contribute to current political policy debates on key social issues related to marriage, family life, and sexuality, and is a frequent commentator in the national media.

In 1968 I was studying sociology when *Humanae Vitae* appeared, causing me personal concern that data on human behavior might contradict the Church's teaching. This led to the practice of investigating the data of threatening research with care. This led in turn, within a year, to the conclusion that authors' personal conclusions often stretched the data beyond what was scientifically appropriate—a lesson repeated again and again on many topics in the social sciences, particularly on matters of sexuality, marriage, parenthood, and family. It taught me the danger of using science for ideological reasons, and affirmed the need to distinguish between the canons of the social sciences and those of philosophy.

I did not set out to serve the Church in doing my sociology: rather what may have happened is that by trying to be faithful to both the sciences and to the

Church, I have repeatedly found "no conflict." However the teaching of the Church raises many issues for the social scientist, causing one to have daring hypotheses: daring because they fly in the face of the academic fashions of the day. Thus the Church helps the researcher overcome the intellectual shortcomings of his time and generates a tension that is good for the sciences, bringing new data to light, data that would have been hidden otherwise. Working on issues of marriage and family, which by nature have the sexual at their core, leads a family-focused social scientist like me into constant debate with the fashions of the sociological profession.

At the same time as I was struggling with *Humanae Vitae*, I became aware of a subtle but profound difference between seeing the Church at the service of the social sciences and seeing the social sciences at the service of the Church. In May of 1968 the Irish theological journal, *The Furrow*, published a homily called "Passionately Loving the World," delivered in Spain six months prior by Josemaría Escrivá. I did not read it until I returned home in October from a long summer bartending in New York, which was a great way to put oneself though college in Ireland at the time: one summer's work covered two years' total expenses. That homily gave me exactly what I was looking for: a way of serving the Church while being a layman "Passionately Loving the World." The simultaneous experience of that piece and the seeming clash of *Humanae Vitae* with the social sciences of the day was deeply formative.

After I had received my graduate journeyman psychologist's degree I went to Canada to gain clinical experience before getting a PhD. The first three years of clinical work were of lasting import because, day after day, I learned there that children thrive or their symptoms disappear when mother and father are united in a happy marriage. By the end of my second year of clinical practice I realized that the child's problems stemmed from within the family and the family's problems stemmed from what was happening between mother and father. As a result I would not see the referred child unless I could see the whole family together, including the father—most families were intact in the early 1970s. Getting the child's father to attend would have been next to impossible if I did not insist on his being there for the *first* visit. After a few family sessions I normally had a fair grasp of where the discord was between father and mother and peeling the couple away to work on their marital issues was easy. Once they were restored to functional happiness all was well. Ninety-five percent of the original identified patients (the referred children) got better—"spontaneously"—without any direct treatment. The rest of my life's work has been a playing out of the insights from those three years of child, family, and marital therapy. The shift from clinical practice to public policy occurred after a move to Washington to do a doctorate in clinical psychology. During the following years I met my wife and started a family, but also saw, up close, how Congress undermined the families of the poor with Family Planning programs that tore them apart. For a clinician this was truly insane and led eventually to a complete switch into public policy on behalf of the family against those, of both the Left and the Right, who were committed to public policies of radical individualism. My tools would remain somewhat the same: using the social sciences well. However, learning to do insight therapy with Congress through the data took a few years to figure out.

An appointment at the U.S. Department of Health and Human Services as Deputy Assistant Secretary for Social Services Policy led (unexpectedly) to the conclusion that all the program-driven social policies were failures, insofar as the problems addressed had not been diminished by government intervention but rather increased the longer government dealt with them. All this led to questions and insights about the nature of social policy and about how society worked, which in turn became the dissertation topic of a second PhD pursued at my alma mater in Dublin.

In turn this has led, in the last few years, to a long-nurtured dream of building a sociometric, demographic model of how society works—optimally through more worship, more marriage, and more children—which model-building is now under way in partnership with my colleague Henry Potrykus. The model's first studies illustrate that marriage is critical to economic growth and that the divorce revolution has, since the late 1970s, been a continuous drag on the growth of our Gross Domestic Product. Because our model will illuminate where, how, and why our society functions well, it will also describe where and why it does not. Thus we will envelop and illustrate the model Planned Parenthood proposes (less worship, less marriage, and less children) and its dysfunctional impacts. We should be able to present to Congress these two competing models and their consequences for the nation. Finally, we will be able to tackle Family Planning with the scientific attention it has never yet received.

16

Anne Hendershott

Anne Hendershott received her PhD in Sociology in 1988 from Kent State University, and spent more than fifteen years as a tenured professor and department chair at the University of San Diego. In 2005 she was invited to become a James Madison Fellow at Princeton University, and in 2008, she moved from San Diego to head the Politics, Philosophy, and Economics Program at the King's College in New York City. She is a frequent contributor to the Catholic press, and has also contributed to the op-ed pages of the Wall Street Journal, San Diego Union-Tribune, *the* Hartford Courant, *and the* Washington Times.

She is currently the Pope John Paul II Fellow in Student Development of the Cardinal Newman Society's Center for the Advancement of Catholic Higher Education. She is the author of five books, including Status Envy: The Politics of Catholic Higher Education *(Rutgers, NJ: Transaction Publishers, 2009);* The Politics of Abortion *(San Francisco: Encounter Books, 2006);* The Politics of Deviance *(San Francisco: Encounter Books, 2002);* The Reluctant Caregivers: Learning to Care for a Loved One with Alzheimer's Disease *(Westport, CT: Bergin and Garvey, 2000); and* Moving for Work: Corporate Relocation in the '90s *(Lanham, MD: University Press of America, 1995).*

Just about a decade ago, in the midst of the clergy sex abuse scandal in our Church, I became concerned about all of the untruths that were being published about the causes. I was especially disappointed that journalists and news commentators were seeking out dissident Catholic activists to analyze the reasons for the abuse in print and media interviews. Most of these self-appointed Church-spokespeople had their own personal agendas to advance. Some of them had spent the previous decades denigrating Church teachings on reproductive rights, women's ordination, and a celibate clergy. Some, like one Boston College theologian, blamed the "all-male" clergy as the cause for the sexual abuse. I began to recognize that if faithful Catholics like myself did not step up and provide sociological data to help people put the scandal into context, the response from the angry dissidents would win the day. This was when I moved from being one who was a consumer of media information about the Church to a committed contributor to the conversation—providing a faithful sociological witness for the Church.

I would not call myself an apologist—even though I have often been described as one by others in the media. Rather, I think of myself as a Catholic sociologist who so loves the Church that I could no longer be silent in the face of the attacks that were being made. Much like I could never allow others to attack my family, I began to realize the Church has been a like a mother to me; she has nurtured me throughout my life. I realized that I could no longer allow the lies about her to continue unanswered.

Since we were living in San Diego at the time, and I was teaching at the University of San Diego, the first thing I did was to publish an op-ed in the *San Diego Union-Tribune*. The piece was called "The Perfect Panic," and it framed the scandal in sociological terms. I drew comparisons between the moral panic that surrounded the clergy abuse scandal of 2002 with the moral panics of the past. Using sociological theory on moral panic, I demonstrated that while there were indeed some cases of sexual abuse by clergy, the inflated numbers and exaggerated "sinister" role attributed to the bishops and the Pope himself were signs that a moral panic was operating. I also demonstrated that one of the reasons that the panic had expanded so greatly was because there were so many who could gain so much by keeping the panic alive. I pointed out that as in all moral panics, those with an agenda to advance promote the panic. I identified many of those involved in promoting the panic—by name—including women who wanted to be ordained, gay men who thought that the reason for the panic was because gay priests had repressed their sexuality, married former priests who wanted to continue to celebrate the Eucharist, and dissident Catholic feminists who wanted access to full reproductive rights—including abortion.

For the past ten years, I have continued to draw from sociological theories and concepts to help others understand the goals and objectives of the progressive social movement that is currently operating within the Church. I identify groups like the American Catholic Council and Voice of the Faithful who continue to lament what they see as the "failed promise of Vatican II" and demand major structural changes in the Church—including erasing the distinction between the laity and the ordained, and allowing parishioners to elect their own bishops and priests. And, although the slogans of these groups claim that they only want to "Change the Church not the Faith," I point out that their real goal is to change Church teachings on a long list of issues—including abortion, homosexuality, celibacy for the clergy, and women's ordination. For the past ten years, most of my publications have focused on exposing the agenda of those involved in this progressive—and very dangerous—social movement within our Church.

Most recently I have changed my focus away from the dissidents to begin to document some of the positive news on the Catholic priesthood. While the media—including much of the Catholic media—continues to ignore it, there is some good news on the increase in priestly ordinations in many dioceses in the United States. I am currently co-authoring a book that explores the reasons for this increase. Drawing from sociological theory on charisma, and identifying sociological indicators of "faithful leadership," we are attempting to make the argument that courageous leadership matters when it comes to encouraging priestly ordinations. In the coming years I look forward to publishing the good news about our Church—rather than continuing to dwell so exclusively on the dissidents.

17

G. Alexander Ross

G. Alexander Ross, PhD, is Professor and Dean of Students at the Institute for the Psychological Sciences in Arlington, Virginia. He received his doctorate in sociology in 1976 from the Ohio State University and has taught at colleges and universities in Michigan, Ohio, Florida, and Virginia. During his career he has pursued a variety of research interests, including the social response to natural disasters and other emergencies, historical demography, the integration of the social sciences with a Catholic understanding of the human person, social change in the family and religion, and the social psychology of happiness.

The hope that sociology might serve the Church, rather than always be used to undermine it, may appear quixotic to many. After all, the man often referred to as the "father" of sociology, Auguste Comte, boasted that his "positive sociology" would soon replace religion. "I am convinced that before the year 1860," he said, "I shall be preaching positivism at Notre Dame as the only real and complete religion" (Lubac 1995, 149). Nevertheless, the hope of serving the Church is shared by the contributors to this volume, and by others as well. My hunch is that, if our academic colleagues today do not oppose us in our pursuit of a sociology founded on Catholic truth with the antipathy and ferocity of a Comte, their indifference and lack of understanding has much the same effect. It is this uncongenial atmosphere that we usually find in our places of employment which leads us to form and join associations like the Society of Catholic Social Scientists.

My experience with sociology began outside Catholicism. Reared in the Episcopal Church, I participated in the Christian faith as a youngster, but fell away in the third year of college, the same year I switched my major to sociology. Twenty years later, my heart and mind finally open to the truths of Christianity, I began the hard work of incorporating my years of training and experience in sociology with a radically altered view of everything important. I must add, however, that although such work has often been difficult, I have found that progress in it has been accompanied by greater joy than I knew before in my work. Because my faith filled me with the assurance that both in my personal and professional life I was being called by the Lord to cooperate with his redemptive work in the world, the word "vocation" took on a meaning it had never before had for me.

During these years, I was drawn more and more to the Catholic faith; and in December 2000, at the end of the Jubilee Year, I was received into the Church. Although my conversion was not motivated by my professional academic interests, I began to see that the philosophical richness of Catholic teaching offered a far more solid foundation for sociological work than anything I was acquainted with in my Protestant tradition. Introduced to the Society of Catholic Social Scientists at about this time, I began to make contacts with other academics who sought to take their faith seriously in their professional work. I have been very grateful for their guidance.

My association with the Institute for the Psychological Sciences (IPS) has been exceptionally important for me. IPS is blessed with a well-articulated mission to develop a psychology grounded in the truths of the faith and an administration, staff, faculty, and student body dedicated to that mission. Unusual in an academic institution today, this authentic, institution-wide commitment to Catholic teaching sustains an environment that consistently encourages the exploration of the relationship of psychology and related social sciences to the Catholic understanding of the human person. In this setting, we are able to work together effectively in the pursuit of our vocations to serve the Church.

Efforts such as the Society of Catholic Social Scientists and IPS are precisely the kind of apostolic activity called for by the Council Fathers of Vatican II. They taught us that it is the vocation of the laity to "seek the kingdom of God by engaging in temporal affairs and by ordering them according to the plan of God" (*Lumen Gentium*, #31). And the field of sociology is in particular need of re-ordering. Consider, for example how instrumental academic sociology has been in promoting a scientism that pits faith against reason, or a moral relativism that denies objective standards of truth. But sociology and other fields of modern thought are not permanently yoked to these distortions; if we embrace instead a Catholic view of the human person, we can more readily produce social research that is helpful to human society because it is true to the nature of man. The Church assists us with resources to do so. Our two most recent popes, John Paul II and Benedict XVI, have been both extraordinarily acute in their diagnosis of the distortions of human reason that plague our modern times and exceptionally inspiring in their invitation to all people of good will to pursue the truth. The call of the Second Vatican Council to engage the laity in evangelizing our culture and the example of these two great popes give us a most timely opportunity to answer a vocation to sociology.

Bibliography

Lubac, Henri de. 1995. *The Drama of Atheist Humanism.* San Francisco: Ignatius Press.

18

Stephen R. Sharkey

Stephen R. Sharkey received his PhD in Sociology from the University of Connecticut in 1980. He is past Dean of Arts and Sciences at Alverno College, and currently Professor of Sociology and Senior Scholar for Liberal Learning at that institution. He is the Sociology disciplinary section chair of the Society of Catholic Social Scientists, and a member of University Faculty for Life.

His main scholarly interests have been the individual and society, social movements, Catholic social thought, and the nature of undergraduate teaching, learning, and curriculum development. For many years he served as a national consultant to campuses and sociology departments on general education, faculty development, curricular reform, and assessments of student learning; he edited and contributed to books published by the American Sociological Association and other higher education organizations on these topics. Recently focusing more on Catholic social thought, his articles and papers include "Teaching for Sociological Imagination in a Social Darwinist Culture," Sociological Imagination, Vol. 41, No.1, 2005; "Unwrapping 'Our Best Kept Secret:' A Critical Review of Popular Textbooks in Catholic Social Teaching," Catholic Social Science Review, November 2004; "Framing a Catholic Sociology for Today's College Students: Historical Lessons and Questions from Furfey, Ross, and Murray," Catholic Social Science Review, November 2004 and November 2005; and "A Catholic Sociology of the Movement for Same Sex 'Marriage' in the United States" presented at the Annual Meetings of the Society of Catholic Social Scientists, October 2009.

I graduated from Colgate University in 1970 during that raucous period when any self-respecting new sociology student opposed the Vietnam War, scoffed at most social conventions, and believed that sociology could be a righteous tool for social change through its critical theory, research, and teaching praxis. Having decided on an academic career, I then attended the University of Connecticut (way before there were NCAA basketball championships), where the sociology graduate program was oriented very traditionally toward producing empirical researchers. Its faculty were largely secular in their outlook; I am sure it was actually more complex than this but at the time they also seemed terribly split down the middle between conservative functionalists on one side and progressives such as early feminists and Marxists on the other. I came down on the left.

My cradle Catholicism and Christian Brothers high school education seemed distant echoes of an unaware past and my adherence to the secular rejection of Christianity was a given. Yet a mysterious quiet reserve remained in the background of my consciousness that did not quite go away—today I might say that God was waiting for me, though I would never have said such a thing at the time. Crucially, I decided I wanted to be an undergraduate liberal arts professor rather than a researcher in a big department. Looking back I can discern in my interests in the nature of student thinking and self-development, in existentialism, and in the sociology of knowledge a commitment to a sort of humanistic sociology that left open doors for later pursuit of religious questions. I became more and more interested in students' meaning-making and college's role in fostering not only specific ideas but broad worldviews. I went to Alverno in 1978 because of its national reputation for educational reform and progressivism: an abilities-based program with a mission to nontraditional populations, small classes, lots of faculty collaboration on teaching and curricula. I was in part hired because of my sociological secularism and commitment to progressive causes.

But over the years, the more I studied sociology and how sociology was framed for students, the more I thought and felt it to be partial and stilted. The materialism of the explanations and the flatness of the vision of the person embedded in the field did not match up with what I saw in students trying to figure out what society was and who they were. Further, a not uncommon process ensued where the god of Marxism failed me personally: I had a spiritual crisis wherein religious faith became plausible for me once more. It became harder for me to be satisfied with traditional sociological conversation and ideas. In my search for alternatives I encountered works of Catholic social teaching and social thought that impressed me enormously—for example, many texts by John Paul II. I read voraciously, trying to make up for years lost justifying my sociologism and Marxism. I "discovered" that one could be an intellectual and a Catholic at the same time! My cradle Catholic wife had followed a similar intellectual and political trajectory in the field of psychology, and at a certain point in the early 1990s we both found ourselves crossing back over the Tiber, making general confessions, and returning full blown to the Church. As it happens I came to use my sociological and academic leadership training to good effect in parish administration for the last two decades, and she has used her expertise to start and run an explicitly Catholic psychotherapy clinic.

I must admit I found the Society of Catholic Social Scientists almost by accident, as I was searching for professional colleagues who could talk both sociology and Catholicism, discerned the tension between the two, and sought some sort of collaboration or synthesis. That was a happy discovery which continues to nourish my ongoing conversion and offer me a kind of haven in a sometimes heartless academic world. At this time I think Catholic scholars are ready to take a fuller place at the broader societal and academic table, and I want to help that along. I have only increased my commitment to sociological teaching and inquiry with a Catholic accent, focused in particular on Catholic higher education, student learning and development broadly defined, and what Catholic social teaching can contribute to contemporary culture and political discourse. My faith influences my professional work very deeply, though often and appropriately in an implicit way. I live aware that whatever I do as a teacher, academic colleague, and citizen can lead those around me either closer to or further away from God. The faith and its intellectual tradition are my rock and my shield.

19

D. Paul Sullins

The Rev. Donald Paul Sullins, PhD, is Professor of Sociology at the Catholic University of America and a Fellow of the Institute for Policy Research and Catholic Studies, the Center for the Advancement of Catholic Higher Education, and the Marriage and Religion Research Institute. He also directs the Summer Institute of Catholic Social Thought at Catholic University, and serves on the board of the Society of Catholic Social Scientists. He has published dozens of articles in major sociological and religious studies journals and over 100 research reports for religious judicatories and agencies. His most recent book (edited with Anthony Blasi) is Catholic Social Thought: American Reflections on the Compendium *(Lanham, MD: Lexington Books, 2009). Formerly Episcopalian, Fr. Sullins is a married Catholic priest with an interracial family of three children, two adopted.*

I first became interested in sociology as a discipline to help make sense of my faith and mission as a priest and pastor. At the time I directed a soup kitchen that had grown into a diverse agency offering a range of social services, including overnight shelter, medical screenings, job placement assistance, and transitional housing. Increasingly we were getting into political issues, community organizing, and partnership and boundary issues with other missions and public agencies. Social science was valuable to me in two ways. First, theoretical models of collective agency and communal understandings of rights and justice provided a valuable context to better understand why we should head in certain directions and not others; and second, once we had decided where to go, random-sample data analysis to test ideas against empirical reality helped decide how to get there, by showing us what kinds of things worked and what did not.

Eventually I moved into the university setting, teaching sociology full time. I really didn't intend to do this; I'm really an accidental sociologist. I can identify three types of Catholic sociology I've been engaged in since coming to the university. First, as time went by I got involved in many research projects for Catholic agencies, dioceses, and school systems, focusing on the second value of social science just noted above. I think good evaluation research is of great instrumental value to the Church and its related institutions; and it's hard for someone who doesn't relate well to the Catholic faith to do such work. Second, I also began to do research to explore hypotheses that support Catholic policy stances or truth claims in the public arena. This is also a kind of applied Catholic social science, though at a higher level of analysis, so with a little more theoretical intentionality. A study that demonstrates, say, the negative social effects of contraceptive use, is motivated and informed by a Catholic perspective in a more particular way than one that advises a Catholic school system where best to place a new school. Third, I have lately moved even more toward exploring the first kind of value noted above, that is, the theoretical structure of an explicitly Catholic social science.

In my view there are good reasons to think that we can talk about a Catholic sociology or social science. We affirm, with all religions and ethical systems, the presence of a moral order (Tao, natural law) which, when not blinded by bias that excludes such knowledge, is readily observable by empirical research. Original sin is easily empirically demonstrable, particularly if you consider that one of its demonstrations lies in the tendency to deny it in the face of overwhelming evidence to the contrary. Catholics also affirm a concrete, sacramental experience of God in the particular person of Christ, which opens us up to matter and the body, and thus social science, in a unique way. Catholic piety, moreover, is distinctly social. A faithful Protestant prays alone in a "quiet time" with God; a faithful Catholic goes to Mass or confession, encountering God by means of others. The Church is necessary and concrete for Catholics in a way that it is not, generally, for Protestants. Above all, there are the social teachings, built around the powerful concept of human dignity and transcendence, which comprise, in a sense, marching orders for a Catholic social science.

The problem in exploring such ideas in terms of sociology is that so much of the contemporary discipline is affirmatively anti-Catholic, or more broadly anti-religious: a widespread rejection of moral truth and even metaphysical knowledge is implicit in the presuppositions and self-perception of most American social scientists. An absence of direct empirical evidence for God has been misunderstood as empirical evidence for the absence of God—a very different matter. Several of the offerings in this book explore these themes.

In fairness, I also have to confess that I'm a little leery of the actual "Catholic" sociologies I've encountered. A Catholic sociology that elbows a place alongside other "interested" approaches, like feminist, Marxist, latino/a, LBGT, seems to miss the point, as does a "Catholic sociology" which is simply the sociological study of Catholics and Catholic institutions, a subfield of the sociology of religion. Such efforts try to refocus or redirect the discipline without addressing the fundamental flaw that makes it opposed to Catholic thought, or to religious thought more generally. I have experienced the perverse product of such efforts, pervasive in Catholic institutions, in a Catholic sociology (so-called) that is itself anti-Catholic.

A genuine theoretical Catholic sociology is possible and would be of great value to Catholics, who are pretty open to social science, but of little use to sociologists, who are pretty closed to things of faith. I see a lot of interest in social science at the United States Conference of Catholic Bishops, but very little interest in Catholic insights at the American Sociological Association. What social scientists need is not so much an explicitly Catholic sociology as an ability to engage perspectives that depart from the orthodoxy of naturalism and relativism. Before sociology can even begin to engage a Catholic sociology, it needs to develop an open mind about religious truth. So as a sociologist I'm not an advocate for Catholic sociology, for a non-anti-Catholic sociology; yet as a priest I'm interested in an unapologetically Catholic sociology. In a real way, I'm back where I started: turning to social science to better understand my faith and mission in the world.

20

Joseph A. Varacalli

Joseph Varacalli received his BA in Sociology from Rutgers, MA in Sociology from the University of Chicago, and PhD in Sociology in 1980 from Rutgers. He is currently Distinguished Service Professor of Sociology at Nassau Community College-SUNY, where in 1999 he created the Center for Catholic Studies.

After co-founding the Society of Catholic Social Scientists in 1992, he was the editor-in-chief of its journal The Catholic Social Science Review *from 1996–1999, and since then has remained a frequent contributor. Active in the affairs of the contemporary Catholic Church, he was on the Board of Directors for the Fellowship of Catholic Scholars from 1993–1995 and then again in 2002. For his outstanding achievements in Catholic culture, he received the Pope Pius XI Award from the Society of Catholic Scientists in 2004 and the Denis Dillon Award from the Long Island chapter of the Catholic League for Religious and Civil Rights in 2007. Since September 2007 he has served on that organization's Board of Advisors.*

His scholarly works have been published in such journals as Faith and Reason, The Homiletic and Pastoral Review, Lay Witness, *and* Nassau Review. *His most recent books are* The Catholic Experience in America *(Westport, CT: Greenwood, 2006); and* Bright Promise, Failed Community: Catholics and the American Public Order *(Lanham, MD: Lexington Books, 2001). He is co-editor of the* Encyclopedia of Catholic Social Thought, Social Science, and Social Policy, Vols. I, II, and III *(Lanham, MD: Scarecrow Press, 2007 and 2012).*

I consider myself a student of two distinguished sociologists, Peter L. Berger and Edward A. Shils, both of whom had strong interests and expertise in the sociology of knowledge. I studied under Berger as both an undergraduate sociology major and graduate student and under Shils while at the University of Chicago. While (literally) awed by their brilliance, my co-natural and integrationist-incarnational-sacramental Catholic sentiments did not allow for me to accept either Berger's sharp Weberian and Lutheran "two kingdoms"-like distinction between the sociological and theological enterprises; or Shils' admittedly broad and expansive secular humanism, refusing, as it did, to ultimately acknowledge the reality of a transcendent realm that had implications for this-worldly existence, including intellectual and academic work.

I have spent my entire academic career as a somewhat professionally marginalized community college sociologist—a consequence, in some part at least, of my heterodox stance affirming the plausibility and mostly latent reality of "Catholic perspectives" in sociology and the social sciences. However I am fully aware of a this-worldly "trade-off" in operation: the margin has certain advantages. Simply put, the community college setting, for all its obvious limitations in terms of individual advancement, working conditions, financial remuneration, status, and, more importantly, ability to influence the academy and society, has nonetheless allowed me to engage and move forward, even if in a fragmentary and unsatisfactory manner, with my "heretical" intellectual projects, viewed at least from the frame of reference of the mainstream sociological profession. Given my intellectual and religious convictions, I understand well that it would have been practically impossible to survive—never mind thrive—with a sense of ethical integrity in a more mainstream sociological academic setting, at least as the latter is presently constituted. An obstinate fellow (no doubt in part a function of the working-class southern Italian entrepreneurial heritage which I consciously embrace), I have begrudgingly accepted the trade-off.

I hope the choice between academic integrity/freedom and a successful mainstream professional career will not be as stark for future generations of serious orthodox Catholic scholars in the social sciences as it has been for me and others in my generation. However, the decision to pursue the idea of Catholic perspectives in sociology has been made infinitely easier given my faith commitment as a serious Catholic (with all the responsibilities entailed therein) and by my good fortune in having been supported all my life by a family offering (almost) unconditional love.

Index